ANGELS AND BELIEF IN ENGLAND, 1480–1700

BY

Laura Sangha

PICKERING & CHATTO
2012

Published by Pickering & Chatto (Publishers) Limited
21 Bloomsbury Way, London WC1A 2TH

2252 Ridge Road, Brookfield, Vermont 05036-9704, USA

www.pickeringchatto.com

BRITISH LIBRARY CATALOGUING IN PUBLICATION DATA

Sangha, Laura.
Angels and belief in England, 1480–1700. – (Religious cultures in the early
modern world)
1. Angels – Christianity – History of doctrines – 16th century. 2. Angels –
Christianity – History of doctrines – 17th century. 3. England – Religion –
16th century. 4. England – Religion – 17th century.
I. Title II. Series
235.3'0942'0903–dc22

ISBN–13: 9781848931459
e: 9781848931466

Typeset by Pickering & Chatto (Publishers) Limited
Printed and bound in the United Kingdom by the MPG Books Group

ANGELS AND BELIEF IN ENGLAND, 1480–1700

Religious Cultures in the Early Modern World

Series Editors: *Fernando Cervantes*
Peter Marshall
Philip Soergel

Titles in this Series

Forthcoming Titles

www.pickeringchatto.com/religious

CONTENTS

ACKNOWLEDGEMENTS

This monograph is founded on my doctoral research, so I would like to extend my warm thanks to the Arts and Humanities Research Council, the Warwick Institute of Advanced Study, and the Warwick Humanities Research Centre for their generous financial support. Intellectually, I have been the beneficiary of the insights and comments of numerous conference, workshop and seminar audiences over the years. I am particularly indebted to the organisers and participants of the 2008 Newberry Mellon Project workshop: a uniquely formative academic and personal milestone. At the University of Warwick I was privileged to be part of a vibrant history department with an incredibly rich research culture, and I would like to extend my gratitude to all the staff and students who made my time there so rewarding.

Two colleagues that I would particularly like to mention are Katherine Fox-hall and Catherine Rider, both of whom generously proofread various sections of the manuscript. I would like to offer special thanks to those that I consider to be the guardian angels of this project. Bernard Capp not only read and offered his expertise on my doctoral thesis, but also generously passed on angelic gleanings from his own research, many of which have been incorporated into this book. Alex Walsham similarly provided constructive and insightful thoughts on my research, and I am also extremely grateful to her for allowing me to read various articles and chapters prior to their publication. Both as my doctoral supervisor and subsequently, Peter Marshall has proven an inexhaustible source of knowledge, advice, encouragement, friendship, and much more, and I thank him for his patience and guidance in helping me to reach this stage.

Finally, I must acknowledge the tireless support, invaluable advice, and persistent optimism of Mark Hailwood, without whom this would be a far worse book. It has been a delight to be able to see the angels off as part of a team. The book is dedicated to my family: Jacqui, S, Rachael and Russ.

Exeter Quayside, October 2011

ABBREVIATIONS

HJ	*Historical Journal*
JEH	*Journal of Ecclesiastical History*
ODNB	*Oxford Dictionary of National Biography*
P&P	*Past and Present*
PS	Parker Society

INTRODUCTION

> A generation of men there is, who would have all the talk and enquiry about Angels
> and Spirits to pass for Old-wives stories, or at best the waking-dreams of persons idly
> disposed ... Now, what pity and shame is it, when the holy Scriptures have told us so
> much and plainly concerning this excellent sort of Creatures, and the good turns we
> receive continually from their Attendance and Ministry, and the admirable vertues
> we have to copy out in their Example; and we Christians profess to expect the happi-
> ness of being made like unto them, and bless'd hereafter in their Society; we should
> yet continue so profane, and sceptical, and indifferent in our belief, esteem, thoughts,
> and speeches about them?[1]

Despite what Protestant minister Benjamin Camfield suggests in this passage,
angels, those spiritual beings that were one step down from God, one step up
from men in the universal hierarchy, were not considered Old-Wives tales in
early modern England. Rather, faith in the reality of their existence was commonplace. Belief about angels was a mainstay of the Christian church, and
numerous responsibilities and theological assumptions were associated with
these evocative and often mysterious supernatural beings.

In recent decades historians of the early modern period have become
increasingly interested in many aspects of the supernatural, and subjects such as
prodigies, portents, miracles and ghost stories have all attracted greater notice,
supplementing the already extensive scholarship on witchcraft and demonology. The result has been a rich body of literature that has greatly expanded our
understanding and appreciation of the early modern world, and the beliefs and
expectations that informed contemporary mentalities.[2] However, the above
lamentation of Benjamin Camfield, in the foreword to his 1678 *A theological
discourse of angels and their ministries*, is one that could be repeated by twenty-
first century scholars, because within the existing literature angels are one aspect
of the supernatural that have remained a diffusely handled topic.

Since it is a commonplace of early modern studies that the mental universe
of contemporaries was infused by Aristotelian contraries, the neglect of the
'good' angels at the expense of the evil is particularly surprising. In *Thinking
with Demons*, Stuart Clark demonstrated that the early modern mentality was
organized around oppositional thought and expression. His suggestion that

contrariety was not only a 'universal principle of intelligibility' but was also profoundly influential for 'styles of argument and communication' was marshalled in support of his thesis that early modern demonism was coherent and rational in its own terms, not an exotic and marginal aberration.[3] However, his contention that opposites 'require each other in order to form wholes and improve understanding' might now be fruitfully revisited with regard to those supernatural beings found at the opposite pole to the demons in his study.

English Religious Cultures

The English Reformation has long been a fruitful area of research, and more recently scholarship has progressed from a preoccupation with the rate, geography and social distribution of conversions to Protestantism, to focus instead on broader questions about the processes of reform and their meaning for early modern society.[4] Tessa Watt's notion that later sixteenth- and early seventeenth-century culture comprised 'a fusion of new and traditional elements', resulting in 'a patchwork of beliefs' that were "distinctively 'post-Reformation', but not thoroughly Protestant" has proven a tremendously useful concept, and scholars have subsequently sought to pinpoint elements of continuity as well as change, recognizing strategies and 'accommodations' adopted by reformers in order to secure the loyalty of the people.[5]

The recent 'post-revisionist' trend in Reformation studies is therefore to see continuity with the past rather than radical dislocation, with the gradual modification of belief and an ongoing dialogue between traditional understanding and innovative reformed ideas. Historians such as Peter Lake, Judith Maltby, Tessa Watt and Alexandra Walsham have argued that considerable overlap existed between the world-views of the reformers and the laity, and attention has shifted to focus upon undercurrents of continuity that eased and alleviated the upheavals of the mid-sixteenth century.[6] Instead of seeing the Reformation as a purely destructive campaign that obliterated inherited systems of tradition and custom, replacing them with radical and disconcerting new precepts, historians now recognize a willingness on the part of Protestant ministers to 'exploit, engage with, and re-channel common assumptions', arguing that such accommodation catered to the intellectual and emotional capabilities of the laity and created points of intersection between old and new ideas.[7] Historians have consequently examined those aspects of belief where old and new ideas intersect, seeking to construct a more nuanced picture of English religious cultures in the sixteenth and seventeenth centuries.

Angels have a strong claim to be examined in a similar light. A persistent belief in angels as protectors and ministers was widespread in early modern England, and angels were the focus of a particularly disparate grouping of assumptions and expectations. The ubiquity of belief about angels in religious cultures, coupled with the great flexibility and diversity of the angelic motif, makes them an excellent unit of historical enquiry. They were a shared cultural 'space', within which contemporaries engaged in theological discourse and worked through complex ideas, as well as an important rhetorical tool for those attempting religious reform. As with demons, an examination of belief about angels therefore has the potential to elucidate early modern mentalities and expectations, and is an excellent means to explore the belief systems that gave structure to the early modern world.

Beginning with Pierre Bourdieu's concept of the 'field of cultural production', this study therefore perceives of angels as a cultural motif that was determined by the way it fitted into the interests and preoccupations of the society that created it.[8] To revisionist historians, angels might seem a symptom of the resilience of Catholic devotion, whilst others have suggested that they served the pastoral agenda of Protestantism, stepping in to replace the saints as the 'ideologically appropriate friends of humanity'.[9] However, neither of these explanations is entirely adequate, as they ignore the continual re-imagining of angels in a variety of different political, cultural and confessional sites. Therefore, this enquiry is not framed as an intellectual history that concentrates exclusively on patterns of thought at the expense of the interests they served and the social and cultural contexts in which they were conceived. Nor is it a narrative of the fluctuating fortunes, or popularity of angels, set against the backdrop of the sixteenth and seventeenth centuries. Rather, this monograph uses belief about angels to throw light on the strategies and methods employed by religious reformers seeking to persuade the laity of the veracity of their particular confessional stance. It emphasizes the relationship between ideas and historical change. Within the text, discourses about angels are disentangled and clarified, and the pastoral and didactic functions of belief about angels are considered alongside the rhetoric of those individuals competing to shape the development of religious cultures in early modern England.

The persistence of belief in angels thus offers an opportunity to explore the survival and mutation of a key component of traditional belief in Reformation England, with angels forming one of the points of intersection and accommodation identified by post-revisionist scholars. An examination of belief about angels speaks to recent debates about how Protestantism was able to enter the hearts and minds of the English laity, and how the populace was able to adjust to the dramatic restructuring of the religious landscape in the sixteenth century. The underlying argument in this study is that although continuity was an integral element of religious cultures, it is important not to prioritize this at the risk of obscuring equally important change. Continuities were complex, and fiercely contested by those of differing confessional stripes. The development of the identities of Catholics, church papists, prayer-book Protestants, Puritans and Presbyterians was conditioned by conflict within and between them. The ways in which people reacted to the 'official' understanding of angels, and how they sought to commandeer angels in defence of their own understanding of what the church should be, needs to be considered. A disparate range of confessional identities emerged and were hardened within the same physical and intellectual environment throughout this period, and this study utilizes angels as a shared theoretical and cultural 'space' in which to understand these processes.

This study therefore perceives of reform as an ongoing process, and uses belief about angels as a means to elucidate and trace the continuing development of doctrine and practice throughout the period of the 'Long Reformation'. The broad temporal scope of the study provides the perspective from which to perceive the ongoing evolution of the Church of England, and provides an insight into change within the context of broader social and political trends. Studying belief about angels contributes to our understanding of how reformers tried to implement change through the institution of the Church, but also how this was re-appropriated and challenged in wider public discourse. It indicates how contemporaries sought to shape and influence the expectations of the laity, as well as their intents and purposes in attempting this in the first place.

Histories of Angels

In 2009, in a review in the journal *Reformation*, Diarmaid MacCulloch described angelology as a theme in early modern Christianity 'which might be seen as even more important' than the 'almost over-researched' witchcraft.[10] In the essay, MacCulloch considered the importance of angels as 'the accredited agent of communication used by the deity', and reflected on two recent works that investigate why belief in angels was important to early modern religious cultures. Both the existence and the content of MacCulloch's essay are testament to the fact that the study of angels has come to life in recent years, following the comparative neglect of this key component of Christian belief in the historiography. However, in this emerging field, there is still no comprehensive, in-depth study of belief in angels in early modern England. This study seeks to address this gap, tracing the evolution of belief in angels throughout the sixteenth and seventeenth centuries, and locating this belief firmly in the context of early modern religious cultures and mentalities more broadly.

Early modern scholars had previously paid scant attention to the cultural and epistemological implications of the continuing presence of angels in English religious cultures. It is striking that in two works which have proven exceptionally influential with regard to scholarship on late medieval and early modern religious cultures, Keith Thomas' *Religion and the Decline of Magic*, and Eamon Duffy's *The Stripping of the Altars,* neither author devoted a separate section to angelic beings, although each recognized the potential significance of their presence.[11] Scholarly interest in early modern angels was limited to the areas of elite ceremonial magic and literary studies, focusing on the occultism of John Dee and his conversations with angels, or offering a limited consideration the significance of belief in order to contextualize an investigation into John Milton's angels in *Paradise Lost*.[12]

From the late 1990s, scholars of the medieval period have shown more interest in the subject. In *Angels and Angelology in the Middle Ages*, David Keck casts the net Europe-wide to provide an excellent, wide-ranging study of celestial beings, illustrating how they became a cornerstone of medieval Christianity.[13] Keck's work is broad in its temporal and geographical scope and serves as a comprehensive, if general, introduction to the importance of the angelic presence and the significance of commonly held assumptions relating to celestial beings. Richard Johnson's *Saint Michael the Archangel in Medieval English Legend* is another more recent work which similarly identifies the value of angels as a unit of historical enquiry, and indicates an aspect of belief that could prove fertile grounds for further examination. Johnson addresses the question of how angelic belief informed personal religious devotion, albeit in association with only one aspect of angelology.[14] Johnson argues that the foundation myths of the various shrines dedicated to the angel provided the main source for popular assumptions about the existence and responsibilities of angels, shaping expectations and serving as a spur to piety.

In 2006, Peter Marshall and Alexandra Walsham published an edited collection that was a reflection of a growing interest in the topic. *Angels in the Early Modern World* convincingly establishes the cultural ubiquity of angels, demonstrating the scale of angelic activity and establishing the groundwork for future scholarship in what is now an emerging field.[15] The collection is very broad in scope: contributors' articles explore the role of angels against the backdrop of the Renaissance, Reformation, and Enlightenment; they cover a large swathe of the globe ranging from Europe to New England and Latin America; and they consider how angels were implicated in the processes of Protestant and Catholic renewal.

Taken as a whole, this recent scholarship has demonstrated the legitimacy and potential usefulness of a more comprehensive and in depth study of the cultural significance of angels in early modern England, but as yet, such a study has not appeared in print. Although the field of angelology has begun to come to life, with recognition that angels are a legitimate unit of historical study, publications within it have retained their literary focus. Faisal Mohamed's *In the Anteroom of Divinity: The Reformation of Angels from Colet to Milton* (2008), concentrates on the theology of a range of canonical Renaissance authors, particularly that associated with the angelic hierarchy, while Joad Raymond's insightful *Milton's Angels: The Early Modern Imagination* (2010) only briefly surveys the development of early modern angelology, before moving on to a detailed analysis of the poet's angelic theology.[16]

This book will provide a more systematic evaluation of the significance of belief about angels in early modern England, firmly locating the concept in the political, social and religious context of the sixteenth and seventeenth century. It builds on the groundwork and insights of recent scholarship on the medieval period, examining how the attitudes and assumptions uncovered by David Keck evolved during an era of exceptional religious turmoil and reform. Similarly, it recognizes that the cult of Saint Michael and the angelic hierarchy are fruitful lines of enquiry, and traces the impact of the Reformation upon these important elements of religious cultures. Moving away from the literary preoccupations of recent work in the field, it will not concentrate exclusively on patterns of thought during the sixteenth and seventeenth centuries. Instead, the book will focus on the social context in which these patterns of thought were constructed, establishing how clergymen reformed and reconstituted their beliefs about angels, and then utilized these ideas in the confessional struggle for the soul of the continually evolving Church of England.

Traditional and Scriptural Angels

Similarly to many other aspects of Christian belief, the angelic motif was a fusion of ancient ideas from several near eastern religious traditions. However, the mainstay of belief about angels was Hebrew and Greek scripture, which provided countless examples of their existence and endeavour, and which formed the foundation of medieval angelology. Angels are first mentioned in the Old Testament in the form of a Cherub, guarding the gates of Eden after the Fall (Genesis 3:24), and thereafter they appear frequently to assist the functioning of God's providence and to serve as 'administrators in a hierarchical bureaucracy of the world'.[17] An angel prevents Abraham from sacrificing his son Isaac; angels carry messages such as those to Hagar and Balaam; prophets often encounter them in visions or episodes, such as Jacob's dream of angels on a ladder ascending to heaven; and an angel offers comfort and instruction to Elijah when he is in the wilderness. They are also particularly prominent in many of the familiar passages of the New Testament, and the narrative of Jesus' life is replete with angelic collaborators. His birth is foretold to Mary by an angel (Luke 1:28) and announced to the shepherds by a heavenly host (Luke 2:9); angels minister to him in the wilderness (Matthew 4:1) and preside at his tomb after the Resurrection (Matthew 28:2, Luke 24:4). Following Jesus' death angels continue to appear in various guises, and they play a vitally important role in the book of Revelation, participating in the destruction of the earth and engaging in a war against Satan and the evil angels (Revelation 7:2). Yet the roles that angels took in scripture were not exclusively those of succour and protection, because they might also act as dispensers of divine justice: the two angels that visit Lot smite the men of Sodom with blindness and proclaim that they have been sent by God to destroy Sodom and Gomorrah (Genesis 19:1); and it is an angel that nearly destroys Jerusalem when God is displeased with David (2 Samuel 24:16).

Tradition provided the basis for other expectations about angels, and gradually general assumptions about them began to emerge. The Greek and Latin Fathers accepted that the angels were creatures that dwelt in the upper heavens, had no natural corporal body and were sexless, despite their usual artistic representation as male. The appearance of the angels can be traced back to supernatural beings in Graeco-Roman culture, which acted as benevolent mediators between men and the gods; the attribute of wings, which has scant scriptural validation, may have been inspired by the image of Iris, a messenger for the Gods found in Greek mythology, or the winged figures found on Etruscan tombs or in frescoes at Pompeii.[18] A text that played a particularly important role in the development of theological ideas about angels was *On the Celestial Hierarchy*, the treatise which outlined the order of angels, translated into Latin in the ninth century. The author is usually referred to as 'Pseudo-Dionysius', because medieval writers confused him with Dionysius the Areopagite who was understood to have listened to St Paul's address to the Athenians, or with St Dionysius, the third century apostle to Gaul. Dionysius' highly influential treatise organized the nine angelic names found in Scripture into three descending hierarchies, comprising of Seraphim, Cherubim and Thrones; Dominions, Virtues and Powers; and Principalities, Archangels and Angels. In doing so he established a hierarchy within which the angels performed specific functions and participated in the order and workings of the universe as a whole. Although not officially verified by the Church, Dionysius's scheme became widely accepted and such luminaries as John Scotus, Hugo of St Victor, Peter Lombard, Bonaventura and Thomas Aquinas all produced commentaries on his work.[19]

One of the results of these theological musings was the association of distinct characteristics with particular orders (often derived from their names) as angels became more individual and less impersonal instruments of the divine will. The first hierarchy were defined by their relationship with God. Following the traditional translation of the Hebrew word 'seraph' as burning, the Seraphim were identified with a fiery love of God, the 'summit of the creaturely ability to contemplate and love the divine'.[20] The Cherubim were particularly associated with the quality of knowledge, and Thrones were considered steadfast and tranquil, illustrating the divine presence, authority and power of the Lord. The second hierarchy had names that hinted at their participation in the ordering of the universe: Dominions presided over the earth, Virtues would operate within the world, perhaps performing miracles, and Powers were thought to be adept at repelling harmful forces. The orders of the third hierarchy were the most active in human affairs: Principalities were responsible for the governance of kingdoms; Archangels directed human affairs, delivering important messages; and the Angels were believed to fulfil the role of guardians to individuals, watching over and ministering to them.

The bible also contributed to the development of distinct angelic identities, providing the names of the three archangels: Gabriel, Michael and Raphael. Michael appeared in scripture as the champion and leader of the angelic host, and his defeat of the 'dragon' in the Book of Revelation ensured his special responsibility for combating evil.[21] He was also crucial to the drama enacted around the deathbed where it was believed the good and evil angels took part in a struggle for the soul of the dying. Michael's role here was that of a vital supernatural ally. The deathbed was in fact one of the most important arenas for angelic intervention on earth, and it was a common conception that angels provided succour for the dying and after death would receive the souls of the saved in order to carry them into Abraham's bosom, as was attested to in the Bible (Luke 16:22). The archangel Gabriel's identity was intimately connected to his relationship with Mary because of his proclamation at the Annunciation; and Raphael, who accompanied Tobit's son Tobias on a dangerous journey to Media, was considered the 'Medicine of God', associated both with healing and offering special protection to travellers and pilgrims.[22] Although not recognized as canonical by the Church, the apocalyptic book of Enoch provided more angelic names, and taken together these sources made it less likely that angels would be perceived as ciphers, mere manifestations of divine providence. This in itself was an important development in medieval perceptions of the divine beings and had important implications for religious devotion.

Scripture emphasized that angels, although excellent, were infinitely inferior to Christ (Hebrews 1:13–14), and warned against offering undue veneration to them (Colossians 2:18). The possibility of the worshipping of angels troubled the church throughout the Middle Ages, as did attempts to harness the supernatural power of the angels for private advantage. Periodically the Church had to act to condemn the unorthodox coercion of angelic power, such as the Roman council that at the end of the fifth century forbade the use of amulets engraved with angelic names, or Charlemagne's ban on the summoning of angels that were not found in scripture.[23]

Despite these contemporary misgivings, this survey of the origins of belief about angels suggests the great versatility and utility of the motif. From these firm foundations in scripture and following the dictates of tradition, angels became an integral part of the religious world view of medieval English people, engaging with a diverse range of belief and doctrine, and prompting a variety of expectations and assumptions. However, the ambiguities in the status of angels were to give them a contested place in Protestant theology, and although indubitably biblical, the variety of rituals, representations and devotions associated with angels occupied an uneasy position between orthodox piety and illegitimate 'superstition' for many reformers. They therefore offer a unique opportunity to examine contemporary structures of belief and the nature of religious change.

Structure

The underpinning logic of this study is that an angel was a culturally constructed motif that reflected the anxieties and preoccupations of the society that created it. As such, it is impossible to provide a comprehensive, universal survey of English angels. Instead, I aim to elucidate the most significant discourses about angels in a wide variety of early modern sources, focusing on printed polemic in conjunction with material evidence. Principally, I examine angels in the light of the strategies and methods adopted by religious reformers seeking to persuade the laity that their innovative theology was in fact representative of the one true faith. The ways in which they took up and utilized the motif of angels, and the meanings they attached to them, reveal much about post-Reformation mentalities and the ways in which change was implemented through the institution of the church.

The long chronology of the study allows for an insight into both the initial impact of reform on belief about angels, as well as a survey of the continual evolution of angelology throughout the 'Long Reformation'. Tracing the development of belief up to the late seventeenth century allows for an investigation of the cyclical nature of the processes of reform, and recognizes that teleological narratives founded on the assumption of the steady processes of 'secularization' have proved insufficient interpretive frameworks for the post-Reformation world. It also makes possible a properly contextualized study of angels that is firmly rooted in wider developments in the political, social and religious spheres, acknowledging the cultural foundation and composition of religious cultures. In the process it unites the historiographies of two centuries that are often artificially separated.

Chapters are organized within a loose chronological framework, though a thematic organization takes precedence. Chapter 1 is a survey of the place of angels in late medieval English cultures, exploring the unique relationship between humans and angels and their perceived roles in the life of the church, establishing their status as a ubiquitous element of the religious landscape. The use of angels for didactic and pastoral uses, and the potential impact of these ideas upon personal devotion will be considered, before wider questions relating to the angels' involvement in the salvation of mankind and the functioning of eschatology are addressed. The chapter lays the foundation for an understanding of how reformed thinking was to radically alter belief.

Chapters 2 and 3 investigate the dramatic religious upheaval of the sixteenth century, and the survival and mutation of belief about angels in the face of religious reform. Chapter 2 establishes those aspects of belief that were vulnerable to reformed thinking in a period when parochial religious culture was transformed by an attack on the principal expressions of communal faith and observers. Traditional understanding of the angels included certain indefensible elements, focused around their assumed roles as mediators between men and the divine, and furthermore angels were compromised by an association with what now came to be seen as objectionable or 'superstitious' Catholic devotional practices. This chapter investigates how these elements were suppressed by the reformers, as well as evidence that the reformers were eager to appropriate the angelic motif, as angels began to form an essential feature of English Protestantism. Chapter 3 continues this line of enquiry, providing evidence of the persistence of a core set of beliefs about angels that endured throughout the sixteenth and seventeenth centuries, beliefs which together could be considered to be the 'authorized', Church of England, angel, well suited to the ecclesiology and religious outlook of the Church. It investigates how belief about angels continued to fulfil important and wide ranging pastoral and didactic functions, and how churchmen utilized the concept of angels in polemic designed to establish Protestantism in the hearts and minds of their parishioners.

Chapters 4 and 5 examine the problematic legacy of the Elizabethan settlement, investigating how angels could become conduits for unorthodoxy in the hands of those pushing at the boundaries of what has been termed an 'Elizabethan consensus'. Because they were theologically malleable, angels were recruited by clergymen of all stripes in support of their particular reformed stance, and these dissenting voices need to be heard in order to gain a more complete notion of the status of angels in early modern religious discourse and in the Church more generally. Chapter 4 therefore considers how Presbyterians, Arminians, Laudians, and Puritans used the angelic motif to argue about what the Church of England should be, as confessional stances emerged and were hardened over the period. Hostility to Catholicism was a formative influence on the English Protestant identity, so an understanding of the significance of angels for those on the opposite side of the denominational divide is also crucial for a more complete construction of post-reformation angelology. Chapter 5 therefore investigates how angels were used to articulate the divide itself. A consideration of angels during the reign of Mary I reflects on wider questions of the tone and effectiveness of Marian Catholicism, and beyond this, the chapter seeks to uncover how the experience of persecution affected the ways that angels were discussed, perceived and utilized by Catholic contemporaries.

Chapter 6 seeks to widen the terms of the debate by examining how the rhetoric of the reformers was received at an individual level. Moving away from the explicitly confessional tone of many of the sources examined in the preceding chapters, it considers evidence of belief in angels amongst the English laity. By utilizing diaries, cheap print and literary sources, it will provide an insight into the place of angels in individual belief. Although by no means a comprehensive survey, this will indicate possible alternative understandings of angels that were in competition with the 'authorized' angel of religious polemic.

The final chapter investigates broad intellectual shifts that had enormous implications for angelology. The threat posed by the rise of mechanical philosophy and experimental science in the seventeenth century threatened to undermine the fundamentals of belief in angels, but the evidence does not support a paradigm whereby people gradually lost all faith in supernatural creatures. This chapter questions the paradigm of secularization, and illustrates how clergymen reacted to the 'new thinking', and to growing fears of heterodoxy and atheism, by mounting a stout defence of angels. This defence could prompt clergymen to go much further than their predecessors in asserting the reality of angelic beings and their participation in life on earth, as a search began to provide the empirical evidence that would prove the existence of the supernatural, and thus disprove the claims of the materialists.

Historians increasingly perceive the English Reformation as a long-term process of negotiation and development, which encompassed an astonishing diversity of belief and where the pace of change was at times bafflingly swift, and at others slow and irregular. The early modern period was thus characterized by ideological eclecticism and fixed confessional identities emerged only gradually, as older assumptions and practice were assimilated and harnessed in the service of novel causes. Through the examination of a particular aspect of theology and devotion, this study seeks to elucidate how these processes were worked through and understood by contemporaries. Utilization of the angelic motif allowed a varied range of individuals and groups to engage in religious discourse and allowed angels to become a concept within which diverse and complicated ideas about the functioning of the universe were played out.

1 THE MEDIEVAL ANGEL, *c.* 1480–1530

Every year, on the Feast of Saint Michael, 29 September, congregations the length and breadth of medieval England would come together to contemplate and give thanks for God's holy angels and the ministry and succour they provided to humanity. The sermons and prayers offered on this day focused the laity's attention on an aspect of belief that permeated numerous areas of religious life, and on concepts and ideas central to the whole community. Angels were a ubiquitous presence on the medieval landscape. The liturgy and preaching of 29 September would have been received in an environment that was imbued with the physical presence of the angels: meditations and music thus building on conceptual ideas with their foundations in the very stone, wood and glass of the church itself. Their principal responsibility of leading men to beatitude meant that the deeds of the angels were as diverse as they were far-reaching; their duties included roles as worshippers, protectors, messengers and guardians, and contemporary understanding and official endorsement of these concepts gave the celestial beings an integral part in the functioning of medieval religious life.

Angelology had a strong scriptural basis, and from here, angels went on to assume their pervasive role in medieval religious culture.[1] For churchmen and theologians, angelic involvement in the scriptural narrative made angels an aspect of belief that could be utilized to explore the mysterious workings of God and the system of eschatology, as well as providing an opportunity to expound such passages as the creation or crucifixion in greater detail. As a result, the study of angelology flourished within the cloister and university, and angels acquired a new place in the fields of philosophy, reason and logic, where rigorous discursive reasoning was applied to reveal the exact nature of celestial beings. As the most marvellous creatures in the universe, it was believed that a deeper understanding of angels could provide insight into the limits of the cosmos and the natural and moral laws that governed it. For the laity, angels also assumed a conceptual importance as they joined humanity in the praise and worship of God, and provided an example of the obedience and love that every man should aspire to. They continued to assume their more practical scriptural roles as messengers and ministers, and appealed to all as protectors and assistants, guiding men on the path to redemption.

The ubiquity of the angelic presence must be understood in conjunction with the religious culture of the Roman Catholic Church. The reputation of the late medieval English Church has recently undergone substantial restoration, and scholars accept that although fifteenth-century Catholicism encompassed elements of belief and practice that offered a tempting target for the evangelically minded, this did not preclude the existence of an enthusiastic, rich and dynamic indigenous religious tradition.[2] Angels were evidently a common element in these medieval religious cultures, and to a certain extent their involvement in numerous aspects of religious life may provide the explanation as to why they have previously been neglected in historical studies. The ubiquitous presence of the angels appears to have been taken for granted. Angels are so much a part of the iconography of the medieval church that their presence has been overlooked by contemporaries and historians alike. Angels are expected to appear in a scene of the Nativity or Crucifixion, so it has not been felt necessary to comment upon their presence. However, it is often the cultural elements that are unquestioned and whose existence are 'assumed' that in fact prove to be most revealing and which can provide the most discerning insight into cultural life. There is no scriptural basis for the appearance of angels at the crucifixion, so the question of why they appear at the very heart of Christian universal history deserves further attention.

The three sections of this chapter seek to locate angels firmly within the framework of late medieval religion, to discover why, and also how they achieved this ubiquitous presence. The liturgy, popular sermon collections, devotional materials, and the lives of the Saints, together with the physical attributes of the church are the principal sources of evidence to be examined. Drawing on these, the first section will establish the extent of the angelic presence within the community. This was the orthodox, public face of angelic belief, and the parish church was the site where men and celestial beings came into contact most frequently.

The second section moves on to look at the impact of these ideas upon personal devotion, and will discuss how representations of angels were interpreted and internalized by the laity, beyond the framework of official doctrine. The struggle for the soul on the deathbed is fundamentally important for personal devotion when it comes to notions of individual judgement, but also relates to belief about angelic involvement in the salvation of humanity. The final section addresses these wider questions, probing the angelic role in the functioning of eschatology, and in doing so locating angels at the very heart of Christian belief.

The Fellowship of Angels

> In the confession of a true and everlasting Godhead, both distinction in persons, and
> unity in essence, and equality in majesty might be adored. Which Angels and Arch-
> angels praise, Cherubim also and Seraphin, who cease not to cry with one voice.[3]

The primary angelic occupation in the liturgy was as fellow worshippers alongside mankind. This was their principal function, because all forms of celestial
ministry had the glorification of God as their ultimate aim. The contemporary
perception of the angelic hierarchy bore witness to this: the upper order, which
enjoyed a position in closest proximity to the divine, was wholly defined by their
relationship with God. It was only the lowest order of principalities, archangels and angels, which descended to earth to interact directly with humanity.[4]
The greatest of the angels therefore existed solely to worship and honour God,
although this was also an important responsibility even for the angels in the lowest order of the hierarchy, and accordingly their intervention in earthly affairs
most frequently involved participation in the liturgy of the church.

The perception that religious services brought angels and men together in
adoration of God was commonly held in the medieval period, and was emphasized by a variety of sources. The regular participation of angels in the divine
liturgy perpetually placed them in the lives of Christians, and created a perception of the relationships between God, angels and men that was fundamental
to the church's angelology. Central to this was the *Sanctus*, the 'angelic hymn'
forming the last part of the Preface to the Mass and sung in nearly every rite, the
text of which was drawn from Isaiah 6:3:

> Sanctus, Sanctus, Sanctus,
> Dominus Deus Sabaoth
> pleni sunt coeli et terra gloria tua
> Osanna in excelsis.[5]

The passage dealt with the prophet's vision of heaven and fittingly it is the seraphim surrounding the throne of God who are the source of the words in the
passage. It was designed to convey the joy of redemption but also indicated the
angelic contribution, the seraphims' cry expressing the 'unmediated experience
of the divine and the proper creaturely response'.[6] The words of the Ferial Preface
itself echoed the same ideas, stating that 'at all times we should give praise to you
God' and again mentioning the angels of the upper orders:

> angels praise thy majesty, dominions adore, powers tremble, the heavens, and the
> heavenly hosts, and the blessed Seraphin unite in one glad voice in extolling thee.
> Together with whom, we pray thee, that thou wouldest command that our voices
> should have entrance, humbly confessing thee.[7]

The request for permission to join the angelic hymn emphasized the subservient position of men, and recognized the favour shown by God in granting that their humble prayers be added to the heavenly choirs' exaltation. It is a theme that was continued in the Preface to Communion itself, which consisted of the well known phrase 'O all ye angels of the Lord: praise him, and magnify him for ever'. Angels therefore provided a model of the veneration that man should show towards the Godhead, an idea that was frequently repeated in many of the services found in the *Use of Sarum*, the liturgical form most frequently employed in the English Church prior to the Reformation.[8]

Many of those passages in the *Use* that preceded great Liturgical feasts also referred to angels. The extract at the beginning of this section comes from the preface for Trinity Sunday and the Sundays leading up to advent, and was part of the liturgical build-up to the greatest feast in the Catholic Calendar. The service for Easter Even contained several references to angels, including an evocation of the 'angelic host of heaven', called upon to exult the divine mysteries. This was evidently a common figurative phrase that embodied the idea of the angelic participation in worship.[9] Accordingly, it was very common for angels to be depicted with musical instruments, such as those that appear on the minstrel gallery in Exeter cathedral. Angels were also particularly associated with the employment of music in the veneration of God, and numerous hymns refer to this role. The sequence on Christmas Day begins with the lines 'All hosts, above, beneath/ Sing the incarnate Lord' continuing that 'Glory to God on high ... Was thundered forth in harmony/ By angel legions bright', and others are similarly littered with dramatic appearances such as this.[10] If the allure of traditional religion was to some extent based upon the sumptuous quality of worship and its captivation of the senses of the common man, the infiltration of the angels into many aspects of church music therefore created an important area of contact between men and the celestial beings.

Evidently an association between angels and men was a common assumption in medieval liturgical worship, and was conveyed to the congregation through the many references to angels in the order of service. In the past historians have questioned the level of comprehension that the laity had of Latin Catholic services, but scholars have shown that in alliance with other textual and visual aids, and in conjunction with clerical instruction, the laity exhibited a religious outlook that incorporated much of the official religious position.[11] It is also true that even for the poorest members of the parish, those who had no access to additional devotional material, the frequently repeated Latin word 'angelus' was similar enough to English for the concept to be communicated to the congregation.

Therefore if it was assumed that the laity understood only the occasional word that issued from the priest's mouth, even this would have been enough for the sacred words of the Liturgy to establish the ubiquitous presence of the angels, thus providing the framework of angelic belief. This framework was built upon by vernacular texts, particularly sermons, which elaborated and gave meaning to the existence of angels, and furthermore, the ritual and decoration of the church gave these concepts a vivid and striking physical presence at the heart of the congregation. Even with a strictly limited comprehension of what the words of the liturgy meant, the notion of the fellowship between God, angels and men was one that could be, and indeed was conveyed to the laity.

Vernacular sermons would have been one of the chief means of disseminating ideas about angels to the congregation, and two collections, which were among the first books printed by William Caxton in 1483, were to have a particularly influential impact upon parish religion. These were Jacobus de Voragine's *Legenda Aurea* and John Mirk's *Festial*. *Legenda Aurea* was a widely read collection of legendary lives of the saints compiled in the thirteenth century, and its arrangement in the chronological order of their feast days was designed to assist clergymen in the composition of sermons.[12] In addition, it is likely that the hagiographical work became a book for private reading and devotion, fulfilling didactic purposes whilst also serving as a prompt to piety. It was undoubtedly a medieval 'best seller'.[13] *Mirk's Festial* was a collection of homilies assembled by an Augustinian Prior in the late fourteenth or early fifteenth century. The sermons betray the influence of the *Legenda Aurea*, but there is evidence that Mirk's motivation in producing the work was his concern over the threat of Lollardy and the low quality of pastoral care offered by unlettered priests. The *Festial* was therefore styled to the less educated elements of society, with a simple structure and uncomplicated language, and frequent recourse to narrative and exempla. Caxton's decision to print the *Festial* was undoubtedly influenced by its popular appeal, and between 1486 and 1532 a further twenty-two editions were produced, making it the most widely read sermon cycle in the fifteenth century.[14] Throughout the country it was also the text that was most likely to be heard or to inform what was said in the pulpit. Both these texts provide an insight into the common themes and perceptions that were associated with angels during the period.

These collections frequently articulate the liturgical idea of angelic participation in worship. It is perhaps significant that occasions when angels are mentioned in the context of worship are also those feast days in which angels appear in the *Use of Sarum*, a conjunction of concepts which would link the sermon with the ceremonial in the mind of the laymen, perhaps prompting greater understanding of the latter. On the occasion of Jesus's birth in *Legenda*, hosts of angels sang 'Glory to God in the highest and peace to men of good will' before the shepherds, and at the Ascension the angels were 'jubilant', and the 'vastnesses of the air' were 'sanctified by the divine retinue' as Christ took his place in heaven.[15] Angels also appeared in the Nativity sermon in the *Festial*, which related: "angeles songen þus: 'Gloria in excelsis Deo'. Þat ys to say: 'Ioye be to God þat ys hegh yn Heuen'", in this instance Mirk helpfully translating for those who could not grasp even this familiar Latin phrase. On Palm Sunday the angels in heaven were said to 'maken moche melody yn Heuen', at Easter 'þe Fadyr of Heuen makyth wyth all hys angelys soo gret melody for þe vpryst of hys sonne'. Music is indeed a continuous theme, and in De Diebus Rogacionum Sermo Breuis, the narrative tells of a boy who was taken up to heaven where 'þer angeles taghten hym forto syng þys song: 'Sanctus Deus, sanctus fortis, sanctus et immortalis, miserere nobis!' These are lines which appear in the 'Improperia of the Office of Good Friday', firmly locating them in orthodox Catholic practice but also providing an example of angels not only joining in prayer with humanity but also providing the words and music appropriate to the rite.[16]

The sermon collections also drew attention to the particular periods of the year when people were encouraged to think about angels: around the time of the Annunciation, when Gabriel performed his crucial function in the narrative of Christian history; or throughout the Nativity when hosts of the angelic beings joyfully proclaimed the birth of the saviour. As already mentioned, the most important date in the Calendar was 29 September, the feast of Saint Michael and All Angels, when the laity were instructed to contemplate and give thanks for the ministry of the celestial beings. Both Voragine and Mirk in their sermons call on the congregation to 'makyþe mencyon of all Goddys holy angels' in their prayers on that day, and the authors use the opportunity to elaborate on heavenly beings.[17] Although the content of these sermons will be considered in more detail in the next section, it is worth noting that Voragine's sermon includes a lengthy passage on the hierarchy of angels, and he is explicit about the fact that the first hierarchy consists of those 'that are close to God, with no intermediary, and are wholly turned to him'. Their primary role is the worship of God, and Voragine urges that parishioners should recognize them as 'our brothers and fellow citizens'.[18]

The idea of angelic participation in worship was evidently deeply ingrained in the theology of medieval religion, hardly surprising given that the central rite of the church, the Mass, is perceived by historians as a 'ritual of social peace among Christians'.[19] In terms of the spiritual society this would include the angels alongside men, and the capacity of the ritual to visibly celebrate the bonds of the community through the 'unitive and corporative dimension of the Blessed Sacrament' resulted in the idea of the angelic co-operation in worship being reemphasized each time parishioners gathered for services.[20] Furthermore, the environment in which this social ritual took place was crucial to its performance, for the very fabric of the church communicated a sense of the physical presence of the angels in the building itself. Angels permeated not only the temporal space of the liturgical calendar, but were ubiquitous to every aspect of the sacred space which the congregation shared with them.

Even a brief survey of the material aspects of medieval religious culture demonstrates the extent of angelic iconography and implies the dramatic influence it could have. Although survival rates for English medieval iconography in general are low, numerous traces of angels remain, many integral to the architecture of the church itself: on the fronts of cathedrals, amongst the roof bosses of vaulted ceilings, on pew ends or in expensive glass windows. There are also many wall paintings that were whitewashed at the time of the Reformation but which have since been uncovered, and other images such as the illustrations in printed texts or the tombs erected within parish churches (which lay outside the purview of reforming iconoclastic commissioners) also provide an insight into medieval surroundings.

There are many portrayals of angels in their role of worshipping, but of particular importance were images of Christ in his majesty. This was a scene that often formed the centre-piece of Doom paintings, illustrations of the Day of Judgement that were painted above the chancel arch in parish churches. Angels were usually found flanking Christ as he sat enthroned in glory, gazing enraptured at his face and often carrying censers or the instruments of the passion. There are examples of such paintings still in existence in varying states of repair at Houghton Conquest, Bedfordshire; Kempley, Gloucestershire; and Clayton in West Sussex, and given the strictly limited rates of survival for such artwork these multiple examples give some indication of the original frequency of similar depictions within parish churches.

The location of the doom painting, dominating the nave where the congregation were seated during services, is also of significance, for its positioning was such that it was likely to catch the eye of worshippers whose concentration was wandering. Angelic worshippers were ubiquitous, and they assumed the role in numerous scenes involving Christ or the saints. Each image served as a reminder of their participation in the rites of the Catholic Church, and of the joining of men and angels in prayer and praise. The layman was literally surrounded by the angels as he worshipped.

This role can also explain some of the recurring imagery associated with angels. The act of censing has already been touched upon, and undoubtedly the common depiction of angels with thuribles, in the process of censing saints or the Holy Trinity, was representative of the act of worship. This was an image that appeared repeatedly in the sculptured capitals, corbels, spandrels, windows and other decoration within parish churches. Incense was generally used to signify a number of functions. It represented sacrifice to God, protection from demons, consecration, purification and prayers.[21] This last idea was drawn from a passage in Revelation 8:3–4, where an angel with a golden censer was given incense 'that he should offer it with the prayers of all saints upon the golden altar which was before the throne'. The smoke of the incense along with the prayers then 'ascended up before God out of the angel's hand', providing the basis for the common belief that angels played an active role in the mass by bearing the sacrifice from the altar on earth up to the altar in heaven. The belief was mentioned by Jacobus de Voragine in the sermon for the dedication of a church, where incense was said to symbolise devout prayer as it 'rises to the memory of God, heals the soul of the past sins by obtaining pardon ... imparts caution to the soul as it face the future'.[22] In this way angels assumed a heavy responsibility within the liturgy as mediators enabling the effectiveness of prayer, particularly during the rite of the Mass.

Images of angels also featured on an array of other church fabric. They appeared on the elaborately decorative vestments of the clergy, an essential part of the ritual of services. Although the laity would probably only receive the sacrament once during the course of a year, there was great emphasis on seeing the mass and in particular the host, because popular belief attested that this would offer the beholder special protection on any such day.[23] The most important and most dramatic moment was therefore the elevation of the host, when the miracle of transubstantiation occurred and the body of Christ was made physically present among the worshippers. At that moment the priest was facing the altar with his back to the congregation, allowing the parishioners to focus on the intricate designs on his richly coloured vestments during the elevation. Surviving examples suggest that the angelic motif was common in the decoration of these liturgical costumes. They were particularly prone to manifestation on the *chasuble*, one of the *veste sacrae* that required the blessing of the bishop before use in church. Angels were again to be found censing the figure of Christ, and generally served as a useful piece of iconography to complete a pattern. Angels are also depicted playing musical instruments, a reminder of their association with the *Sanctus* and their role in singing the heavenly praise of God.

The conceptual and physical presence of angels was evidently ubiquitous in the public worship performed within parish churches throughout medieval England. The laity were prompted by the temporal cycle of the liturgy to focus their thoughts on angels at certain times of the year, but the physical manifestation of angels on the rood screen, within the doom painting and in the furniture and decoration of the church would have crystallized the perception of constant celestial companionship in the minds of the congregation. The location of angels in these prominent sites made their presence palpable to the laity and establishes their importance to the medieval Catholic faith as fellow worshippers in the religious community.

The Ministry of Angels

> There are many reasons for our honouring and praising the angels. They are our guardians, our servants, our brothers, and our fellow citizens; they carry our souls into heaven; they present our prayers before God; they are noble soldiers of the eternal King and the consolers of the afflicted.[24]

The ubiquitous presence of angels in medieval Catholic culture had a wide-ranging impact on personal devotion and influenced many aspects of individual belief. Taking their cue from scripture and the lives of the saints, people harboured various expectations about the heavenly ministry. The above extract from Jacobus de Voragine's Saint Michael sermon summarises these hopes, articulating the belief that angels were sent to men to 'inflame our hearts with love ... enlighten our understanding and ... strengthen any weakness' and to ensure that the souls of every individual 'make progress in gaining grace'. Angels were chiefly thought to assist men on the path of the salvation through their role as messengers and protectors, mediators of both God's providence and mercy. This inspired a broad and inclusive understanding of the angelic mission.

As worshippers alongside humanity angels contributed to the merit of prayer, but also provided the laity with a model of the loyalty, respect and honour that was owed to God. To illustrate this point Voragine referred the reader to Saint Gregory, who had shown how characteristics of the different orders of angels might be used as role models for a good Christian life. In relation to the lowest hierarchy, Gregory suggested that brothers who had little knowledge were the equivalent of angels; brothers who grasp and make known the secrets of the heaven are archangels; and those who perform wonders are 'assumed among the Virtues'. At the second hierarchical level, those who put the evil spirits to flight through prayer are Powers, those who surpass and rule over the elect are Principalities; and those who dominate all vices and achieve purity are Dominations, 'Gods among men'. In the upper hierarchy, those who represent God's power on earth as rulers of the church correspond to the thrones; those who are filled with love of God are the Cherubim; and finally, there are those who are 'fired with the love of contemplating the things of heaven and pant with the sole desire of their Creator', those who reject earthly things and who 'love and burn and in that very ardour find rest'. These exceptional few will find their place among the Seraphim.[25]

The concept of heavenly beings therefore served as an important spur to piety. In the *Legenda* several of the saints were described as aspiring to angelic status – John the Baptist was compared to the cherubim and seraphim because he has 'fulfilled the offices of all the angels'; and in the sermon on the feast day of Paul the Apostle, Voragine invited comparison between saint and angels, describing the apostle as 'winging his way, as it were, over Greece and the lands of the heathen'.[26] The humility and obedience of heavenly spirits were considered the ideal for monastic life, but angels were particularly associated with chastity, an aspect which had further implications beyond the cloister walls.[27] Angels often appeared in the lives of those saints whose virginity contributed to their sanctification. Virginity was 'the sister of the angels', and was 'dear to God, related to the angels'. In addition, it was common to find angels protecting the pure status of chaste saints: Saint Agnes declared that she had with her 'a guardian of my body,

an angel of the Lord' and guardian angels prevented a lustful lady from enter-
ing the bedchamber of Saint Eusebius and corrupting his 'virginal life'.[28] Perhaps
most significantly, the archangel Gabriel was intimately associated with the most
holy Virgin of them all, through his Annunciation to Mary.[29] These ideas had
implications for personal devotion – although it was unrealistic for people to
attempt to live an angelic life, angels certainly served a didactic function in lion-
izing the status of virginity with the intention of encouraging sexual restraint.

Angels also influenced personal devotion in more direct ways by fulfilling
an instructive function and facilitating greater understanding of the narrative
of scripture. Angels appeared frequently in the bible, and even when not explicitly mentioned, it seems that it was natural for artists and authors to assume the
angelic presence and depict them regardless. At the beginning of the Old Testament, it was a Cherub that was set to guard the entrance to paradise after the
Expulsion of Adam and Eve, a passage that was usually represented in artwork by
two wretched figures being driven away by a stern looking angel with a sword.[30]
Other scriptural scenes were treated in similar ways, and wall paintings, bosses
and misericords also depicted the appearance of the angel to the shepherds
following the birth of Jesus; warned Joseph of Herod's intentions; and were
frequently depicted in scenes at Jesus' tomb following the Resurrection. They
were even found within scenes of the Resurrection itself, and in the widespread
image of Christ emerging from the sepulchre they appear flanking his figure,
arms raised in joyful celebration of events.[31]

Eamon Duffy has shown that in the later medieval period the clergy were
aiming to surpass the modest thirteenth-century aim of equipping the people
with merely the bare essentials of belief by providing more sophisticated instruction and a more extensive religious education. Literature was written to assist
the priest in his pastoral obligations, and the spread of literacy among the laity
encouraged the production of aids to understanding such as books of hours.
Collections of prayers and devotional material of a moral, catechetical, and
hagiographical character coexisted in these texts with secular elements such as
astrological information, divination techniques and charms. Duffy describes
this as a 'cruder, less inward piety' than that of the more learned members of
the congregation who might use Latin primers to assist their understanding of
belief and practice, but it was piety nevertheless, and there was much overlap
between the catechetical concerns of the two media. The sources demonstrate a
shared interest in religious instruction and spiritual improvement on the behalf
of layfolk.[32] Angels contributed to this growth in private prayer and personal
devotion through the ways in which they informed religious understanding.
They were implicated in these processes of education because they were instantly
recognizable and familiar figures, whose capacity to mediate between men and
the divine functioned not only in a literal sense, but also in a theological one,

because angels made the divine more accessible and perhaps more appealing to the lay audience. The possibility of direct experience of God was inconceivable for ordinary men, but interaction with angels was a more foreseeable prospect. Angels were infinitely more approachable, they could be comforting, inspiring and faith affirming, and they were symbols of the continued care and interest that God had for his creation. Thus angels could be used as a tool by the clergy to explain the nature of God's covenant with man and the story of his fall and redemption. Complex theological ideas about the nature of sin and salvation and the quality of God's mercy were made more comprehensible through association with the familiar concept.

For instance, angels were involved in explaining a pivotal episode in the narrative of Christian history. The Annunciation was the best known example of an angelic apparition and is one of the two scenes in which angels were most commonly depicted, with significant implications for individual faith.[33] This biblical episode infused Christian worship: Gabriel's salutation to the Virgin Mary forms the basis of the *Ave Maria* and images of the archangel's greeting are ubiquitous in the visual imagery of the church. Many wall paintings of the scene survive, often located in the holiest precinct of the church, the chancel, such as those at Little Melton, Norfolk; Chalgrove, Oxfordshire; and Martley in Worcestershire. The location denotes the significance accorded to the episode, as do numerous depictions of the scene in clerical vestments, roof bosses, stained glass and misericords. The scene was also represented within *Mirk's Festial* and *Legenda Aurea*, in the rare woodcuts that accompany the most important narratives in the text.[34]

This image reminded the laity that news of the incarnation was communicated to men through angels, and it illustrated the working of God's will, but its widespread popularity was certainly due to the growing importance of the cult of the Virgin Mary, a devotional development that was central to personal belief. From the eleventh century the increasing emphasis on the humanity of Jesus had led to a corresponding growth in awareness of his birth and therefore the importance of his mother, leading to the establishment of new feasts in her honour such as the 'Compassion of the Virgin' and the 'Presentation of the Virgin'. Angels benefited from this new interest in Mary by virtue of their involvement in her history and the Angelic Salutation and saying of the Rosary became increasingly important forms of personal devotion.

Allegiance to Mary was demonstrated by the production of numerous apocryphal writings on her life, and altars and chapels dedicated to the 'Lady' were to be found in churches throughout the country. As well as the proliferation of feast days in her honour, prayers and mediations on the Joys and Sorrows of the Virgin were a favourite form of Marian piety and were a staple of books of hours and primers.[35] In general terms, this meant that the presence of angels became more pronounced and parishioners were increasingly likely to see the image of an angel when they entered their parish church or opened a devotional book. The angelic responsibilities in Mary's life also provided more opportunity for reflection on celestial beings, and sermons delivered on the feasts of the Birth of the Blessed Virgin, Annunciation of the Lord, and the Assumption of the Virgin in both *Mirk's Festial* and *Legenda Aurea* all seized the chance to expound on the angelic nature.[36]

These developments had a more specific impact upon angelology. Unsurprisingly, they chiefly emphasized the angels' position as God's messengers. This was a responsibility reflected in their name, which was derived from the Greek *aggelos* meaning 'messenger', and which found many expressions in scripture and sermons on the saints' lives.[37] Angels also brought messages that led to the establishment of new observances in honour of the saints: an abbot had a vision revealing the holy status of one of the monks in his monastery; the day of Mary's birth was revealed to a holy man, who heard 'joyous choirs of angels chanting solemn paeans' on that particular day; and an angel appeared to a churchwarden to reveal that on All Saints 'the saints come together to intercede universally for us' and to tell him to establish a day in honour of these saints.[38]

Within the narrative of Mary's life, the angels provided 'techyng and ynformacyon' so that she might believe the archangel's message, and offered her comfort by advising 'be not adrede, but be glad and blythe' at the birth of her son. They were sent to provide an 'assurance of victory over the corruption of death', and an association with song is again evident, when angels 'token up a song of swete melody and heuynly mynstrelcy'.[39] The Annunciation also contributed to the development of the archangel Gabriel's distinct identity, because the Mass of Saint Gabriel in the *Use of Sarum* attributed him with the power to dispel 'the darkness of the Christian people' through his visitation and salutation.[40] However, although Marian devotion was central to the development of angelology, it conversely also ensured the angels' subordination in the heavenly hierarchy. David Keck suggests that because Mary, as the Mother of God, took the title 'Queen of the Angels' the angels began to be perceived as increasingly inferior.[41] Their presence authenticated the innovations of the cult of Mary but at the same time reduced their relative importance, and iconography and sermons sources reflect this shift. The common arrangement of the Annunciation scene sees Gabriel looking and often pointing towards Mary, indicating where the focus of attention lies for the viewer. Sermons provide similar evidence, 'we are invited to salute Mary by Gabriel's example' and Mirk related that when Gabriel approached Mary 'he knelyd downe, and worschepyd hur as hym oght forto do hys Lordys modyr' speaking 'mekely' to her.[42] Mary's arrival in heaven at the Assumption makes these relative positions abundantly clear, the angelic role in the passage below is solely to offer honour and worship to Mary for the perceptible influence she had on the fate of humanity:

> Today the heavens welcomed the Blessed Virgin joyfully, Angels rejoicing, Archangels jubilating, Thrones exalting, Dominations psalming, Principalities harmonizing, Powers lyring, Cherubim and Seraphim hymning and leading her to the supernal tribunal of the divine majesty.[43]

The association between Mary and angels also provides an insight into wider debates about the latter's relationship with the cults of the saints. If association with Mary caused the subordination of angels, the presence and status of the saints in late medieval religion also tended to divert attention away from angels and place limits upon the influence they had on individual devotion. Late medieval religion was characterized by dedication to the saints: they were a pervasive presence in the theology and iconography of the church. Saints were considered to be invaluable mediators and protectors, offering spiritual comfort to the laity, and they appeared to be charged with similar responsibilities to angels. Although it would be misleading to suggest that angels and saints were held in equal regard by medieval parishioners, the fact that archangels had names and more developed biographies undoubtedly contributed to their relative popularity, and there are indications that devotion to Michael, Gabriel and Raphael could resemble the pattern of other saints' cults. It is particularly significant that the *Use of Sarum* included separate masses for each of the angels, describing the specific characteristics of each.[44] However, there is no sense that saints and angels competed for the loyalty of the layman. Rather, the cult of the saints was just one of the numerous areas of religious life where angels did not fear to tread, and in their frequent appearances in the narratives of saints' lives, such as the life of the Blessed Virgin, they offered a distinctive contribution to forms of devotion.

Through their ministry the angels were believed to offer 'gret helpe and seuice' to mankind, and the more specific notions of angelic ministry are underpinned by the common aim of providing succour and protection for humanity.[45] The saints, given their intimate relationship with the divine, were particularly likely to experience this ministry, and their lives provided evidence of the circumstances where angels were expected to intervene. In many cases these notions can be traced back to the biographical details of the archangel Michael, and it appears that popular perceptions of the roles of angels were rooted in these legends as well as in scriptural appearances.

The foundation myth of the shrine to Michael on Mount Gargano in Italy provided an association with healing that had its roots in the early Christian era and was corroborated by the lives of the saints.[46] The shrine was established following apparitions of the archangel, and at the spot a 'sweet clear water' flowed from a rock. If drunk after communion this water ensured that people 'were cured of whatever diseases they had'. Voragine's sermon continued the curative theme with a miracle story relating how a seriously ill man dragged himself to the site of Michaelium near Constantinople, and there saw an apparition of Michael who conveyed medicine to him to rid him of his ailment. The healing powers of angels similarly appear in Mirk's sermon on the Legend of the Cross; an angel came to venerate a tree that had grown from the wood of the crucifix, and 'steret þe watyr' at the base of the tree. The first person to enter the pool afterwards 'was heled of what maner euell þat hym greuet'.[47] The traditional understanding of Raphael's Hebrew name was 'Medicine of God' and the book of Tobit provided many examples of his medicinal miracles. Furthermore, the belief was also attested to in the *Use of Sarum*, particularly during The Mass of the Archangel Raphael, which called upon the archangel to 'convey unto us the health of body and soul' to 'avoid the dangers of this present life and ... reach securely the joys of heaven'.[48]

Raphael also had special responsibility for the protection of travellers, an association derived from his guidance of Tobias on his journey to Media.[49] Raphael's Mass propagated these ideas by unusually prefacing the rite with an explanation of when it would be appropriate to perform:

> The following office of the Archangel Raphael can be celebrated for pilgrimages or travellers, that as he conducted and re-conducted Tobias safe and sound, so he would also bring back others in safety. It can also be celebrated for all infirmities, and also on behalf of demoniacs; because the angel is the angel of healing, who restored sight to Tobit, and delivered Sara, the wife of his son, from a devil.[50]

Within the *Use* there are also services for travellers and pilgrims, both of which make numerous references to angels, and mention Raphael by name.[51] The association of the angels with these particular functions was reinforced by these repeated references to his ministry, and undoubtedly people would have looked and prayed for angelic protection during times of sickness or at the commencement of a journey.

Michael's most prominent function was combating evil and acting as God's standard-bearer. As the leader of the heavenly host, Michael was the defender and protector of the elect, a role he assumed when he cast the fallen angels from heaven, and which will climax when he kills the Antichrist at the Lord's command, as foretold in Revelation. In the *Legenda* his protective responsibilities are represented in his victory over the dragon and his ability to save men from the temptation of evil demons, who come down to test us and 'are innumerable, like flies, they fill the whole air'. The wider repercussions of these beliefs for medieval eschatology will be considered below, but the idea of angelic protection also had important implications for individual devotion, because Michael and the angels were believed to curb the demons' power by impressing the memory of the Passion in men's minds, by removing obstacles to doing good and leading men back to the path of penance, and by strengthening weakness and enlightening understanding.[52]

Reprising their role of comforting Jesus in Gethsemane, angels often offered consolation to saints during their trials. So that Bartholomew 'schuld not be wery of hys gret trauayle', God sent angels 'forto kepe hym and to comfort hym', and they appeared to Katherine to bid her to be 'stedfast yn þe byleue'.[53] Angels are also credited with participation in many scriptural passages: Mirk ascribed to Michael the responsibility for accompanying Moses and Aaron into Egypt where the archangel is presumed to have worked many miracles (including the parting of the Red Sea), and he even credited angels with assisting Noah at the time of the Flood, when 'al maner of bestys, as God bade byfore, werne jbroght byfore Noye by help of þe angelys, and don yn þe schippe'.[54]

The elaboration of the idea of protection also resulted in the emergence and proliferation of the concept of the guardian angel, a personal spirit designated to each soul at birth, or perhaps conception, and which accompanied an individual throughout their life. The idea of specific guardian was based on two passages in the bible, was affirmed by the scholastics, and was later incorporated into the liturgy with prayers and votive masses dedicated to guardian angels.[55] Prayers to the guardian angel were a feature of the *Horae*, and there were vernacular translations which ensured their reception and use amongst the laity. Voragine's work again disseminated these ideas: he dedicated a lengthy section of his Saint Michael sermon to the function of angels as guardians and the benefits that this brought mankind. Voragine's understanding was that each man was designated a good and bad angel whilst still in the womb. The bad sought to deceive men through false reasoning and seduction, but the good countered this and attempted 'to instruct and direct him against falsehood, to exhort and incite him to good and defend him against cajolery, and to protect him against violent oppression'. The fruits of these efforts were to instil penance, to prevent sin and to combat the devil by curbing his power and reminding men of the Passion of Christ.[56] Testifying to the widespread diffusion of this concept, guardian angels were assigned to the protection of saints. In his sermon for Saint Paul, Paul's custody of Christendom is likened to the angels' protective role, as 'it has often happened that this or that people has been placed under the care of angels'. Similarly, several of the saints' individual angels are referred to within the text: 'the companion and guardian' of the admirable Saint Paula is called upon to testify to her sanctity and Saint Gregory has several encounters with a being who claims 'I am his [Gregory's] angel, and the Lord sent me back so that I might always protect you'.[57]

The most likely site of interaction within the *Festial* and *Legenda,* was when angels offered succour and protection to saints during their sufferings and persecution. Angels were often responsible for the release of saints from imprisonment. Angels set free Saints Remy, Secundus, Peter the Exorcist, Primus and Felicianus, Vitus and Modestus, James the Greater, Quentin and Theodore, and others ministered to prisoners by providing physical and spiritual nourishment. When Saint Vincent was in prison the darkness of the dungeon was dispelled by dazzling light, as the saint enjoyed 'the solace of angels ... and joined in the angel's chant', a sight which converted his guards. Meanwhile the throng of white men that came to Saint Theodore through the closed doors of his cell caused his jailers to flee in terror.[58] The popularity of this motif makes plain its importance, as does its theological origin.[59] The episodes were evidence of the special protection enjoyed by those dedicated to doing the Lord's work, but they also conveyed a further meaning. The angel that released Saint Remy from his cell opened the door without damage to its seal, recreating one of the circumstances of the Resurrection, and the conversion of guards was a similar common motif. Accordingly these narratives may deliberately echo the central drama of Christian history. An allegorical reading of these events would be that the saints are imprisoned by their heathen captors, but by God's will they are easily saved through the power of his grace and his promise of salvation, mediated to men through angels. There is other evidence to support this suggestion: in Voragine's Saint Remy sermon an angel tells Remy that the door of the prison will be opened forthwith 'so that you may know that the door of heaven is opened to you'; and the *Use* documents how an angel 'burstest prisons', whilst the 'Mass for One in Prison', gives thanks that 'the Lord hath sent his angel, and hath delivered me'.[60]

There are also numerous instances where angels intervene to thwart the cruel methods of martyrdom devised by the enemies of Christendom. An angel shattered the wheel that Saint Juliana was stretched upon and restored her broken bones, and Saint Christina was thrown into the sea by her heathen father 'but immediately angels bore her up' and placed her safely on dry land.[61] Angels also played a significant role in the martyrdom of Saint Katherine, a saint with a sizeable cult following and impressive presence in medieval devotion. A special torture on a wheel had been devised for Katherine but 'anon þer come an angyll from Heuen, and smot al þe wheles into peces ... and slogh anon ryght foure þousand' bystanders. Following her eventual death by beheading, angels continued to carry out their ministry:

> anon þerwyth come angeles, and token hyr body, and beren hit vp ynto þe eyre, and soo forth xx[ti] dayes iourne þennys to þe mownt of Synay, and þer buryet hit wyth gret worschyap wher God haþe wroght mony gret myracles.[62]

Depictions of Saint Katherine often included images of angels. An impressive wall painting at Sporle, Norfolk, depicts twenty-five scenes from the martyr's life, representing them in various guises: ministering to the saint in prison, or breaking the wheel and intervening at the end of her life. Such imagery emphasized the close relationship between saints and angels, proliferating belief about the ministry and responsibility of the celestial beings whilst also indicating the separate, but complementary roles of the two groups of intercessors.

The saints' lives therefore provided numerous examples of specific angelic protection, ideas that were conveyed to the congregation and would have informed their religious outlook, instilling the expectation that the celestial beings could provide spiritual comfort to beleaguered women and men. The regular appearance of angels at the time of a saint's martyrdom, like the description of the transportation of Saint Katherine's body in Mirk's sermon, alluded to an area of angelic belief that was integral to individual devotion and popular perceptions of the angelic ministry, but which also engaged with theological conceptions of the angels and their participation in eschatology. The contribution of the celestial beings at the time of death and the events succeeding it was a fundamental motif which linked the individual's struggle for salvation – enacted in the good and evil angels' battle for the soul around a man's deathbed – with God's gift of human salvation and the ultimate redemption of humanity. The final section will trace this involvement of angels in the 'Last Things'.

The Afterlife

The deathbed is recognized by historians as an important source of evidence for cultural and religious change, the belief and perceptions underpinning the ritual enacted there providing a valuable insight into contemporary religious mentalities.[63] Mortuary culture in late medieval England was informed by both secular and spiritual concerns and the management of the rites of dying, mourning and burial, and the theological understanding of the immediate and ultimate fate of the souls of the dead reveals these underlying currents. Angels have a pervasive role in these 'Last Things', and this involvement was profoundly influential for religious cultures. Beliefs about death and salvation influenced personal devotion relating to the fate of the individual, but also had greater didactic and theological connotations in the wider context of the functioning of God's mercy and the ultimate redemption of mankind, each of which will be considered in this section.

The transportation of Saint Katherine's body to her final resting place is part of a wider theme which sees angels intervening to assist in the performance of burial rituals of various saints. In a similar fashion, Saint Secundus' decapitated corpse was taken by God's angels who 'with praises and chants gave it burial'.[64] It is particularly apt that following the martyrdom of the influential angelologist Saint Dionysius, his body 'stood up, took his head in its arms, and, with an angel and a heavenly light leading the way, marched two miles ... to the place where by his choice and God's providence he rests in peace'.[65] These narratives are indicative of the importance of the burial ritual in medieval religion, a fact that is stated explicitly in the sermons: Saint Quiricus and his mother Julitta are cut up by their persecutors so that Christians cannot give them a proper burial, although the intention is thwarted because 'the pieces were 'collected by an angel and buried at night'.[66] These notions can be traced back to an apocryphal narrative of Adam's death, where an angel was thought to have appeared to Adam's surviving relatives. The angel carried the message that 'it es my lordes will, I sal teche here зоw vnto, How зe with þis cors sall do ... Gers beri þam in erth or stane'.[67] Thus the angels are credited with instructing mankind in the correct form of Christian burial, an association that would have been confirmed by the involvement of the celestial beings in the last rites: in the *Use of Sarum* a prayer 'For a Person very near to Death', the prayer 'Before the Day of Burial' and 'The Office of the Dead' all invoked the angels.[68] The association of angels with the Last Things was also closely related to the Cult of the Virgin Mary, where it gained further expression in narratives of Mary's life. According to the sermons on the Assumption in both *Legenda Aurea* and *Mirk's Festial,* angels announced to Mary her imminent death and participated in her funeral procession, 'filling the whole earth with the sweet sound of her song' and defending her body from spiteful Jews who attempted to disrupt the ceremony.[69]

The angelic role at the time of death was not limited to an association with funeral rites and management of the corpse however. Narratives of the Assumption were probably an important source for a motif that was central to medieval angelology and was one of the most important angelic responsibilities – the belief that angels carried the souls of the dead to heaven. In Assumption sermons, Christ appears 'and fache þi soule wyth multitude of angelys, and bere hit vp ynto Heuyn wyth gret joy and blysse', an image depicted strikingly in many editions of Voragine's *Legenda Aurea*. The belief is further attested to in the sermon for Saint Michael and All Angels, where angels are said to 'beron vp sowles ynto Heuen', this being one of the chief reasons that humans should honour the celestial beings.[70]

The expectation that angels would carry the soul to its final resting place was originally derived from the parable of Lazurus and the rich man (Luke 16:19–31), where the soul of the beggar was said to have been carried by angels to Abraham's bosom. It also appeared in the *Sarum Use* in the 'Postcommunion Before the Day of Burial', where God is implored to 'cause the soul of thy servant *N.* to be received by the angels of light, and to be carried to the habitations prepared for the blessed'.[71] The notion of angels as carriers of souls gained its fullest artistic expression within depictions of the Assumption, a scene that pervaded medieval religious art despite there being no scriptural warrant for the episode. It was a common subject for stained glass windows such as the two excellent examples at Beckley, Oxford, where Mary is surrounded by six angels, four lifting her heavenwards whilst a further two are censing; it appears in misericords at

Lincoln and Saint Michael's in Occold, Suffolk; and it is a very popular subject for roof bosses such as those at Norwich and Winchester Cathedrals.[72]

The association also demonstrates how Marian devotion could enhance the theological and physical presence of the angels within religious culture, but once again the celestial beings were subordinate to the luminous presence of the Queen of the Angels herself. This subordination was emphasized by her Coronation, an episode that was believed to have followed the Assumption and which therefore often accompanied depictions of Mary's ascension. Within these scenes it was common for the artist to give an angel the role of placing the crown on Mary's head, graphically suggesting the ordering of the heavenly hierarchy – with the celestial beings below the mother of Christ.

Jacobus de Voragine used the idea of angelic stewardship of the soul extensively in his sermons on the lives of the saints. Saint Anthony the Hermit witnessed 'angels bearing the soul of Saint Paul heavenwards', and Saint Martha 'heard the angelic choirs bearing her sister's soul to heaven'.[73] The motif was equally familiar in Mirk's collection, after Saint Thomas died 'angeles broghten hym befor God' and bystanders at Saint Margaret's martyrdom 'saw her sowle come out of her body as a mylke-whyte coluer; and angelys token hit, and beren hit ynto Heuyn'.[74] The theme frequently recurred in medieval iconography: several of the angels in the Lincoln Angel Choir bear souls in their arms; the woodcut accompanying Voragine's sermon for the Feast of All Soul's depicts two angels carrying a number of souls heavenwards, and angels were a pervasive presence on the tombs and monuments of the period.

Tombs are particularly significant sources as they represented sites that related to the individual salvation of their patrons, but which were also a public memorial and reminder to the congregation of theological understandings of the nature of death and redemption. In the same way, the presence of the angels on these memorials represented their engagement in the personal struggle to live a pious Christian life, but also testified to their expected participation at the climax of Christian history, the Resurrection. The persistence of the image of angels in mortuary culture can therefore also be accounted for because of their perceived role in combating evil and engaging in a ceaseless battle with the evil angels for the salvation or damnation of humankind.

On a personal level, the struggle between good and evil was at its most intense at the end of life when men were most weak and vulnerable, but this was also the moment that angels had the potential to be most beneficial to mankind. The deathbed was a chief battleground, because there good and evil angels were thought to compete for the custody of the dying man's soul. Good angels were present to prevent the human from succumbing to the diabolical intentions of the devil, who would seek to tempt the dying into spiritual complacency or even despair. Angels provided hope and encouragement, and were a comforting reminder of God's grace and the possibility of spiritual salvation: the 'Office for the Dead' beseeched God that 'thou wouldest not deliver it [the soul] to the hand of thy enemy, nor forget it at the last, but that thou wouldest command it to be received by the holy angels, and be carried to the land of the living'.[75]

The anticipation of a cosmic struggle at the moment of death inspired a genre of texts known as *ars moriendi*, handbooks of dying that provided a guide of how to achieve a good Christian death. These aids to personal devotion were replete with the angelic presence and confirmed belief in the angelic role at the deathbed.[76] William Caxton's 1490 treatise on the 'arte and crafte to knowe well to dye', is a perfect example of this – the reader is encouraged to 'calle on the holy angellys' for assistance, that 'the right splendaunt companye of angelles be atte thy departynge and mete the', 'that ye delyuer me myghtily from the awaytes and fallaces of my aduersaryes', and that 'the goode angelles of god maye accompanye the in thy comynge to glory'.[77] The woodcuts illustrating these texts provided further support for the notion; angels are depicted exhorting the dying to remain steadfast in their faith and they receive the soul of the deceased to convey them to their final resting place.

The importance of a 'good death' was attested to in Voragine and Mirk's sermons, which often also documented the presence of angels at the deathbed. It is no surprise to find them discussed in Voragine's Assumption sermon: this time in the context of Mary's anxiety after the angel informed her of her coming death. The angel reassured her that her victory over the corruption of death was not in doubt, but still Mary gathered her friends to tell them to 'be watchful, because when someone is dying, both the godly power of the angels, and wicked spirits, come to the death-bed'. Other saints were equally vulnerable: while on her deathbed saint Elizabeth was often visited by a little bird that sang to her, 'this bird we take to have been her angel, who was delegated to be her guardian and also to assure her of eternal joy'. There is also a vivid account of a vision that Saint Fursey experienced in his final hour, where three angels succeeded in carrying his soul to heaven, despite the obstacles that numerous demons placed in the way.[78] The angelic presence at the deathbed signalled the working of God's grace, those who fought the temptations of the evil demons and who strove to achieve a pious and repentant life were thus assured of safe passage to the next.

It is likely that the sword-bearing angel leading Fursey on his perilous journey was Saint Michael, who was commonly depicted in martial apparel and who was believed to be present at the deathbed in his capacity to combat evil. The more general expectation of angelic presence around the deathbed also found its origins in scripture: a passage in Jude 9 named the archangel when he contended with the devil over the body of Moses. Sermons delivered on Michael's feast day also emphasized this role; Mirk thought that God turned to the archangel when he 'wold do wondurfull þyng or dede' because he was 'victoryus yn his feghtyng', furthermore 'Mychaell and his angelys foghten wyth Lucifer ... and drof out of Heuen þe dragon and all hys feres', and 'he schall sle þe Antecryst yn þe mownt of Olyuete'. Voragine similarly referred to the scriptural passages, describing how 'the standard bearer of the celestial host, marched up and expelled Lucifer and his followers ... and shut them up in this dark air until the Day of Judgement'; and anticipating how 'the great prince ... will rise and stand forth, a valorous aid and protector against the Antichrist'.[79]

The image of Michael's defeat of the dragon was symbolic of his ongoing battle against evil and also anticipated his participation at Judgement Day. The battle was an integral part of medieval visual culture and was consequently likely to have been one of the most familiar images for the average parishioner, causing them to look to Michael and the other angels for protection against the forces of evil, particularly around the time of their death.[80]

It has already been noted that the angelic responsibilities for healing and the protection of travellers were in part derived from the foundation myths associated with shrines to Saint Michael. These legends also confirmed the angelic role of battling evil. Voragine's sermon documented the common belief that Michael had appeared at the shrine at Monte Gargano in Apulia to assist in the military victory of the Sipontus over the pagan Neopolitans. Mirk elaborated on the tale, describing the 'arowse of fyre and boltes of thondyr' that engulfed the battlefield, and the conversion to Christianity of all the survivors of the day.[81] The visual imagery in combination with the beliefs which proliferated in association with Michael, who significantly was the only angel also privileged with sainthood, ensured the proliferation of his cult. The importance of his feast day was given extra weight because Michaelmas was also the occasion for reckoning of accounts at the end of the agricultural year, a fact that would have etched the significance of the date in the minds of many parishioners.

There was also a second feast in Michael's honour in the Roman Kalendar, commemorating his appearance on Monte Gargano on May 8. Either of these dates would have been occasions of particular devotion to the archangel, whose name would have been invoked in prayers and whose deeds, as we have seen, were venerated in sermons. The feast days might also have been the occasion for a pilgrimage to the shrines where Michael was believed to have appeared and which were dedicated to his memory. In France a vision of the archangel had led to the founding of Mont-Saint-Michel in Brittany, a genuinely popular pilgrim centre which may have been accessible to the more well off medieval English parishioners. However, the expense of such a journey would probably have made it more feasible to visit the English alternative situated at Saint Michael's Mount, Cornwall.[82]

Although the popularity of the cult of Saint Michael appeared to be waning in the latter part of the medieval period, there is evidence of its persistence: churches continued to be dedicated to the archangel and his image was still a popular motif in the decorative schemes of manuscripts and architecture. Loyalty to the archangel was sustained and evidently benefited from association with developing religious piety.[83] After her death Mary may have 'merited a throne above the Cherubim and Seraphim', but Christ had privileged Michael with special responsibility for carrying Mary's soul to this final resting place.[84]

The perception of angelic protection from the malevolent forces at work in the Christian universe was clearly a popular idea that had a unique influence for personal devotion. Whether in conjunction with beliefs about Mary and the saints, or with Michael, the standard bearer of the celestial army himself, the understanding that angels existed 'in accord with the kindness of God' with the aim of meeting 'the neediness of mankind' underpinned common late medieval conceptions.[85] The angelic role at the end of earthly life was particularly important, as this was a time of great spiritual vulnerability for the laity when the neediness of humans was at its height.

There was one final aspect of the angels' association with the 'Last Things' which had profound implications for religious culture. Involvement in the Resurrection incorporated many aspects of the celestial duty and represented the climax of the angelic ministry through participation in human redemption itself. At a personal level, the concept of the guardian angel was a recurring element in perception of the Final Judgement, as it was a common belief that the battle between good and evil forces continued at the Resurrection. Mirk's homily for Advent Sunday described how a soul will be brought before Christ 'hys domesman' with 'hys angyll on þat on syde tellyng hym redely wher and how of he haþe don amys; on þat oþer syde fendes chalenchyng hym horres as by ryght'. A guardian angel accompanied a man throughout life not only as a source of protection and strength, but also as a representative of God's omnipotence, and a reminder that each man would be called to account for his actions in life at the time of Judgement. This idea had a scriptural basis in Job 20:27 which stated that 'the heavens will reveal his [the soul's] iniquity', and Voragine elaborated on the idea, saying that the witnesses at the trial are God, conscience, and 'his own angel assigned to be his guardian; and the angel, knowing everything he has done, will bring testimony against him'. This was yet another way in which beliefs about angels could serve as a spur to piety and as a reminder of the need to live a Christian life. Of course, the guardian angels would also stand as witnesses to the better side of man's nature, a function they are called upon to fulfil in Voragine's sermon for Saint Paula. Angels would not only present prayers to God during earthly life, but were present as intercessors to plead on the behalf of the soul at its end.[86]

Presiding over this judgement is Saint Michael in his capacity as the weigher of souls, the office that was probably most well-known to the medieval congregation. The importance of the Doom painting to medieval visual culture has already been discussed with reference to the appearances of angels in depictions of Christ in his majesty,[87] and it was also typical of these judgement scenes to include an image of Saint Michael holding the scales used to weigh a man's soul, which determined if the man would be granted salvation and entrance to heaven. Michael as the weigher of souls would have been one of the most familiar depictions of an angel in any medium. This was particularly fitting, considering that this was Michael's most profound responsibility. Images would have popularized this aspect of the angelic role, and furthermore they gave the celestial beings an integral position at the heart of the biblical narrative, locating them in the centre of the main drama of Christian history.[88]

In his comprehensive survey of English medieval sculpture, Arthur Gardner suggested that as the medieval period progressed angels became a 'stock motif of decoration', serving merely as attractive features for the brackets and bosses of parish churches and filling the spandrels of cathedral choirs.[89] However, images of Saint Michael and the other angels participating in the Resurrection and Judgement directly contradict this view. Angels may have been becoming more popular as decorative objects, but this evidently did not preclude their involvement in scenes with special theological importance. Equally, alongside a decorative function, the wider context of angelic iconography might imply other meanings: an angel could hold a coat of arms on the tomb of a nobleman, but the association with the grave and death would undoubtedly have imbued the sculpture with further meaning, calling to mind the importance of the angelic ministry in the enactment of the 'Last Things'. Returning to the image of Michael in the Doom paintings, it is clear that the angel is to be found here in an allegorical role. The archangel appears as God's agent, representing the concept of his mercy and illustrating to the unlearned congregation the possibility that mere men might be granted God's great gift of salvation. The presence of angels at the Expulsion, after Adam and Eve have committed the original sin, had associated celestial beings with the fall of man, but it is also an angel that completes the cycle and facilitates mankind's redemption from sin in the doom cycle. As well as their representation in the figure of Saint Michael, angels performed other duties drawn from the account of Resurrection in Revelation: they swooped down blowing trumpets to herald the commencement of Final Judgement, they roused the dead from their graves, ushered them towards their final trial and welcomed redeemed souls into heaven. The angelic participation in Judgement is depicted in numerous surviving wall paintings: they blow trumpets at Rotherfield, East Sussex; Hales, Norfolk; and Broughten, Buckinghamshire; at Clayton, West Sussex and Bacton, Suffolk they lead the blessed to paradise; at Stoke-by-Clare, Suffolk they assist the rising dead; they welcome souls to heaven at Trotten, East Sussex and Chesterton, Cambridge; and at Chelsworth, Suffolk, an angel swoops down to do battle with a demon that has claimed a soul.

Angels were therefore used in the iconography of the church as a tool to explain God's covenant with man and to convey complex ideas about the nature of sin and salvation. Once again good and evil struggle for precedence, this time in the opposite pans of the weighing scale, and the message of the scene is simple: living a pious life will tilt Michael's scales in the soul's favour and the gates of heaven will open to them. Alternatively, the sinful must be wary of Mirk's 'fendes chalenchyng hym horres', because the devil and his minions are also central players at judgement, attempting to tilt the scales in their favour in readiness to drag the wretched souls down to hell.

The functioning of man's salvation and the nature of the covenant with God also provided the impetus for another of the devotional innovations of the late medieval period. Ultimately it was the Incarnation and the Passion that made redemption attainable and which formed the Good News of the Christian message. Along with dedication to Mary, meditation on Christ and his suffering therefore became an increasingly important part of official and personal religion. Angels were to reap the benefits of an association with the increasingly Christocentric flavour of religious culture. This realignment of devotion was expressed in similar ways to the Marian influence, in the establishment of new liturgical feasts such as those of Corpus Christi, the Crown of the Thorns, the Name of Jesus; and the cult of the Five Wounds, which was also accompanied by a commemorative feast. The cult nurtured an intense piety based on meditations of Christ's sacrifice for mankind. The objects of the Passion – the spear used to pierce Christ's side, the sponge dipped in gall and held to his lips, and the other instruments of torture – were the iconography associated with it, important for angels because they were credited with the role of gathering the instruments of the Passion in preparation for judgement.

The assembly of the instruments of the Passion is a role that Voragine mentioned in his homily for Michael and All Angels, where he attributed this responsibility to Michael alone with the statement that 'it is he who will present the cross, the nails, the spear and the crown of thorns at the Day of Judgement'.[90] This belief therefore makes intelligible another popular aspect of medieval visual culture: the proliferation of series of angels holding the objects of Christ's Passion. These sculptures again contradict Gardner's assertion that angels became 'little more than fairies whose functions are to hold up the scrolls or shield of arms, and to minister to the glorification of human masters'.[91] On the contrary, the dramatic figures of these angels performed the same function as the image of the crucifix in visual representations of the struggle at the deathbed: they reminded the viewer of the mercy of God in allowing the possibility of redemption, whilst at the same time sanctioning the damning to eternal punishment of those who denied the Passion. Angels carrying Instruments of the Passion are ubiquitous in medieval art: they appear in doom paintings at Ashamptstead,

Berkshire; Pickworth, Lincolnshire; Broughton, Cambridgeshire; and Blythe, Nottinghamshire and on bosses at Tewkesbury Abbey; Lechdale, Gloucestershire; Salle; Christchurch, Hampshire; Newbury, Berkshire and Wells Cathedral. Hammer-beams decorated by angels are particularly common in Cambridgeshire, Lincolnshire, Norfolk and Suffolk. St Wendreda in March and St Mary's at Doddington in Cambridgeshire; Holy Trinity, Blythburgh, Suffolk; and St Michael-at-Plea in Norwich, Norfolk are impressive examples.

God's mercy and justice was represented in these simple visual reminders of the narrative of the central covenant of Christian history. Consequently, although it is true that the hammer-beam angels which survive in numbers across eastern England were a useful and attractive means of finishing the roof of the parish church, these sculptures were evidently constructed with the clear intention of providing people with an experience of awe, wonder and spectacle, as well as being designed to communicate central aspects of the Catholic Church's teaching.[92]

Angels were further associated with growing devotion to Christ because it was believed that Raphael had provided the order of service for a new feast of 'The Five Wounds of Our Jesus Christ', a belief that Voragine reiterated in his homily for the day. This mass was indulgenced by Innocent VI (1362) or John XXII (1334), and provided further support for the idea of Raphael as 'God's medicine'; the archangel provided a seriously ill Pope Boniface with the Office for the mass and informed him that if he repeated the words sixty-five times he would receive health.[93] 'The Office of the Five Wounds' therefore indicated how angels might contribute to the authentication of novel religious practice and endorse further devotion to Christ, whilst also reinforcing their position at the heart of Christian theology.

Summary

Analysis of the numerous areas of medieval religious life where angels were to be found has revealed the versatility and utility of this aspect of devotion for medieval religious cultures. Angels were useful because they were familiar figures to the unlearned laity; their presence was imbued with meaning, and acted as an aid to devotion and piety whilst also fulfilling many didactic functions. Their varied contribution to numerous aspects of religious life makes angelic belief diffuse, but these qualities are also the characteristics that make angels a rich source of evidence, and which provide a compelling insight into medieval religious culture more broadly.

This survey has shown that the average medieval layman in all probability entertained various beliefs about angels' existence and ministry. The medieval church was well equipped to convey these complex ideas via media that were accessible to their audience. The abundance of material evidence in this chapter has indicated how the dissemination of these ideas was achieved, and is a testament to the enthusiastic deployment of the angelic motif in the visual culture of the medieval church. Vernacular sermons were an important means of conveying to the laity the more complex aspects of angelology, but this was complemented by visual sources such as the detailed depictions of the Nine Orders of Angels that still survive on the Rood screens at Barton Turf, Southwold and in the stained glass of Spurriergate, York, and Malvern Priory.[94]

Consideration of the nature of medieval angelic belief has also demonstrated that the angels were intimately associated with the saints, and has shown that they might carry out similar roles. In times of sickness, at the outset of a journey, prior to a battle and particularly at the end of life, angels were prayed to and their special protection was invoked, and lurid descriptions of the doom, in manuscripts, sermons, and writ large on the chancel arch, conveyed a vivid and powerful sense of the participation of the angels at the heart of Christian history.

Saint Michael was the standard bearer of the celestial host, a medieval hero who had rich metaphysical existence and incorporeal individuality that provided the foundation for a cult in his honour. However, his capacity as the weigher of souls also represents the essential qualitative difference in the ministry offered by saints and angels. Whereas saints acted primarily as intercessors, assisting the laity in times of need and acting as somewhat indulgent protectors, angels assumed these responsibilities but also undertook a parallel function as the instruments of God's justice. They were the agents of God's providence, and they were expected to inflict punishment on unrepentant sinners and to smite the wicked alongside their more benevolent roles as guardians and defenders in the fight against evil. This is a theme that runs through *Mirk's Festial*, his angels maintain a stern countenance, and there is repeated emphasis that sin 'is right fowle in Goddys sight and all his angeles', and that the pious man should struggle to avoid those 'stynkyng wedys of vyces...þat makyþe our angelys eschew our company'.[95] Saints were a source of comfort and protection; angels were more complex beings, channels both of God's mercy and stern justice.

Although this chapter has focused on the 'positive' aspects of late medieval angelology, in accordance with the surviving evidence, it should also be acknowledged at this juncture that the belief and practice associated with angelology might in some cases serve as a source of anxiety for the church. The superstitious invocation of angelic names and use of prayers summoning celestial protection were areas that might on occasion shade into unorthodoxy. These problems could be traced back to ancestral traditions and the assimilation by the early churchmen of older non-Christian beliefs. Lesser deities had been refashioned as celestial beings subordinate to the one true god, fulfilling a need for protection against evil demons and 'replacing other possible sources of supernatural enchantment with a Christianized form of magical control'.[96] Churchmen would always have been aware that compromising with earlier ideas could open the way for pagan survivals, and these concerns, combined with evidence of such continuing unorthodox activity, inspired attempts by the medieval Church to suppress questionable practices. A Roman Council at the end of the fifth century ruled against amulets which invoked the names of angels, insisting that they were the names for demons, and Charlemagne and Ansegisus had to forbid the calling upon angels by names that were not scriptural.[97] Once removed from their ecclesiastical setting, churchmen struggled to control these formidable creatures, and some areas of personal devotion show the signs of the abuse or manipulation of their supernatural power. These struggles were to resurface in the mid-sixteenth century, and these anxieties will be examined in greater detail in the following chapters.

Finally, although this study does not propose an extensive investigation of the significance of angels in secular drama (particularly the mystery plays), it is likely that the appearance of angels in this context helped to formulate and enhance belief outside the ecclesiastical setting. Secular drama aimed at rendering the truths of the Christian faith graphic and compelling, and in these 'living books' the cosmic scale of events was never far from the surface.[98] Because of their extensive role in the narrative of Christian history, angels were to be found in many of the key episodes within the plays, and their presence there confirmed many of the roles suggested by the medieval liturgy and sermon sources, and were a literal illustration of the expectations and belief that contemporaries harboured about the celestial beings. The civic importance of the mystery plays has also been explored by scholars who see them as public demonstrations of 'civic pride and community effort', encompassing complex layers of symbolism.[99] Thus the constant coming and going of angelic figures on the stage, and their integral part in the narrative of Christian salvation was a reminder of their responsibility as worshippers alongside men. It was not only the social body that was manifested within the play cycle, but the entire body of the universal church, angels and men included. Differentiation was also an important element – the privileged position of angels as agents of God's providence at the top of the universal hierarchy was indicated by the presentation of these creatures on stage, and they were set apart by their costume and actions. However, ultimately these angels were still integral members of the society on its pilgrimage through life, just as they were implicit in mankind's eventual redemption.[100]

The process of Reformation, beginning in the sixteenth century, profoundly altered the religious landscape in both a physical and theological sense. A survey of late medieval religious culture has demonstrated the ubiquity of the angelic presence, but it is subsequent events that have the potential to reveal the full significance of the angelic role and the importance of the heavenly beings for the functioning of the religious universe as a whole. The next chapter will seek to discover whether reformers were forced to compromise their theological principles in the face of a resilient collection of beliefs that would prove difficult to erase. It will attempt to answer the question of whether angels were allowed to survive because they performed what might be termed a 'load-bearing' function in religious culture, providing the laity with much-needed succour and protection and functioning as an essential support for the system of eschatology.

2 THE PROTESTANT ANGEL, *c.* 1530–80

The dramatic restructuring of the religious landscape of sixteenth-century England was to have a profound effect on belief about angels. The decades between 1530 and 1580 witnessed the transformation of parochial religious culture as the authorities struck at the heart of the principal expressions of communal faith and observance. The papacy, mass, monastic institutions, intercessory prayer, purgatory, and the cult of the saints came under sustained attack, and traditional religion was comprehensively overhauled. From the perspective of reformers committed to the principles of *sola fidei* and *sola scriptura,* traditional understanding of the angels themselves involved certain indefensible elements, focused around their assumed role as mediators between men and the divine. Furthermore angels were associated with Catholic devotional practices that to the reformers reeked of 'superstition', and there was intense anxiety about the veneration accorded to them, particularly those with names and cult followings. As Peter Marshall and Alexandra Walsham note in the introduction to their collection of essays on celestial beings, 'angels had been badly compromised by their collaboration with many of the worst excesses of the late medieval devotional regime'.[1]

However, albeit somewhat altered, angels survived the vicissitudes of the profoundly destructive English Reformation, and went on to assume a new status in the post-Reformation era. The fundamental reason for this was their sound scriptural credentials. These provided reformers with undeniable proof of their existence, and they were therefore obliged to find a place for angels in the reformed universe they were in the process of constructing, regardless of what they would perceive as the more distasteful rituals and belief that were associated with them. The reformers rejected some aspects of angelology, whilst they retained and elaborated on others, giving the angels a new, reformed identity, tightly bound to the evidence furnished by scripture. It is possible to explain this process and to uncover why the reformers were happy to embrace some elements of the angelic personality but not others, by examining the intellectual constructions and the reformed principles that gave rise to the realignment of belief.

The persistence of angelic belief thus offers a unique opportunity to explore the survival and mutation of a component of traditional belief in Reformation

England, and to examine an aspect of devotion where negotiation with older understanding was at least a possibility. Although historians have paid surprisingly little attention to this particular element of the reformed supernatural universe,[2] in his book on the European Reformation Diarmaid MacCulloch does acknowledge that angels occupied an important position in developing religious cultures. In fact, he conceives of the survival of angelic belief not as an accommodation on the behalf of the reformers, but rather as the eager appropriation of these creatures as a convenient weapon in the struggle to convert the laity to the true faith. MacCulloch argues that angels took over the intercessory and protective functions previously ascribed to saints, providing a Protestant alternative to a popular Catholic devotion and clearing the way for the rise of the angels as 'the ideologically appropriate friends of humanity'.[3]

Put crudely, this amounts to a suggestion that angels were substituted for saints and it speaks to recent debates about how Protestantism was able to enter the hearts and minds of the English laity, and how the populace adjusted to doctrinal revolution as a permanent fact. The recent 'post-revisionist' trend in Reformation studies is to see continuity with the past rather than a radical dislocation, with the gradual modification of belief and an ongoing dialogue between traditional understanding and innovative reformed ideas.[4] It is possible that belief about heavenly beings formed one of these points of intersection and accommodation: certainly MacCulloch's suggestion that angels took on the responsibilities previously shouldered by the saints would fit neatly into such analysis. The reformers' categorical rejection of the intercessory powers of saints, along with the abolition of purgatory and prayers for the dead, left the laity bereft of devotional mechanisms that had previously provided them with succour and comfort, and undermined the hope and means of achieving eventual salvation. Angels had the credentials to fill this emotional and spiritual void, and their scriptural presence made them a potentially useful pastoral resource for the reformers. However, there is also evidence to suggest that the angels were *enthusiastically* adopted by the reformers, not least due to the scriptural evidence of their ministry, and their enshrinement in several reformed confessions.[5]

This chapter will therefore explore the survival of angelic belief in light of the post-revisionist understanding of the Reformation, seeking to test MacCulloch's hypothesis, but also to investigate how far, if at all, reformers were forced to compromise their theological principles in the face of a resilient collection of beliefs that could not be suppressed, or at least could not be suppressed without great difficulty. With this in mind, the first section will examine the initial impact of reformed theology on angels, identifying areas that were the focus of controversy and exploring the extent of continuity and change with regard to late medieval perceptions. The second section will broaden the scope of the investigation by examining the influence of iconoclasm on the physical manifestation of angels, whilst the third will seek to uncover new theological emphases in angelology as a result of the processes of reform. Confessional identities became increasingly complex during the post-Reformation era, and angels offer to shed some light on the complicated mix of religious ideas and motifs that were beginning to form the essential features of English Protestantism.

Compromised Belief

We ought not to invoke, honor or pray unto angels and saints, or to fast, kepe holy day, sing or hear masses and the sacrifice or make any [illegible] in the worship of any saint or angel, nor yet to byld any temples of [sic] altars or to make any service for them or to worship and serve them many dyvers ways / to take them for patrones or defenders, to seeke help for all manner of things of them and to byleve that every one of them hath a peculyer proper vertu by himself ... for it is very more idolatry for to doo for as such honor is peculiarly due to God only and to no other.[6]

The principle of justification by faith, allied with belief in predestination and the abolition of purgatory, had profound implications for angels. Reformed thinking had an immediate impact upon angels in the liturgy, the collection of formularies for the conduct of divine service which was the foundation of the seasonal cycle of fast and feasting, ritual and festival, which shaped the religious life of early modern communities. The liturgy shaped peoples' perceptions of angels, and it remained one of the principal means by which belief was formed. Eamon Duffy has identified the variety of levels at which the liturgy functioned, providing spectacle, instruction, communal context for affective piety, and serving as a stimulus to personal devotion. It was central to lay religious consciousness and was also utilized as a means to negotiate social relations, its processions and ceremonies supplying the opportunity for the 'sacramental embodiment of social reality'.[7] The gradual introduction of the vernacular into the liturgy transformed the laity's experience during attendance at church, and the books of common prayer (the first promulgated by both the ecclesiastical and secular authorities in 1549), were particularly important in this respect. Streamlining the various Roman service books and different uses that had previously provided the basis of the liturgy, the book was published with the professed intention of removing all 'uncertain Stories, Legends, Responds, Verses, vain Repetitions, Commemorations, and Synodals' from the text.[8] Although angels had less of a presence in the 1549 *Prayer Book* than they did in the *Use of Sarum* (a presence that was set to diminish in the 1552 and 1559 editions respectively) the fact that angels appear with relative frequency is a clear indication of the esteem that they continued to be held in, and signals that they were not to be condemned in any of these categories. It also means that initial omissions, and subsequent revisions, to the Prayer Books can provide the historian with an indication of the evolution of reformed ideas about angels. The evidence shows that that there were some aspects of angelology that were rejected outright, but it is clear that there was much ambiguity over many of the angelic qualities.

For example, it is surprising to find that the 1549 *Book of Common Prayer* incorporated a moment in the mass when the priest entreated God to accept the prayers that the community was offering and that the angels would carry up to heaven. The passage runs: 'we beseech thee to accept this our bounden duty and service, and command these our prayers and supplications, by the ministry of thy Holy Angels, to be brought up before the Holy Tabernacle before the sight of the divine majesty'.[9] However, this text was eradicated from the 1552 and 1559 editions of the prayer book, and with good reason. Although other areas of angelology provoked internal discussion and disagreement amongst the reformers, they were united in denial of angelic acts of intercession or mediation.

John Calvin made this explicit in *The Institutes*, writing 'Away, then, with that Platonic philosophy of seeking access to God by means of angels, and courting them with the view of making God more propitious', and reminding his readers that 'it is solely by the intercession of Christ that the ministry of angels extends to us'.[10] Although in Scripture celestial beings descend and ascend the ladder in Jacob's vision, this is only possible due to the presence of God at the zenith, directing the ministry. Other influential reformers were in agreement; in his sermon on good and evil spirits Heinrich Bullinger wholly endorsed the existence and ministry of angels, but warned that angels are causes 'further off' whereas 'God is the nearest and most principal cause'. Like Calvin, he was keen to emphasize that 'Jesus Christ is the only Mediator and Intercessor for all the faithful', rejecting any rival claimants to this role, whether saints or angels.[11] Again, in *A Booke of Christian questions and answers*, translated into English in 1572, Theodore Beza discussed praying to angels, asking 'howe may that bee done in faith, seeing we know not ... nor finde anye worde or example of it in the holy Bible', 'there is none to be compared, either in power or loue towards us, unto Christ God and man'.[12]

Continuing their traditional deployment as a useful didactic instrument, churchmen were prone to using angels to emphasize the central Protestant tenet that salvation could only come through Christ. There were numerous catechetical works similar to Beza's *Booke of Questions* that echoed the opinions of the reformers in this respect. For example, in Edward VI's reign, Edmund Allen's catechumen asks if he is permitted to use the help and intercession of the holy angels, but receives the stern reply that 'we oughte to seeke nor use none other meanes to obteyne the favour of God ... than alonely suche as the Lorde hymselfe hath appointed in his holy worde: but to put all our trust and confidence in God, and in our lorde onely'.[13] The trend continued later in Elizabeth's reign when Edward Dering noted in his discussion of the second commandment that 'in spirite and truth we must worship God alone, and beside no other: No Saint, no Angell, no creature'.[14]

The presence of angels in these catechisms is worthy of note. Ian Green has highlighted the importance of catechizing in the dissemination of religious ideas, and he argues that these books of elementary instruction provided manuals of belief for ordinary people, conveyed in a medium well suited to a religion of the word. For the reformers, the genre was a means of instilling a new faith in the hearts of the people, particularly timely given that many of the older forms of instruction – wall-paintings and sculpture, elaborate priestly rituals and vestments, confession and religious drama – were being dismantled in the name of reform.[15] Catechizing was intended as a means to tell false doctrine from true, and to promote a life of Christian virtue free from vice: as Green states 'a good catechism was a guide to piety as well as knowledge and understanding'.[16] Of course it is difficult to tell how successful this strategy was; there was great variation in the type and form of catechisms, and how far people had access to these resources, particularly given low levels of literacy and high levels of poverty, is open to question.[17] In his exhaustive monograph Green addresses these problems, and he provides convincing evidence that there was a 'moderately frequent, moderately conscientious' level of catechizing in the late sixteenth century, usually using the 1549 *Prayer Book* text as the basis for learning, and taking place in the church or local school. He believes that the *Prayer Book* and catechism effectively provided 'the basis of a liturgical-cum-spiritual odyssey, from baptism in infancy ... to full participation as an adult'.[18] Alongside evidence from other sources, catechisms can therefore prove instructive about the changing perception of angels.[19]

Further evidence that reformers were emphasizing Christ as the only mediator in contrast with the angels can be found in numerous other sources. In a sermon preached at Bexterly on Christmas day in 1552, Hugh Latimer declared that 'we are not bound to call upon the angels, when we hear that they serve us; but rather to give God thanks in them ... therefore learn only to hope and trust in the Lord'.[20] In his exposition on the first epistle of Saint John, William Tyndale went so far as to imagine a conversation with an angel on the topic:

> Now if an angel should appear unto thee, what wouldest thou say unto him? If thou prayedst him to help, he would answer: 'I do. Christ hath sent me to help thee ... If thou desiredst him to pray for thee, to obtain this or that, he would say: 'Christ hath prayed, and his prayer is heard ... If thou desiredst him to save thee with his merits, he would answer that he had no merits, but that Christ is Lord of salvation.[21]

The motif recurred in the work of John Bridges, a clergyman who discussed the definition of prayer in 1573, saying that 'except it be made to God, it is no true praier'. Given that invocation is prayer, 'inuocation therfore vnto saints, angels, or any creature besides God, is neither true nor Godly'.[22] Indeed, these uncompromising warnings against idolatry, and constant reminders that Jesus was the sole mediator, are evidence against MacCulloch's suggestion that angels were perhaps embraced by the reformers as a convenient substitute for saints. Although they might still serve as the protectors and ministers of mankind, there is no sense in which angels took on the intercessory role of the saints – this was a point on which the reformers were explicit.[23] The initial impact of reformed thinking was therefore to reject completely the angelic role of intercession. Angels were no longer to be thought of as mediators between men and the divine, and their traditional role of bearing the sacrifice and prayers from earth to heaven was entirely anathema to the Protestants.

However, a prayer 'For the help of God's holy angels', included in the 1553 Primer and reprinted several times afterwards, is a reminder that praying *to* angels, and praying *for the assistance of* angels were altogether different. It was legitimate to ask God to send his angels to assist men, as this was how he interacted with his earthly kingdom. The prayer itself acknowledged this fine distinction, entreating that the Lord Christ 'send thou me *thy* blessed and heavenly angels', for 'thou, O Lord, hast devoured hell'.[24] The emphasis is on Christ's role as the mediator of salvation, and his ability to send angelic assistance if he wishes, rather than the independent action of angels themselves. For the reformers, angels as a symbol of God's mercy, love and continual care for mankind were acceptable, whereas anything that hinted at the veneration of angels was not. The reformers' main anxiety was that angels were a temptation to idolatry: orthodox prayers such as the one above were uncomfortably close to unorthodox prayers to angels themselves. Given that angels were a ubiquitous conceptual idea in the late medieval era, with foundations in the very fabric of the church itself, it was unsurprising that the reformers were deeply concerned that vivid depictions of the angels might lead people to worship these beings rather than God.

Wherever angels are mentioned by Protestants, they are usually accompanied by a warning against undue veneration. Calvin remarked that because the refulgence of divine glory is manifest in angels, 'there is nothing to which we are more prone than to prostrate ourselves before them in stupid adoration, and then ascribe to them the blessings which we owe to God alone'.[25] Bullinger's warning was comparable: 'we must here take heed lest, contrary to the nature of true religion, we attribute too much to angels; that we worship them not, that we call not upon them, nor serve them'.[26] The worship of angels is referred to as idolatry in the Geneva catechism, translated and published in 1550, where it is stated that 'if we shall haue recourse vnto Aungels or anye other creatures, puttynge any parte of oure confidence or truste in them: we commyte therein damnable Idolatrye'; or Dering's version in 1575: 'make no image of any other thyng, eyther to worship the Image itselfe, eyther God, Saint or Angell'.[27]

The scriptural precedent that was often offered in support of these propositions was that God had explicitly warned against offering worship to angels in the book of Revelation, when John fell to the ground in reverence of the angel that appeared to him.[28] The angel admonished John and reminded him that praise is owed to God alone. This passage was cited as proof of the reformers' position on idolatry; in his catechism Thomas Becon referred to the passage and quoted the angel's words, 'Look that thou do it [worship] not, I am the fellow-servant of thee and of thy brethren ... Worship God'.[29] In the *Homilies*, ordered to be read in every parish church on the authority of Queen Elizabeth, it is remarked that 'when the saint John fell before the angelles feet to worship him, the angel woulde not permit him to do it, but commaunded him that he shoulde worship GOD'. This was cited as proof of the Protestants' main argument on idolatry, 'that the saintes and angels in heaven, wyll not haue vs do any honour vnto them, that is due and proper vnto God'.[30]

Further evidence that angels were proving useful in the battle to establish a reformed faith in England can be seen in the more involved discussions of image worship. The Catholics' 'lewde distinction of Latria and Dulia' is also mentioned in the *Homilies*: *latria* being the supreme worship that was due to God alone, and *dulia* the inferior veneration or honour paid to lesser beings.[31] Reformers rejected this distinction, viewing any veneration of a creature as 'a spoyle of God's honour'. Again, Revelation is cited as evidence that saints and angels 'can not abyde, that as muche as *any* outwarde worshippyng be done or exhibited to them'.[32] William Fulke argued along the same lines, saying that Saint John worshipped the angel with 'civil' worship, the worship due to honourable men, not with any form of 'religious' honour, 'worship, which is called Doulia, as well as that which is called Latria, is due onely to God'.[33]

Reformers therefore rejected entirely the association of angels with mediation, and were not hesitant when it came to forbidding any sort of veneration. Angels were not one of the major battlefields upon which the struggle for the soul of the Church of England was fought, but it is evident that the ubiquitous concept of the angels was implicated in and contributed to significant theological disputes of the era. Thomas Cranmer provided another example of this: stressing that Scripture was the sole source of divine authority and lambasting the idolatrous practices of the Catholics, he related that they:

> allege revelations of angels, or our lady and saints, and dead men's souls appearing to divers men and women, bidding them to cause certain masses, trentals, pilgrimages, and offering images and relics of this and that saint ... that they should be delivered from the fire of purgatory.[34]

Angels are thus enjoined in an invective against Catholic accretions that had introduced corruption into the Christian church. Cranmer was insistent that 'neither the visions of angels, apparitions of the dead, nor miracles, nor all these together joined in one, are able or sufficient to make any one new article of faith, or stablish any thing in religion, without the express words of God'.[35]

Cranmer's words show that the reformers were also anxious about what they considered 'superstitious' practices associated with belief about angels. There were various aspects of late medieval angelology that in themselves were 'without the express word of God', and these unscriptural accretions now came under scrutiny. For example, devotional preoccupation with named archangels, in appearance similar to devotion to the saints, caused considerable unease. The separate masses to Michael, Gabriel and Raphael which appeared in the *Use of Sarum*, had no place in the reformed liturgy, and the cult of the archangels also suffered when the Protestants rejected the books of the bible without a Hebrew original (those books that only existed in a Greek version were considered Apocryphal). As a consequence they removed the book of Tobit from the Protestant canon. As the sole source of the angelic name Raphael, this demoted belief about the third archangel. The *Book of Common Prayer* again provided verification of the progression of reformed thought on this aspect of belief: the 1549 edition alluded to Raphael both in the 'Solemnization of Matrimony' and in the 'Order for the Visitation of the Sick', asking God to comfort and protect the ceremonies' participants 'as thou didst send thy Angel Raphael to Thobie and Sara ... to their great comfort', and 'as thou preservedst Tobie and Sara by thy Angel from danger'.[36] In the subsequent 1552 and 1559 editions these references were erased entirely.[37]

Belief in angels was also undermined because much of the traditional belief about angels was unfortunately either founded upon, or received much support from the lives of the saints. The importance of such sermon collections as *Legenda Aurea* and *Mirk's Festial* in disseminating ideas about angels has been established, but the notion of *sola scriptura* and rejection of the cult of the saints led to the elimination of such material. Because his was the most mature of the angelic cults, and due to his special status as a saint, Michael particularly came under attack. Interestingly, the feast of Saint Michael and All Angels was not purged from the ecclesiastical calendar,[38] but the shrine in his honour suffered the same fate as other monastic establishments in the 1530s.

The abbey on St Michael's Mount had previously been a cell of Syon Abbey, and although the 1492 visitation of the Exeter diocese by Archbishop Morton gives a picture of what historian A. L. Rowse describes as 'general decay', an inventory from the time revealed that the shrine located at the site was flourishing. The image of Saint Michael was particularly lavish:

> his image was of silver gilt and weighed ten ounces; there were two bonnets for him, one of tinsel satin embroidered with gold, the other of blue velvet fringed with gold; he had two coats, one of cloth of gold, the other of purple velvet embroidered with IHS. He wore a chain of gold, a baldric of silver gilt, a flower like a rose, of gold of Venice set with pearl and stone, and a little silver bell.[39]

The shrine was suppressed in 1538, and it is unlikely the reformers had any qualms about putting it down.[40] The gifts and tokens listed in the inventory represented an impressive haul; including 43s. 6d. in money, five ships of silver, 43 silver rings, and a little golden image of Saint Michael valued at 51s 8d. There were also further items to provoke the reforming ire: a sword and pair of spurs that had belonged to the sainted Henry VI, and the jaw-bone of Saint Apollyen, enshrined in silver and gilt.[41] The reformers were evidently keen to eradicate from angelology any suggestion of a link with the abolished practices of the traditional spiritual regime such as those represented here.

The suppression of Saint Michael's Mount also sheds an interesting light on Diarmaid MacCulloch's suggestion that angels took over the intercessory and protective functions previously ascribed to saints.[42] It seems eminently plausible that Protestants might employ angels as a familiar and reassuring spiritual resource for a laity facing the future without the safety mechanisms of purgatory and prayers for the dead, but the suppression of Saint Michel's Mount, in combination with the intense hostility of the reformers to the idea of angels as intercessors, provide serious objection. It would also appear that although the medieval tradition of angelology created many similarities between devotion to angels and saints, it was often precisely such associations that vexed the reformers the most, as they highlighted the potential for angels themselves to become the objects of idolatrous worship. Despite the superficial similarities between angels and saints, devotion to the two groups had always in fact been distinct.

In Eamon Duffy's opinion, saints were 'first and foremost perceived as friends and helpers', encouraging neighbourliness and being depicted as kind and unassuming.[43] In late medieval England it was normal for people to 'cultivate relations of intimacy and dependence' with the saints, observing their feast day and honouring their image, and a client might base special affectionate dependence upon their name saint, or the patron of their church or occupation. Although there were the three named archangels with more developed biographical narratives, devotion to angels did not usually follow the same pattern. Duffy admits that often it was the vivid and spectacular legend of a saint that prompted particular loyalty, and, perhaps in part due to a lack of these legends, angels did not appear to inspire the same feelings of empathy and intimacy that specialist saints invited.

This discrepancy points to the essential difference between angels and saints: in reality it was more natural for people to look to saints as intercessors by virtue of their shared humanity. This common ground contributed greatly to their appeal: saints were loving friends who understood the weak nature of flesh and blood, and for mortal sinners they were more sympathetic figures than distant celestial beings who had never shared the temporal and earthly reality with men. Jacobus de Voragine in fact made this explicit in the sermon for the feast of All Saints when he described why saints should be honoured. He noted that saintly virginity should be held in higher regard, because angels do not face the same earthly temptations and daily struggles that saints must experience. Their 'victory is greater than the angels, because angels live without flesh but virgins triumph in the flesh'.[44] The immediacy of the saints therefore provided the basis of the 'neighbourly community' that Duffy describes as 'one of the most striking aspects of the cult of the saints in general'.[45] Although angels were part of the religious community as fellow worshippers alongside mankind, they lacked the personal touch and proximity of the vividly drawn saints. Peter Brown in fact sees the search for 'the face of a fellow human being, where an earlier generation had wished to see the shimmering presence of a bodiless power' as a central reason for the rise of the cult of the saints in the first instance.[46] Brown maintains that the religious sensibilities of men had long been 'molded by an intense dialogue with invisible companions': in the third and fourth centuries this meant a sense of the self as a hierarchy, with its peak directly below the divine where an invisible protector, a personal *daimon*, or the *guardian angel* was to be found. By the fifth century however, people began increasingly to turn to invisible beings who were fellow humans for friendship, inspiration and protection, enabling them to conceive of the relationship with the intercessor in terms 'open to the nuances of known human relations between patron and client'.[47]

This projection of clearly defined relationships onto the unseen world was obviously problematic when it came to nebulous heavenly beings. Whereas the saints were accessible and human, angels were comparatively more remote and unapproachable, most having few defining characteristics with the potential to provide the foundation for personal devotion. Neither were angels unambiguously benevolent powers. As well as demonstrating the benign nature of their ministry, scripture also cast celestial beings as dispensers of divine justice, such as when two angels proclaim that they have been sent by God to destroy Sodom and Gomorrah (Genesis 19:1), or when God intervenes to prevent an angel destroying Jerusalem when he is displeased with David (2 Samuel 24:16). The vital angelic role in the book of Revelation and anticipated participation in the destruction of the earth, along with the ambivalent role of angels at personal judgement, similarly contributed to the singular nature of heavenly beings.

The capacity of angels to act as dispensers of divine punishment was one that was to later gain prominence in post-Reformation England, but it was not a capacity that was shared by saints, who were merely instruments of God's mercy.[48] This again altered the nature of the devotion directed to them. Angels generally lacked the miracle-working relics that were the impetus for countless spiritual journeys across the country, and which provided the focal point for shrines. The purpose of a pilgrimage was to seek the holy, concretely embodied in a sacred place or relic, or privileged image, and saints were able to leave numerous material traces of their presence in ways that angels did not: there was therefore no angelic substitute for the power of the saints, as channelled through their sacred artefacts.

Combined, these disparities demonstrate that although angels and saints were similar, devotions to each remained different. The human status of saints allowed for regular forms of dedication, and it was more natural for the laity to look to fellow humans rather than to the more detached figures of celestial beings for assistance. Thus, the Reformation was not simply the moment when angels emerged from the shadow of the saints, stepping into the shoes of their more brilliant and compelling, but now evicted, heavenly co-inhabitants. Rather, reformers realigned belief about angels, building on their unique qualities to bring them into harmony with their new worldview. This also provides an explanation as to why reformers were anxious to separate the celestial nature from the human, and why they placed much emphasis on the peerless status of Christ in contrast to flocks of heavenly beings.[49] Angels were dehumanized to bring them closer to their representation in scripture: they were to be perceived as entirely distinct from the downgraded and theologically perilous saints, as well as from the son of God, the only true intercessor. Hence, there is no sense that the reformers were being forced to compromise their principles in light of the concerns and needs of 'popular' religion in their dealings with angels: the same standards were applied to both angels and saints, and, as has been seen, both groups of the heavenly company were often referred to together when it came to a condemnation of seeking any intercessor apart from Christ himself.

Further evidence that the reformers were seeking to sever links with late medieval tradition can be found in the reformed attitude to both the Cult of the Five Wounds, and the popular Cult of the Virgin Mary. Because neither had scriptural justification they were areas of parochial religious culture that the reformers were keen to suppress. In fact the former was particularly vilified because, as is confirmed by the Sarum Missal in the preface to the 'Office of the Five Wounds', it was a common belief that the mass had been given to Pope Boniface I by the Archangel Raphael. This would have been enough for reformers to condemn it as a Catholic innovation, but even worse were the claims the angel made for the mass' efficacy: a priest who celebrated the mass devoutly five times for himself or any other person 'shall receive health and grace, and hereafter shall possess eternal life'. Alternatively, if the mass was for the soul of someone deceased, then after it had been said, 'that soul shall be freed from punishment'.[50] Cranmer's invective against idolatrous Catholic rituals could have been written with this example in mind. The legend of the mass of the five wounds encapsulated several of the reformers' chief concerns: both about the elaborate Catholic ritual and belief that had become attached to articles of faith; and their concerns that the laity were being led astray by Catholic promises that good works such as the celebration of masses, the offering of prayers for the dead or the buying of indulgences would secure salvation. It is therefore unsurprising to find that the mass was strictly censured in John Foxe's *Actes and Monuments*, arguably the most important Protestant work of Elizabeth's reign. Foxe affirmed the 'great absurditie, wicked abuse, and perilous idolatry of the Popish masse, declaring how and by whom it came in, clouted and patched vp of diuers additions'. That the office of the Five Wounds was based on a vision was reason enough 'why it is to be exploded out of al churches', for 'the masse is an hinderance to the true seruice of god, and to the godly lyfe of men'.[51]

In a similar fashion, the angels also sustained collateral damage through their prior association with the cult of the Virgin Mary. The temptation to conceive of Mary as a mediator and to seek her assistance was perhaps even greater than in the case of the other saints, and the reformers were eager to abolish the cult, dismantling the great shrines in her honour at Abingdon, Glastonbury and Walsingham in the 1530s. This further reduced the presence of angels in religious culture and undermined the significance of Gabriel's role as God's messenger. What is more, the reformers were unsurprisingly particularly troubled by the 'Ave Maria', the prayer based on Gabriel's salutation to Mary at the Annunciation and which called for the intercession of Mary. Numerous authors denounced the prayer, Hugh Latimer was typical in his argument that although the Ave Maria was 'an heavenly saluting or greting of our lady, spoke by the Angel Gabriel ... yet it is not properly a prayer, as the pater noster is ... saluting or gretyng, laudying or praysyng, is not properly prayeng'. The Danish theologian Niels Hemmingsen expressed similar objections in a sermon written for the feast of the Annunciation, translated into English in 1569. Of the angelic salutation he said 'how foolish are they that will make a prayer of it, wherewith they call upon the blessed virgin, contrary to the manifest woord of God'.[52]

Angels were also compromised by the link between heavenly beings and the enforcement of celibacy in the monasteries. Although reformers accepted that angels provided an example of the pious and loyal life that each believer should strive to emulate, there was an understanding that angels represented the ideal, and that in reality men could not hope to achieve such spiritual dedication. The reformers derided an institutionalization of chastity that they thought had no basis in scripture. John Bale demanded to know why chastity was thought godly, for vows were 'neyther workes nor offyces of that gospel to that glory of god, but wicked wayes of sinnefull mens inuencion ... to apere more holy than that common sort'. Bale maintained that the truth was that when monks claimed to 'leade an Angels life', the reformers were 'able to codempne your saynges by dayly examples of their buggeryes and other beastly occupienges'.[53] This is a theme that is to be found in Foxe's *Actes*, in the letter of Hildebrand of Soana (later Pope Gregory VII), who asked why men 'should be coacted to liue as angels, that is, to perfourme that, whiche nature dothe not geue'.[54]

There were also various practices and commonly held beliefs relating to angels that the reformers considered to be 'superstitious accretions'. The association of angels, particularly Raphael, with magical healing was one such area of concern. Eamon Duffy gives an example of the type of quasi-magical practice that caused unease, describing 'an elaborate formula for conjuring angels, for purposes of divination, into a child's thumbnail' that appeared in the commonplace book of rural artisan and church-reeve Robert Reynes.[55] The reformers took action against such practices: as mentioned above, the name of the archangel Raphael was erased from the 'Order for the Visitation of the Sick' in the 1553 and 1559 *Prayer Books* following the rejection of the book of Tobit, and it seems that this may also have been indicative of a wider attempt on the behalf of the reformers to suppress the association of angels with charms and healing. This attitude is succinctly illustrated by the words of William Bullein, in *Bulleins bulwarke of defence against all sicknesse, soareness, and vvoundes*:

> I knew in a towne called Kelshall, Suffolk a Witch, whose name was M. Didge, who with certain Aue Maries vpon her Ebene Beades, and a waxe Candle, vsed this charme folowyng for S. Anthonies fyre, hauing the sicke body before her, holding vp her Hande saying: there came two Angels out of the North east, one brought fyre the other brought frost, out fyre and in frost. In nomine patris. &c. I coulde reherse an. C. of sutch knackes, of these holy gossips, the fyre take them all, for they be Gods enemyes.[56]

Bullein was originally a Protestant clergyman, resigning his post in 1554 at the beginning of Mary's reign, and going on to write several medical books whilst a practising physician. They proved popular, being reprinted in the 1580s and 1590s.[57] The spell that Bullein describes in the *Bulwarke* is interesting both because of the use and repetition of the *Ave Maria* to make the charm effective, but more obviously because the spell calls on angels to heal the afflicted. This is precisely the kind of 'magical' ritual that the reformers believed typified Catholicism and which they were seeking to eradicate. It was also a further blow for Raphael: as the 'medicine of God' he was particularly vulnerable to any attacks on the angelic association with healing. Questions of charms or oaths using the names of angels were a further area of concern.[58]

Theological Realignment

It is evident that angels were compromised both because of their previous roles as intercessors and mediators, but also because of their close association with earlier forms of devotion and popular practice that were subsequently rejected by the Protestants. Reformers often found fault with, or at least expressed equivocal attitudes over some of the more elaborate traditions in angelology, because they regarded extensive, convoluted debate on the precise attributes and purposes of angels as redundant and unnecessary. They were anxious to emphasize that enquiry into the angelic nature should 'keep within the bounds which piety describes' lest the people are led away from what Calvin described as 'the sim-

plicity of the faith'. As for those matters 'which tend little to edification', it was
a duty 'to remain in willing ignorance', for as Bullinger stated with reference to
good spirits, 'that which is not delivered in the scriptures cannot without danger
be inquired after, but without danger we may be ignorant of it'.[59]

A revealing manifestation of this concern is the reformed attitude to the
celestial hierarchy. Although the names of the nine orders of angels were to be
found in scripture, there was a paucity of detailed biblical evidence beyond this.
Therefore, Calvin was entitled to ask 'how is it possible from such passages to
ascertain the gradations of honour among the angels to determine insignia, and
assign the place and station of each?', because there was no precise guidance on
the matter.[60] This was also acknowledged by Bullinger, who accepted that there
were various distinctions between the different types of angels, and that orders
existed, but that 'what they are, and what they differ between themselves, I know
not'. This did not cause him any distress however, as he continued by stating that
'neither truly do I think myself for the ignorance thereof to be endangered' as the
scriptures 'minister unto us all things necessary and healthful'.[61]

Reformers therefore generally accepted that there was a hierarchy and different orders of angels, each with allotted responsibilities and names; however,
it was unusual for a Protestant theologian to assert anything beyond these bare
facts, and they poured scorn on the elaborations of the medieval tradition.
Calvin urged his readers to avoid 'frivolous questions' in favour of 'solid piety',
stating that 'those who presume to dogmatise on the ranks and numbers of
angels, would do well to consider on what foundation they rest'.[62] Calvin was
particularly scathing about the Dionysian hierarchy, condemning the church-
man's formulation of the angelic order as 'shrewd and subtle dispositions' and
declaring 'when you read the work of Dionysius you would think that the man
had come down from heaven, and was relating not what he had learned but what
he had actually seen'.[63] This scepticism was likely to have been fuelled and confirmed by the discrediting of Dionysius in theological circles. The Renaissance
saw a movement away from the traditional identification of Dionysius with St
Denys and from the belief that Dionysius had heard St Paul preach on Mars'
Hill.[64] The significance of the rejection of the book of Tobit can also be con-
strued from the Protestant attitude to the orders of angels. Raphael's message
that he was 'one of the seven holy angels who present the prayers of the saints
and enter into the presence of the glory of the Holy one' was not only perceived
as an invitation to intercession, it was understood by the reformers as an additional, and equally dubious speculation on the celestial hierarchy.[65] William
Fulke, in his response to the publication of the Catholic Rheims Testament in
1582 by biblical translator Gregory Martin, certainly took this line:

> and for the orders and patronage or protection of angels by God's appointment, we
> have sufficient testimony in the canonical scriptures, that we need not the uncertain

report of Tobie's book to instruct us what to think of them. But as for the hierarchies and patronage of angels, that many of you papists have imagined and written of, neither the canonical scriptures, nor yet the apocryphal books now in controversy, are sufficient to give you warrant.[66]

Guided by the Protestant canon, the reformers therefore rejected the nine orders of the Dionysian hierarchy. The result of this shift was to endorse a trend which tended to depersonalize angelic beings. The Dionysian hierarchy had supplied names and characteristics for angels, but references became more general as allusions to names, roles and responsibilities now disappeared from religious cultures. The liturgy was a prime example: there were frequent references to the glorious order that God had ordained, but there was no differentiation between angels. The collect for the Feast of Saint Michael and All Angels is a good example:

> Everlasting God, which hast ordained and constituted the service of all Angels and men in a wonderful order: mercifully grant, that they which always do service in heaven, may by they appointment succour and defend us in earth: through Jesus Christ our Lord &c.[67]

In a similar vein, Henry Bull included in his collection of prayers 'An other meditation of the blessed state of felicitie of the life to come', in which he listed the personnel that will be present: 'the Archeaungels, Aungels, Thrones, powers, Dominations, cherubins, ceraphins' included, but there was no hint of the traditional order of precedence amongst the esteemed company.[68]

With regard to the celestial hierarchy, it is therefore evident that reformed 'theological pruning' brought about a shift of emphasis that affected the representation of angels in religious cultures. The same processes can be seen in the Protestant attitude towards guardian angels. The relevant scriptural passages were Jesus's blessing of some children whose 'angels do always behold the face of my Father in heaven', the second the disciples mistaking the newly escaped Peter for 'his angel'.[69] These could be interpreted as evidence that all humans were assigned a specific, guardian angel to watch over them during their lifetime, although, as with the angelic hierarchy, the evidence is by no means explicit. Reformers were divided over the question: Luther appeared to countenance the idea, whereas second generation reformers such as Calvin remained unconvinced, and there were concerns that this belief might prove a temptation to idolatry. Therefore Calvin accepted the biblical precedent when Daniel 'undoubtedly intimates that certain angels are appointed as a kind of president over kingdoms and provinces', and agreed that when Christ says that the angels of children always behold the face of the father in heaven 'he insinuates that there are certain angels to whom their safety has been intrusted'. However, he stated that he could 'not positively affirm' if each believer had a single angel assigned to them. Rather, it was the 'vulgar imagination' that found such an idea comforting, whereas the true believer should be satisfied in knowing that there was a whole host of heavenly beings assigned by God for the protection of mankind, 'that all with one consent watch for our safety'. Indeed, those 'who limit the care which God takes of each of us to a single angel, do great injury to themselves and to all the members of the Church'.[70]

Calvin's attitude undoubtedly contributed to the tendency of writers in this period to refer only to general notions of the protection of angels, rather than to debate the existence of guardian angels. As with the angelic hierarchy, the drive to link angelology more closely to scriptural evidence, and the quiet stifling of aspects of belief that were less scripturally sound or less edifying to reformed sensibilities, once more had the consequence of depersonalizing the angels. Angels were likely to be depicted as abstract representations of God's power and mercy, the protection they provided dependent not on a familiar winged figure, with distinct characteristics, but rather linked to the providential working of God himself. This realignment of understanding came naturally to reformers, because stripping angels of distinctive features not only reduced the potential of angels to prove a stimulus to idolatry in the first place, but also redirected the gratitude and praise prompted by the angelic existence onto God alone. Thus Bullinger emphasized that angels appear 'for a time for the weakness of our capacity'.[71] In other words they were generously provided by a God who was not averse to catering to the shortcomings of his beloved people.

The Protestant position on the angelic hierarchy and guardian angels therefore represented aspects of angelology where there was marked contrast with the late medieval tradition. Evidently, although angels were an article of faith, they remained a problematic area for reformers, and belief in celestial beings did not remain impervious to the dramatic changes that were sweeping the country. The reformers were coming to an altered understanding and appreciation of heavenly beings, and this was reflected in the attitudes they held towards them and the responsibilities that they credited them with, but this understanding did not negate the usefulness and ubiquity of angels in early modern religious cultures.

Incomplete Iconoclasm

Although the average layman might have little understanding of the complexities of reformed thought on the Dionysian hierarchy, there is no doubt that he or she would have been aware of the impact of reformed theology on the physical fabric and customs of his parish church. Late medieval belief had been generated and sustained by the rich imagery and visual allusions that were a pervasive part of the decorative schemes in medieval ecclesiastical institutions, and the transformation of the setting and ritual of worship is important evidence of how the new understanding of angels was conveyed to and disseminated amongst the population.

The iconoclastic purges initiated by Henry VIII and Edward VI created many angelic victims. Although not the focus of particular controversy for the reformers in comparison to the holy trinity and saints, angels did represent a potential focus for idolatry. They were also especially vulnerable because of their ubiquitous presence in traditional religious culture: although images of angels in themselves *might* have survived the rigours of the initial, destructive phases of the English Reformation, angels disappeared because visual paraphernalia that was not directly linked to angels suffered in the name of reform. For instance, the white-washing of churches to rid them of wall paintings meant that doom illustrations and those biblical narratives featuring angels were lost. The disappearance of elaborately decorated clerical vestments accounted for other pictorial representations, and the dismantling of rood screens resulted in the removal of the angels that prior to this had been found flanking the crucifix and the figures of Mary and John. Images of angels themselves did in fact also come under attack, such as the angels on a screen at Southwold in Suffolk, whose faces have been viciously scratched out. The revolutionary changes to the interior of the parish church therefore encompassed a great reduction in the prominence and extent of the angelic presence.

For the layman, the symbolic impact of this destruction and the oral messages delivered from the pulpit and through the medium of the catechism would have combined to denote the changing status of angels. The fact that angels no longer appeared alongside the saints on the rood screen signified Christ's role as sole mediator, whilst the removal of the images more generally was a reminder that veneration was to be directed to God alone. The suppression of the cult of the Virgin Mary and the cult of the Five Wounds, damaging to the angels by proxy, were a further reminder to the laity that alternative devotions could in no way assist in the attainment of salvation, and that reliance upon anything but faith was mistaken, and placed one's soul in jeopardy.[72]

Yet despite the savage and occasionally frenzied attacks of the reformers, images of angels endured. In fact they were *never* explicitly identified in the ordinances and laws issued by the Tudor monarchs. Moreover Elizabeth I issued a proclamation in September 1560 which condemned the defacement of any monuments, tombs or graves; effectively exempting mortuary artwork and the winged figures that adorned many effigies and memorials from iconoclastic aggression.[73] The proclamation was intended to protect those monuments that 'only show a memory to the posterity of the person there buried', and was ostensibly prompted by concerns that the destruction of such monuments would corrupt 'the true understanding of divers families in this realm'. As a result, angels were still a common sight in parish churches, so much so that art historian Fred Crossely was able to identify and categorize the regional 'types' of angels produced by different medieval workshops and placed on monuments.[74] Their survival deserves closer attention.

The evidence supports the reasoning of Tessa Watt, who has argued convincingly against Patrick Collinson's suggestion that there was a 'watershed' in English visual culture in the 1590s, when iconoclasm transmuted into iconophobia.[75] Instead, Watt maintains that the pictorial remained an important element in the Protestant approach to moral and spiritual truths throughout the period, and that the laity were not cut off from all Christian imagery.[76] The fact that William Dowsing, whose journal provides the most systematic evidence of the new wave of iconoclasm of the 1640s, was able to obliterate or order the destruction of hundreds of surviving angels during his 'cleansing' of churches in Cambridgeshire and Suffolk 1643-4, is an excellent example of the survival of Christian imagery in the churches of England.[77] One of the chief explanations for this may be simple expediency: angels were often situated in positions that made it particularly hard for the most enthusiastic reformers to remove them. Thus, even the relentless zeal exhibited by Dowsing could not entirely obliterate images of heavenly beings, and angels remain to this day in many of the churches he visited.[78] Roof angels provide the most obvious example of the practical difficulties of directing iconoclastic attacks against angels, but stone spandrels, bench ends and stained glass windows (the latter being very expensive to replace), all posed problems for the potential iconoclast. The very ubiquity of the angelic image in traditional visual culture meant that their presence was virtually impossible to eradicate.

If, however, the pragmatic difficulties could perhaps have been overcome, there was a further obstacle to the removal of images of angels. In her article on the place of angels in the evolving visual culture of early modern England, Alexandra Walsham points out that 'scriptural passages left a loophole within which depictions of angels could, at least in the eyes of some Protestants, continue to exist'.[79] Angels were involved in theological debates over religious imagery, because scripture recorded that the deity himself commanded images of cherubim to be placed on the tabernacle and in Solomon's temple.[80] The presence of an image of a supernatural creature on the ark that housed the tables of the Law was potentially a severe embarrassment for the reformers and was often cited by Catholics seeking to defend their visual inheritance, as they interpreted the passage to mean that it was lawful to make images. James Calfhill vehemently refuted this; he argued that scripture gave no indication that these images were to be worshipped, and that it was not intended that the images on the tabernacle should even be seen by the people. The cherubim were 'but a peculiar ordinance of God', and did not prejudice what the reformers saw as a universal law.[81] The *Homilies* collected by John Jewel also countered Catholic claims, stating that images were forbidden in the first instance due to the tendency of 'heathens and infidels' to worship them. Thus it was no contradiction for God to command images of cherubim on the tabernacle, as 'the cherubims stood not in the temple in the sight and presence of the people, but within the veil of the tabernacle ... therefore there was in it no danger of idolatry'.[82] Cranmer concurred, there were two cherubs of gold on the tabernacle, which much was made clear in scripture, but 'that was in such a place as the people never came near, nor saw'.[83]

Walsham traces the other debates on the validity of pictorial representations of celestial beings, concluding that there remained an ambiguity in reformed attitudes towards depictions of angels. At a time when reformers were concentrating on putting down those images that played an active part in Catholic worship – those that were 'abused'[84] – decorative images of angels were bound to be less offensive than the more promiscuous saints, and were therefore less likely to attract the Protestants' notice.

Walsham's account goes a long way to explaining the resilience of images of angels in English parish churches. Scriptural evidence regarding representations of angels was by no means conclusive and theological uncertainty was reflected in the patchy nature of iconoclasm. The suggestion that it was only the most objectionable images of angels that were destroyed during this period also draws attention to those representations that were attacked, as these indicate those areas of belief that were abrogated by reform. The Protestants' dislike of the named angels and their associated cults can, for example, be read in their attitude to images of Saint Michael. Michael was often explicitly mentioned when reformers warned against the dangers of venerating angels, such as when Thomas Rogers included in a list of now forbidden images 'Also of God his creatures; as of angels, always with wings, sometimes with a pair of balance, as St Michael'.[85] Cranmer similarly asked

> what teachethe the picture of sayncte Mychael waying soules, and our lady putting her beades in the balaunce. Forsoth nothing els, but superstitiousnes of beades, and confidence in oure owne merites, and the merites of saincts, and nothynge in the merites of Christe.[86]

If it is accepted that the images of angels that were removed were those that were thought likely to encourage idolatrous behaviour, it seems that this was an accurate reflection of the Protestant priority when it came to reforming celestial beings. Margaret Aston has pointed out that consideration of the physical proximity of idols was also thought to be an important factor when it came to promoting idolatrous behaviour, and that a distinction was often made between less offensive narrative representations and unacceptable individual devotional images.[87] Although this distinction may reflect more pragmatic concerns rather than strictly reformed theology, it nevertheless remains true that individual images of the members of the nine orders of angels, or of Saint Michael in his role of defeating the dragon or weighing souls, were anathema, whereas the numerous decorative and ornamental angels, often situated high in up among the eaves of a church, or in the corners of windows, were allowed to survive.

What is more surprising is that new depictions of angels were being produced in this period, in the frontispieces to both *Actes and Monuments*, and vernacular versions of scripture. There are also examples of tombs erected in the 1580s on which angels appear; at Leigh in Kent there is an effigy of an unknown women, 'surrounded by an angel' produced c.1580, and in Heston, Middlesex, the 1580 brass to Constance Bownell depicts her in bed with her dead child, and an angel at her side.[88] New images of angels provide evidence in support of Tessa Watt's contention that traditional piety was modified, resulting in a 'patchwork of beliefs' that were 'distinctively "post-Reformation", but not thoroughly Protestant'. Watt defines the 'Protestant' parts of this patchwork to include an emphasis on the importance of faith in the achievement of salvation, a marked absence of saints, an interest in Protestant martyrs and a tendency to emphasize the lessons and characters of the Old Testament over the New.[89] The attitude of the reformers to angels betrays many of these characteristics and is an example of the fusion of new and traditional elements of popular piety. What is more, the new images of angels conform to Watt's suggestion that biblical figures that were not associated with cults of devotion, and allegorical or symbolic images were in fact acceptable to some reformers. Alexandra Walsham actually makes this point in direct reference to angels, noting that that images of angels 'might be deemed to fall into the category of acceptable allegorical signs' and providing substantial evidence against Patrick Collinson's thesis that England suffered from a form of 'visual anorexia' in the early modern period.[90]

Walsham concludes that the survival of angels were an emblem of the 'ongoing theological, liturgical and cultural quarrels' that were the most enduring legacy of reform.[91] Protestants certainly did disagree as to whether depictions of angels were admissible, but there were other aspects of the angelic existence where there was more consensus and where reformers of all stripes, from the more conservative through to the more radical, discovered that angels were a useful weapon in the struggle to establish the new religion. The presence of new images of angels may not therefore represent half-completed reform, but rather may reflect the realignment of the theology relating to celestial beings, and the fact these new images were decorative and symbolic would appear to support this argument. The treatment of images of angels reflects a wider ambiguity and is indicative of the fact that after the initial curtailment of the excesses of late medieval angelology, new roles for angels began to emerge and new trends developed: the 'depersonalization' of angels appears to have been an important part of this process. The incidence of symbolic images of angels will therefore be considered within the context of other developments in angelology in the next section, which explores how the Church of England was able to utilize angels in the struggle against false belief.

Protestant Angelology

If the survival of images of angels is taken as an indication of the continuing importance of celestial beings, a further examination of their significance in reformed religious cultures certainly supports this understanding. Angels continued to appear in familiar roles and took on traditional responsibilities throughout the period, and they evidently retained an important position within the functioning of the reformed universe. The promise of angelic protection and succour, and a shared responsibility for worship of the godhead extended naturally into the post-Reformation era. However, the pastoral applications of angels, and the fundamental significance of their existence did undergo considerable modification through the processes of reform. New understanding and shifting emphasis resulted in the growing prominence of a strain of ideas that had previously held an unassuming place in late medieval angelology, but which now began to come to the fore.

Despite reformed anxiety over the excesses of late medieval angelology, there were still many scripturally sound aspects to the angelic existence, and angels were to prove the natural allies of the reformers. Protestants encouraged parishioners to contemplate their ministry, and they continued to regard them as a useful devotional aid. Familiar ideas recurred in a variety of sources. For example, the idea that angels joined with man in the worship of God remained significant and occupied an important place in the *Book of Common Prayer*. The preface to communion taught people to laud the name of God 'with Angels and Archangels', and the *Te Deum* functioned in a similar vein, the 1549 text asking that 'ye Angels of the Lord, speak good of the Lord, Praise him and set him up for ever'.[92]

Taking their cue from this official representation of celestial beings, there are many other sources that similarly stress the importance of joining with the angels in prayer. In his Christmas Day sermon Hugh Latimer asked his audience to consider 'that whensoever or wheresoever the word of God is preached, there are the angels present, which keep in safe custody all those which receive the word of God and study to live after it', and Thomas Becon in a sermon on the nativity, suggested that 'we be receaued with the holy Angells ... which are now ioynte felowes with us: so that we may well boste, that in this childe we are come to the moste familiar felowshippe of the Angells' who 'are not proude, but glad with all their hart, that suche sinners are come into their felowshippe'.[93]

This was a traditional understanding of the role of angels, and it was commonly linked to the perception of heavenly beings as devout examples of the pious existence that all men should strive for. The Lutheran author Johann

Habermann noted that 'an easie matter is it, for one to attaine to their [angels'] nature, dignitie, wisedome and understanding, if al his life time, he give himselfe wholy unto praier, and the seruice of God', and Hemmingsen also linked the two ideas, saying that 'wee may learn of the Angels and shepherds togither, too confesse this to Christ. Finally wee may learne too glorifie God, and too sing with the angels'.[94] This is a theme that reappears in catechisms frequently, in expositions on the Lord's Prayer, to explain the phrase 'Thy will be done on earth as it is in heaven'. Authors hold up 'the holy Angels and Sainted in heaven' as examples of how God's will is to be carried out, as Cranmer elaborated:

> Nowe the angels in heauen fulfyll Gods wyll most perfectlye, bothe with moost feruent loue and moste perfyte obedience. And there is not in anye of the heauenly spirites any euell desier, to do any thynge contrarye to gods wyll, but they be whollye inflamed with moste perfecte loue towarde God. Euen so oughte we also to be that dwell here in earth.[95]

Angels were useful as a model of godly living, and this evidently struck a chord the reformers. However, as we have already seen, the Protestant attitude towards angels as an example of holy chastity has suggested that their position as a role-model in this instance compromised their status.[96] Of course, Protestant responses to Catholic insistence on monastic celibacy may signify nothing more than defensive polemic: the Protestants were obliged to find fault with those men attempting to live the life of angels. However, there is other evidence that there was a wider significance to this hostility, and that the attitude was part of a broader trend encompassing angelology as a whole.

Although references to the fellowship of men and angels, and the function of angels as models of devotion, were common perceptions amongst reformed clergy, it appears that there were limits placed on the value of comparisons between the earthly and the divine. The relative celibacy of men and angels is one example of this, and reformed deliberations on the finer points of the relationship between Christ, the angels and men, form part of the same trend. The not infrequent reminders to the laity that Christ took the form of a man, not an angel, provide a good insight into the process. For reformers, conveying the fundamental differences between the son of God and celestial beings was paramount. The idea appears in catechisms such as that by Edmund Allen: Christ 'hathe receyued euen after his mans nature, a power and honor aboue all Angels and creatures', or Beza's *booke of Christian questions*: 'as he is man, so is also God, and therefore higher than the Angelles'.[97] In his nativity sermon, Becon even went so far as to relate the opinion of the fathers that it was angelic jealously, stirred up because God had chosen the form of a man instead of an angel, that led directly to the fall of the angels:

God should become man, and for that cause [the devil] enuied at man, and began to hate God, because he had not chosen rather to become an Angell, than a man, and that for this enuie and pride he was caste out of heaven.[98]

The effect of this emphasis on the differences between angels and the form that God chose to take on earth was not only to differentiate angels from saints, but further to disseminate the function of Christ as sole mediator. Christ's unique status, higher even than the angels, and part-man, part-God, set him apart from the celestial beings and explained why it was he alone who could mediate between mankind and the godhead. Reformers were anxious that the angelic nature was to be properly understood as scripture intended, not confused and obscured as the Catholics were wont to do when they honoured angels in 'pictures of winged and fethered men'.[99] Frequent contrasts with Christ in the form of a man served as a reminder that angels, glorious and wonderful beings though they were, still remained inferior to the son of God.

Protestants continued to define angels to include within their remit many pastoral responsibilities. Calvin believed that the one thing all could know for certain about angels was that they 'are ministering spirits, whose service God employs for the protection of his people and by whose means he distributes favours among men', and other reformers followed suit.[100] After all, reformers were in agreement that angels were provided by God to pander to man's inherent weakness, and late sixteenth-century religious literature is imbued with the notion that angels existed as evidence of God's mercy and goodwill towards men. Thus it was particularly fitting that angels were involved in the Annunciation to Mary as well as taking on the responsibility of announcing the good news of mans' salvation to the shepherds. As Richard Taverner preached in his 1542 sermon, 'it was mete that an highe angel shulde be sent which shulde bringe tydynges of him that was highest of all', an opinion that Hemmingsen endorsed in a sermon of his own, saying 'it was conuenient that a good Angell should bee the first messenger of the restorement of saluation agein'.[101]

Again, there does not appear to have been any notion of a compromise on the part of the Protestants: traditional notions of angelic protection and succour, with firm scriptural roots, simply remained a notable presence within religious cultures. In *The Institutes*, Calvin established the pattern when he noted that the scriptures especially insist that 'angels are the ministers and dispensers of the divine bounty towards us', 'imparting the gifts of his benevolence', and that angels are given to men 'in accommodation to the weakness of our capacity'. Thus when God employs angels it is because of man's inherent frailty, 'that we might at times be filled with alarm, or driven to despair, did not the Lord proclaim his gracious presence by some means in accordance with our feeble capacities?'[102] Scripturally sound angels retained a significant role in the Protestant mindset. There was also a sense in which they naturally proved an antidote to the more disquieting aspects of the Protestant message. The very existence of angels was heartening to the laity, evidence, if any were needed, of God's continued interest in and care of his people, and they were a reminder that every man might potentially achieve salvation.

Hemmingsen's sermon, delivered on the feast of Saint Michael and All Angels, therefore expressed a typical reformed attitude, suggesting that the occasion had been appointed by the church 'too the intene wee might learne Gods benefites towards us, who hath given his Angels to bee our keepers'.[103] Echoing this sentiment, Bullinger described angels as 'an exceeding great token of his [God's] fatherly care and regard towards us ... because he frameth himself so sweetly to our capacities and dispositions', heavenly beings forming yet another example of the 'innumerable and greatest benefits of God'.[104] The idea that angels were used by God as a demonstration of his special care and protection of mankind was particularly common, and it evidently remained an important trope within Elizabethan religious cultures. It appears in the 1553 Primer in the passage for the feast of Saint Michael, with the request 'that they which always do thee service in heaven, may by thy wonderful appointment succour and defend us in earth'.[105] John Foxe similarly expressed his belief in the idea when he called on his readers to 'give thanks unto god, which hath given us his Angels to be our keepers and defenders, and with more quiet minds, fulfil and do the office of our vocation'.[106] Perhaps Richard Taverner summed up the attitude best in his Michaelmas sermon:

> The good angels do continually minister unto god and serve for our behouf ... and theire office is to execute gods busyness and to take charge and cure of us mortall men. They defend and protect I say al good folke from the assaultes and violence of the deuyll, they nourish concord, peace, virtues, good studies, artes, sciences, polecie, common welthes, discipline, and shortly to speake, mans helth and salfgard.[107]

These were not new ideas, but were firmly rooted in the medieval tradition of angelology. Unlike angelic mediation and intercession, this aspect of belief did not prompt a conflict with reformed sensibilities: to the reformers angels could be a perfect symbol of God's grace, and focusing attention on their presence also served as a reminder to the laity of God's infinite mercy and justice.

Taverner's Michelmas sermon goes into some detail about the character and purpose of angels, and is an indicator of other important themes. Emphasis was on the comfort that angels can provide for men, although this was of course dependent upon living a godly life such as that described in scripture. 'If we be then pure and good, doubt we not, but god hath given commaundement to his angels over us, that they shuld kepe us in all oure wayes', therefore 'Let us endeuour our selfe to be suche lowly and humble persons as our Saviour Christ here speaketh of, that we may haue suche aungels to conducte, leade, defend and kepe us'. Angels are also provided by God to 'direct us, to rule us, to monish us, to governe us ... for the correcting of our doinges and obteyning of mercie for us'.[108] Taverner's writing demonstrates that reformers were not hesitant when it came to encouraging contemplation about the proximity of the angels and their natural love for mankind.[109]

Taverner also referred to 'saynte Peter whiche was led out of prison by an angel'. This scriptural reference was enough to ensure the continuance of the particular belief that angels took special care of prisoners, a belief also attested to elsewhere. John Northbrooke, a puritan clergyman whose *Breefe and pithie summe of the Christian faith* nonetheless was characterized by a conformist outlook, mentions that the apostles were released from prison in Jerusalem by 'the angell of the Lord' who 'opened the doores of the prison and brought them foorth', and he went on to discuss also the episode involving Peter, saying that 'as soone as the angell smote Peter on the side and waked him, his chaines fel of from his handes'.[110] Thomas Becon similarly considered the idea, urging men not to despair because 'God being mightier than all tirannie and power of the world sent his Angell, and delivered Peter out of prison'.[111]

Of course the basis for the association of angels and prisoners was scripturally sound, but given that the idea had been popularized mainly through the accounts of the lives of the saints,[112] it is interesting to find it proclaimed with such confidence by the reformers. Their use of angels as a pastoral resource lacked self-consciousness, they were clear both about those areas of angelology that they disagreed with, as well as those that were an important part of the complex rational structures that constituted their spiritual universe. The reformers were not disposed to ignore the evidence drawn from God's word, but at the same time they were extremely reluctant to draw any wider conclusions or to elaborate on the basic references provided by scripture. The application of the principle of scriptural austerity to angelology therefore resulted in angels becoming a less defined presence, since the passages in the bible relating to angels are brief and lacking in specific detail. Theological pruning was again found necessary to correct the laity's corrupted understanding.

An excellent example of this process is seen in the developing role of angels in the belief and ritual associated with death. This was perhaps the most theologically resonant aspect of late medieval angelology,[113] but was also the aspect that appeared most vulnerable to the processes of reform, given that these processes had abolished purgatory and prayers for the dead. There were various elements of traditional belief that had no place in reformed culture and which disappeared from late sixteenth-century religious literature: allusions to the angelic role of conveying the corpse to the final resting place no longer appeared, and the suppression of the Cult of the Virgin Mary and of devotion to the Five Wounds resulted in the loss of this source of affirmation for the ministry of the angels at the time of death. Most obviously, the rejection of the angelic role of intercession meant that invocations of angels around the deathbed also disappeared from liturgy and *ars moriendi* tracts alike.

The principles of justification by faith and double predestination would seem to have made redundant the notion of a cosmic struggle between good and evil for the custody of the dying person's soul, because official theology dictated that the deathbed was no longer the scene of the final battle for salvation. However, Peter Marshall has illustrated that the perception of the end of life struggle persists as 'a tremulous subtext of Protestant writing', as did the belief that angels were important participants in the fight.[114] Marshall's discussion of the prayer books and primers of Reformation England demonstrates that despite the eventual removal of angels from liturgical services, reformers, particularly those authors of *ars moriendi* literature, continued to give prominence to the biblical evidence that angels would carry the souls of the dead to Abraham's bosom.[115]

These conclusions are borne out by the sources: Cranmer's 1547 collection of sermons calls attention to Lazarus' experience when God, 'by the ministry of Aungels, sent hym unto Abraham's bosome', and the poor man is also mentioned by Becon, as his lucky soul 'immediately after his departure was moste tenderly and ioyfully borne of the blessed Aungels of God into the bosome of Abraham'.[116] However, there was a shift 'from a pattern of dying inviting human effort and invocation, to one totally dependent upon divine initiative'. Thus although angels remained a significant presence at the end of a layperson's life, there is no doubt that the ministry of angels had become a less prominent theme of mortuary culture after the Reformation.[117] Thus angels are present to comfort Christ on the cross, and are mentioned in 'A prayer to be sayed for all suche as lye at the point of deathe', but they are now a comforting presence rather than militant warriors against evil.[118]

Angels also retained their role at judgement, and descriptions of the last days are replete with references to angelic participation. A sermon by John Bradford related that 'with Angells of thy power, with a mightie cry, shoute of an Archangell, blast of a trompe' the end of the world is brought about.[119] The angelic duty of standing witness during personal judgement was not forgotten either, as Richard Day mentioned in 1578: 'my sinnes shal be opened in ye sight of so many Angels, and not my misdeeds only, but thoughts and words', and Bradford also anticipated similar events in his deliberations, when judgement would be 'done against thy lawe, openlye and before all Angells, Saintes and Devilles'.[120] These references also graphically demonstrate the alterations in belief about guardian angels – whereas earlier the angel standing at the weighing of souls would have been understood as the specially assigned guardian angel, these passages merely refer to the presence of angels in the plural, reflecting the prevailing reformed distaste for the concept. The disappearance of guardian angels from the deathbed, documented by Marshall and notable by their absence in post-reformation religious sources, is further evidence of the impact of reformed ideas on this aspect of belief.[121]

The alterations to the angelic role in mortuary culture offer an intriguing insight into the impact that new theological understanding had on the pastoral role of angels. Angels continued to fulfil an important responsibility of providing comfort and succour to a beleaguered laity, just as they always had, despite the presence of new limitations. The Elizabethan 1560 proclamation[122] prohibiting iconoclastic attacks on tombs must also have contributed to the survival of numerous depictions of the heavenly beings, cementing their association with mortuary culture, although it is clear that reformed thought did make some impact in this area. Peter Marshall concludes his discussion by remarking that the treatment of angels around the deathbed is not an example where 'traditional motifs almost unconsciously seep through the top-soil of religious reform', rather these sources were created by educated Protestants whose insistence on the ministry of angelic angels served an important polemical service. He argues that when 'Abraham's bosom' was regarded as a straightforward synonym for heaven, then the angelic ministry at the deathbed and role of carrying the soul to its final resting place drew attention to the abolition of purgatory. In light of this, the emphasis on angels need not be seen as a concession or accommodation on the part of the reformers.[123] The treatment of angels in mortuary culture, an area of belief where reformers were likely to tread carefully given the weighty soteriological matters involved, nevertheless does not show any variation from the treatment of other aspects of angelic belief. Once again, the result was to remove the more distinctive characteristics of the heavenly beings, bringing a more general understanding of the angelic role to the fore.

Somewhat surprisingly, there is also evidence of the persistence of aspects of belief that did not have the direct support of scripture. In the evidence cited in support of his representation of the angelic presence, Taverner points out that 'the good fathers were holpen and benefited of them, as in the Olde testament', and he goes on to talk of Abraham, Jacob, Elizabeth, and 'Tobie' (amongst others). This is interesting because Protestants had rejected the book of Tobit from the Protestant canon, removing the scriptural evidence for the archangel Raphael, whose role it was to assist Toby.[124] Of course, Taverner's sermon was published in the early years of the Reformation, and as such would not be expected to reflect later developments. However, the reference could have been omitted without difficulty, given its controversial nature, and further investigation confirms that this was an area of ambiguity.

For example, the evangelical author Roger Hutchinson (who was deprived of his Eton fellowship in Mary's reign because he was married),[125] in the context of a discussion of angels in *The image of God*, 1550, remarked that 'Raphael, one of the seven angels that stand before God, saith unto Toby 'I have offered thy prayer before the Lord'. This is surprising both because of the mention of Raphael, and because of the idea of a being other than Christ offering prayers to God. Hutchinson quickly elaborated on the latter, 'whereby is meant that they be ministering spirits for their sakes which shall be heirs of salvation, not, that God learneth our need by them, who knoweth what is necessary for us, before we ask it of him', but he did not find it necessary to excuse his use of the book of Tobit or Raphael.[126] Similarly, collections of prayers published throughout the period continue to mention Toby and Raphael. Becon's *Flour of Godly Praiers*, also published in 1550, contained a reference in a prayer for the protection of travellers, asking God to 'take charge of them and shadowe them under thy merciful wings ... yea as thou diddest send thy holy angel with Abraham and Tobye ... be thy guide and defender'.[127] The traditional belief that Raphael would provide protection from travellers was evidently a particularly persistent one. It also appeared in an anonymous collection of prayers published in 1574, where it was noted that 'Against the going of the young Toby into a straunge countrey didest thou provide thy Angell and messenger to be his guide' and it is asked that 'thy holy Angell may be with me, to direct my feet into the waye of peace, trueth and health'.[128] Placed alongside these other impeccable scriptural references, the reference to Toby, and by implication to Raphael, could provide authority and approval for continuing belief in the special angelic protection of travellers and in the named archangel himself.

Significantly, the story of Toby is singled out by Tessa Watt as evidence for the continuing presence of images in early modern life. Arguing that images were more acceptable in domestic, as opposed to ecclesiastical settings, Watt maintains that painting on cloth or walls, or the pasting up of ballads and other forms of 'cheap print', was a widespread practice in alehouses, taverns, and domestic interiors throughout the period. With regard to the content of these illustrations, she argues that there was a 'core of narrative pictorial themes' that recurred in a wide range of settings, and that were relatively unobjectionable to the reformers. The biblical stories identified as most popular by Watt included the tale of Tobias, along with the story of Susanna, and the parables of Dives and Lazarus and the prodigal son.[129]

Watt's explanation for the continual depiction of the story of Tobias is convincing.[130] The surviving references and illustrations of the episode involving Toby indicates the high esteem that apocryphal books continued to be held in despite their rejection from the official canon. Although these books were not to be used as the basis of doctrine, they were nevertheless valued as a source of spiritual knowledge and they continued to be bound (albeit separate from the official canon) in Protestant editions of the Bible. This all helps to explain the Protestants' apparent lack of concern over residual belief with reference to the book of Tobit. Intriguingly, Watt posits that it was precisely the non-scriptural status of selected images that made them acceptable to reformers, as the temptation to worship was less where depictions were purely narrative in function, rather than providing a static target for idolatry. Thus the images that were produced moved down a 'ladder of sanctity': depictions of figures from the New Testament were anathema (although parables, being mere stories, were viewed with less aversion), those taken from the Old Testament were not quite so 'dangerous', and those purely narrative tales from the Apocrypha, removed from their ecclesiastical setting, could serve a useful instructional purpose.[131] Watt's argument provides a plausible explanation for why a tale taken from the book of Tobit did not simply disappear from popular religious cultures after its rejection from the Protestant canon. It is also evidence of the ambiguity that characterized the reformers' dealings with angelic creatures: there was clearly no direct correlation between more forthright opinions of leading reformers such as Calvin, and the continual development of angelology at lower levels. Less scripturally secure elements of belief continued to be affirmed by reformed clergymen.

However, there is one aspect of this area of belief that is noticeably different from traditional angelology, and that is the contrast in tone and content. The story of Raphael and Toby's journey is described by Peter Marshall and Alexandra Walsham as 'the bible's most affecting account of human-angel interaction'.[132] However, the later, post-reformation references to the tale are more fleeting in tenor, containing no discussion of the companionship of the angel and the man, and rarely mentioning the archangel by name. The depictions of the story remarked upon by Watt are instructional and narrative in form. It appears that these references to angels were treated with the same caution as was reflected in the persistent reminders that the angelic nature was not to be confused with that of men, and with the curbing of support for the angelic hierarchy and guardian angels. The marginalizing of the personal interaction between Raphael and Toby, and the consistent employment of the episode merely as an example of the care and protection that God has for his people, is further evidence of the ambiguity that marked many aspects of the reformed celestial beings.

This trend has been detected elsewhere, and recurred in aspects of angelology that, although they had been present in traditional religious cultures, now received greater emphasis and became more integral to belief in angels as a whole. After the initial curtailment and adjustment of perceptions of the angelic beings, reformers therefore began to focus their energies on those aspects of belief that had a more positive contribution to make to the emerging Protestant nation, and this is nowhere more evident than in the evolution of ideas about angels as agents of God's providence.

Providential angels are found in various polemical writings by eminent churchmen, but their most frequent appearances in this context are in sermons, catechisms and most prominently in the forms of occasional prayer that were issued by the government, as a response to national events. Alexandra Walsham's work on providence in early modern England has established the importance of the concept to the Protestant identity,[133] and unsurprisingly there are many instances where angels are described as the agents of God's will. For example, Niels Hemmingsen described how God 'never dealeth with man by his bare woord'; He was considered more likely to 'send angels to give men knowledge of his will'. Similarly James Calfhill noted that angels 'have been by God's providence a defence of the faithful, and overthrow of the wicked', and Latimer talked of 'how diligently the angels do God's commandments' in a sermon on the Lord's Prayer.[134]

With regard to providential angels and protection, a significant theme emerges from the literature. A recurring and important concept was that 'angels pitch their tents round about us', a biblical metaphor drawn from Psalm 34:7, which reads 'The angel of the Lord encampeth round about them that fear him, and delivereth them'. The notion appeared in the prayer 'For the help of God's holy angels' in the primers, where God was called upon to defend the petitioner against the numerous evil spirits by sending 'thy blessed and heavenly angels, which may pitch their tents round about me and so deliver me from their tyranny'. The idea was also found in books of religious instruction, such as the 1572 *Briefe and Necessary Catechism*, where the student, when asked to comment upon the comfort that men receive from God, replied that 'al ye good angels of god shal watch over me, and pitch their tents about me', ensuring that neither devil nor man can cause hurt 'but when, and so farre as god will permit them'.[135] Further examples can be found in John Foxe's *Actes and Monuments*. A letter from the martyr Rafe Allerton, in which he seeks to comfort his fellow sufferers, begins with the hope that 'The angel of God pytch his tent about us, and defend us in all our wayes'. Similarly, shortly before his execution, Richard Roth tells his brethren to 'wayte you stil for the Lord. He is at hand, yea the angel of the lord pitcheth his tent rounde aboute them that feare him'. He then goes on to link the concept with a notion of God's providence by saying that the angel 'delyuereth them which way he seeth best, For our lyves are in the Lordes handes'.[136]

In this chapter, references to angels in Foxe's *Actes* have been mentioned in various contexts, often in association with angelic belief that was regarded with disapproval by Foxe and other reformers.[137] However, as these references to angelic protection indicate, Foxe's attitude was not always so hostile. Foxe in fact subscribed to and espoused the view that God had given men angels 'to be our kepers and defenders' and he similarly included references within his work that demonstrated an awareness and appreciation of other traditional benefits of the angelic existence. For example, the scriptural passage relating to the release of Peter from prison forms part of John Lambert's defence of his reformed religious views, and the idea that angels minister to those under lock and key was again implied when Rowland Taylor, imprisoned before his martyrdom in 1555, described the fact that during his confinement 'he founde suche an Angell of god, to be in his company to coumforte him'.[138] The persistent belief that angels would carry the souls of the saved to heaven was also attested to: in one of John Hooper's letters he reminded his fellow brethren that the angels 'be ready always to take you up into heaven', and correspondence with the prisoners in Newgate attempted to fortify the resolve of the condemned with the expectation that 'the holy angels of your heavenly father are alredye appoynted to conduct your swete soules into Abrahams bosome'.[139] The common association of angels with mortuary culture is also displayed by references to the angelic witness of the punishment of sinners at Judgement, and is given emotive substantiation in the prayer of John Hullyer, when he calls upon God for strength at the time of his martyrdom, pleading that

> at this present time, when most nede is ... send down thy holy Aungel to comfort, assist, aide and succour me, to prosper my iourney, and safelye to bring me through the straight gate and narrow way, into thy most ioyful, heauenlye, and euerlastynge rest.[140]

Familiar themes are therefore indicated by the references to angels in *Actes and Monuments*, although the emphasis on providential angels was a new development.

It is particularly interesting to find the persistence of belief in angels within what is this immensely important Elizabethan publication, as this provides a poignant example of confessionalized angelic beings and their place in the reformed universe. However, a decisive assessment of the importance of Foxe's *Actes and Monuments* to popular religious cultures has proved elusive for historians, despite an outpouring of scholarly writing on the topic: accordingly the presence of angels amongst its pages is difficult to evaluate.[141] Yet by considering the book in the wider context of reformed angelology, and with regard to the book's creation and publication, it is still plausible to identify some underlying themes which may in turn shed light on the development of angelology.

Scholars are now likely to reject William Haller's premise that Foxe was an Anglocentric writer, intent on promoting the idea that England was a New Israel or an Elect Nation under the special protection of God. The argument that Foxe's *Actes* was a patriotic Protestant history was fostered by a particular edition, edited and published by Timothy Bright in 1589. Bright was a physician whose experience of the St Bartholomew's Day Massacre in 1572 had encouraged his perception that England benefited from the special protection of God. His edition of the work appeared just a year after the defeat of the Armada and he added a preface entitled 'The speciall note of England', which glorified the nation's achievements and depicted the country as the true fount of the Reformation, concluding that England was 'the first that embraced the gospel ... the first reformed'. Recently, Bright's work has been subject to revision, with scholars suggesting that his abridgement was a conformist defence of the Elizabethan settlement, rather than a strident outpouring of national feeling, and it also appears that his abridgement was not a particularly popular edition. However, for our purposes Foxe's original intentions are less important than the popular reception and legacy of his work.

As a consequence of this more recent scholarship, Foxe is now seen as a Protestant internationalist, far more concerned about erecting the true church than pushing a brand of patriotism.[142] Patrick Collinson sees the apocalypse, and particularly John Bale's reading of Revelation in *The Image of Two Churches,* as providing Foxe with the idea of 'using martyrology as a line upon which to hang a history of the conflict between the True church and the false', with his work therefore reflecting universal rather than regional concerns. However, David Loades suggests that there were elements of Foxe's work which would have permitted an Anglocentric interpretation, and it is generally accepted that *Actes and Monuments* was associated with an emerging Anglo-Protestant consciousness through the appropriation of Foxe's legacy subsequent to his death.[143]

The idea of the book acting as 'religious imperialist propaganda' remains credible, albeit not in the way originally envisaged by Haller.[144] Collinson has also provided a timely reminder that although Foxe was a 'highly proactive editor', whose authoritative stamp was in evidence throughout the work, in reality 'many hands and voices contributed to "Foxe"' and the whole represented 'a highly collaborative literary venture'. Collinson argues that the book itself therefore represents the godly community 'constructing itself by both writing and reading, rehearsing these stories', and also that the resulting construction was essentially 'inclusionary', that is to say it did not have a separate message for the committed (or Elect) in contrast with the message for all the rest.[145] Although Collinson also calls for more research into the mass reception of the *Actes*, it seems apparent that the book has a wider significance, and if, as Collinson maintains, the essential constituents required for the construction of national sentiment are 'a shared language, expressed in written vernacular literature, and a shared religious identity', then Foxe's *Actes* unquestionably fits the bill. There is certainly no doubt that the work allowed Englishmen to see themselves as the faithful members of an embattled nation surrounded by enemies of God. In these circumstances it was perhaps natural to expect the angels to come to the defence of God's chosen people. This sentiment was perfectly expressed in a letter from Bishop Hooper, reprinted in *Actes and Monuments*: he says 'remember what lokers upon you have, to see and behold you ... God and all his holy angels, ready to minister to you, 'if you be slain in this fight'.[146]

Further evidence demonstrates how this understanding might inform religious cultures: five forms of prayer issued in the course of the Anglo-Spanish war contain a reference to angels pitching their tents (no doubt it was also a popular turn of phrase due to the martial association). By these means providential angels became associated with the security of the nation, either as guardians, or as the instrument of the destruction of the enemies of the state. God is accordingly beseeched to send 'good and honourable victories', as he did to Abraham, and by means of 'an host of Angels to scatter their armies both by sea and land'.[147]

Perhaps the best example of this can be found in a prayer of 1590 on the part of the French king Henry IV, issued before he decided that Paris was worth a mass and underwent his final conversion. The prayer asked for God's protection against the 'multitude of notorious rebels that are supported and waged by great forces of foreigners', meaning the Catholic League and the Spanish, who were disputing Henry's claim to the throne. It asked for a holy angel to circuit the realm, so that the numerous enemies might see the 'unresistable army of angels' fighting alongside the Protestants, forcing them to recognize that God was 'the help of the humble, the defender of the weak, the protector of them that are forsaken'. The prayer conveys a strong sense of an embattled godly minority that would nevertheless prevail due to God's special protection.[148] For a relatively small and vulnerable Protestant European power, the notion that God was onside with a mighty celestial army to do his bidding was evidently a comforting one.

Even where angels are not specifically mentioned, often the imagery and metaphorical language of religious literature seemed designed to bring them to mind. One of the prayers discussed above desired the angels to pitch their tents among men 'that we may know thine holy hand stretched out for our help and strongly set against them', and a later prayer of 1597, for the success of her majesty's forces and navy, started by asking that the forces might be defended by 'thy strong and mighty arm' and went on to request 'thy providence secure them, thine holy Angels guard them'.[149] The idea of the 'holy hand' or 'arm' of God is here clearly associated with angelic power, and is also reminiscent of the second book of Samuel 24:16, 'and when the angel stretched out his hand upon Jerusalem to destroy it, the Lord repented him of the evil, and said to the angel that destroyed the people, It is enough: stay now thine hand'. Although the activity the angel undertook in the scriptural passage is destructive rather than protective, there is no doubt that the references to the holy limbs of the Lord were closely associated with angelic activity, and therefore where further references appear it might be assumed that this would recall angels to the congregation's minds. Numerous prayers incorporated this theme and some also referred to the working of God's providence, which we have seen fell under the angels' jurisdiction. For example, 'A prayer made by the Queen at the departure of the fleet' in 1596, says 'Stretch forth, O Lord most mightie, thy right hand over me, and defend me from mine enemys'.[150]

Although it could be questioned whether mentioning the holy hand of God was a reference to angels, the latter prayer also mentioned wings, a more concrete allusion. There are several similar prayers which provide further evidence for the association, one from 1594 offering a pertinent example:

> Our shield and defence belongeth to thee (O Lord of hosts)...both prince and people dwell still under the shadow of thy wings, protected by thy power, preserved by thy providence, and ordered by thy governance.[151]

The reminder that God is the Lord of the hosts, combined with the references to both wings and providence, would again have linked these ideas in the audience's mind. It is also worth noting that the angels were here used to bolster and legitimise the monarchy, and it is under the shadow of the wings of God that Elizabeth 'hath not miscarried'. A later prayer also noted that God 'hast appointed Kings and Princes as thine Angels and Lieutenants, full of wisdom and beauty, to rule and govern in thy Name, the people on the earth committed to their charge', evidence that the monarchy was not averse to appropriating the special status of the celestial beings to its own advantage.[152] It is also possible that there is a connection here with the passage in Daniel 10, which suggested the existence of national guardian angels. Interestingly, although Calvin had rejected the notion of the personal guardianship of angels,[153] he was rather keener on the idea that each *nation* had a special angel guarding it, presumably because the scriptural evidence was less obscure on this point. In the *Institutes* he said that Daniel 'undoubtedly intimates that certain angels are appointed as a kind of presidents over kingdoms and provinces', and this notion may well have informed these forms of prayer, calling on God to send his angels for the national defence.[154]

Clearly the angelic role as agents of God's providence had popular currency. Although this *had* been an aspect of medieval angelology, it had merely been one of many diverse strands, and its noticeable prominence in the sixteenth century therefore represents a shift in emphasis on the part of the reforming churchmen. Once again, the alteration in the treatment of angels, and the self-conscious association of angels with notions of providence, and their re-imagining as powerful extensions of God's providential will, fitted in with the theological trend which sought to minimise notions of the personal ministry of angels and instead concentrated on more general ideas of angelic protection. Reformers again can be seen emphasizing the angels' role as servants of God, created at his whim to act as agents of his will. Thus those aspects that might tempt people to the damnable sin of idolatry were suppressed, whilst the angels' primary function of magnifying the glory of God was secure. This was firmly in agreement with Calvin's notion that although scripture illustrated the existence of 'this noble and illustrious specimen', it only provided firm evidence that angels are 'the ministers appointed to execute the commands of God', nothing more.[155]

The increasing interest in angels as examples of the functioning of divine providence also has a greater significance. Alexandra Walsham has established that providential belief was a fundamental element of continuity that united English religious cultures of the period, and in its various forms these beliefs provided another of the foundations for the forging of a Protestant nation. It functioned as 'cultural adhesive uniting disparate groups at moments of communal emergency and crisis', and combined with anti-popery and xenophobia it created a potent brand of patriotism that in turn helped to create confessional identities.[156] The idea that the processes of reform contributed to a distinctive English Protestant identity has also been explored by David Cressy in his study of the development of a new ritual calendar following the jettisoning of many Catholic annual feasts. Cressy's contention was that the Elizabethans and Stuarts developed a yearly calendar that was based on and gave expression to 'a mythic and patriotic sense of national identity'. The processes of reform introduced a new national devotional framework that was firmly centred on commemoration of the life of Christ, but which also began to incorporate the anniversaries of monarchy, linking parishes in loyal celebration of the fortunes of the reign. Along with the dates of royal accession, Protestant deliverances were prominent in the new calendar, the anniversaries of the Armada and Gunpowder Treason being well known examples of this.[157]

The idea that providence was a concept central to the Protestant worldview, alongside the notion that providential events contributed to a growing sense of national identity through the absorption of these events into a new ritual calendar, is therefore increasingly familiar. Yet to date, there has been little attention to the role angels played in these processes. There was no additional day of celebration dedicated to angels, although Cressy does note that the feast of St Michael and All Angels survived the drastic reduction in the number of feast days that the Injunctions of 1536 entailed. However, although he sees Michaelmas as a 'pivot of the year', this is not because it is one of the remaining ecclesiastical festivals, but as 'a crucial date in the *secular* calendar': more important to the cycle of the economy and government than in the liturgical cycle of the church.[158] Admittedly Michaelmas *was* a fundamental secular date: it lent its name to the university and Inns of Court terms, it was the usual day of elections in local government, and it fell at the end of the agrarian year, making it the occasion of the settling of rents. However, the date also retained religious significance and was an important element in the devotions relating to angels. It continued to be a fixed date when the congregation was invited to reflect on the nature and purpose of angelic beings, and it was a regular occasion for the delivery of sermons devoted to contemplation of celestial beings such as Hemminsgsen's sermon 'Upon the feast day of St. Michael the Archangell' or Richard Taverner's sermon 'On Michelmas daye'.[159]

Angels also participated in the developing national calendar through their repeated appearance in occasional forms of prayer. Churchgoers' perception of angels would have been informed by these prayers, and in the course of a year they were exposed to their recurring themes. So although a particular military victory may not have been ritually celebrated year after year, prayers for the protection and aid of the angels remained constant elements, and the notion that angels acted as agents of God's providence leading them to intervene directly in the affairs of the state, would have been instantly recognizable. Thus it could be argued that these forms of prayer contributed to the emergence of the English Protestant identity in the same way that annual celebrations have been seen to, as they established an integral role in the functioning and temporal understanding of the reformed universe. It is also true that angels could appear in precisely those new annual celebrations that Cressy singles out in his work. *A Psalm of thanksgiving*, issued following the defeat of the Armada in 1588, says of the Spanish:

> The Angel of the Lord persecuted them, brought them into dangerous, dark and slippery places, where they wandering long to and fro, were consumed with hunger, thirst, cold and sickness.[160]

Evidently in the hour of the nation's greatest need, God had seen fit to stretch out his hand, sending his angel to destroy the enemies of the state and providing celestial beings with an enduring legacy in the emerging Protestant nation.

Summary

Recent post-revisionist scholarship on the English reformation is inclined to view the phenomenon as a fluid process, whereby older assumptions were assimilated and harnessed, and accommodation was made with existing belief. This survey of the religious reform in the sixteenth century provides evidence that in part supports this idea, but which does not entirely synchronise with the 'post-revisionist' paradigm. It is true that notions of the ministry of angels continued to contain much that had firm roots in medieval religious traditions, but close examination of particular aspects of belief, combined with an appreciation of the elements of traditional angelology that were casualties of reform, illustrates that these changes were not the result of 'accommodation' on the part of the reformers. Rather, a process has been revealed whereby older belief was stripped of its non-scriptural features and dubious legacies were quietly suppressed, with the result that the remaining, thoroughly reformed perceptions of angels could be endorsed without scruple by the Protestants. Admittedly the reformers were eager to promote the benefits of these wonderful celestial creatures, scripturally sound tokens of God's mercy and love for his people, but it was simply fortuitous that this turned out to coincide with early modern sensibilities. Despite the incongruous presence of Raphael and Toby in religious cultures, there is no real evidence that this was a self-conscious attempt to assuage the preoccupations of 'popular' culture in the early modern world. Instead, old ideas engaged with reformed theology to produce a novel and distinct understanding.

Consequently although the notion of angels as intercessors and any practice or belief that might tend towards idolatry was rejected outright by the reformers, angels retained a significant pastoral role as the comforters and protectors of mankind. The guiding theological principles of *sola fide* and *sola scriptura* had prompted the reformers to curb the excesses of medieval angelology and to adjust their understanding of the angelic beings. Calvin led the way with these words on medieval angelology:

> In this way the glory of Christ was for several former ages greatly obscured, extravagant eulogiums being pronounced on angels without any authority from Scripture. Among the corruptions which we now oppose, there is scarcely any one of greater antiquity.[161]

However, as long as a belief or practice could be firmly backed by scriptural evidence, angels continued to perform traditional functions, and although this did not mean that they stepped into the shoes of the saints, it is true that some of these functions had previously been shared with these other members of the holy company of heaven. The ubiquity of references to angels in the bible in fact meant that heavenly beings were to prove a particularly useful tool to the reformers, and they were eagerly enlisted as a tonic to the potentially alarming implications of the rejection of purgatory and endorsement of double predestination.

Over the course of the period, it is also apparent that angels were not only utilized as examples of God's mercy and care of his people, but that they were increasingly useful in providing support for the Protestant message and for the reformed perception of the functioning of the universe. One of the most persistent references to angels in every form of religious literature relates to the biblical passage Galatians 1:8, when Paul warns though 'an angel from heaven, preach any other gospel unto you than that which we have preached unto you, let him be accursed'. It is not surprising to discover that this is a passage that is constantly reiterated by Protestant authors as further proof against popish innovations, and evidence that only the bible contains the true word of God. Foxe's *Actes and Monuments* contains several references to the same. For instance in his defence before Bishop Bonner, Thomas Iveson refused to recant with the words:

> I doe appeale to Gods mercie, and wyllbe none of your churche, nor submitte my self to the same: and that I haue sayde, and will saye agayne. And if there came an Aungel from heauen, to teache me any other doctrine, then that whiche I am in nowe, I woulde not beleue him.[162]

In this instance, the angels are utilized to emphasize and disseminate the central tenet of Protestant thought, and it is a pattern that is repeated elsewhere. Accordingly, angels were invoked in arguments against monastic chastity and the cult of

Mary, and they were a common presence in arguments against the existence of any mediator aside from Christ himself. The understanding of the providential angelic role and the emphasis that angels, as with all things created, were entirely dependent upon the will of God, was particularly important in this respect: angels drawing attention to God's position as the sole creator and ultimate power in the universe, whilst also providing support for the central Protestant tenet of predestination and confirming the workings of God's providence. Angels were an important concept in emerging 'Protestant' religious cultures.

This new emphasis on angels as mighty instigators of God's power also contributed to, and reinforced the overall trend in angelology to depersonalize heavenly beings.[163] This trend was directly linked to the paucity of scriptural detail relating to celestial beings, and was also reinforced by the rejection of the angelic hierarchy and more dubious elements of traditional belief, such as guardian angels. However, the persistence of references to Toby demonstrates the variety of attitudes that the reformers harboured about celestial beings, and is a reminder that despite theological pruning, there were still areas of ambiguity and disagreement. By the 1580s, belief about angels clearly remained a strong and significant strain in English religious cultures, but various aspects of belief, particularly relating to named angels and the viability of depictions of winged figures, suggested potentially dissonant features that might prove a problematic legacy.

3 THE CHURCH OF ENGLAND ANGEL, *c.* 1580–1700

Despite the upheavals of the mid-sixteenth century, belief about angels was evidently an enduring aspect of English religious cultures. Angels did not merely survive the turmoil of the early years of reform, but also persisted as an important element of belief that played a part in many significant theological discussions of the era, in the process contributing to the emergence of a distinctly 'English' Protestant identity. The legacy was to endure, and become a permanent feature of post-Reformation England. This chapter examines this legacy, tracing the evidence for a core set of beliefs about angels that persisted throughout the sixteenth and seventeenth centuries, beliefs which together could be considered to be the 'authorized', Church of England, angel. It investigates how belief about angels continued to fulfil important and wide ranging pastoral and didactic functions after the Reformation, and how churchmen utilized the concept of angels in polemic designed to establish Protestantism in the hearts and minds of their parishioners. The result of this was that particular aspects of belief were elaborated upon to create an 'orthodox' angel that was well suited to the ecclesiology and religious outlook of the Church of England.

The first section of the chapter explores the ongoing consolidation of the processes outlined previously. It will first demonstrate how the compendious works of prominent English churchmen, with their strong Calvinist theology, reinforced the concept of the 'reformed' angel, with distinctive characteristics and qualities, before exploring how these ideas were secured in a broader range of texts and over time. In the second half of the chapter, the endurance of these elements of belief will be traced through the latter part of the seventeenth century, indicating the persistence of the 'Protestant' angel in post-Reformation England.

Consolidation

Thus far, discussion has focused on the differences between the pre- and post-reformation understanding of the nature and responsibilities of angelic beings, highlighting areas of ambiguity but also identifying continuities with the past, and the positive employment of angels in the conversion of the laity to the reformed faith. However, the development of Protestant angelology was an ongoing process, and although not every historian would go so far as Patrick Collinson in asserting that 'the Reformation was something which happened in the reigns of Elizabeth and James I', it is undoubtedly true that the processes of reform did not end with the settlement of 1559 but continued for many decades after.[1] The official Protestant perception of an angel, as derived from the writings of the major continental and English reformers, continued to be expounded upon and perpetuated in the literature published in the formative years of the Church of England.

A second generation of English reformers, many of them born in the 1550s were publishing works that sought to summarise and consolidate the 'new thinking' during the late Elizabethan and Jacobean period. William Perkins, Andrew Willet, and George Abbot, may stand as representative of the fully reformed Church of England rejecting the extremes of separatism, nonconformism, and anti-Puritanism.[2] These men were establishing the boundaries of moderate churchmanship for a broad readership, and through the customary inclusion of celestial beings within their comprehensive works, they were also perpetuating the reformed perception of angels.

William Perkins (1558–1602) was an influential Church of England clergyman and his works are replete with references to celestial beings, where he discussed at length the practical implications of their existence. A detailed exposition of their nature and functions can be found in *A golden chaine,* Perkins' investigation into the unalterable order of creation from the angels through to the most simple organisms. Here Perkins began with a description of angels as 'spirituall and incorporeal essences', who attended to God in the highest heaven, adoring and praising him continually: their office was 'partly to magnify God, and partly to performe his commandements'.[3]

Following this general introduction to angels, Perkins then focused upon their functions and responsibilities. He argued that angels were wise, mighty, swift and innumerable, and explained in detail the occasions when they took visible shapes and forms, as well as unravelling the mysterious quality of their excellent knowledge and understanding. He specified the ministry of the angels: protecting and preserving the temporal lives of men and women, comforting and directing them, assisting at the end of life by carrying souls to their final resting place and participating in the Final Judgement. He allowed that there was a hierarchy of angels, although of course 'what be the distinct degrees and orders of Angels, and whether they are to be distinguished by their natures, gifts or offices, no man by scripture can determine'. He did not shy away from the less comforting aspects of the angelic existence either, describing also how angels executed judgements on wicked sinners and depicting the serried ranks of celestial armies that awaited to inflict punishment on the impenitent.[4]

Perkins' description is firmly rooted in earlier reformed perceptions of angels, but its importance does not hinge on its originality. Recent reassessments of Perkins' career have shifted his reputation from that of an influential Elizabethan Puritan to an apologist for the Church of England, therefore Perkins' objectives in his writing and preaching are of significance.[5] W. B. Patterson has argued that Perkins considered the Church of England sound in liturgy, polity and doctrinal standards, but that he 'saw it as his vocation to win the ignorant, the superstitious, the uninformed ... to a religious faith that would transform'.[6] That this was his intention is endorsed by Lori Anne Ferrell, who has argued that the explicit visual character of *A golden chaine*, which makes the story more accessible by representing the functioning of salvation in diagrammatic forms alongside the text, indicates Perkins' wish to appeal to the middling sorts in whom a new intellectual capacity was awakening.[7]

The presence of a long section on angels within this work is therefore significant as it represents a format whereby a Protestant clergyman sought to convey these ideas to a broader audience. Angels were not to become the preserve of theologians arguing over fine details such as whether angels could eat or speak, rather their treatment here gives support to Patterson's suggestion that 'by appropriating ideas and practices of the traditional pre-Reformation religion of the island, while defining them in a way consistent with Protestant, particularly Calvinist, theology, he [Perkins] helped to win his compatriots to a reformed faith'.[8]

Perkins' was acutely aware of the pastoral expediency of angels: he portrayed a 'patterne of Angelicall obedience ... propounded for our imitation'.[9] Interestingly, Perkins believed that the benefits of this approach were not to be gained by those 'who account zeale in religion, affected preciseness', a statement which provides support for Patterson's understanding of Perkins as an apologist for the Established Church. 'Zeale' and 'preciseness' were two of the adjectives closely associated with the radical element within the Established Church, those pushing for further reform of the liturgy and hierarchy who were also often charged with hypocrisy for failing to live up to the strict moral standards they advocated. In Perkins' mind, only those 'who call God father in *sinceritie*, must set before them the obedience of the holy Angels, as a patterne for their imitation', implying the exclusion of the 'busy' godly element.[10]

Perkins' work therefore provides convincing evidence that celestial beings remained an important part of the reformers' arsenal when it came to the consolidation of orthodoxy amongst the laity. Similar attitudes can be traced in much of the literature published at this time, many distinguished authors following him in devoting a substantial portion of text to discussion of heavenly creatures. Excellent examples are Lancelot Andrewes (1555–1626), Andrew Willet

(1561/2–1621) and George Abbot (1562–1633), all of whom were committed and influential supporters of the Church of England in the early part of this period, albeit from varying stances of 'churchmanship'. A sermon in Andrewes' *The wonderfull combate betweene Christ and Satan* comforted the audience with the promise that angels 'defend vs in all our dangers, and succour vs in all necessities, spreading their winges ouer vs, and pitching their tents about vs'.[11] Andrew Willet used angels to demonstrate a 'heresie reuiued by the Papistes: for they doe maintaine the worship and adoration of Angels', a practice he then condemned in no uncertain terms, and he discussed their nature and purpose at length in several of his other works.[12] George Abbot pursued a similar course; he expounded the angelic existence, concentrating on the celestial hierarchy and the extent of human knowledge relating to it.[13]

The works of these leading clergymen illustrate the unity of Church of England clergymen with regard to celestial beings. Despite their differing churchmanship, these men were united in their opinions and expectations about angels. This point is further endorsed in the work of Richard Hooker (1553/4–1600), particularly in the first major English work that sought to consolidate reformed doctrine: *Of the Lavves of ecclesiasticall politie*. The professed purpose of the work has been described by one historian as 'resolving the consciences or enlisting the affections of those who could or would not accept the religious settlement of 1559 … a continuation of Hooker's earlier pastoral efforts'.[14] The inclusion of celestial beings in its pages indicated the continuing esteem in which angels were held. Hooker's exposition contained no surprises, his 'immateriall and intellectuall' creatures are perfect in their obedience to God's law, 'being rapt with the loue of his beautie, they cleaue inseparably for euer vnto him'. Indeed he identified their chief actions in relation to love, adoration and imitation, and mentioned several traditional motifs, including the notion that angels are 'lincked into a kinde of corporation amongst themselues, and of societie or fellowship with men'.[15]

It is particularly interesting to find these traditional ideas appearing in Hooker's work, because the clergyman's theological outlook was not entirely in line with his contemporaries. The *Lavves* came into their own only after Hooker's lifetime, and were destined to become a favourite of Anglican churchmen in later centuries. His tendency to endorse medieval continuity and sacramentalism was distinctively un-Puritan in tone. However, although historians continue to probe the religious convictions of the man, it is clear that Hooker's understanding of angelic beings did chime with earlier Protestant teaching, and more generally with the Elizabethan ordering of the universe. When it came to this aspect of belief, Hooker was in agreement with his peers.

The utilization of angels in these ways demonstrates the willingness with which the angelic motif was appropriated and employed in polemical writing, as in the examples of Willet and Abbot, who were both penning explicitly anti-papal works. It is suggestive of the important place that angels assumed in the reformed mentality. However, this understanding of angels was also perpetuated in other contemporary literature and can be traced through many contemporary genres. For example, in a prose and poetical commonplace book entitled *Politeuphuia: wits common wealth*, edited by Nicholas Ling in 1598, the section 'On Angels' provides a succinct summary of angel lore: they are diuine messengers beholding the face of the heavenly Father, they are created 'immortall, innocent, beautifull, good, free and subtile', they comfort, instruct and reform men, and they intend two things, 'the glory and seruice of God' and 'the health and saluation of hys Chyldren'.[16]

Collections of prayers also remained an important medium when it came to the dissemination of Protestant ideas about celestial beings. The moderate Puritan and Church of England clergyman, Thomas Tuke, included in his prayer compilation supplications asking God to 'command the guard of thy holy Angels to pitch their tents about vs, and preserue vs both sleeping and waking', and beseeching the lord to assist men in striving to do his will 'ioyfully, readily, faithfully and with a constant heart, as thy Saints and Angels in heauen performes it'.[17] John Norden (*c.* 1547–1625), a prolific author of devotional works, incorporated many references into *A poore mans rest founded vpon motiues, meditations, and prayers,* appealing to God that angels might 'compasse the bed whereon I rest', 'direct me in all my wayes' and 'driue away the deadly enemy'. He finished by confidently asserting that 'Angels shall be ministering spirits for my good'.[18]

In these and other writings, themes and perceptions that formed the foundations of the Protestant understandings of angels recurred frequently, creating and sustaining existing trends. The controversy over the angelic hierarchy also resurfaced. In *Synposis Papismi*, Willet allowed that there were nine orders of angels, but argued that to 'enquire of them more subtilly' was 'a point not onely of foolish curiositie, but also of vngodly and daungerous rashnes'.[19] In his commonplace book, Ling also mentioned the nine orders, listing the scriptural names but keeping within orthodox teaching on the hierarchy and desisting from further speculation.[20] A scries of lectures on Paul's 'Epistle to the Colossians', published by the clergyman Robert Rollock in 1603, displayed similar concerns, saying of the hierarchy 'if God haue not reuealed it, be not curious to search it, let it be, leaue off questioning of things that God hath not reuealed'.[21] Rollock also included a list of the arguments which 'false teachers vse to moue men to worship Angels and Saints departed', pronouncing such persuasions as 'Popish antiquitie', 'foule and false a head of doctrine'.[22]

The Church of England clergyman Thomas Bastard (1565/6–1618) also associated his work with earlier deliberations on angels in his *Twelve sermons,* published in 1615. In a discussion of the wonderful, yet limited range of angelic power, the author noted the responsibility of the angels to 'sit vpon the Spheares of Heauen, and to bring the Sunne to his daily course: to vphold the earth, to dispose seasons and times, to inflict famines and pestilence'.[23] This passage illustrates a continued understanding of the angelic role in the functioning of God's providence, a theme explored in chapter two, where it was argued that the notion of angels as the agents of God's providence became an integral part of the emerging English Protestant identity, a process closely linked to the development of a distinctive national calendar.[24] Evidently this remained a significant trend, as Perkins perpetuated it with a reference to the Spanish Armada in a discussion on the consolations granted to men by the existence of the holy angels. Asking how England came to be saved from the huge navy just off the coast, Perkins expressed the opinion that 'it was the Lord, no doubt by his Angels that did keepe our coasts, and did scatter our enemies, and drowne them'.[25]

There are also other instances where angels were associated with plague, which was often interpreted as a providential punishment visited by God upon his unrepentant people. Henry Holland in his *Spirituall preseruatiues*, issued in the plague years of 1593 and 1603, discussed the scriptural psalm that provided the basis for this association. He noted that an angel of God slew many thousands in David's kingdom, until God commanded it to hold its hand, before going on to discuss the angelic involvement in a plague epidemic at length. Holland understood the angelic role to include 'a speciall charge and commission from God to preserue his faithful people', but also thought that the evil angels were 'Gods speciall instruments in the pestilence', licensed to smite the wicked.[26] Two works published a year after the 1603 epidemic pick up the theme: Henoch Clapham analyses the 'Angells stroke' which he understood caused the infection, using a mixture of scriptural evidence and logic to explore the justice of the Lord and his power and might which 'appeares and is more manifest in this great evil, than in any other'.[27] Francis Herring adopted a slightly more traditional approach, arguing that although 'the angels are vsed as instruments and ministers to inflict this iudgement and plague of the plague [*sic*] for the sins of men', some plagues were thought to have natural origins.[28] Either way, the strong link between angels and providence remained an important strand of angelology in the period.

The expedient nature of the angelic trope was not overlooked either, since the pastoral importance of angels was appreciated by authors throughout the period. Joseph Hall (1574–1646), who went on to occupy the bishoprics of Exeter and Norwich, considered the angelic role in his *Contemplations vpon the principal passages of the holy story*. He emphasized that 'it is one of the worthy imployments of good Angels, to make secret opposition to euill designs', pondering the many evil acts that celestial creatures hindered and encouraging his audience to attempt the same: 'to stop the course of euill, either by disswasion, or violence, is an Angelicall seruice'.[29] The clergyman Thomas Taylor (1576–1632), loyal to the Church of England throughout his career and equally hostile to popery and Arminianism as he was to separatism and antinominalism,[30] began one of his books by imagining the great field of God which made up the world, 'in which Michael and his Angels fight against the dragon and his angels'. Angels went on to play an integral part in the text: Taylor listed the benefits that their presence bestowed on mankind, warned against the 'new-found' distinction between *dulia* and *latria* which revealed nothing but the 'grosse ignorance' of the Church of Rome, discussed the legality of the use of images in religious worship and also debated at length the implications of the angelic existence for men. He maintained that the presence of angels should serve as a reminder that 'we doe not speake any thing without many witnesses', thus we should take care of our behaviour; and this should also prompt us to 'giue to God the honour of our saluation and safety', for this 'is not by chance, nor by our prouidence and policie, but by Gods charging his Angels to saue and keepe vs'.[31]

Another persistent theme in this early literature is the role of angels around the deathbed; again, the literature reflects broad continuity.[32] The sources are replete with references to angelic participation at the end of life. John Smith reminded his readers that there are 'Angels round about the beds of the faithfull to carry their soules into heauen, which is a maine benefite we now haue', a notion common in religious writing throughout the period.[33] They are particularly pronounced in prayers for the sick or dying that were a feature of works in this period. In a prayer for those that are present at the 'death-pangs' of any, appearing in a devotional book in 1591, the supplicant asks God to 'Sende vnto him thy holy Angelles, that they may bring to him the fellowship of al Angels', and in the same year the renowned preacher Henry Smith beseeched God to 'let thine Angels carry up my soule to heauen, as they did Lazarus, and place mee in one of those mancions which thy sonne is gone to prepare for me'.[34]

This was also a theme that Nicholas Byfield, a godly conformist clergyman, explored in his work. He pointed out that death was a far more enticing prospect than the misery of earthly life, arguing that the society of innumerable angels was only one of the delights awaiting the faithful. He repeated the sentiment in *The marrowvv of the oracles of God*, where he urged his readers to 'consider the perfection of the creatures, whose communion we shall enioy'.[35] Stephen Jerome dedicated a chapter of his *Seauen helpes to Heauen* to 'Comforts against the feare of Death', in the course of which he mentioned the angelic joys awaiting the saved at the day of Judgement and the fact that they would 'carry thy flitting soule, as they did Lazarus his, into the seates of the blessed', alongside the many consolations offered by their ministry in earthly life.[36]

Persistence

Following the consolidation and confirmation of the belief about angels in English Protestant discourse in the formative years of the Church of England, the concept was to remain stable throughout the rest of the seventeenth century. Although broader social and cultural events were to influence the tone and emphasis of angelology, the fundamental elements of belief were to persist, and were reproduced for decades to come. By these means, Protestant divines found a natural affinity between the angelic motif and their duty of providing their parishioners with edification and instruction.

The most significant emphasis in the majority of treatise and sermons on angels in the seventeenth-century was the insistence on the great benefits that God offered to mankind through them. In 1646, the parliamentarian Henry Lawrence peppered his *History of Angells* with prompts and reminders to the reader of the wider benefit and meaning that angels represented.[37] Lawrence's advice was for people to 'walke both as Christians and members of Churches, that the Angells may discharge themselves of their worke', and men may receive the benefit of it.[38] Lawrence also indicated how angels could perform instructive roles. He exhorted his readers to 'feare and please God', the provider of the angels, and to 'grow into a greater league and familiarity with them', for this would provoke holiness and obedience in men.[39] Ultimately, angels should inspire men to 'fight manfully the Lords Battailes' and to 'walke reverently in respect of the Angells even in your bedchambers', for the angels were created to 'helpe you in all your wayes'.[40]

In 1659 Samuel Clarke, a Presbyterian cleric, detailed the scriptural evidence of the roles and responsibilities that angels undertook towards men, describing how angels were 'Physicians to cure their maladies', 'Guides to direct and keep them from wanderings', 'souldiers to guard them', 'Prophets or Teachers to instruct them', comforters, punishers and fellow worshippers.[41] These questions are often the subject of discussion in the devotional literature of the time for authors with pastoral provision on their minds. For example, John Gumbleden wrote a sermon on the 'effectual ministry of angels', and described how they comforted those in distress, fought against God's enemies, and were set to guard 'and carefully to watch over all faithfull believers'.[42]

Clarke was keen to stress that God used the ministry of angels not out of necessity, but 'to declare his abundant love' and care of mankind, and relayed how the presence of angels could be a great comfort to men 'when we see our own weaknesse and impotency on the one hand, and the multitude, power and policy of the enemies on the other'. Finally, Clarke moved on to consider what lesson his readers should learn from this God-given gift. He advised people to 'blesse God that hath thus honoured us', and urged them to 'take an holy State upon us, and to think our selves too good to abase ourselves to sin ... seeing we have Angels to attend upon us'. He called on the laity to imitate angels, and to stand ready to execute the will of the Lord, 'with chearfulnesse, sincerity, and without wearisomness'.[43] J. A. Rivers similarly suggested that 'For pleasure, not for want of power or skill, He makes the Angels', and Gumbleden attributed their existence to 'Gods great love', 'for when our God hath a purpose to do us good, he neglects no means'.[44] Other authors were equally keen to promote the benefits of the angels, Edward Leigh hoped that men would learne humilitie' from the angels, 'by comparing ourselves with these excellent spirits' and also suggested that we should 'imitate the Angels'.[45]

Perhaps the most comprehensive discussion of angels in this period was by the Puritan minister Isaac Ambrose in 1662 – his extensive treatment began by listing other authors' works and opinions on celestial beings before considering the spiritual nature of angels and the scope of their ministry.[46] The most interesting section of the treatise concerned the 'reasons for the ministration', because it was here that Ambrose explained the importance of God's provision of angels. He discussed this with regard to God, angels and men. It was God's 'will and pleasure' that the angels should minister, and by his command. For angels, it was their duty to 'act and move as the Lord appoints', it was their 'delight to attend the Saints', and furthermore it was an 'honour to wait on the saints', bearing in mind that it was men, not angels, that had received the gift of salvation. With regard to the Saints themselves, the angelic ministry was 'for their consolation, a mighty comfort', and it was 'for their benefit, both of body and soul'. Ambrose then enlarged on this last point, describing the myriad ways that angels benefited mankind. His different 'uses' included the use of encouragement, for although the wicked were left to fend for themselves, the godly were given 'Tutors, and Governors, and Guardians' to assist them. This claim was supported by scriptural evidence, and details were provided of angelic aid on journeys, during battles, when facing oppression and persecution or when 'under the tyranny of wicked men', or when 'maligned, censured, imprisoned and condemned'. Other uses were that angels should provoke admiration of 'the kindness of the Lord', promote magnanimity, and encourage exhortation and communion with God.[47]

The second book of Ambrose's work went on to examine in detail the special use of direction – 'what they do in their times, and then what we must do in our times, in answer to them and their ministration'. The structure is further evidence of Ambrose's intention to edify and instruct through the employment of the angelic motif. He exploited the diverse range of beliefs that were associated with angels to create a Christian guide to behaviour throughout life, beginning with 'the first Period wherein the Angels minister to Heavens Heirs ... from their quickening in the womb, till their Birth'. After describing how angels 'keep, preserve, defend, deliver, sustain and strengthen babes', he provided cases where this type of ministry had been experienced in recent years, and then related the duties that the laity were expected to assume because of this.[48]

Ambrose proceeded to use this approach in relation to infancy and child-hood, 'from their Birth to their youth, or riper years'. At this time angels kept children from evil, kept them in health, and 'teach and tutor' them. Ambrose also provided examples of these activities, describing several incidents where chil-dren fell into rivers and ponds but were found, miraculously unscathed, or where a starving mother discovered 'a suck-Bottle ... full of good Milk' at a fortuitous moment.[49] Finally Ambrose addressed the ministration 'in our riper years unto their death', whereby a person's body was kept from evil. Angels 'help to remove disease, and to conserve bodily health' and 'carefully furnish us with all other nec-essaries for this life'. With respect to the soul, angels 'declare to us what is the will and mind of God', 'repel temptations, or prevent occasions of sin' and 'quicken our dullness, encourage our weaknesses, and comfort us in our sorrows'.[50]

Ambrose's work provides an informative and comprehensive account of both scriptural and experienced angels, but his intention is clearly more pastoral than polemical – he sought to provide his audience with a greater appreciation and understanding of the ministry of divine beings, and his ultimate aim was that people might gain spiritual aid and education through them. Other works also included a substantial amount of material designed to instruct and edify. These continued to build on the foundations of many years of reformed writing about angels to confirm their important pastoral roles and responsibilities. Benjamin Camfield's 1678 *A theological discourse on angels* is a good example of this. His approach was similar to Ambrose's: he began by outlining what angels were – their nature and substance, their intellectual and physical power, their number, distinction and order.[51] However, the main focus, and the longest section of the treatise, was reserved for a consideration of the offices of angels: 'whereunto God hath appointed and commission'd them'. Camfield himself expressed a desire to 'promote our duty and comfort, more than to satisfie speculative curiosity', and in the pages that followed he provided a comprehensive account of the roles and responsibilities of the celestial creatures that he had just described.[52] Camfield's concerns were apparent in his text, he was insistent that angels were:

> ready Messengers to receive his [God's] commands, observe his orders, go upon his errands and embassies, and fulfil all his will; thus to serve and obey him, in whatso-ever he shall send or imploy them about.[53]

His text supplied the evidence of what exactly these employments might encom-pass, and paid particular attention to 'the Ministry of the Angels unto the Faithful', which Camfield understood to include three main areas: 'instruction and admonition', 'defence and preservation', and 'comfort, help, deliverance and supply'.[54]

In 1668 the ejected Church of England minister John Maynard focused his discussion on the employment of angels, which he thought was to 'attend on the Lord, and give him praise', obey God's command, defend the church and its members, and to execute God's judgements.[55] Maynard included much in the way of instruction and consolation – angels offered 'great assistance, and protection' and their example was expected to stir people up to obedience and good.[56] Maynard's work in fact bears a suspicious similarity to Isaac Ambrose's in that he also listed the spiritual 'uses' to which angels might be put: they should encourage people to 'mediate up on this excellent work of the All-sufficient Creator'; people should endeavour to 'let the perfections of the Angels teach thee humility of spirit', and all should 'be thankfull for that Protection which the Lord giveth thee by these'.[57]

Richard Baxter, writing towards the end of the century, also provided instruction to his readers. He was of the opinion that 'the Angels of God are not useless to us; but their Ministry is one of Gods Means for our Preservation, and we owe them, Love and Thanks for all their Love and Service'. He also thought that their ministry 'should always keep the Souls of the Faithful in joyful gratitude, for the work of Regeneration, Grace, Justification and Salvation'.[58] Throughout his career Baxter was committed to pastoral oversight, and his ideals and zeal are reflected in his *Gildas Salvianus: the Reformed Pastor*, first published in 1656 and reprinted many times thereafter. His work reflected not only concerns about irreligion, but also about the well-being of souls, and he evidently thought that angels were an effective means to address both these issues.

There are numerous other examples of authors employing angels to provide instruction to their readers, further evidence that this remained an important function for most, despite a climate of intellectual change.[59] The rector of a Huntingdonshire parish, William Johnson, in *A sermon preached upon a great deliverance at sea* in 1664, noted God's promise that 'he will send his own royal guard, the Militia of Heaven, his holy and glorious Angels, to be our Guardians'. Johnson hoped that his parishioners would welcome these good angels 'with a joyful, but a thankful Spirit,' for they were 'happy opportunities of grace', and he called on people to be thankful for this demonstration of God's mercy.[60]

Others also employed angels to encourage and educate their parishioners. One of the practical tracts published by the Church of England clergyman Clement Ellis was a catechism that asked several questions about the nature and relevance of angels to the catechumen, concluding that they were 'innumerable', 'subject to Christ' and 'ministering spirits'.[61] The nonjuring bishop of Bath and Wells, Thomas Ken, in his *Manual of prayers for the use of the scholars*, included angels in many of the entries, beseeching God to 'give Thy Angels charge over us, to protect us from all sin and danger', and reminding his readers that 'even the Good Angels ... fall Prostrate and tremble' before God.[62] The clergyman Richard Allestree wrote a series of moral and devotional works, including *Scala sancta*, which included many set forms of prayer. As well as asking for angelic protection 'For safety in childbirth' and 'Before Journey', in 'A Prayer for Protection in all Dangers' Allestree called on God to:

> Give thy Angels charge concerning me, and my habitation, that I may be reserved and kept in all my waies, and that no evil happen unto me, no plagues come nigh my dwelling, no terrours of the night, no arrows of thy vengeance by day may disturb my peace or safety: Let thy ministering Spirits bear me in their hands, and keep me from precipice, from fracture of bones, from dislocations, noisom or sharp diseases, stupidity and deformity.[63]

Some authors were more extensive in their treatment of the angelic presence. Anthony Horneck, a church of England clergyman who contributed an appendix of Swedish cases to the second edition of Joseph Glanvill's *Saducismus triumphatus* in 1682, evidently placed great value on celestial beings because they were a feature of *The happy Ascetic* of 1681, where Horneck pronounced his intention to 'call Man away from the Shadow, to the substance of Religion … from a notional to a practical Belief of the Gospel'.[64] In a section entitled 'The Ordinary Exercises of Godliness' Horneck urged his readers to spend half an hour each day 'thinking of Good things'. His recommended topics often contained angels – on Sunday, when considering the Kingdom of Heaven, Horneck evoked the 'Guard-Royal of Angels, shining in Robes of Light' that would greet the saved on their arrival, and on Monday the topic was the Last Judgement when Jesus would be revealed 'with his mighty Angels, in flaming fire'. Horneck also called on his readers to show humility, which 'makes us like unto the Angels of God', and asked 'How hath he honoured thee in that he hath charged his Angels to guard thee?'[65]

As a pastoral resource, angels had more uses than merely demonstrating the benefits that God had bestowed upon mankind, and alongside their employment as illustrations of God's mercy, angels were also utilized as a means to demonstrate his justice. A traditional concern and preoccupation, punishing angels abounded and persisted – their involvement with Final Judgement no doubt kept the angelic association with the events of the Second Coming firmly in people's minds. For instance, the minister John Spencer thought that 'at the last day, the Angels shall be the Ministers of his [God's] justice, and increase the terrours of his coming', and also affirmed that 'God sometimes made use of evil Angels as the *Executioners* of his judgements'.[66] In a brief treatise on the pestilence, it was an intrinsic part of William Kemp's argument that the plague had been sent by God as a punishment for the sins of the nation, and furthermore that 'Angels march in the Head of his Troops, whereof he hath thousand thousands'.[67] Indeed, in the plague literature that poured from the presses during the 1665 epidemic, there were many texts that subscribed to the idea that the disease was a judgement from God, inflicted by angels. John Edwards thought that 'the destroying Angel [had] gone forth to smite' and called for 'all to mourn for the crying and raigning sins of this Land', and many of the leaflets that were published throughout the seventeenth century, listing the bills of mortality, also reproduced a verse reminding readers that 'the judgements God hath sent even to cite us / Unto repentance, and from sin to fright us ... For God hath given unto his angels Charge / To strike and to forbear as he sees fit'.[68]

The tumultuous events of the 1660s provided an excellent opportunity to reflect on this, more daunting aspect of the angelic ministry. The use of angels as instruments of providence was a long-standing perception, and it was no doubt reinforced by these observations on the disaster that had befallen London. The Great Fire of 1666 similarly provided the opportunity for commentators to evoke the destroying angel, as the scholar Edward Waterhouse did when he compared the events of the conflagration to those in the book of Revelation, when 'the fourth Angel powred forth his Vial upon the Sun, and power was given him to afflict men with Fire'.[69] These associations are also a reminder that clergymen were not merely cynically exploiting angels as a useful means to an end, nor were they reluctantly promoting angelic responsibilities as part of a broader reforming campaign. Rather angels, in all their roles, were an integral part of their universe, and as such it was natural for them to refer to them when instructing or offering guidance to others.

Contemplation of the angelic involvement in Revelation is also a reminder of the importance of angels in mortuary culture. Angels and the afterlife remained a dominant part of late seventeenth-century angelology, and they were frequently referenced in funeral sermons and devotional treatises. Authors were keen to exploit the comforting and consoling aspects of angels, another area of continuity with earlier belief and practice, although some shifts of emphasis can be discerned. For instance, many drew attention to the traditional expectation that angels would carry the soul of the deceased to heaven. The clergyman Thomas Gouge, in a 1668 work designed to awaken the consciences of the ungodly, reminded his readers that the soul 'is instantly conveighed by the Angels into Abraham [sic] bosome, as is expresly noted of Lazarus'; by contrast, those of the wicked were 'seized upon by wicked Angels'.[70] John Flavel's phrasing was a little more fanciful: his opinion was that 'when once you have loosed from this shore ... your soul will be wafted over upon the wings of Angels, to the other shore of a glorious eternity'.[71]

Published funeral sermons also helped to foster and endorse the association of angels with mortuary culture. The clergyman and ejected minister Thomas Vincent affirmed that the soul of Henry Stubbes, 'immediately after its separation had the attendance of Angels upon it to be its convoy into the heavenly Paradice'. In another sermon 'preached at the funeral of that eminently holy man

Mr. Henry Stubs', Thomas Watson also mentioned that 'no sooner did Lazarus die, but he had a convoy of Angels to carry him to Abraham's bosom'.[72] At the funeral of Thomas Gilson in 1680, yet another ejected minister, Samuel Slater, commented on the 'happiness of the servants of Christ', for 'when they have once put off this thred-bare wornout garment of flesh, they shall immediately be conveyed with all possible speed by the holy Angels into those blissful mansion, where they shall be *present with the Lord*', and William Bates in 1692 reminded his audience that 'the Angels transport the separate Souls of the Righteous to Heaven' in a sermon preached after Richard Baxter's death.[73] The use of the angelic motif by these non-conformist ministers gives no hint of hesitation or caution when promoting the pastoral utility of celestial beings.

Other roles that angels were expected to assume around the time of death were also incorporated into these sources. Many made mention of the fact that angels would greet souls as they entered heaven and that the afterlife would be spent in their company. The Church of Ireland bishop George Rust thought that 'it must needs be a matter of unspeakable pleasure, to be taken into the Quire of Angels and Seraphims' after death, and John Bunyan stated his belief that 'they that shall be counted worthy of that world ... are equall to the Angels, and are the children of God'.[74] Samuel Slater also made use of this comforting aspect of doctrine in another funeral sermon of 1682, he thought that the prospect of the 'innumerable company of Angels and Spirits of Just men' should 'quiet us, under those Breaches which Death makes in our Families and Relations'.[75]

Evidently the association of angels remained an important element of mortuary culture, and clergymen were adept at utilizing the angelic motif to provide consolation and encouragement to their parishioners. The notion that an angel would carry one's soul to heaven at the end of life, and the vision of heaven that was conjured up by these authors were designed to offer pastoral support to their audiences.

Summary

This broad survey has established the persistence of beliefs examined in the previous chapter, beliefs which would provide the backdrop for new developments in religious cultures. The authors of the sources drawn on here, particularly those higher up in the ecclesiastical hierarchy, represent the broad spectrum of churchmanship, from the avant-garde Hooker and Andrewes, to the godly Perkins and Willet. In this context it is legitimate to note that despite harbouring diverse opinions with regard to some of the more controversial aspects of religious cultures, these churchmen were united when it came to notions of celestial beings. Whilst appreciating that terms such as 'orthodoxy' and 'conformism' are virtually impossible to apply to individual members of church in the years after the Reformation without heavy glossing, when it came to the treatment of angels these prominent clergymen were all singing from the same hymn-sheet: it would not be going too far to describe their harmonious representations of angels discussed in this chapter as the 'official line' of the Church of England on this matter.

Within the examined sources, the themes and issues that were prominent in the years immediately following the Reformation evidently retained their importance, Restoration ministers were as confident as ever in the angels' ability to edify and instruct. Furthermore, the concerns and anxieties that were expressed and fiercely debated amongst intellectual elites in the latter part of the century do not appear to have had a discernable impact on the core set of perceptions about angels at lower levels.[76] The pastoral value of the notions of protection and ministry; the participation of angels in worship alongside men; the integral role of angels in mortuary culture; and the utilization of angels as tools to pronounce on controversial areas of doctrine such as the worship of images or the existence of godly intercessors, can all be discerned from the religious literature of the sixteenth and seventeenth centuries.

The wide range of genres that encompass aspects of angelology – from the commonplace book of Nicholas Ling to the polemical writings of George Abbot – also indicates the ubiquity and broad appeal of the angelic motif. Angels could consolidate orthodoxy in two ways, both through their use to attack aspects of 'papistry' and to support a more positive projection of the benefits on offer from reformed angels. They are an example of how the processes of reform could transform a traditional element of culture into a vehicle for religious change, through new emphasis in combination with distinct and novel understandings.

4 THE CONFESSIONALIZED ANGEL, *c.* 1580–1700

In post-Reformation England, angels were familiar figures on the religious landscape. Although not a central or fundamental area of belief, they were nevertheless an important pastoral resource. As with their evil counterparts, the demons, throughout the sixteenth and seventeenth centuries, clergymen found angels good to think with – they turned to them to provide religious instruction and guidance, and angels were evidently useful allies in the battle to establish the true faith in England. Thus far I have offered a description of belief that prioritizes the harmony and consistency of reformed ideas. The core of official Protestant angelology was undoubtedly solid, its rejection of mediation, intercession and worship, and emphasis on angels as instruments of God's providence, dispensing justice and mercy, were common to all English reformers, and were perfectly suited to the outlook of the Church of England. However, it is also important to recognize that the ambiguities of earlier decades were never fully resolved, and that belief about angels continued to reflect all sorts of wider religious, cultural and social themes, tensions and developments. The Elizabethan legacy was to prove problematic, and even angels could become conduits for unorthodoxy in the hands of those pushing at the boundaries of what has been termed an 'Elizabethan consensus'. Because they were theologically malleable, angels could also be recruited by clergymen of all stripes in support of their particular reformed stance, and these dissenting voices need to be heard in order to gain a more complete notion of the status of angels in early modern religious discourse and in the Church more generally.

This was a period when religious controversy fuelled wider cultural transformation, and which saw the church become a battleground for rival visions of what English society should be. Historians are in agreement that the failure to reconcile these differing visions culminated in the eventual outbreak of Civil War. These events were to leave their mark on English angelology, and this chapter acknowledges this, sketching out shifts in the tone and emphasis of belief that were intimately connected to broader events, and putting Protestant angelology into a broader social and political context. Churchmen continued to write about and examine belief about angels in the maelstrom of the mid-seventeenth century and after it. This chapter therefore begins by considering those alternative confessional stances that were in competition with the officially authorized version of Christian religion, examining how Presbyterians, Arminians, Laudians, and Puritans employed the angelic motif in opposition to the 'orthodox' understandings documented in the previous chapter. The first part explores the ways in which angels could become the focus for confessional controversy, a consequence of the divergent ways that their scriptural foundations were interpreted. The second part focuses on those areas where less explicitly confessional concerns were to the fore, and where belief about angels to become entangled in social and political matters.

Part I: Challenging the Consensus

Church Government

Debates about the nature of the Jacobean and Caroline church have been pursued extensively elsewhere, and although it is not my intention to replicate those arguments here or to attempt to locate angels in an exact position on a confessional spectrum, drawing on the themes and concerns thrown up by this scholarship will help to highlight the issues that were at stake in the presentation and utilization of the angelic motif. Even as notions of angels were being consolidated in the official canon, they were also being unsettled and readjusted in the broader religious imagination, and this evolution reveals much about larger processes and their complexities during the period. Perhaps precisely because they were not the focus for intense religious controversy, angels could be the conduit for ambiguity and unorthodoxy in many published works.

Confessional controversies in the late sixteenth century demonstrate how this process might work, as authors adapted the angelic motif in support of a range of religious standpoints. Following the appointment of Archbishop Whitgift in 1583, there was renewed confrontation with nonconformists, and a Presbyterian movement emerged which aimed at pushing reform further in England. Angels became involved because the address to the seven stars and angels of the seven churches of Asia (Revelation 1–3) was frequently interpreted as a reference to the organization and government of the church. Accordingly, both the Presbyterians and their conformist opponents picked up on the angelic motif to provide support for their positions. For example, Thomas Bilson, the bishop of Winchester, confirmed the validity of the status quo when he stated that 'the vocation and function of Bishops was an Apostolike ordinance, and consequently confirmed and allowed by the wisedome of Gods spirit', pointing out that in Revelation Saint John addressed letters to the 'seuen stares and Angels of the seuen Churches of Asia, that is, to the seuen Pastours and Bishops of those seuen places'.[1] This is indicative of the way in which the passage was employed by conformists in defence of the Elizabethan settlement, and it recurs often elsewhere.[2] As late as 1644 the dean of Saint Paul's, John Barwick, was expressing similar sentiments, arguing that 'the Angels of the seven Churches, according to all reason, from the Text it selfe, and by the testimony of Antiquity, are seven Bishops of those seven Churches understood', making them the successors to the fixed authority of the apostles and the model of what the Church should be.[3]

The angels in Revelation were also utilized by individuals that had given up on the possibility of further reform from within the Church of England. For instance the English separatist John Robinson, who relocated to Amsterdam in 1609, also drew on the passage from Revelation to support his vision of the church. He argued that simply because John addressed his letters to the 'Angels' of the Churches, this did not mean that 'the reformation of abuses ... and disorders' within the institution should be left to the officers (angels) alone, as the conformists often argued. Rather, John sent these letters to the chief officers of the Churches because it was his intention that the matters would be made public and 'published to the whole body of the church, he 'willeth all men to heare, and take knowledge what the spirit sayeth to the Churches', in order that 'every freeman be to speak to, and consent in the busines'.[4] Thus Robinson's interpretation of the angels in Revelation provided a conflicting explanation of their significance and supported a Presbyterian style of church government such as that in the pilgrim Church that Robinson founded at Leiden: there a community of Christians voluntarily united to serve God, without the corrupting presence of Episcopal government.

Henry Ainsworth, an exile who became the 'teacher' of the Ancient Separatist Church of Amsterdam,[5] also employed the seven angels in his writing, although in this instance it was in opposition to John Smyth, a fellow separatist. Smyth had renounced the Ancient Church, criticizing its use of English scriptural translations in worship and suggesting that the role of the church elders was wrongly defined. In his reply to Smyth's censures Ainsworth responded that it was wrong to suggest that an Angel signified a 'college of pastors' or 'the company of the most sincere and holy men', because Ainsworth took this to mean merely 'Special persons'. He went on to use the angelic motif to support the legitimacy of a church structure that encompassed elders, pastors, teachers and rulers, using the passage to prove that such organization is not 'mans device' alone.[6]

Later in the century, this trope resurfaced. It is implicit in Smectymnuus' 1641 work *An answer to a booke entitled An hvmble remonstrance* that although the angelic hierarchy might be presumed from scripture, angels there 'are not literally to be taken, but Synechdochically, as all know'.[7] This argument provided the grounds needed for the rejection of the seven angels of the seven churches from Revelation as evidence for Episcopal government of the church.

> let us suppose ... that the word Angel is taken individually for one particular person
> ... yet nevertheless, there will nothing follow of this acception, that will any wayes
> make for the upholding of a Diocesan Bishop, with sole power of Ordination, and
> Jurisdiction, as a distinct Superior to Presbyters.[8]

The pamphlet is of particular interest because the author, 'Smectymnuus', was the acronym adopted by a group of Presbyterian ministers that were involved in the controversy over church government during the Long Parliament. The authors were actually Stephen Marshall, Edmund Calamy, Thomas Young, Matthew Newcomen and William Spurstowe, and the pamphlet challenged Joseph Hall's *An Humble Remonstrance* which had defended the existing liturgy of the church and its Episcopal structure. As well as criticizing the 'many Additions and Alterations' to the liturgy, a central purpose of the pamphlet was to deny that episcopacy in its present form derived from the apostles. Their gloss on Revelation was therefore intended to further their argument that there was no basis for the Episcopal structure in scripture, despite what their opponents might argue. In 1649 William Prynne argued along similar lines, discounting the idea that the Angels in scripture provided evidence for the Church of England's organizational structure. He stated that he could not 'find the name of a Bishop in any of St. Iohn's Writings, but the title of Presbyter or Elder very frequent.'[9] Both these works therefore utilized a scriptural passage that was also a favourite source for their religious opponents, in order to provide validity for their distinct understanding of the reformed church.

Church Ceremony

Throughout James I's reign historians have recognized that a more relaxed atmosphere prevailed in religious cultures, with the king himself encouraging a wide range of theological opinion and churchmanship for the sake of preserving Christian unity. James I's reputation has recently undergone rehabilitation from the bungling 'Wisest fool in Christendom' to a delicate and diplomatic ruler, who skilfully manipulated power in order to ensure a peaceful and prosperous regime. His ecumenical outlook meant that the broad umbrella of the Jacobean church sheltered a great diversity of belief.[10] Many of the sources discussed in the previous chapter therefore need to be put in the context of a literature of a young Church seeking to forge a religious consensus and develop a distinctive set of doctrines that recognized the authenticity of many expressions of Christianity, a process in which the king was to take an important part. However, this situation altered following the accession of Charles I with a change of direction in ecclesiastical affairs. The shift was indicated by the types of 'anti-Calvinist' churchmen that the king favoured; royal restrictions on 'new opinions' and 'unnecessary disputations'; increased attempts to try to control the non-conformist clergy; the reissuing of James I's *Book of Sports* in 1633 and the development of Laudianism, a new style of churchmanship. The latter encompassed efforts to promote more reverent and sacramental worship in churches, with bishops issuing orders for the restoration of many places of worship, and more controversially still, a campaign to have the communion table railed off and placed permanently at the East end of the church in an 'altarwise' orientation.

There is a rich historiography concerned with religious developments after Charles I's accession in 1625, not least because of the contribution of religious factors to the eventual outbreak of Civil War. Nicholas Tyacke has discredited the traditional idea of a 'Puritan Revolution' in the 1640s, arguing instead for an 'Arminian Revolution' in the 1630s, which was led by Archbishop Laud and which insisted on reverence and order in worship and exalted the status of the clergy in opposition to long-established Protestant traditions.[11] Other scholars have complicated the picture by questioning how far ceremonial changes can be interpreted as symptoms of Arminian theology, and by speculating on the responsibility that Charles himself had for the change in devotional emphasis. What all are in agreement on is that the 1630s did see reform in the worship and theology of the church. This process was again one in which angels were called upon to support and validate innovative practice.

As early as 1603, William Covell, a clergyman who was the author of a number of anti-Puritan writings, drew on angels to argue in favour of 'Church attire (meaning Surplesses)'.[12] Listing the occasions in scripture when angels appear 'clothed in pure and bright linen', in 'a long white garment' or in 'white apparel', he maintained that Church attire 'liuely resembleth' such garb and that therefore 'it suteth fitly' for ceremonial. Angels themselves 'could not easily deuise a garment of more decencie for such a seruice'.[13] Although historians have usually seen the placing and arrangement of altars, and doctrines of grace and salvation as the cornerstone of the 'Laudian' identity, preoccupations about the order and beauty of worship, clericalism, and anti-sabbatarianism also had a part to play.[14] Significantly, Covell's concerns are reflected by several authors publishing in the 1630s who also used angels to verify and substantiate their shift in devotional emphasis.

Robert Shelford, a clergyman with known Laudian sympathies, cited the presence of angels as one of the many reasons why decorum and respectful behaviour was essential in church, 'for it is as certain that angels are present in Gods house'. He was also convinced that 'where Christ is in the Eucharist, there is no want of angels', and that as a result the laity should reverently cover their heads when in church 'lest the holy angels in the congregation should be offended at the womens irreverent carriage with bare heads and long hair, and at the mens hats on their heads'.[15] The traditional notion of the presence of angels at worship is therefore adopted by the clergyman to support his own ceremonial preferences, their existence a perfect example of the importance of 'good orders and manners' when it came to the church. Other authors similarly emphasized the significance of the presence of heavenly beings. The clergyman Jasper Fisher noted that 'a woman must be covered in the Church, because of the Angels', whilst Sir Thomas Baker repeated the sentiment and also warned his readers that 'we ought to discover our thoughts by words, because of the Angels, for angels know not our thoughts but they heare our words' which should then 'giue them cause of rejoycing'.[16]

By these means, belief relating to celestial beings was employed to advance the Laudian agenda, with angels taking a central position in some of the most controversial aspects of religious cultures in the early seventeenth century. Old ideas could be reiterated, albeit to support innovations in worship and doctrine. The future Laudian bishop Richard Montagu advanced these trends in 1624, arguing in no uncertain terms not only that 'euery Christian man, at his Birth, or at his Baptisme, hath his Guardian Angell deputed to him', but also that 'At all times, some of them pray for the particular estate of some priuate Men, Cities, States, Societies or Countries'. Montagu repeated these opinions in another tract, where he asserted that 'touching Inuocation, the Case of Angels Guardians is peraduenture different' and therefore that in some instances prayer to angels was acceptable.[17] Both of these assertions were significant departures from the official Protestant line on angels.

The use of old ideas to support religious innovation can also be seen in the common comparison between priests and angels, a customary notion that gained a new currency in the period. This was partly the logical outcome of interpreting the seven angels in Revelation as the pastors and bishops of those churches, as discussed above. Thomas Bilson equated the two when he noted that Angels of the Churches 'ought not to be vnderstoode to be any but the Bishops or Rulers of the Churches', although he also conceded that 'the preachers in the Scriptures are sometimes called Angels'.[18] However, this interpretation gained more significance in Fisher's narrative when he stated that 'I am sure, consecrated Priests may be counted Angels: And there is a majesticall and more then humane splendour in both Offices, and a dutifull submission due to the dictates of both persons'.[19] Fisher's intention is evidently to valorise and extol the position and status of the clergy, an aim that fits with so called 'Laudian' priorities concerned with the conduct and behaviour of churchgoers.

Evidently earlier, customary understandings of the role and responsibilities of angels could be employed for myriad purposes by a range of Protestants, each with their own priorities and preferences when it came to religious worship and devotion. In many cases, this served to further promote belief in angelic beings, because authors were often sidetracked into lengthy discussions about heavenly spirits. Thomas Bilson took the opportunity to comment on the angelic responsibility as messengers and protectors; William Covell took his discussion of angelic attire further to consider also 'their attendance'; and in his sermon on the proper form of conduct in church, Robert Shelford digressed into extended commentaries on the essence, nature, responsibilities and fall of the angels.[20]

The emergence of Laudianism also indicates another way in which belief about angels was changing in some circles, because Laudian attitudes to ceremony and the beauty of worship also encompassed a re-evaluation of the validity and status of images. Indeed, Alexandra Walsham has found 'much to suggest that angels became implicated in the evolving programme to restore the beauty of holiness' as they were 'natural allies in the aesthetic refurbishment of churches that became synonymous with the style of churchmanship and worship promoted by William Laud' in the 1630s.[21] Walsham shows that angels appeared in the artistic and architectural schemes sponsored by Laud himself: on an arch at St John's, Oxford; in the roof of the Lincoln College chapel; and in windows in the chapel at Lambeth. The 1620s and 1630s also saw their inclusion on altars and altarpieces, such as in various chapels in Cambridge where pictures and hangings of angels were erected. This was particularly contentious as it associated angels with the new doctrinal emphasis on the sanctity of the chapel and the mystery at the heart of the sacrament, which to some opponents appeared to represent a shocking slide back to the Roman mass. Walsham also documents the reintroduction of angelic imagery into parish churches across the country, from wooden angels on communion rails in Barking, to a stone statue of Saint Michael holding a cross in Canterbury.[22] This evidence demonstrates that those of the Laudian persuasion had a more lenient attitude towards images of angels. These were acceptable if they were not abused, because they had the capacity to adorn places of worship and provide instruction to the laity.[23]

By these various means, angels remained a significant, if ancillary, presence in religious cultures. Although not central to the theological and ceremonial debates played out during the Stuart and early Caroline periods, there is no doubt that they became deeply implicated in some of the most significant religious controversies, with reformers of differing outlooks recruiting them in defence of their particular position. However, the response to these Laudian innovations indicates the cyclical nature of this process, as angels were to become the victim of a Puritan backlash against the recent shifts in devotional emphasis. The evidence suggests that angels suffered because the introduction of new images reawakened and brought into sharper focus old doubts about the acceptability of depicting them. They were caught up in a tendency for the opponents of Laudianism to see popish survivals lurking in every corner of the land, and in some eyes, even those angels who served merely decorative purposes were now suspect.

The Godly Perspective

Ceremonial innovations seem to have been disliked by the majority of the laity and the situation was exacerbated by the anti-popery that pervaded the national consciousness and which appears to have been a crucial element in the development of a distinctly 'English' Protestantism.[24] In the 1640s the paranoid atmosphere fuelled a widespread belief in an imminent Catholic uprising, and this was exacerbated by the behaviour of the king, the conspicuous presence of Catholics in the capital and at court, and the resurgence of Catholicism on the Continent. In this context, it is unsurprising that the new innovations, closely linked to Arminianism, were taken to be part and parcel of a popish plot, nor is it hard to comprehend why angels became more vulnerable, a reflection of wider processes in religious cultures.

The shifts in emphasis are reflected in religious literature. From the mid 1620s there was a growing tendency for religious writers to dwell on the potential of angels to lead individuals into error, alongside expositions of the benefits that they could offer to mankind. Significantly, the pamphleteer William Prynne, in a work published before his conviction for seditious libel, voiced concerns over the depiction of angels. In his censure of the work of the 'Laudian' Bishop of Durham, John Cosin, Prynne began by objecting to the very frontispiece of *a collection of private deuotions* (1627) as 'meerely Popish'. He singled out the 'three Capitall letters; (IHS) incircled in a Sunne, supported by two Angels', asking 'what is this all but an undoubted Badge, and Character of a Popish, and Iesuiticall Booke'?

Prynne may well have had a point: Julie Spraggon has shown how the letters 'IHS' were to become a target of the iconoclastic campaigns of the 1640s, when they were consistently referred to as the 'Jesuits Armes' and were seen as symbolic of the Jesuit order, and Anthony Milton has described Cosin's 'deep attachment to the Catholic tradition' and 'deep interest in the writings of the moderate Jesuit Maldonatus'.[25] Here angels have perhaps suffered from their association with other elements of religious culture, but Prynne's later invective against Cosin's collect 'desiring the MEDIATION OF ANGELS' is a direct attack.[26] Prynne took issue with this, and his interpretation of Cosin's writing was that he allowed 'that men may adore the Persons, and Images, of Saints, and Angels', and that 'he approoues the making of the Images, and Pictures'. The suggestion of mediation was considered by far the worst however: in Prynne's eyes it was 'to the disgrace, and scandall of our Church; and the great advantage of our Aduersaries'. For Pyrnne, these notions were all 'new Deuotions' and there was not 'in the Common Prayer Booke any such trash ... as his Prayer to God for the Mediation of Angels'.[27]

Although in slightly less vociferous language, other authors reiterated Prynne's concerns about the worship of angels and the possibility they might be called upon to mediate between men and the divine. In a sermon preached before the Commons in 1624, James Ussher, Archbishop of Armagh, stated plainly that 'Christians ought not to forsake the Church of God, and goe and inuo-cate Angels', as had been decided at the Laodicean Council.[28] Francis White, the future bishop of Ely and an anti-Catholic polemicist, espoused similar opinions when he reminded his readers that invocation, vows, oaths, offerings, adoration and confidence in the merits of Angels 'hath no foundation expresse or infolded in divine Reuelation, and the Primitive Church did not appoint or practise the same'. His conclusion was that 'we may not esteeme it lawful'.[29] Objections to the worship and invocation of angels were of course nothing new, but they were more prominent in the 1620s and 1630s than in previous decades. The dean of Exeter, Matthew Sutcliffe, thought that people had been 'mistaught by popish Priests' to honour angels, and expressed his contempt for such practices when he asked, 'are they [the papists] not made to pray vnto such as they know not?'[30]

Other aspects of angelology drew similar opprobrium, and familiar concerns over belief associated with Saint Michael the Archangel resurfaced. For example, as part of his diatribe against the worship of angels, Ussher noted that it was a continuing folly of the 'popish' to maintain 'many Churches of Michael' and 'Oratories' dedicated to his memory.[31] One of the reasons that the clergyman Lewes Hughes took exception to the *Book of Common Prayer* was because of the retention of Michaelmas day, when 'the twelfth Chapter of Revelation, from the seventh verse to the thirteenth, is appointed to be read for an Epistle, it being no Epistle'. Hughes' interpretation of this was that it was 'of purpose to pervert the meaning of our Saviour Christ, by misse-applying to Michaell and all Angels ... the victory that Christ hath'.[32]

These sources convey a growing sense of anxiety over the presence and func-tion of angels in religious cultures on the part of the 'godly'. The fact that the Catholics had enthusiastically recruited angelic beings in their Tridentine offen-sive against the Reformation,[33] combined with the tendency for angels to be associated with 'Laudian' and 'Arminian' ideas, left heavenly creatures vulner-able to a renewed assault on those aspects of their existence that the reformers objected to most strongly. Images of angels and suggestions of invocation and mediation therefore became more contentious, and stern warnings and rebukes about the dangers of undue reverence for celestial beings regularly issued from the presses and pulpits. This was part of wider processes whereby earlier questions and ambiguities, present since the Elizabethan Settlement in 1559, resurfaced in the political and religious climate of the time. Particularly pertinent was the ten-dency to discover 'popish' survivals in all aspects of religious life, a trend which undoubtedly damaged the angelic reputation for some.

The culmination of these anxieties can be seen in the renewed iconoclasm and new legislation of the 1640s, when the agenda of the godly was able to come to fruition because of the political split between King and Parliament, and the out-break of Civil War. Orders for the suppression of 'Innovations' and monuments of 'Superstition and Idolatry' were issued in 1641 and 1643 respectively, and in the early 1640s, images of angels were again being openly rejected by some: the inhabitants of Allhallows, Barking, petitioned against superstitious ornaments in their church in 1640, including little wooden angels on the communion rails, and in 1643 workmen were paid to cut down angels in St Martin Queenhithe and St Michael's Crooked Lane.[34] The controversy that erupted over the demolition of Cheapside Cross also provides evidence of the growing anxiety over representations of angelic beings. A letter was published containing the opinions of George Abbot which suggested that the replacement for the cross ought

> best to be some *Pyramis* or matter of meere beauty, and not any Angell or such like whatsoever, for although in truth that deserveth no reprehension, yet by avoyding of that the mouthes of the Adversaries may be stopped.[35]

Abbot's words are indicative of a growing concern with images of angels, but also confirm that they were not yet completely rejected. The development of the iconoclastic campaign also indicates a progression in attitudes. Spraggon notes instances of sites where angels were allowed to remain untouched, such as St Helen's Bishopgate, where a door pediment contained the royal Stuart arms supported by twelve reclining angels. Doubly surprising because of the intact representation of royal authority, Spraggon suggests that this might have been because symbolic representations were not as objectionable as representations of the persons of the Holy Trinity, but she also sees a trend in the evidence that suggests images of angels in 1641 were only condemned if they were in close proximity to the altar, such as on the altar hangings in the chapel at Peterhouse College, Cambridge.[36]

However, the shift in perception, fuelled by the emergence of Arminianism and Laudianism, had undoubtedly weakened the position of angels in visual cultures. As a result they were to become victims of a new bout of iconoclasm. This was ensured by the Parliamentary Ordinance of 1644, which specifically mentioned angels by name and called for their destruction.[37] Alexandra Walsham has convincingly argued of depictions of angels that, 'like surplices, free-standing crosses, and altar rails, they came to be regarded as a symbol of England's imperfect Reformation', they were thought to be the first stage in a plot to reconcile the nation to Rome. The 1644 ordinance and subsequent image-breaking certainly supports this.[38] The effect on church interiors is best documented by William Dowsing's journal from his years as the parliamentary commissioner in East Anglia. As we have seen, Dowsing made celestial beings a target during his 'cleansing' of parish churches in the 1640s, recording many instances where the removal of angels was ordered or their destruction carried out.[39] Along with other 'superstitious' imagery, hundreds of angels were removed from bench ends, roof beams and stained glass windows, whilst many others had their faces and wings hacked off in this iconoclastic bout.[40]

The zeal with which Dowsing and his deputies approached their task indicated the anxiety and hostility of the godly element of society at the changes that had taken place. The entries convey the passion of the Suffolk yeoman as he 'gave order to deface' the fonts in numerous parish churches, 'pulled down divers pictures, and angels' at Christ's College, 'beat down about 110 superstitious pictures, besides cherubims and ingravins' at Queen's College, both in January 1644, and 'did downe two angells' in Bourn, 7 March 1644.[41] However, the journal also reveals the diversity of opinion that existed when it came to physical representations of angels and religious imagery more generally. Firstly, by following in Dowsing's footsteps and visiting the East Anglian churches that the parliamentary commissioner documented, Trevor Cooper has uncovered discrepancies between what the godly reformer ordered to be taken down and the destruction that actually took place. Various entries make it clear that without the threatening presence of Dowsing and his soldiers, some clergymen and their parishioners were reluctant to carry out his orders. This might indicate the practical difficulties of such iconoclasm, but the survival of angels in accessible locations (such as the bench end at Withersfield St Mary depicting Saint Michael weighing souls), perhaps indicates a theological or even cultural motivation for the failure to comply.[42] The suggestion seems more plausible when viewed in the light of the resistance that Dowsing met with at Pembroke College, where 'we broak 10 cherubims'. Some of the fellows protested:

> Others alledged cherubims to be lawfull by scripture (Deut.iv.12, 16 and vii. 5, 25, 26, xii.2) and that Moses and Solomon made them without any command. I deny'd it and turned to Exod.xxv.18, 22. Then they said, Solomon did make them without any order from God. I answered, he received a pattern from David, and read to them, I Chron.xxviii.10, 11 to 18, 19.[43]

The controversy over the appearance of cherubim on the tabernacle has already been discussed;[44] evidently it was still a point of ambiguity and contention. Dowsing went on confidently to assert that God had required the destruction of all religious pictures without exception, but the episode indicates that this was not the only opinion current at the time. Spraggon documents evidence both of angels that were destroyed, and others that were ignored or replaced at a later date.[45] Alexandra Walsham believes that the 'patchy implementation' of the 1644 Ordinance, which called for the destruction of images of angels in churches and open places, is indicative of divided opinion on the issue of representation, and this evidence provides more support for that interpretation.[46] Nonetheless, Dowsing's actions represent the culmination of the debates surrounding the legitimacy of the traditional roles and responsibilities of angels, part of wider processes by which the country had descended into Civil War.

The 'Hotter Sort' of Angelology

Angels remained a useful means of articulating both novel and traditional concepts during this period, and they persisted as a useful cultural resource to be figured and reconfigured in numerous ways. They were connected to the religious and political fluidity of the period, and how they were utilized to think creatively about a range of issues that formed the preoccupations of these decades. I have argued that angels were being used by those unhappy with the official boundaries of English religious cultures, and employed as a 'space' in which to consider questions about both doctrine and ceremonial and to make statements about what the Church should aspire to be. Building on this understanding, I will now examine the new ideas and perceptions that accumulated around angels in order to understand how they contributed to attempts to reconstruct the institutions of society following the trauma of the war and death of the King.

In 1645, as the royalists suffered crushing military defeats in the field, the Independents gained the upper hand in Parliament, and the New Model Army was formed, traditional social values were swept away and the institutional safeguards of these values crumbled. With the abolition of monarchy and the collapse of the established church, there was a great overturning, questioning and re-evaluating of fundamental beliefs and assumptions, and what is more, the breakdown of censorship ensured that radical new ideas circulated and were disseminated throughout the population as never before. Christopher Hill has described the 'glorious flux and intellectual excitement' that characterized the period, and which threw up a flood of new ideas and saw the emergence of a plethora of radical groups, each with their own political and social solutions to the nation's troubles.[47] While the Presbyterians and Independents struggled for supremacy in Parliament, various groups such as the Baptists, Quakers and Muggletonians offered alternative religious solutions to the English people.

The 1640s and 50s saw the reinvigoration of publishing about angels, with many authors of sermons and treatises mentioning them in their title pages and dedicating large sections of their work to them. It is also significant that this era saw the publication of two treatises exclusively dedicated to angels: Henry Lawrence's *An history of angells* (1646) and Robert Dingley's *The Deputation of Angels* (1653).[48] Given that this study is predicated on the premise that angels were a ubiquitous feature of early modern religious cultures, it is worth reiterating that printed works dealing explicitly with the nature, responsibility and meaning of God's generous gift to mankind were rarely forthcoming. John Salkeld's *A Treatise of Angels* had been published in 1613, and although Jeremias Drexel's Catholic treatise *The angel-guardian's clock* had been translated into English in 1630, Protestant authors had remained reticent in tackling the topic directly since early in the century. The thirty-three year silence was broken in the 1640s, however, when two treatises on celestial beings were published in quick succession.

The appearance of these treatises is intrinsically interesting because of the contrast with what had gone before. To the uninformed outsider, it would be easy to attribute the sudden spate of writing to the collapse of censorship – Archbishop Laud, the head of the licensing system, had been imprisoned in 1641, the same year that Star Chamber and High Commission were abolished and the Stationers' Company collapsed. These works could therefore easily be mistaken as indicative of the 'torrent of print' that Joad Raymond has charted at the beginning of the 1640s, with treatises of angels being published in the new, more tolerant atmosphere of the times.[49] However this scenario does not entirely ring true for a number of reasons. For example, it has also been a contention of this study that in themselves, angels were hardly a controversial aspect of religious cultures, and that they only became the focus of reforming ire through the Protestant association of them with the more dubious and extravagant aspects of traditional religion. Thus, aspiring angelologists hardly needed to wait for the collapse of censorship to pen a treatise on angels, as it would be perfectly possible for an orthodox member of the Church of England to produce a theologically sound work with a useful pastoral and didactic bent.

This suggestion also fails to account for the shift in attitude that is expressed through the publication of these works. As discussed above, the Parliamentary Ordinance of 1644 had mentioned angels by name and called for their destruction, and angels had suffered because of their close association with Arminian and Laudian innovation during the 1640s. The resurgence, endorsement, and re-engagement with belief about angels was a distinct contrast to what had gone immediately before and it is clear therefore that the causes of the flowering of angelology in this period cannot be limited to the immediate effects of the collapse in censorship. It is therefore necessary also to take into account the identity of the authors involved in this revival, and the expressed and implicit motivations behind their interest in and deployment of angelic motifs, in order to understand how belief in angels continued to develop.

Although clerical discussions of angels have already been discussed in the context of the 'orthodox' Protestant themes and ideas in the previous chapter, several of the works from this period also indicate a shift in understanding and attitudes, and it is this more than anything that signals the appearance of a distinctively Puritan, pastoral theology. As has been established, reformers had previously been very reluctant to positively affirm the existence of guardian angels.[50] However, the reformers remained divided in their opinions, and belief in guardian angels had previously been endorsed by those clergymen of a more conservative bent. For example, John Salkeld documented the ancient and esteemed heritage for the concept, and the style and tone of his treatise, which might be described as crypto-Catholic, indicated his acceptance of the belief.[51]

Henry Lawrence's *An history of angells* is typical of the shift in attitudes towards guardian angels. Born in 1600, Henry Lawrence proceeded MA at Cambridge in 1627 and the next year married the daughter of Sir Edward Peyton of Iselham, a noted puritan and future parliamentarian. From 1631 to 1636 he was the landlord of Oliver Cromwell, to whom he let Slepe Hall, before fleeing to the Netherlands in the late 1630s, seemingly to escape religious persecution. He remained there until returning to England in 1646, whereupon he published his treatise.[52] The dedicatory epistle to his mother revealed the rationale behind his work, which grew from the political circumstances of the time. The ongoing Civil War had given Lawrence cause to meditate on the accompanying spiritual warfare that these events entailed, in which struggle he maintained that men were supported by 'aides and assistances from without', although men seldom paused to acknowledge this. Thus, although men considered God's role in the spiritual drama, they passed by the benefits of:

> those hoasts of Angells, which on either side more immediatly managed and improoved this warre, as they are spirituall and invisible beings, so they passe with us, unseene, and undiscerned ... and we, who are the subjects of this warre, and whose interests are especially concern'd in it, by not knowing or considering, can neither improve our most active, and most powerfull friends, or enemyes, to our advantage.[53]

His treatise was intended to rectify this problem, to illuminate the angelic participation in this world both by demonstrating 'what influence the evill Angells have upon us ... though few enough know or consider it', whilst also advising people of the presence of good angels, 'the proper armes for this holy warre', and 'the right wearing and using of them'.[54] Lawrence's avowed intentions allowed him to explore the didactic uses of angels within the treatise and are indicative of a wider trend that saw the emergence of what might be termed the pastoral Puritan angel.

In the treatise, Lawrence figured angels as a consoling presence, and the best ally that a person could have in spiritual warfare. Throughout the piece the underlying tone is one of edification, and generally the themes and associations that Lawrence included conform to the traditional concerns of angelology, albeit with a distinctly Protestant emphasis. What stands out however is the section on guardian angels. Lawrence's discussion of this aspect of belief in fact bears some resemblance to John Salkeld's, in his 1613 work. He began by noting that 'the doctrine of Angell Gardians [sic] hath bene exceeding antient, not onely amongst the Christians, but the heathens also'. In the argument that followed, Lawrence's belief in guardian angels was apparent, if not explicit – although he maintained only 'that it is *probable* that every elect hath his peculiar Angell deputed as his keeper and companion', he nevertheless went on to discuss the specifics of this guardianship in some detail. As with Salkeld, Lawrence's treatment of guardian angels acknowledged that this was an area of controversy, yet his writing ultimately supported the doctrine.[55]

Lawrence also affirmed the probability that provinces and communities had guardian angels, and provided the scriptural evidence that had led him to conclude this. Furthermore, he declared that he was not satisfied with the usual objection to guardianship, which was that its critics 'thinke it is a derogation to the goodness of God to his people, who gives them the heavenly host amongst them and to them all', for if each person had a particular angel, 'yet so as extraordinarily many may be sent to his ayde' – Matthew 18:10 was cited as proof of this.[56] It was of course Calvin who had provided the original objection, writing in *The Institutes* that 'those who limit the care which God takes of each of us to a single angel, do great injury to themselves and to all the members of the Church.'[57] Lawrence's refutation of this, combined with his discussion of when exactly guardians are assigned to men, illustrates the differing positions of the two on this point: Lawrence evidently declined to take Calvin's advice that 'it is not worthwhile anxiously to investigate a point which does not greatly concern us.'[58]

Henry Lawrence's divergence from Calvin's thought is unexpected, particularly since previously the affirmation of guardians, although not an acid test of commitment to Catholicism, certainly might have indicated some divergence from the 'official line' of the Church of England. What are we then to make of Lawrence's enthusiasm for the notion? The key point is the proviso that Lawrence, unlike Salkeld, adds to the proposition. The ministry of guardians for Lawrence is conditional – he is clear that it is *only the elect* that receive the companionship of the angels. In emphasizing this he gives the doctrine a distinct Calvinist twist, verifying the truth of predestination and indicating his views on salvation. The spectre of 'accommodation' is lurking behind Lawrence's work here. It might be suggested that, when confronted with the confident proclamation of the benefits of the guardian angels by Catholics imbued with the post-Tridentine spirit, Lawrence felt compelled to address the issue, admitting that the existence of these beneficial creatures was acceptable in the Protestant universe, but adjusting the specifics to emphasize the central reformed tenet.

However, although Lawrence's work might be viewed in this light, the suggestion of accommodation to earlier belief is not in keeping with the tone of the treatise more generally. The work reads as a confident assertion of the benefits of angels and uses scripture impeccably to back up each of the points made. Lawrence's elaboration of the doctrine of guardian angels can instead be read as a sign of an increasing self-assurance on the part of English Protestants. There is a sense that the anxiety previously expressed by the reformers over angelic hierarchies and guardians was no longer so immediate. Lawrence may have felt able to delve deeper into this aspect of angelic existence because he was less concerned that this might lead the laity astray – his focus was on the pastoral benefit that these considerations might offer them. His concerns and confidence are also reflected in many other works in the period.

Perhaps most importantly, in the other treatise published in these decades and dedicated exclusively to consideration of angels, guardians were made the centrepiece of the work. In doing this, Robert Dingley's 1653 *The Deputation of Angels or Angell-Guardian* went further than Lawrence in staking a claim for the sound Protestant credentials of this aspect of angelology. His debt to Lawrence is clear however, as he quite literally built on the foundations that his predecessor has laid, 'borrowing' large sections of Lawrence's text throughout his treatise.[59] Many parts of Dingley's argument were distinct though, and his discussion of the existence of guardian angels far more forthright and elaborate than Lawrence's.

Dingley was born in 1618/9, and Anthony Wood claimed that that he cynically turned Presbyterian in the early 1640s after initially being an enthusiastic supporter of ceremonies. In 1648 he was presented to the rectory of Brighstone on the Isle of Wight, and it was there that he published *The Deputation*, which was dedicated to Colonel Sydenham, the Governor of the Isle at the time.[60] The epistle, and the treatment of angels in Dingley's work suggest that the clergyman's priorities differed from Lawrence's, as he chose to use angels as a means of commenting on the social and political issues that were facing society at the time. In his work, angels were handled as a model of how society should be ordered; they were used to support Dingley's understanding of ecclesiological matters and to enable further investigation into the relationship between church and state.

In his discussion of guardian angels, Dingley made his intentions plain from the outset, stating 'I will not write of angels: of their creation, conformation, place, nature, number, amity, offices and degrees' – he was chiefly concerned only with the deputation of angels itself. This was a topic that in his opinion had been overlooked: in his foreword he warned that he walked 'in untrodden places where little hath been said before me', a negligence that he thought was rooted 'chiefly in opposition to the See of Rome'.[61] This particularly provides further evidence in support of the notion that authors were choosing to write about this aspect of belief not in a fit of reactionary anxiety, but rather because guardians were undergoing some form of rehabilitation. The writers in the 1640s and 50s did enjoy greater freedom of the press than previously, which undoubtedly made it more likely that they would publish their more unorthodox thoughts relating to angels. However, this was not the only trend that was affecting the boundaries of belief. It also seems that Protestants were more willing to salvage those parts of Catholic angelology that had previously been rejected because of their less savoury associations. Dingley's foreword expressed this sentiment clearly – he stated that he did not intend 'to gratifie Romanists, or derogate from Calvin and other learned Protestants', but that he wanted to reclaim those aspects of belief that previously had been considered dangerous.[62] What is more, he did this with a clear conscience, for:

> a man will take the Fly out of his Glass, before he drink the wine; and we have here rejected the Popish additions to the truth.[63]

What follows is a lengthy discussion that seeks to establish the verity of guardian angels, whilst also demonstrating the utility of the belief. Through a detailed exposition of Acts 12:15, which deals with Peter's arrival at the house of Mary, where he is mistaken for 'his angel', Dingely concluded that the text was 'an infallible demonstration, that there is some such thing as a particular and Guardian Angell'. From this he deduced more widely that 'every Elect person hath his Guardian-angel, who by particular Designation is allotted to be his faithfull Keeper, and Tutor, and vigilant Associate to his lives end'.[64] The evidence that Dingley marshalled in support of this was rich and diverse. Like Lawrence, he documented the persistence of the idea from the time of the 'heathens' and primitive church, as well from the scriptural evidence. He argued that there are many things 'firmly believed' that scripture mentions only occasionally, guardian angels finding their place alongside heaven, the holy trinity, the Lord's supper, infant baptism and the Christian Sabbath. Dingley went so far as to argue that because guardians are mentioned in both the Old and New Testament, they were in fact better scripturally supported than some of these others.[65]

Dingley's enthusiasm for guardians, however, was always tempered by his attempts to fish the fly out of the wine. He did more than Lawrence to emphasize that guardian angels are only assigned to the elect, 'I say Elect persons, and such only … they are to attend the Heirs of Salvation'. Dingley also conceded that 'many rich Mysteries are lockt up in the Nature of Angels', a thing which stopped him from too great elaboration on their nature, and which was also a (perhaps contradictory) nod to Calvin's 'minimalist' stance on angelology. Protestant rejection of all forms of idolatry was a theme; he stated 'we abhor with greatest Detestation the Adoration of Angels', a point that is included 'to silence our Adversaries of Romish Interest, who may hope that the Needle of this discourse inclines to draw in the rotten Thred of Adoration'.[66] What is more, after rebutting 'all the Objections that I ever yet met withall', Dingley listed the Romish additions and errors so that all might know the mistaken Catholic beliefs associated with angels. He rejected the idea that Michael was the protector and keeper of the church, for the reason that Christ alone held this distinction. He also explicitly denied the idea that *every* man had a guardian angel, arguing that although 'good angels may have treated with evil men', only the elect were blessed with this privilege.[67] Evidently, although Dingley was happy to confirm the existence of guardian angels, his Protestantism meant that he distinguished between an acceptable understanding of what this meant and unacceptable and invalid elaborations on the doctrine, and he was keen to distance himself from the Catholic understanding of guardians, stressing repeatedly that his was 'no Novel or Heterodox opinion'.[68]

The emphasis that the provision of guardian angels was for the elect only is the crucial element of these new formulations. Both Lawrence and Dingley were comfortable sanctioning the pastoral uses of angels, and both authors recognized the potential of the angels to appeal to and instruct the laity on a range of issues – as Dingley stated 'here is comfort for you, for your Children, and for the Nation'.[69] However, this pastoral application was given a distinct Calvinist gloss in the insistence that it was only the elect that were to reap these benefits. By these means, angels were transformed into a vehicle for a paramount Puritan doctrine, one which lay at the heart of their perception of the world and their identity. Fittingly Dingley closed his treatise with the words:

> Every *Believer* hath invincible guards of Angels to help, and relieve him in all his streights, but one hath speciall Comission still to be with him, and watch over him: Wheresoever thou goest, this Angel moveth, marcheth after thee, ready to counsel and comfort thee, resolved to stay by thee in the greatest extremities.[70]

The concerns that preoccupied Lawrence and Dingley are echoed in the literature published in the period, as other authors also affirmed the existence of guardian angels. For example, Zachary Bogan was a scholar who in 1653 published a work on the threats recorded in scripture, writing that although people had 'just cause to feare the helpe which they have of Angels', because God often used them to inflict punishment, this was alleviated by the fact that 'God's children have not onely each of them his Angel (as Peter had)', as well as an army of angels 'such as Jacob had for his guard'.[71]

John Gumbleden, in a sermon on Acts 10:3, 'preached before the university, at Oxford, some years hence', described the soldier Cornelius' vision of an angel, declared ''tis not altogether improbable, that every particular *faithful* Man, hath his particular tutelar Angel assigned to him of God, to defend, and protect him'. He cited the scriptural passage relating to Peter's angel in evidence of his opinion that 'each hath from his birth an Angel appointed, peculiarly to guard him'. It was also true that '(when there is most need) many Angels, by Gods command, are ready to protect, and defend, even one single *faithful* Man'.[72]

Ideas relating to guardian angels appeared in a variety of genres throughout the period, and it is noticeable that the tone and discussion within these works was remarkably similar, despite the differing contexts. The prevailing ideas were that it was highly likely that each individual had a guardian angel, although this did not preclude the assistance of more than one in a time of necessity, and also that it was only the faithful, God's children, or the 'Believers' that were to be the lucky recipients of angelic attentions. Contrasting the sentiment in Gumbleden's sermon with the Arminian Jeremy Taylor's thoughts on guardian angels illustrates this last point. In *A discourse of baptism* published in 1653 while he was a bishop in the Irish church, Taylor noted that it was 'generally and piously believed by very many eminent persons in the Church, That at our Baptism God assigns an Angel Guardian', and he claimed 'I insist not on this, though it seems to me hugely probable'.[73] Taylor's work was polemical, intended as a defence of the sacrament of baptism, but at no point does he suggest that the guardianship of angels was strictly limited to the elect. The guardian angel is in fact utilized by the bishop on more than one occasion – in his devotional treatise of 1657 he included a 'Prayer for Baptism' that implored God to 'send his Holy Angel to be the Guardian of this child, and keep him from the danger and violence'. In these works both political and pastoral concerns were to the fore, as Taylor asserted the validity of baptism in the face of unorthodox ideas that were circulating about the sacrament in one, and provided devotional encouragement to the laity in the other, but again, there is no insistence that it was only the heirs of salvation that were to receive the benefit of these celestial creatures.[74]

The overlapping ideas in these sources are instructive as they demonstrate the closing of the gap between Catholic and Protestant belief about angels. However, this should not be exaggerated – the Protestant authors' insistence that only the elect could receive the benefit of guardian angels, and their attempts to reconcile these novel ideas with the writings of Calvin, illustrate that there continued to be distinct understandings of the angels on either side of the confessional divide.[75] It also shows how reformers were able to rescue the notion of guardian angels, reconfiguring it along Calvinist lines, to give it a place in what could be described as a Puritan practical divinity. The sources illustrate that angels provided an excellent opportunity to provide the laity with didactic and practical instruction about how to live a good Christian life. Guardians therefore indicate one of the ways in which churchmen were beginning to think creatively about angels, developing a Puritan pastoral theology that might also provide an antidote to despair or complacency. If a guardian angel was assigned at the start of life, and it was impossible thereafter to lose its assistance, this was a comforting and consoling doctrine and demonstrates succinctly how angels played a role in providing a bulwark against despondency and helped to build assurance in an uncertain and precarious time. This was an appealing aspect of Puritan theology – something that historians have traditionally failed to discover in the beliefs associated with the 'hotter sort' of Protestantism.

Puritan affirmations of the existence of guardian angels in the mid-seventeenth century may also be indicative of a self confidence and optimism not present prior to, or after this point. Perhaps unsurprisingly, it appears that Puritan pastoral angelology all but disappeared from the 1660s, when the re-establishment of the Church of England saw the trope fade into the background again. Guardian angels were still discussed, and in many cases endorsed by clergymen in their writings, but few elaborated on this to emphasize that only the elect could expect the lifelong companionship of a specific guardian angel.

For instance, Jeremy Taylor thought that 'some wise and good men have piously believed', that at children's confirmation 'a special Angel Guardian is appointed to keep their souls from the assaults of the spirits of darkness'. His opinion was that the 'supposition is not disagreeable to the intention of this Rite', and thus that the allocation of a specific angel to each person was probable.[76] His conviction that it was at confirmation that the angel was allocated is also revealing, as angels were thus recruited to provide support and validation for the institutional church, whose ceremonies were the means through which access to angels was channelled. Indeed, the notion of a decline in the Puritan guardian angel can be better understood in the context of the Restoration Church's priorities and personnel. John Spurr has emphasized the importance of Latitudinarianism within the newly established Church, and although he is keen to stress the shortcomings of this label, Spurr identifies a group of moderate Restoration clergymen that were pursuing a 'middle way': reacting against the radicalism of the 1640s and 50s, and seeking to divorce the Church from Calvinist soteriology. Thus 'the dominant temper of Restoration Anglicanism' was the 'renunciation of the old orthodoxy', and a distaste for the hopelessness of the doctrine of predestination.[77] Spurr also sees this as a reaction against the determinism of Thomas Hobbes's thought, part of a wider Anglican 'revulsion against theological and philosophical opinions which appeared to rob man of his autonomy and dignity'.[78] In a similar vein, Blair Worden has argued that 'science' caused an 'intellectual adjustment' that led to the sidelining of ideas about man's natural sinfulness.[79] There is no doubt that the dissolution of the association of angels with the doctrine of predestination was the outcome of these shifts.

Thus the nonconformist minister John Bryan in 1670 described 'besides this common attendance, a peculiar Guardian of Angels', but failed to state precisely who this was intended for, and Richard Baxter in the same year remarked that 'nor yet may we pretend to know what particular Saint or Angel is deputed of God to our protection', again endorsing the notion of a guardian angel but without the Calvinist implications that have been seen previously.[80] Towards the end of the period some authors seemed to offer an echo of the trope – the Whig politician Sir Robert Atkyns in 1693 stated that 'Scripture tells us, that the good Angels are Ministers of God for good to the Elect', and the Calvinist clergyman John Edwards in 1696 wrote that angels were ministering spirits, 'and employed for the good of Mankind, especially the choicest part of them, the Heirs of Salvation', but these references were far less common than previously and it was more likely for authors to endorse the general concept of guardian angels without elaborating further on this.[81] Interestingly, although Spurr's contention that 'English congregations did not suddenly hear new doctrines from the pulpits in 1660' is undoubtedly true when it came to the essential truths of the faith, the treatment of angels demonstrates a means by which shifts in the tone and content of the Church's orthodoxy might be conveyed, indirectly, to the congregation.[82]

Part II: Political Contexts

National Government

Belief about angels therefore remained a vibrant and versatile religious resource, a means to articulate confessional divides and to engage in theological debate. Their significance was not confined to the religious sphere however; as angels might also become engulfed in areas where religious, political and social concerns came together. Parliamentarians and Royalists found characteristics of the angelic society that they were able to draw parallels with, and accordingly angels took their place in ongoing debates about how the state should be organized,

Robert Dingley's treatise provides an insight into these processes, through his discussion of the belief that guardian angels might also be assigned to communities and nations. Lawrence also considered the question, stating 'it is very probable' that 'there are Angells deputed to the care and protection of Provinces and Countries', as well as those 'Communities very deare unto God', and Dingley's views were similar: he argued that communities had guardians, along with 'Cities, Shires, Provinces, Islands, Churches and Kingdoms', and more pointedly that, 'each Republick hath an Angel to be its protector'.[83] Admittedly, the reformers had always been more prepared to countenance belief in guardians for nations or provinces (as opposed to personal guardians) because the scriptural evidence for this notion was less ambiguous, a distinction that Calvin himself had made. However, this aspect of doctrine was realigned during this period in order to support and legitimise a diverse number of social and political claims, providing further evidence of the growing confidence when it came to dealing with angels within Puritan circles, and also reflecting the peculiar social context of the 1650s.

Dingley's treatise is perhaps the best example of the wider significance of these assertions. The key to fully understanding the intent behind the work is to be found in its underlying agenda, which Dingley made no attempt to disguise. He dedicated *Deputation* to Colonel Sydenham, the Governor of the Isle of Wight, fittingly describing in his dedicatory epistle the 'Angelicall services' that the Colonel was employed in as a friend and protector of the isle.[84] Dingley marked the fact that at the time of writing, 'Liberties and Properties' had now been secured, 'faithfull Ministers not a little encouraged', and that the 'Heavens also have Relented', and he called on the governor to take the opportunity to eliminate atheism, profanity and heresy within the territory.[85] The significance of Dingley's wheedling epistle only becomes completely clear in the closing pages of the treatise. Following his discussion of the care of angels for particular cities and nations, he asserted that if at any time 'pillars of Kingdoms be shaken, and the wicked striving to bear sway and trample Religion, Order, and Government', the angels would be a great comfort to all. It must likewise be acknowledged that 'when things are tolerably carried in these evill Times, that it is not effected without the Ministry of Gods Angels', and more significantly, the laity were called upon to pray to God that he 'would cause his celestiall Principalities and Powers to encircle those who sit at the *stern'* at such times.[86]

Dingley's angelic treatise therefore culminated in a double plea to both laity and rulers to 'mistrust not the continuation of Divine Providence over us'. He used the angelic motif to demonstrate God's continual care for his people, despite the political and social trauma of recent times, and utilized the appealing and comforting aspects of angels in order to claim that 'this may quiet us in the many great mutations and changes in the frame of civill Administrations'. He called on the English people to accept that 'the workings of Providence are very mysterious', and hoped to seal 'this Truth, that Republicks and Kingdoms are overruled and disposed by Angels, silence and hush all peevish and mutinous complaints'. His contrast between London, as a refuge to persecuted ministers 'therin to God as the Aple of his eye', and Rome, 'that Idolatrous City' where 'those evil Angels that are in and over ... shall not be able to shield her from the wrath of God', was a particularly striking and potent image.[87]

This exhortation to the English laity was also complemented by a call to those at 'the stern', the magistrates that were steering the country through the radical 1650s. All men were encouraged to imitate the angels' 'swift, constant, and most cheerfull obedience', but magistrates were singled out, and a special responsibility was conferred upon them, that they might 'be Defenders of the Faith', cherishing the Godly and punishing the wicked. Dingley is insistent in this matter. He provided a large section detailing exactly what the implications of this were for those ruling the country: like the angels the magistrates were expected to protect, cherish and provide for the souls of the people, to cause the word to be heard, suppress wickedness, and more specifically employ the poor, set up judges and be ready in case of invasion.[88] Moreover, their responsibilities did not end there – it was also their duty to disarm heretics either by reason, banishment, imprisonment, or in the most extreme cases, death. The necessity of this had been demonstrated to all during the Anabaptist regime at Münster, where one of the 'seditious Lawes enacted' was 'let no man be subject to Magistrates and Princes'.[89]

Finally, Dingley digressed into a diatribe on religious toleration; he declared that it would be impossible to uphold peace and order if the magistrates did not do all they could to stamp out error, for 'there can be neither, in a Generall tolleration'. God had forbidden diversities in worship and hated 'an impure medly and mixture in Religion', which was the root of 'innumerable and incurable evills', and which, if not quenched, 'Run and spread in the Tinder of the multitude'.[90] Dingley did gloss this denunciation though, adjoining two 'necessary cautions'. He pointed out that 'some latitude must be given to peaceful souls', for not all errors would 'raze the foundation'. He also suggested that not every difference in doctrine was heresy, 'therefore if foundationall stones be secured, and all necessary truths maintained; both Magistrates and Ministers must wink at all Lesser dissentings'. He went on to advocate toleration for the Jews, provided that they did not 'openly blaspheame Jesus Christ', nor 'suffer Christians to come unto their Worship', they were to be pitied, and besides, 'they shall undoubtedly be Restored and converted in Gods due time'.[91]

Dingley's double appeal to the laity and magistrates is an excellent illustration of how angels continued to be relevant in the new political and social atmosphere of the 1650s. He was able to utilize an aspect of belief about angels which had previously been neglected and suffused with ambiguity, as a vehicle through which he could offer advice to those responsible for making decisions about the direction that the country was moving in. The figure of the guardian angel was adopted in order to project Dingley's version of what he wanted England to become, and to put forward his opinions on the value and extent of toleration, one of the central concerns of the Republic. By addressing his treatise to Colonel Sydenham, Dingley was able to use the angelic motif to appeal to his local political overlord and to engage with wider discourses relating to the state. Dingley was emphatic on this point: 'Magistrates must protect the Good, and therin imitate our Guardian-Angels, yet they must not give like Protection to Wolves and Foxes'.[92] What is more, Dingely also concluded his work by speaking to Ministers, 'who are called Angels of the Churches; They are like unto Angels in name and employment, for they carry Messages from Heaven and Glad-tidings to men'. Dingley believed that this similarity should also be borne out in twelve respects, including that they should strive to 'sparkle as Angels in sound Doctrine'. 'Angels keep close unto their charge, and so must Ministers unto their people', angels are creatures of another world, 'so Ministers should not be delving and rooting in this, nor intangled in the Thicket of Secular Affairs'. Dingley also reminded his audience that 'the chiefe charge of Angels is over the Elect, and so the Ministers of the Gospel are chiefly sent to call home, and build up the Elect of God'.[93]

Dingley's work demonstrates that in a time of great social experiment, when the foundations of society were undergoing structural shifts, angels remained a valuable cultural resource which could be used to articulate opinions that went to the very heart of contemporary controversies. Although previously a preference for guardian angels might have indicated unorthodoxy or a predilection for traditional religious tastes, this doctrine could just as easily be manipulated to support a more radical vision. It could contribute to ecclesiological debates, another indication of the how the flexibility of ideas about angels permitted and encouraged their employment in a variety of disparate ways. Despite the fact that angels had often been used in the past as a bulwark for the traditional ordering of society and to legitimise its governing institutions, this did not make them redundant during the Civil War and Interregnum.

The treatment of the angelic hierarchy in the 1640s and 50s supports this suggestion. It is perhaps surprising that although guardian angels were experiencing a sort of 'rehabilitation' in the period, the same cannot be said about the angelic hierarchy. Protestants were still willing to countenance the idea of a hierarchy, but they were usually not prepared to posit any more than that there was order amongst the angels. Throughout the 1640s and 50s, this remained the dominant position, and although authors were still willing to refer to the hierarchy and affirm its likely existence, they were very reluctant to take this any further. For example, John Spencer included an entry on 'Order to be in the Church of God' in his store house of sentences, which maintained that:

> AS there is an *Order* in God himself ... so in the whole Creation, *Angels* have their Orders, Thrones and Dominions, Principalities and Powers, and an Arch-angel, that at the last shall blow the Trumpet.[94]

This was a positive affirmation of the concept, but it did not elaborate any further. Peter Heylyn provided more discussion, describing not only how God had divided his angels into 'several ranks to make them differing in degree', he also listed the names of the nine orders, arguing that their names were to be found in scripture. However, unlike earlier authors, Heylyn did not specify or even record what he understood as the roles and responsibilities of these orders, nor their specific place in the hierarchy (as for example John Salkeld had), writing only that 'these several names do serve to signifie and distinguish those several orders'.[95]

This is interesting in light of the more liberal attitude towards guardian angels. The reason for this discrepancy may be that the scriptural evidence for guardians was more convincing than that for the hierarchy. But it also suggests that political expediency could influence attitudes towards angels. The notion of an angelic hierarchy had particular appeal as a model of social organization, and fitted well with the angelic role as exemplars. The laity had previously been exhorted to see the merit in and to emulate the angelic hierarchy, with its lower orders of angels, whose responsibility was to labour on earth for the good of mankind, to those in the top echelon, who were the governors of regions and territories. Of course in the Republic, the model of the angelic hierarchy was unsuitable, and this perhaps explains the lack of interest in it. As we have seen, Robert Dingley was able to use his discussion of guardian angels as a cover for an appeal to the authorities to continue to reform society along the lines that he thought best. In contrast, it was far more difficult to manipulate the idea of the hierarchy in favour of a republic.

References to the angelic hierarchy therefore persisted in the literature, but did not achieve the same level of interest as guardian angels.

This suggestion is supported because the invocation of the angelic hierarchy as a model of good government which could be imitated on earth returned in Restoration England. A royalist army officer named Matthew Carter pondered just such concerns in 1660, offering the opinion that 'Philosophy tells us of Angells, and the Supream Heavens being immediately Governed by the Maker of all things ... Kings are in like sort of Government'.[96] The bishop of Lincoln, Thomas Barlow, in 1671 demonstrated the 'Necessity and Excellency of Monarchy' with a similar angelic comparison: 'consider the Angels, and you shall find one Archangel above the rest, as the Angels Monarch'.[97] Following the overthrow of James II and the accession of William and Mary to the throne, the constitution of the state again dominated the political stage, and several authors evoked the angelic motif in their discussions – the Church of England clergyman and political writer George Lawson compared the ministry of angels to 'Deputies and Vicegerents', those who 'bear the Sword to protect the good and punish the bad'.[98] However, these comparisons were not always a straightforward and wholesale endorsement of the system of monarchy, and Lawson reflected the unstable political circumstances of the time when he tempered his enthusiasm with caution, warning that 'an absolute and pure Monarchy is a very dangerous form of Government, very inclinable and propense to Tyranny', because although it has the potential to be the best form of government, men were not the same as Angels but were full of 'imperfection and corruption'.[99]

Praise and Patronage

Angels therefore persisted as a useful means of articulating both novel and traditional ideas. They might also be co-opted in other ways to convey political messages. In particular, it was common for supporters of one political figure or another to use the motif to heap praise upon their patron, therefore descriptions such as Arthur Wilson's of James I 'who is not only the wisest of Kings, but the very *Image* of an *Angel*, that hath bought good tidings, and settled us in the fruition of all good things' were commonplace, because comparisons with angelic beings associated the patron with all that was good about these wonderful creatures.[100]

It was indeed a prominent trope to compare the deceased to an angel in a funeral address, as this was a convenient way to convey their purity and holiness. For example, George Rust related how the subject of his sermon, the bishop of Down, 'made his hearers take him for some young Angel, newly descended from the Visions of Glory'.[101] Thomas Vincent described an earlier, pre-mortem visit from the recently departed Henry Stubbes, claiming that 'I were unworthy to receive such a one under my roof; and methought his face did look like the face of an Angel', and Thomas Watson's words were in a similar vein when he affirmed that 'he is as rich as the Angels, though he hath lost his life, yet not his crown'.[102]

Thus a comparison with angels, or intimation that the recently departed were now enjoying celestial company, could serve as short-hand for the impeccable character and purity of the deceased. There were some circumstances however, where the context might supply these comparisons with added meaning. This is fairly straightforward with reference to the funeral sermons and elegies that proliferated after the death of Queen Mary in December 1694. These eulogizing texts were eagerly rushed into print, and it is reasonable to assume that alongside their desire to immortalise their lamented Queen in print, the authors were also keen to obtain the favour and patronage of the surviving king, who had become deeply attached to his wife and was inconsolable after her death. The favourable comparison of Mary with angels could therefore become politically charged. For instance, the bishop of Gloucester Edward Fowler prefaced a treatise reflecting on the workings of providence with 'some observations, touching her [Mary's] excellent endowments, and exemplary life'. In this he described her conduct during her last illness, when she was suffering from smallpox. Fowler related that she was so composed throughout her last sickness, that 'One of Her *Physicians* (a very Worthy Gentleman) was so Affected with the Observations he then made of Her, as since to say, *She seemed to me, more like an Angel, than a Woman*'.[103] Fowler was evidently keen to retain the esteem of the monarch, and his 'observations' were designed to garner William III's support. Other clergymen adopted comparable strategies: Samuel Wesley wrote an elegy to the Queen that included the lines:

> The *Angel,* who no more cou'd stay,
> *Bows,* and *beckons* her away.
> Gladly the *Message* she receives,
> Gladly all but *WILLIAM* leaves.
> This only her firm *Virtue* tries,
> No *pains* she felt, or cou'd all pains *despise,*
> But what her *Royal Heart*
> Endur'd, with *him* to *part:*[104]

It is also noticeable that it was not only clergymen who were hoping to secure royal approval. Daniel Defoe made a contribution entitled *The Life of the incomparable princess, Mary*, in which he described how 'Angel-Trains the welcom'd Angel greet'.[105] The playwright Thomas D'Urfey published *Gloriana, funeral pindarique poem*, in which he described:

> Four Cherubs that on th' Angel came to wait,
> Whose awful Looks a Power display'd, superiour to Fate,
> Went up where *England's* Guardian Regent sate,
> Her seiz'd; then with their precious Load withdrew,
> And thro' the wide expanding Air, to their Third Heaven flew

Once in heaven the Queen was soon pronounced blest, and a 'Heavenly Seat' of highest degree was fixed for her – 'She needed but a small Translation there; The Angel was more than half perfect here'.[106] Thus in the context of these tributes, angels could be enlisted to allow the authors to laud and extol the virtues of the departed Queen. It also appears that deliberate echoes and associations were being drawn with earlier beliefs about he roles of angels in the Assumption of the Virgin Mary.

Angels could also be used to praise or perhaps censure individual political actors. The ambitious bishop of Worcester and staunch royalist John Gauden lamented the ejection of 'those good Angels, such as our English Bishops have been', from their positions in the 1640s, and lauded the mercy of God for sending other good angels 'even the King, and his faithful forerunner (who are in this respect as Angels or Messengers of God) to stop those Lions mouths'.[107] The anonymous tract *England's black tribunal*, which included an account of the trial of Charles I and the gallows speeches of many royalist prisoners, was replete with references to angels. The royalist officer Colonel Eusebius Andrewes beseeched the crowd to offer prayers 'to help those Angels that are to convey my soul to Heaven', where he would rejoice with them forevermore, and the royalist conspirator Peter Vowell looked forward to 'the spangled Heavens, where the holy Angels dwell, where God himself is rounded with thrones, Principalities, Powers'. Others called on the angels as witnesses to their sufferings – James Stewart, the seventh earl of Derby, proclaimed that 'I love Monarchy as the best government' saying 'if it be my crime, I here confess it again before God, Angels and men'; and the inclusion of Archbishop Laud's final speech in the treatise testified to his desire to 'die in the presence of Almighty God and all his holy and blessed Angels'.[108] The utilization of angels in this collection of speeches is another example of how angels were commandeered in order to endorse and add authenticity to a cause. The rapidly shifting political circumstances which had seen the re-establishment of Church and monarchy fuelled comparisons of the executed king with a good angel just as it promoted the publication of sermons commemorating the 'martyrdom' or 'execrable murder' of the monarch.[109]

In other instances, angels might also be appropriated to endorse more unconventional individuals. The possibility is raised by a narration of the fate of Sir Archibald Johnston, Lord Wariston. Wariston was an unusually devout Scotsman, who had used his skills as a lawyer to assist in the drawing up of the National Covenant of 1638. At the Restoration he was singled out for punishment and eventually arrested by Charles II's government and hanged at Mercat Cross in Edinburgh in 1663. A 'short Narration of the Lord Wareston's Carriage' on the scaffold published in 1664, was a typical example of the gallows speech genre as discussed by Peter Lake and Michael Questier, amongst others.[110] The author elaborated on Wariston's 'most convincingly Christian' behaviour, relating that 'during the whole time of his Imprisonment the Lord keeped him in a most spiritual tender frame, even to the conviction of some that hated him formerly'. When he received his sentence it was 'with exceeding meekness, to the admiration of all', and he was 'quieted in his mind' on the eve of execution. On the scaffold itself he delivered a speech 'with very much undaunted courage, audacity, and quiet of mind', in which he first confessed his sins, and then affirmed his faith in God and the Covenant. Afterward he went calmly to his death, although not before exhorting the watching crowds to '*be encouraged to do, and endure, in suffering for him, and his Interests; for I assure you in the Name of the Lord he will bear all your charges*'. At his death there was '*a very lamentable Cry of many thousand Spectators*', as 'without the least motion, trembling or shaking of body, which is most ordinary in that condition, [he] peaceably slept away to glory', upon which his son wept that 'you are very highly honoured this day'.[111]

This affecting tableau was highly stylized and bears all the hallmarks of the 'gallows speech' genre. The representation of Wariston as a dedicated and godly Christian, quietly assured and steadfast in his convictions, is expressed through his comportment and behaviour: from his meek acceptance of his sentence, his stoic behaviour leading up to his death, right through to the fact that he does not struggle when he is turned off the ladder – this is the quintessential 'good death'.[112] The significance of this with regard to angels can be found in the commentary that followed, written by a self-confessed 'Favourer of the Covenant and work of reformation'. The text figured Wariston as a 'Witness for Christ', and furthermore it expressed an expectation that Christ would offer such people assistance that will enable them to perform their 'great and honourable piece of Work'.

> Without all doubt it is then to be expected, when sealing his Truth on a Scaffold or Pillory for his sake: Comforts run most sweetly and abundantly in that hour. When Jesus is to suffer, *Luke* 22. 43. an Angel is sent to comfort him.

Thus one of the rewards for the steadfast faith and adherence to principle that Wariston demonstrated was the assistance and ministry of angels. Those that suffer for the true religion were to be singled out for the special attention and care of God, for 'if his face was as the face of an Angel, *chap*. 6. 5. O how chearfull hath his countenance and lovely smiles been now?'[113]

This scriptural evidence was therefore employed in such a way as to associate angels with this martyr for the covenanters' cause, both through the expectation that angels would assist the victim in their 'great work' and through the implication that they might then be translated to an angelic state. It also entangled angels in the interplay of power and authority surrounding the scene of an execution. The notion of gallows as sites which provided protagonists access to, and the potential means with which to harness the emotional energy that was released there, has been touched upon in previous chapters, and also overlaps with the concerns of more 'popular' beliefs about angels, discussed in chapter six.[114] It is evident that, at the end of the seventeenth century, these sites still functioned as foci of power and that the angels were called upon to endorse particular political and spiritual positions as fragmented groups struggled for agency. It is particularly significant because it demonstrates how angels were evoked to provide legitimacy and vindicate the authenticity of a confessional group – as people struggled to affirm that God was on their side, the angels could function as evidence of divine support. This can also be traced in other sources.

For instance, angels appear in another 1660s text which was constructed as a defence of the covenant. *The speeches, discourse, and prayers, of Col. John Barkstead, Col. John Okey, and Mr. Miles Corbet* included a description of how the aforementioned men were apprehended, and also related the cause they claimed to die for. It then reproduced some of their letters and speeches on the scaffold. The prisoners affirmed that 'it was in *pursuance* of the *Covenant* that we acted, and that in *defence* of it now we do suffer', and there was a long discourse on the nature and aims of the covenant, summed up as 'the preservation and Reformation of the true *Protestant Religion*, both Personal and National'.[115] Barkstead's comportment in prison was exemplary, he wrote scriptural verses on his cell's walls and went with 'readiness and chearfulness' to the gallows on the morning of his execution. Miles Corbet exhibited a similar willingness to acquiesce to his fate, stating 'the more *ignominious* our Death, the more *conspicuous* will our Honour be, while we are made *spectacles to Angels and men*', and he looked forward to 'an innumerable company of Angels' after his death. His final prayer concluded '*take the Soul of thy poor worm into thy Bosom, and let thy holy Angels be in readiness to receive it*'. Both his and John Okey's scaffold speeches also invoked angels; Corbet entreated God that 'when our poor souls shall be coming to thee, we pray thee give thy Angels charge over us, and strengthen us against the fears and terrors of Death'. Okey expressed a similar supplication, 'we beseech Thee for Christs sake, that Thou wouldst now let us see (as *Stephen* once did by the eye of Faith) even Heaven opened, and the Lord upon the Throne ... and the glorious Angels receiving our souls into thy everlasting Mercy'.[116]

Once again the good deaths that these men achieved were marshalled as evidence of the legitimacy of their cause. The discussion of the covenant, the behaviour of the victims, and the arrangement of the material in the text conveyed a picture of self-assured and utterly dedicated martyrs for the Protestant cause. Nowhere is mention made of the fact that both Barkstead and Okey served as commissioners at the trial of Charles I, or that all three of these men's names were on the King's death warrant. In the text they are figured as martyrs for their religio-political beliefs, despite the fact that in the eyes of the government they were participants in 'execrable treason' and were to be put to death for their crime. The references to angels reinforce the construction and message of the text, indicating these regicides' belief that they were witnesses for a true cause – their hopes and expectations that angels will soon welcome them to the heavenly Jerusalem evidence that they were the beneficiaries of divine favour.

Other sources employed the angelic trope in support of nonconformity. Theodosia Alleine's account of the life and death of her husband, the ejected minister Joseph Alleine, related how, when he was imprisoned for preaching his separatist beliefs, he was 'joyful to suffer for the Name of Jesus and his Gospel'. In prison he endeavoured to convert his fellow prisoners, saying that:

> *The Eyes of GOD and Angels are upon you, and the eyes of Men are upon you; now you will be critically observed. Every one will be looking that you should be more Holy than others, that are called forth to this his glorious Dignity, to be the Witnesses of Christ Jesus.*[117]

Theodosia documented that 'The Guard of God's Angels' was one of the seven 'choice Tokens Christ had sent him', and on his deathbed angels were again in Alleine's thoughts, as he told his friends that were present that 'we shall be as the Angels of God in a little while: Nay, to say the truth, Believers are, as it were, little Angels already, that live in the power of Faith'.[118] Angels also appeared in an anonymous pamphlet relating the dying speeches of Protestant martyrs. This included narratives from three men executed for plotting against Charles II. Henry Cornish, a politician, pronounced his conviction that 'I am going to the Kingdom of God, where I shall enjoy the presence of God the Father ... and of all the Holy Angels', and similarly John Hickes looked forward to a 'perfect Peace and concord, the innumerable company of Angels, and this Spirits of Just men made perfect' after his demise. Richard Nelthorpe in his last speech also pronounced his conviction that his actions had divine approval when he beseeched God 'in the needful hour of Death, give thy Angels charge over my poor Soul, that the Evil One may not touch nor hurt it'.[119]

However, the flexibility of the belief surrounding angels also meant that this comparison could be turned on its head, as when Ezekias Woodward described Archbishop Laud as 'a seeming Angell of light at his death'. In no way intended as a compliment, this referred to the ability of Satan to transform himself into an Angel of light, and Woodward was certainly of the opinion that the Devil held 'fast and full possession' of Laud in life.[120] Opponents of the crown and royal policy could also be demonized in a quite literal sense, resulting in their representation as evil angels or devils, a stark contrast to their angelic adversaries. An account of Charles I's trial, recorded by John Nalson, a Church of England clergyman and vigorous defender of the reputation of the executed king, described the rise and fall of the 'Impostors' of the 1650s in these terms:

> the Vizard by continual use was at last worn so thin, that the ugly and real *Devil* began to appear through the painted *Angel* of Light; and those Reforming Saints, began to tread so heavy upon the neck of the *Nation*, that they found they had mis-

taken shrewdly; and that it was a *Cloven-foot*, with which these high pretenders to the *Cloven-tongues*, trampled upon, and broke in pieces, the Government, Ancient Laws, Liberties, Properties, and even Religion it self.[121]

John Gauden had a similar perception of Oliver Cromwell, he described him and his men as 'Gods Butchers, the unjust Executioners of his just vengeance; as the evill and destroying Angels sent among us for a time'.[122] The impulse to adopt angels as a means to project a political message evidently continued to characterize the literature of the period. Angels could therefore be enlisted as support against political and religious enemies alike, and the angelic motif was utilized in order to debate and pronounce on issues of social order and hierarchy within the church and community.

Oaths

Angels were also employed in the religious and political debates that resulted from the continued fragmentation of Protestantism and the presence of many sects that were still active in the country. Fears about the proliferation of such groups and concerns over the heterodoxy that they represented were commonplace at the time and represented genuine concerns. For example, angels were frequently evoked in the controversy surrounding the swearing of oaths that was the focus of debate throughout the later seventeenth century.

The subject had become particularly contentious following the Restoration for a number of reasons. Most obviously the Corporation Act of 1661 forced the issue to the top of the political agenda by calling for all members of cities or corporations to take part in the Lord's Supper and to swear the Oaths of Allegiance and Supremacy before they took office. In turn this was motivated by a desire on the part of the government to bring nonconformists in line or to exclude them from public offices if they were unwilling to be coerced. The fact that some sects, including the Quakers, objected to oath-taking no doubt contributed to the anxieties surrounding the questions of allegiance and loyalty in a nation that had only recently emerged from the turmoil and aftermath of a bloody civil war. Angels in particular were of significance to the controversy over oaths because of a particular passage in Revelation when a mighty angel descended from heaven 'And sware by him that liveth for ever and ever' (Rev. 10:5). This was cited as evidence both for and against the practice.

For example, Henry Denne, a Baptist minister, wrote a tract to the conscientious-objectors who were incarcerated because of their refusal to take the oath, asserting the lawfulness and antiquity of it. Denne maintained that 'An Angel swears' in the bible, therefore the oath 'is warranted, not onely by practice, but by precept also'. 'If the Quaker say, the Light within forbideth him to swear' and he 'pleads the Scriptures, you see how weak it is'.[123] John Gauden also made reference to the passage, stating that 'we read the *Angel* in the *Revelation* by his example justifying the *lawfulness* of *some* swearing, for he is brought in thus, *lifting up his hand to heaven,* and *swearing by him that liveth for ever and ever, &c.* after the same manner as the *Angel* in *Daniel* did *swear lifting up both his hands to Heaven'*. It was unthinkable to Gauden that good angels in both the Old and New Testaments might 'appear on record' to endorse an action that Jesus had expressly forbidden.[124]

However, their opponents took it upon themselves to respond to this criticism. Samuel Fisher, a Quaker preacher and disputant, acknowledged the Scriptural passage but asked 'What's that to us?' and countered with the passage 'If an *Angel from Heaven should preach any other Doctrine then what is preached by, and received from Christ and the Apostles, let him be accursed'. Fisher firmly asserted that angels were merely 'ministers', and that 'this is no President for them who are under the Doctrine of the Son himself'*.[125] Francis Howgill, a Quaker activist who played an important role in the development of the movement, offered similar objections to Fisher, stating that 'both Angels and their Ministration are to give way unto Christ, and he must be worshipped; and no example of either Angels or men ought or can violate the Commands of Christ'.[126] In 1673 parliament passed the Test Act, which extended the oath to all those filling any office, civil or military, provoking further contributions on both sides of the debate. In an anonymous tract of 1676, since attributed to Edward Fowler, the minister in the dialogue gave the example 'of the Angels swearing' stating that 'we need not fear any thing that is done in Heaven, where nothing but the will of God, nothing evil and unholy can be done'. Furthermore, angels were 'propos'd to us as patterns for our imitation', 'joyned in the same fraternity', so taking an oath was indisputably acceptable in the eyes of God.[127] A quick reply came from Thomas Ellwood, a Quaker who had been imprisoned for refusing to take the oaths of allegiance and supremacy. He argued that the passage from Revelation could not be taken as an example to men on earth, for it 'was not done in Heaven, but on Earth, for the Angels which swore *stood upon the Sea, and upon the Earth'.* After dismissing this as evidence, he wondered if Fowler:

> doth ... imagine then, that there is Swearing in Heaven? What! if there were not Truth enough in men, does he think there is not *Truth enough in Angels neither,* to make their *bare* Testimony of *sufficient* Credit! what a strange Notion hath he got of Heaven and Angels.[128]

With regard to the argument that angels are 'Patterns for our imitation', Ellwood also gave this short shrift, arguing that if this was to be taken as a literal meaning covering all the angelic actions found in scripture, then 'by parity of reason, it is lawful for us to have a Censer as they had under the Law, and to offer incense thereupon to the Lord', because 'we read that Angels so had and did'. However, if his opponents were of the opinion that 'to use such as Censer now would be Iewish and unlawful, notwithstanding the Angel used one, then to use an Oath now, would for the same Reason be Iewish and unlawful, notwithstanding the Angel used one'.[129]

These examples demonstrate how angels could still become entangled in the political and religious controversies at the end of the seventeenth century, evidence of how close these two aspects of society were. Personal religious identities were intimately linked to the safety and stability of the nation, and the controversy over oaths of allegiance touches on questions of individual freedoms, the rights of the monarch and government as well as aspects of personal belief.

Summary

This chapter has ranged broadly across the full spectrum of late sixteenth- and seventeenth-century religious cultures, revealing that the fortunes of angels varied wildly depending on the context and meaning applied to them by those of differing religious stripes. In the right circumstances angels might be on the defensive, under attack from the puritan element for their close association with Arminian and Laudian 'innovation' and tainted by their appropriation by the leaders of Tridentine reform. However, these circumstances serve to underline the important role they played during the period, as angels were called upon to play a part in the hardening of religious identities, a range of Protestants, anti-Calvinists and the godly, each as willing as the other to promote belief relating to angels. Angels evidently remained an important ideological resource – seldom the direct focus of controversy, they were nonetheless compliant enough to be used to support controversial positions, their legitimacy and scriptural credentials often proving the basis of their appeal and providing a means to promote a particular agenda. As such, they allowed reflection on wider questions of religious identity in a young Church that was itself still in a state of flux, revealing how larger tensions and controversies were played out at the time.

This preoccupation with angels therefore appears to be another example of the resurfacing of issues that were not satisfactorily settled by the Elizabethan settlement, taking its place alongside the questions of religious ceremonial and hierarchy that continued to cause consternation in the years after 1559. However, the evidence examined here suggests that angels had a wider significance. Firstly, the ubiquity of celestial beings, and the malleable set of traditional understandings that were associated with them, allowed angels to be utilized in such a way that they contributed to both questions of ceremonial and organization, as well as fundamental doctrinal debates, because they were employed by those pushing at the official boundaries of English religious cultures at some of their most sensitive points. Thus, when Richard Montagu argued that it was acceptable to pray to angels in some instances, or when William Dowsing ordered the destruction of ranks of hammerbeam angels in an East Anglian church, each was making a statement about their personal vision of the church, and in the former instance, certainly breaking the 'rules' of what had previously been some form of Elizabethan consensus. On their own angels were unlikely to inspire a radical vision of what the English church should be, but the angelic motif could be utilized as a 'space' in which fundamental questions about doctrine and ceremonial could be conceptualized, articulated and argued out. They were so deeply rooted in all aspects of religious culture that they had proved excellent tools to subvert as well as protect confessional identities. More fundamentally, a survey of the ways in which angels became entangled in political discourse is a reminder that the concept of an angel – the binary of the demon – was continually proving an important pillar in the structure of the Protestant rational universe.

5 THE CATHOLIC ANGEL, *c.* 1550–1700

A treatment of angels in early modern England would not be complete without an examination of their place in Catholic cultures, a much neglected aspect of English Reformation studies. A survey of the Counter-Reformation (and the Marian Church, as its spiritual forebear) not only engages with an intrinsically important area of study, but given its position as an oppositional and persecuted movement, can also offer insight into the mentalities of the majority on the other side of the confessional divide. Although angels were certainly recruited as supporters of the established status quo, we have seen how the angelic motif continued to be utilized by those endorsing competing confessional identities. This was nowhere more true than when it came to the English Catholic community. There are a number of reasons why a closer investigation of this minority makes sense at this juncture. The abundance of works refuting Catholic doctrines and traditions, some of which have been discussed above, and the propensity to identify popery in all aspects of daily life, are a reminder that hostility to Catholicism was a formative influence on the English Protestant identity, a fact acknowledged by many scholars.[1] Before the first decades of the seventeenth century, a consensus had emerged among English clergymen that the Pope was antichrist, a fact that united occasionally fractious reformers in opposition to a common enemy. Identifying the evolution of Catholic perceptions of angels will not only allow for a more complete reconstruction of post-reformation angelology, it also informs our understanding of how angels became one of the motifs used to articulate the divide itself.

Marian Angels

In order to appreciate how developments in Catholic angelology were interwoven with and reacted to the processes of religious reform within the country, it is necessary to begin in the mid-sixteenth century and Mary I's reign. An understanding of the Marian perception of the roles and responsibilities of angels also speaks to debates about the potential effectiveness of Mary's religious policy, and the revisionists' claim that her reign was a period of fruitful Catholic restoration which foreshadowed many Tridentine reforms. The treatment of angels during

Mary's reign may provide an insight into processes which resulted in the sharpening of confessional identities and the clear establishment of lines along which confessional battles of the future were to be fought.

Traditionally, historians perceived Mary I's religious policy as misdirected and inappropriate, based on a fundamental misunderstanding of both the situation in England at the time of her accession, and a complete inability to discover any spiritual sincerity on the part of the reformers.[2] Various factors were assumed to have contributed to the 'failure' of the regime: the conservative and legalistic approach adopted by Mary and Cardinal Pole, the counter-productive burning of 300 martyrs, and the failure to appreciate the importance of printing as a propaganda tool being significant elements. However, historians have more recently advanced the case for constructive and far-sighted Marian reform, which failed perhaps only because there was not time for policies to bear fruit before Mary's premature death.[3] Various aspects of religious culture have been rehabilitated as a result. Lucy Wooding has argued that Marian Catholicism drew on a strong tradition of Catholic humanist reformism, which made the Mass central to its religious devotion.[4] Jennifer Loach was able to demonstrate that contrary to previous perceptions, the Marian regime did produce a large amount of printed religious material, albeit instructional rather than polemical in tone. Marian churchmen turned to the press with 'zeal and enthusiasm', producing catechisms, primers, printed sermons and homilies.[5] An investigation into the presence of angels in this religious literature will engage with this scholarship, using angels to examine the religious cultures in Mary's reign and beyond.

Marian religious literature would generally appear to offer a perception of angels that was distinct from that of late medieval Catholicism. The tone was set by Edmund Bonner in what Eamon Duffy has described as 'one of the most remarkable books of the reign, a neglected masterpiece of Tudor catechesis', *A Profytable and necessary doctryne*.[6] In this exposition of the fundamentals of the faith, angels were utilized in traditional ways to support and explore the narrative of religious history. They are mentioned in conjunction with the second article of the Creed ('I believe in Jesus') when they appear to Joseph to advise him of Jesus' birth, and in the seventh article which deals with the end of human history ('he shall come to judge the quick and the dead') when Bonner reminds his reader that the exact time of the Day of Judgement is 'hidden from men and angels'.[7]

More significantly, Bonner also invoked the traditional idea that men and angels join in fellowship during worship, pronouncing that there was no greater treasure in the world than the Catholic faith, which makes 'the men partakers of the euerlastynge enheritaunce with the holye Angels'. Bonner also discussed angels in the context of the doctrine of soteriology. He made several references to the angelic participation at the day of reckoning, 'where is the company of blessed angels, and the elect and chosen of God', whilst acknowledging their role at Judgement, when men will come 'in the maiestye or presence of hys father, and of the holy aungelles'.[8]

However, in Bonner's works celestial beings appear only in conjunction with expositions of the essentials of Christian catechesis. Bonner is not concerned with an exploration of the wonderful benefits supplied to mankind by way of the angels, and makes no attempt to offer a comprehensive synthesis of heavenly beings. In fact, the opposite is true, as he asked 'how vaine a matter it were for vs here buselye to reason, howe God or Aungell, coulde appeare lyke man? and whether they had trye bodyes or no?'[9] This reluctance to engage in a detailed examination of celestial beings bears a perhaps surprising similarity to the reformed tendency to eschew the wild elaborations and speculative nature of late medieval angelology. This shift in tone and emphasis can also be seen in other, officially sanctioned Marian literature, most prominently in the primers.

Eamon Duffy has explored the piety on offer in the Marian primers, concluding that they were a remarkable blend of old and new, in which 'the ancient pieties, to Sacrament and to saint, have their place, but where they are subordinated to a strong emphasis on the centrality of the Passion of Christ'.[10] The belief attached to angels within the primers supports his argument. Angels again assumed their traditional roles in the scriptural narrative, helping to explain the unfolding of human history, and emphasizing that the incarnation was the means by which God offered his people salvation. A passage about the Annunciation was inevitably included in the section on the Gospels, and angels also were mentioned delivering the good news to the shepherds, and accompanying Mary and Joseph in their flight from Egypt.[11]

The primers also often included images which were designed to convey the fundamentals of Christian history. Significantly, the first publication of a Sarum primer in 1554, initially in Latin, was the most extensively illustrated. The images where angels were present included those of the Annunciation, Saint Michael, the visit to the shepherds, the flight out of Egypt, and the Assumption of the Virgin Mary. These illustrations were often accompanied by an English verse, a device perhaps designed to convey didactic instruction to those unable to follow the Latin text. For example, in woodcuts depicting the Annunciation in various Marian primers, the archangel Gabriel points at a shining dove, descending from heaven to the virgin Mary. The dove would have been a familiar trope to the early modern audience as it was derived from scripture and was often used to symbolise the holy ghost, the means of transmission of God's grace. The pictures therefore demonstrate how complex ideas about the nature of soteriology and the processes by which mankind were saved by God's mercy might be communicated to the unlearned laity via the use of familiar motifs and figures. Angelic manifestations to the shepherds during the nativity, accompanying Mary and

Joseph during their flight from Egypt and crowning Mary following her ascension underline the point.

The primers also emphasized the traditional notion that the primary occupation of the angels was to praise God, the Te Deum providing the basis for supplications such as 'Praise ye the lord of the heavens, Prayse ye hym all his Aungels', and 'to the crie forth all angels, the heauens, and al the powers therin'.[12] Similarly, the Litany was to be a reminder of the roles and responsibilities of the angels, asking Michael, Gabriel, and all angels to pray for men, and beseeching them to intercede on mankind's behalf.[13] The feast of Saint Michael also remained a part of the ritual church calendar, the anthem dedicated to the archangel calling on him to 'com for to succour the people of God, and I sall geue the prayse in presence of angels'.[14]

The primers also contained references which hinted at a broader angelology, less reliant on the dictates of the books of scripture, such as the narrative of the Assumption. These were evidently considered important enough aspects of faith to pronounce upon, often in direct contradiction of reformed principles. For example, Catholics were comfortable relating the means by which Mary was conveyed to heaven: 'tyll that by aungelles her blessyd body, to her sonne was exalted to glorye', and they also included Raphael in the Litany.[15] Angels also assumed other familiar responsibilities in association with the end of life. They can be found receiving the body of the glorious virgin and martyr Katherine 'to be caryed by thyne aungels in to the mounte of Synay'.[16] They appeared in discussions of the deathbed, and they can be seen exhorting and encouraging the dying in the woodcuts included with the text.[17]

However, despite the continuity that some of these themes represent, the general tenor of the primers is qualitatively different from pre-Reformation angelology. Duffy describes these primers as 'much more austerely and theologically "correct" than the pre-Reformation books': marked by a silence about indulgences and miraculous legends, they are sparser and more sober in tone.[18] The belief associated with angels within their pages certainly bears this out. In contrast with earlier elaborations that drew on the Lives of the Saints and traditional notions of the practical benefits offered by angels, the Marian primers generally employed angels for didactic purposes and to emphasize the central importance of the incarnation, and the process by which mankind achieved both collective and individual salvation. Thus the more comforting tone of pre-Reformation Catholic angelology is subordinated.

These concerns and preoccupations can also be traced in other literature from the reign. One of the more prominent themes is the employment of angels in works buttressing the central significance of the Mass. In a homily published in 1556, the clergyman Leonard Pollard declared that during the mass 'Seraphins stande rounde about ... and al the incorporal powers prayeth then with the prist for thee'.[19] The Bishop of Lincoln, Thomas Watson, propounded a similar view:

> the holye angels of God, in the time of this oure sacrifice do assist the Priest and stand about the hoste, thinking than the meetest tyme to shewe their charitie towards vs, and therefore holding forth the body of Christ pray for mankinde.[20]

Miles Huggarde, perhaps 'the most effective of the regime's propagandists', also picked up on this theme in several of his works.[21] In a treatise published in 1554 Huggarde pictured 'a priest deuout/ Whiche brought with him the holy sacrament/ With many Angels compassinge him about'.[22] The inclusion of angels in these texts is a device which valorizes the sacrament of the mass (as well as the status of the priest), emphasizing the intense spiritual significance of the rite, when angels themselves were thought to be present. The work of the artisan Huggarde, an unusual religious polemicist because he was not a member of the official church hierarchy, has been explored by Joseph Martin. He has lauded Huggarde's 'propagandist's feel for a situation' and his tendency for brevity and simplicity in his tracts, which were 'mindful of the interests and capabilities of laymen readers'.[23] Huggarde exhibited these talents throughout his nuanced discussion of the relative status of men and angels, in a tract published in 1555. The motif of the angels recurred frequently: God created angels and made man similar to them out of his great love and mercy: 'Where angel is a substance spiritual, But in soule a man is to angel equal'. However, when Jesus took the form of a man this marked mankind out as superior to heavenly beings: 'When Gods sonne was first for man incarnate ... by which coniunction mankinde did attayne, In nature aboue all angels to raygne'. This promise was then made flesh at the Last Supper when Jesus broke bread with the apostles:

> And he that doth eate my flesh fruitfully,
> I in him, and he in me truely shal dwel,
> By this mans nature doth angels excel.[24]

By making use of simple language and familiar motifs, Huggarde was able to guide his reader through the complexities of the sacrament of the mass, imbuing it with meaning and instructing on its wider significance. The comparison of the angelic nature with that of men is used to bring the reader to awareness of their privileged position and to demonstrate the broad, encompassing nature of God's love and mercy.

In utilizing angels in these ways, Huggarde was similar to other Catholic polemicists. Pollard repeated the opinion that 'mans sowle came from God hym selfe, and is of substaunce and nature lyke unto the Angels', and it is a notion that the clergyman Roger Edgeworth returned to in his sermons. Edgeworth stated that man was a 'reasonable creature, little vnder the angelles in the excellencie of his nature'; that 'the humanitie of Christ was so exalted and set alofte ... that it was preferred and set aboue the excellencie of all the Aungels of heauen'; and that 'God made the IX orders of Angels, al reasonable creatures, and the tenth is mankinde, which was by sinne gone at large out of the folde of Paradise'.[25] These ideas were also connected with another recurring concept in Marian literature. Edgeworth indicated this prominent belief when he stated that 'after the general resurrection men and women shall ... be as Goddes Aungelles in heauen'.[26] In association with this was the belief that, through Jesus' passion, God had 'restored agayne the blessed and gloryus quiers of angelles, not creating new angelles, but mercyfully placing penitent soules in the high orders of the blessed angelles'.[27] Here angels demonstrate the wonderful mercy of God, but also communicate the glorious destiny that awaits all those who remained true to the doctrine of the Catholic Church. This was a cheering and consoling message following years of religious turmoil, and in these texts, as the theologian William Peryn stated, 'the cheafest and high glory and ioye of the goodness of the good angels is perfectly to consider the clemency, mercy and benefites of god, and also his unmesurable goodnes'.[28]

The Marian perception of angels therefore does not exhibit the same primary preoccupations as pre-Reformation Catholic angelology. The latter's insistence on the benefits offered by angels, their responsibility in ministering to mankind, and the comfort and succour their existence brought was a long way from the Marian focus on the association of angels with central aspects of Catholic doctrine. In many ways, this supports those historians who have defended the Marian regime's use of the printing press. Recently scholars have recognized that contemporary Catholics demonstrated a commitment to providing instruction and instilling in people the fundamentals of the Catholic faith by exploiting the media, albeit in a manner distinct from the Protestants. William Wizeman has argued that Marian authors created 'a literary programme for religious renewal' in England, concentrated around Christ and his redemption, the reiteration of papal authority, the crucial role of the church in soteriology, and the central role of the sacraments as a means to salvation.[29] The association of angels with the incarnation, the repeated contrast between the wonderful nature of angels and the more superior nature of mankind, and the lionization of the mass, reflected these priorities and gave celestial beings an important role in Mary Tudor's church. This located them within 'the vanguard of the theology, spirituality and strategies of Tridentine Catholicism'.[30]

Marian representations also fit in with Duffy's suggestion that 'the blasting scurrilities of Bale or Becon' were not considered by the regime to be the best model for establishing truth, or for stabilizing the religious life of the people. Rather the way forward was the re-establishment of the beauty of worship, which underpinned 'a regular and solidly grounded pattern of parochial instruction'.

The utilization of angels in these sources fits with these aims and objectives.[31] In fact, there is explicit support for this idea, when the special spiritual authority of the angels was harnessed to promote the extra-ordinary status of the priesthood. In a passage that endorsed the importance of the sacrament of confession, Watson also pointed out that it was onto the priesthood that Jesus had endowed the power to remit sins, and that 'thys power our Sauiour neuer gaue to Aungelles nor Archaungelles nor to no worldlye Prince, but oneley to hys Apostelles and those that haue in hys Churche the order of Pryesthode'.[32] In a similar vein, Edgeworth argued that 'no angel, nor archangell, neither anye other creature, but the very holy ghost himself hath disposed this order', although he was also at pains to point out that 'a priest must nedes be of such pure sanctimony and holynes, as thoughe he were set euen in the heauen and stoode euen in the middle amonge the angels of heauen'.[33] This topos was of course a traditional late medieval one,[34] but the prominence and promotion of the idea in Marian literature certainly indicates the relative importance of the notion and its continuing significance.

Angels appear in these texts in support of the Mass, the priesthood, the workings of salvation and the narrative of Christian history, staying away from those aspects of angelology that might lead the laity into error or confuse them with unnecessary detail. Edgeworth comes close to stating this explicitly in a sermon on the gifts of the holy ghost: 'Of Angels what maner thinges they be, and howe God speaketh to them and one of them to another', 'a hundred such things must be considered in the scriptures, whiche it is but vain labour to teach children, neither to them that be childish, and leud in condicions'.[35] The emphasis on the sacrament of the Mass and other elementary aspects of Catholicism with regard to the angels thus looks like a deliberate policy, part of the 'creative reconstruction' that Duffy has argued for. It supports other scholars who have seen continuity between the policies of the Marian regime and the decrees enacted at the Council of Trent.

Post-Reformation Catholic Angels

It is not surprising to find that the demise of Mary I and the accession of Elizabeth I had a significant impact on the subsequent development of Catholic angelology. Catholics had to adjust to their new status as a church 'under the cross', as they became a small embattled minority in a young Protestant nation. Alterations in the treatment of angels may therefore offer insight into the struggle for survival and the mutations that Catholicism underwent in the years following the Elizabethan settlement. A discussion of Catholic perception of angels also engages with recent scholarship on the Catholic community in post-Reformation England. Early historians considered the survival of a 'backward' creed like Catholicism irrelevant to a Whiggish understanding of the development of the

Protestant nation, and the limited work that did exist was distinctly confessional in tone. However, academic priorities shifted following the publication of an article by John Bossy in 1962, which marked the first attempt to assimilate Catholics into a complex religious landscape.[36] In the *English Catholic Community* Bossy subsequently described the death of the medieval English church and the complete reformulation of Catholicism. Bossy's key contribution was therefore the identification of a 'discontinuity in the historical sequence' whereby medieval 'survivalism' died out to be replaced by a 'seigneurial' Catholicism, characterized by separatism and located almost exclusively in gentry households.[37]

Bossy's work fostered a new appreciation of the significance of the topic and prompted an outpouring of scholarship. Initially, historians such as J. C. H. Aveling endorsed Bossy's model, describing a religion where the gentry formed the 'solid trunk of the papist community'.[38] Christopher Haigh was inclined to see continuity with the past, arguing for widespread potential support amongst the commons immediately following the Elizabethan settlement, as evidenced by the slow pace of reform and the growing recusancy of the 1560s and 1570s, before missionary activity had an impact. Ultimately Haigh's argument still supported Bossy's paradigm however, as he believed that the Jesuit focus on the gentry and their concentration in the Southern parts of England failed to capitalise on this residual support.[39]

More recently scholarship has supplemented Bossy's seigneurial model by identifying novel forms of Catholicism. Jack Scarisbrick finds evidence of a 'plebeian' religion that existed outside of the manor house, whilst others have sought to reinstate the political importance of this dissenting minority, contributing more sensitive readings of what it meant to be Catholic following the Reformation and investigating the relative importance of Church papistry and the nature of conversions to and from Rome.[40] Peter Lake and Michael Questier have scrutinized the elaborate state ceremonial enacted at the execution of Catholic 'traitors', and in doing so illustrated how the ritual opened up space for the victim to contest the state's version of events.[41] This theme of Catholic agency was further elaborated in *The Antichrist's Lewd Hat*, where a variety of locations are explored to reveal the means which both Protestants and Catholics employed strategies in an attempt to 'reach and capture a genuinely popular audience'.[42] Events in prison and on the gallows provided both Catholics and Protestants alike with the abundant material needed to produce edifying and appealing 'cheap print' texts aimed at securing a wider audience for their particular confessional standpoint.

Lake and Questier's nuanced reading fits well with Alexandra Walsham's argument that popery and the printing press should not be situated in stark opposition but that 'English Catholicism engendered its own extensive, cosmopolitan and astonishingly rich culture of print. It too can lay claim to be described as a religion of the book'.[43] Lucy Wooding has charted the changing tone of post-Reformation English Catholicism, arguing that an initial humanist and idealist emphasis came to be replaced following the arrival of the Jesuits, the onset of greater persecution and the influence of the decrees of the Council of Trent.[44] This section seeks to locate Catholic responses to celestial beings within the framework of this rich scholarship. It will trace shifting attitudes to angelic beings and investigate their part in the defence of an embattled faith and the role they assumed in the counter-offensive.

The defensive and offensive purposes that Catholic angels assumed were made explicit by the inclusion of angels in the polemical writings of those defending the Catholic faith – if the Protestants were happy to importune the assistance of angels in the fight against heresy then this was no less true of their opponents. This is shown to good effect in the writings of William Rainolds, an English rector who converted to Catholicism in 1575 and who spent the remainder of his life as a Catholic apologist in Douai and later Rheims.[45] Rainolds was involved in the translation of the Rheims bible, and in his reply to William Whitaker's assault on the edition he counter-attacked by referring to the 'brainsicke conceite' which led the Protestants to 'rent out of the bible so many partes which our auncient fathers deliuered vs, and we hold fast as sacred and canonical'.[46] Whitaker styled the Protestants as 'beaters and circumcisers, and gelders, and manglers, and defacers, and corrupters of those holy bookes' for omitting various texts, including the story of Tobias, and disdainfully inquired whether it was not equally possible to raise objections to every other book of scripture. He was equally incredulous with regard to the reformers' assertion that 'We passe not for that Raphael mentioned in Tobie, nether acknowledge we those seuen angels whereof he maketh mention. Al that differeth much from Canonical scriptures ... and sauoureth of I know not what superstition.[47]

Rainolds's discussion of the rejection of the book of Tobit from the Protestant canon illustrates how the ubiquity of the angelic presence might easily result in their involvement in confessional wrangling on both sides of the denominational divide. This was underlined when Rainolds returned to celestial beings later in his work with a nuanced argument relating to the intercession of the saints: he mentioned that because Christ said that the saints will be advanced to the state of angels, it follows that, like the angels, the saints can also succour and aid men, and 'heare our praiers and help us'.[48] These were questions – the status and authority of scripture, the significance and position of the saints and issues of mediation – that spoke to the disputed theology at the heart of the Reformation, and they demonstrate the expediency of heavenly beings for the Catholic cause.

The fact that angels also featured prominently in the works of other leading apologists provides further support for this idea. Angels secured the attention of the early superior of the Jesuit mission in England, Robert Parsons, who discussed them at length in *The first book of the Christian exercise* in 1582, the revised editions of which were to become well known as *The Christian Direc-tory*.[49] In the text Parsons reiterated many familiar angelic tropes: he argued that the true Christian life should be 'angelicall'; noted that the highest occu-pation of the angels was praising God, whom 'Cherubims and Seraphins doe daylie honour and celebrate'; affirmed that angels 'doe come to take the sowle and to bringe her before the iudgement seate'; and offered the opinion that these angels are 'in number and perfection so straunge and wounderfull'.[50] More con-troversially, in 1606 Philippe Numan used the scriptural example of Saint John's adoration of a visiting angel to support his contention that angels and saints 'may be worthely honoured, worshiped and adored'.[51] The sentiment was echoed in 1613 by Thomas Fitzherbert, who wrote that scripture 'forbiddeth only to commit idolatry to Angels, and not simply to pray to them', asserting that angels 'also do continually assist vs as well with their prayers' and that 'we may lawfully craue their assistance'.[52]

Texts were also circulating in which Catholic authors pronounced on other controversial areas of angelic belief. In a compendium of encyclopaedic, commonplace tales, by the Spanish dialogue writer Antonio de Torquemade (translated into English in 1600), the author concluded that 'God, for our good and benefit, hath ordeyned to each one of vs a good Angel to accompa-nie us' whilst 'we also haue at our left hand an ill Spirit, which stil is solliciting, perswading and alluring vs to sin'.[53] Belief in both a good and evil angel, situ-ated respectively at the right and left hands of each individual went against the general consensus of Church of England clergymen, as did the Jesuit Thomas Fitzherbert's conclusion that the ancient Fathers 'do thereupon teach expressely that we haue euery one of vs from our nativity a proper Angell, who protecteth, and defendeth vs, and prayeth to God for vs'.[54]

Angels were also included in narratives relating to prisons and sites of execu-tion, locating them within the 'arenas of ideological contest' explored by Lake and Questier. In 1587 the Jesuit Robert Southwell, who was himself to be imprisoned and later executed by the state, penned *An epistle of comfort* for incar-cerated priests. The text included a reminder that the souls of the faithful would be 'ordeyned to the fellowship of Angels in eternal bliss'.[55] Heavenly creatures also played an important role in Thomas Alfield's report of the martyrdom of Edmund Campion and two other priests at Tyburn in 1581. Alfield was another Jesuit and future martyr, and his affective verse account of the deaths employed the angelic trope very effectively. Alfield made the angels witnesses to the great crime being perpetrated, so whilst 'the riuer *Thames* a while astonied stoode/ to count the drops of *Campions* sacred blood', 'Angels and saints desired leaue to cry'. Playing on the words of Saint Paul, Alfield declared of Campion's exemplary behaviour at his death 'a pacient spectacle was presented then/ in sight of God, of angels, saints and men', and he completed the celestial imagery by imagining

Campion's 'humble cheare a shining angels face/ his feare, his griefe, his death and agonie/ a ioy, a peace, a life in maiestie'.[56]

In these sources, the angels – God's representatives on earth – are witness to crimes enacted upon the faithful, they provide a point of comparison for the behaviour of Catholics, and they are a comforting presence, a reminder of the superior state of bliss that awaits all those who adhere to the true faith. These texts therefore reveal Catholic clergymen associating angels with their cause, utilizing traditional ideas about angels in support of ideological and political notions. Angels are accordingly implicated in the interplay of power and authority that Lake and Questier perceive within gaols and at the gallows, both of which are perceived as sites which provided opportunities for the 'criminal' to impose their own meaning and understanding on the events enacted there. At the gallows, Catholics were therefore able to harness the release of emotional energy and put it to use for their own ends. In a similar way, the farcical laxity that marked the government of privately run institutions resulted in gaols becoming centres of spiritual power, a fact that was 'compounded by the sacramental grace, spiritual counsel and saintly examples on offer' to those that resorted there.[57] In both these arenas Catholicism found its highest expression, and the presence of angels at these locations involved them in the complex interplay of forces at play there.

This utilization of angels for the purposes of polemic has a wider importance in the context of recent historiography. These bold theological statements relate to precisely those areas where Catholicism was under attack and which represented fundamental Reformation battlegrounds. This is illustrated in microcosm in the concepts of guardian angels or the celestial hierarchy – despite Protestant doubts and anxieties about these traditional ideas, Catholics were forthright in reasserting their beliefs. They had enough faith in the authenticity and potency of the angelic motif to exploit it. This is an illustration of the importance that angels assumed in Catholic counter-offensive, and is also in keeping with the decrees of the Council of Trent, ratified in 1563, where the invocation and veneration of saints was declared to be a good and useful occupation, with the potential to secure great profit for the supplicant.[58]

The suggestion that these authors were part of the Tridentine tradition echoes understandings of Marian angelology as the forerunner of the attitudes and intentions expressed in the Tridentine decrees. However, the tone and content of Marian angelology was qualitatively different from later Catholic representations. During Mary's reign the angelic motif reflected attention towards central religious doctrines, its usefulness was perceived to lie in its didactic capacity. Accordingly the more mundane, earthly benefits of angels, as well as their more controversial aspects were subordinated in preference to these central truths. By contrast, these later authors did not back away from employing angels in support of disputed areas of belief, and they became involved in polemical debates and in the highly charged arenas of the gaol and gallows.

The contrast between Marian angels and later representations can be more clearly seen where they were utilized as a pastoral resource by authors seeking to instruct and guide a persecuted and embattled minority (which of course had not been the case in Marian England). In the *Christian Directory*, Parsons mentioned angels repeatedly in his account of the 'reconinge day', noting that Christ's coming will be accompanied by hosts of celestial creatures, and relating the various responsibilities that angels assume at the Final Judgement. He also reaffirmed the traditional association of angels with the Last Things, when he described how angels 'shal come to take the soule and bring her before the judgement seate', after which 'the iust mans soule goeth out of his bodie with greate ioye and comfort, the good Angels accompaininge her, with exultation'.[59] This element of overlap with conformist Protestant angelology is similarly attested to in a translation of the Dominican theologian Luis de Granada's works. In *The sinners guyde*, he suggested that angels 'beare the righteous in their armes ... and this they doe not onely in life, but also in death', citing the story of Lazarus and the 'rich glutton' as an example of a soul 'carryed of Angels into Abrahams bosome'. He also described the last agony of death when 'the angels guard is most necessary, that they may deliuer us from the fierie darts of the devil, and carry our soul when it is gone out of the prison of our bodie'.[60]

More unconventionally, the Jesuit Girolamo Piatti described the 'most quiet and sweet death' of William Elsinston, admitted into the Society of Jesus as a youth. On his deathbed the Scotsman was 'always wonderful chearful ... thinking that he could neuer thank God enough, that he dyed in Religion'. As the youth neared the hour of his death:

> He cryed out: O glorious death attended by so manie Angels! And expressing exceeding ioy, he sayd further; Doe you not see, doe you not see the Angels?[61]

As discussed above, Peter Marshall has demonstrated that the attendance of angels at the deathbed persisted as a subtext in Protestant writing, and these sources indicate a similar trend in Catholic writings.[62] However, what followed in Piatti's account did represent a significant departure from the conventional Protestant understanding of events at the deathbed:

> And calling vpon his good Angel, he spake with him for a while, as if he had beheld him with his eyes; and related, that he told him, he should passe through Purgatorie, but not stay long there. Whervpon one asked him, in what shape he saw his Angel, and he pointed at a youth that stood by, and sayd: He was like him.[63]

There are several details in this account which indicate the distinctiveness of Catholic angelology. The invocation of angels would have been compounded by the fact that this was the youth's 'good angel' – his particular guardian. This was precisely the sort of perception that the Protestants had tried to stamp out – a personalized angel, the fostering of close relations with a 'guardian', and the imagining of angels in the form of men. All of these elements were presumed to encourage the likelihood of a person falling into idolatry, and went against the Protestant emphasis on heavenly creatures as agents of God's providence and extensions of his will. As if this were not enough, the youth also discussed with his guardian the length of time that he was to spend in purgatory – for reformers this was knowledge that God alone was privy to, although this was incidental given that they had rejected the realm entirely.[64]

In more general terms, Luis de Granada was eager to promote the comfort and succour that heavenly beings offered, emphasizing the 'watch and guard' of angels, and sketching out the positive benefits conveyed by the fact that 'where Prayer is, there ... are the Angels especially present, that they may help vs in our prayer, that they may transport our praiers into the presence of the Lord, that they may defende vs from our enemy, and from all others'.[65] The notion of angels joining in fellowship with men was a familiar trope in both traditional and reformed angelology,[66] although this is also another example of a distinct Catholic understanding: the endorsement of the angelic transportation of prayers to the Lord suggesting an element of mediation that was absent from Protestant theology. This idea was elaborated on by the Spanish Carthusian Antonio de Molina in his discussion of the central importance of the mass. He asked 'What Christian can doubt but that in the tyme of Consecration ... the Quires of Angels assist', again a notion that would not have been out of place in reformed angelology, but his utilization of the angelic motif to stress the sacrificial nature of the Mass and to support his understanding of the sacrament as 'the thing most Venerable, that is in the Church', would have attracted the disapproval of reformed clergymen. Molina used the heavenly beings to call attention not only to the sacrifice, but also to the special status of those conducting it:

> Many millions of Angells kneele with great reuerence about the same, adoring the most holy Sacrifice, and the hands of the Priest that holds it, acknowledging his dignity in this regard to be greater than theirs, seeing to none of them such power and authority was euer giuen.[67]

Using angels to extol the special virtues and authority of priests again indicates how angelic beings could be taken up and used to punctuate controversial aspects of religious life. The acceptance of angels on both sides of the confessional divide and the ambiguous nature of the scriptural detail relating to angels meant that they were malleable enough to be employed in support of other, more contentious areas of belief. Molina's treatise also serves as a reminder of the interaction between English and Continental Catholicism, reflecting as it does a fundamental concern of the Counter-Reformation papacy, that is the insistence on the special status and importance of the members of the Church hierarchy, from the pope down to the parish priest.[68] The employment of angels in the Catholic cause was not always so contentious though, mainly because there was such overlap between the traditional and reformed thinking on angels. There was general agreement that 'The angels of the Lord protect/ All those that are the Lords elect', that it was God's will 'Angels should be ready to doe vs seruice', and that they were 'administring spirits for vs'.[69]

The unflinching adherence to traditional Catholic notions of the roles and responsibilities of angels exhibited in these texts is noteworthy. The fact that later Catholic belief about angels adhered closely to medieval precedents also emphasises the contrast with the utilization of angels in Mary's reign – clerics were evidently aware that their beleaguered followers were in need of encouragement and comfort in trying and difficult times, and angels fitted the bill perfectly as representations of God's mercy and love for his people as well as the purveyors of more direct forms of spiritual succour, comfort and protection. So although post-Reformation Catholic angels could be employed in polemical works for the defence of those aspects of the faith that had come under attack by the reformers, equally important was their pastoral role in offering spiritual nourishment to a persecuted minority.

The first major English Catholic work to provide a comprehensive summary of post-Reformation angelology was a translation of Jeremias Drexel's *The angel-guardian's clock*, published in 1630, and its contents and tone illustrate this point well. It encapsulated the themes discussed above, and in the process demonstrated the continuity in Catholic angelology throughout the late Elizabethan and early Stuart periods. The Jesuit's exhaustive treatment of celestial beings saw him lay out the roles and responsibilities of heavenly creatures, most of which are familiar: angels were expected to protect believers facing the dangerous agony of death, and bring souls to felicity after it. They were 'our aduocates without number', they cure the sick, refresh the weary, quickly comfort the afflicted, exhort to do well and 'encourage those that pray'.[70] Their nature was also formulated in the traditional way, they are 'voide of all corporall dregs' and endowed with 'the full and hidden knowledge of all things, except only the secret of man's hart'.[71]

Unsurprisingly there was also much in this text that reformers would object to. Raphael featured repeatedly, his particular status as 'the medicine, By whome our soules, which are infected, May healed be, our deedes directed' is discussed alongside the function of Michael 'the Angel of peace', and Gabriel, 'the Angel strong' who is expected to visit frequently.[72] Drexel also detailed the nine orders of the hierarchy, listing their names and distinct functions, from the Angels in the lowest order who 'serue the needy, the poore, and pilgrims', through to the Seraphims at the pinnacle, 'who loue God with their whole harts, and are inflamed with the loue of their enemies for God's sake'.[73] It was also implicit in the text that one of the primary functions of angels was intercession; their 'five-fold' office was comprised of their roles as singers, supplicants, ambassadors, protectors and 'warre-like conductors'. Their responsibilities as supplicants were envisaged to 'offer to God men's prayers and good wishes', and a prayer in commemoration of Saint Michael asked that 'the glorious intercession of S. Michell thy Archangel may euer and euerie where protect vs', also calling on Michael to 'be mindefull of vs, and intercede for vs' so that 'what we cannot obtaine through our owne deserts, may be supplied by his intercession'.[74] There were also various prayers directed to the angels themselves, calling on them for protection and assistance. A good example was in the form of 'An ardent Aspiration': 'holie Angels of God: succour and preuent me in all extremities: and when I shall not be able to implore your assistance, forsake me not'.[75]

Drexel's text is intrinsically important, representing as it does a comprehensive overview of Catholic angelology and accentuating how it differed from the official understanding of the Church of England. It is significant for this study because it epitomized the Catholic approach to heavenly beings in the seventeenth century – the tone is confident and assured, and it does not play down those aspects of traditional belief that had attracted the scorn and derision of the reformers. It can also be contrasted with literature produced by the Marian regime, which lacked the repeated references to and occasionally lengthy discussions of the advantages that the angelic presence offered to mankind.

The contrast between the Marian treatment of angels, and that which dominated in the decades after Mary's reign speaks to Alexandra Walsham's thesis about the role of the printing press and texts in post-Reformation English Catholicism. Walsham suggests that the press became a 'surrogate for the personal pastoral discipline exercised by the Tridentine episcopate and parish clergy on the continent', an 'alternative instrument of sacerdotal control for a church struggling to resist its abolition'.[76] Normal structures of authority and communication could not function for the underground English Catholic community, so texts assumed vital importance in sustaining the faith, and religion developed along lines that differed from Catholic nations elsewhere. The shift in emphasis and changing depiction of angels after Catholicism became a minority religion in England might therefore be indicative of a religion that was to become centred on recusant households, and which was 'primarily inward-looking and devotional in tone', rooted in prayers and 'self-regulated programmes of spiritual exercise' rather than one dependent upon the presence of a priest.[77] The treatment of angels reflected these trends, with initial emphasis on the mass and the status of the priesthood giving way to a plethora of traditional and more pastorally focused representations: in a similar vein, Fernando Cervantes has demonstrated that the early Franciscans in Mexico drew deeply on traditional angelology in their quest to evangelise the indigenous people.[78]

Summary

It is apparent that the development of belief about angels within Catholic literature can contribute to the historical understanding of the construction and presentation of Catholicism in England. The sources examined above demonstrate a willingness to engage with and promote traditional perceptions of heavenly creatures, as, like their Protestant counter-parts, Catholic clergymen were alive to the potential didactic and evangelizing power that the angels embodied. Celestial beings were included in polemical writings, where they were employed in defence of doctrine and ritual, as well as in more pastorally minded works which offered comfort and instruction to an embattled confessional group. However, as the areas of overlap between traditional, Tridentine and reformed understandings of angels has illustrated, there were many areas of angelology where compromise and ambiguity could enter into debates, betraying the integrated nature of traditional and evangelical belief following the Reformation.

6 THE PEOPLE'S ANGEL, *c.* 1550–1700

In sixteenth- and seventeenth-century England, angels were ubiquitous in the strategies and methods employed by a variety of religious reformers seeking to shape and influence the beliefs of the laity. Previous chapters have outlined both the intents and purposes, and the rhetoric employed by these contemporaries, and the significance of belief about angels has been traced in the context of the ongoing evolution of the Church of England. This chapter seeks to widen the terms of the debate by moving beyond the more explicitly ecclesiastical tone of the sources examined previously, to explore the diffusion of belief about angels amongst the English laity. Although by no means a comprehensive survey, the discussion is intended to demonstrate the cultural pervasiveness of belief about angels, and the main emphasis and expectations that people harboured at a popular level. By utilizing personal diaries and letters, 'popular' cheap print such as ballads and pamphlets, and visual and performance art, it will give an indication of how far reformed notions penetrated into the cultural life of the nation, and will sketch possible alternative or unorthodox ideas held by the populace in competition with official religious polemic. We have seen what reformers and religious activists wanted the English people to believe, and how they sought to convey their message to the people: this chapter will begin to address the question of how successful these methods were on the ground.

Angels in Everyday Life

In August 1647, the Yorkshire yeoman Adam Eyre recorded in his 'dyurnall' that his wife had suffered from a restless night with a bad foot, which had prevented him from sleeping. He wrote that on this occasion:

> sundry wicked worldly thoughts came in my head, and, namely, a question whether I should live with my wife or noe, if shee continued so wicked as shee is; whereupon I ris and prayd to God to direct mee a right. And, after, I read some good counsell of Lawrence concerning the assistance of Angells ... I prayed God again to direct mee, ans [sic] so slept til morne quietly, praysed be God.[1]

Relations between Eyre and his wife Susan were often fraught, beset as they were by severe financial difficulties, Susan's poor health, and Eyre's predilection for tobacco, gambling at bowls, and bouts of heavy drinking.[2] Keith Wrightson interprets this disturbed night as the crisis point in their troubled relationship – other nearby references in the diary, one in cipher, to Eyre's 'sore temptation', do suggest that this was indeed a moment of acute spiritual vulnerability for him.[3] During this worrying time it was to Henry Lawrence's *Treatise of our Communion and Warre with Angells* that Eyre turned to for guidance and comfort, finding in its pages practical advice that quietened his thoughts and allowed him to get back to sleep.

Fifteen years later, in December 1662, on Christmas Day, Samuel Pepys noted in his diary that Bishop Morley had 'preached upon the song of the Angels, "Glory to God on high, on earth peace, and good will towards men"'. Although Pepys thought Morley 'made but a poor sermon' – too long, and failing to capture the 'true joy that shall and ought to be on these days' – he did not object to the theme selected, and its fittingness for the day. Pepys was again in a critical mood the next August, when a Mr. Mill preached on the authority of ministers, saying that that 'if a minister of the word and an angell should meet him together, he would salute the minister first'. Pepys remained unimpressed by this lofty assertion, which 'methought was a little too high', indicating both that he had listened carefully throughout, but also that sermons delivered in church were not simply absorbed unthinkingly by the congregation.[4]

In 1665, parliamentary army officer John Hodgson, a close friend of the Quakers, was imprisoned at Bradford on suspicion of continued involvement in planned anti-government disturbances. Whilst imprisoned, an act came from Oxford, ordering them to keep a monthly fast for plague-ravaged London. Hodgson recorded that fortunately on that occasion 'God was amongst us, and did hear the prayers of the destitute for that city, did cause the destroying angel to put up his sword'.[5]

These three extracts are taken from the subject's personal diaries, and they give a glimpse of angels outside of their normal ecclesiastical confines, indicating three possible sites where the laity might come across or assert a belief in angels. Adam Eyre's experience is a touching example of the solace and comfort that was inherent in the belief; Pepys's of the potential for the laity to critically engage with the 'orthodox' views espoused from the pulpit; and Hodgson's an indication of how common scriptural material and references had become in everyday life. These anecdotes are evidence of the ubiquity of notions of angels, and they demonstrate how a belief that was not central to Protestant doctrine, had nevertheless made inroads into the cultural life of England and had become important in personal devotion.

But questions remain about how representative these brief extracts are. Can these anecdotes really be held up as evidence of the cultural pervasiveness of angelic belief, and what, if anything, does this tell us about the achievements of the reformers? The sources suggest the potential ubiquity of belief about angels, but they need to be placed in a broader cultural context in order to fully evaluate their significance. The greater part of this discussion will therefore focus on identifying those aspects of belief about angels that had the most prominence in more 'popular' religious cultures. It will supplement the evidence of personal diaries with material drawn from 'cheap print', literary sources, and visual culture. Whilst acknowledging the limitations of the available source material, and the obvious difficulties in seeking to uncover the early modern layperson's beliefs through them, it is nevertheless still possible, I will argue, to use this eclectic and diverse mix of sources in order to sketch out the contours of a more 'popular' angelology.

Definitions

In the dictionary published in 1676 by the lexicographer Elisha Coles, 'Angel' appears as a headword, followed by the seemingly perfunctory definition, 'messenger'.[6] Many other dictionaries contained similarly brief entries: John Baret's English, Latin and French dictionary of 1574 stated that 'Angel, is borrowed of the latin woorde Angelus, which is also deriued of the Greeke ἄγ γελος, signifieth a messenger'; and John Kersey the Younger, in his English Dictionary of 1702, defined an angel as a 'messenger from Heaven'.[7] However, references to angelic characteristics were not limited to entries under 'angel' in early modern dictionaries. Elsewhere in Coles' word lists can be found 'Arch-angel, Prince of Angels', 'Ave Marie, Her salutation by the Angel', 'Gabriel, the strength of God', and 'Seraphim, (shining or flaming) the highest order of Angels'.[8] Collectively, these dictionary entries would suggest that the key aspects of belief about angels were that they were messengers, and that they were organized into a hierarchy, where different orders of angels, and even individual, named angels had distinct functions. Thomas Blount's *Glossographia* of 1656 provided the most expansive definition of angelic hierarchy:

> Hierarchy. A sacred principality, or holy government, as that of the Church, &c. The holy order of Angels, which containing nine degrees (as some affirm) is a mystical resemblance of the Blessed Trinity, there being in nine [sic], thrice three and in every three thrice one. So that there are three superior, three inferior, and three middle degrees. The superior are Seraphims, Cherubims, and Thrones, the middle, Dominations, Principalities, Powers: inferior, Vertues, Arch-Angels, and Angels.[9]

Although stricter reformers might have objected to this definition, the insertion of 'as some affirm', and the absence of specific functions from the description probably would have made the definition inoffensive to most. Other lexicographers also mentioned the hierarchy, or included entries relating to particular orders. A good example is Edward Phillips' general English dictionary of 1678, which stated that 'Seraphical' meant 'celestial, bright, divine; like *Seraphim*, i.e., one of the highest order of Angels; so called from the fervency of their love to God, the word signifying in the Hebrew, fiery or burning'.[10] There are also references to the two archangels named in scripture: Michael is defined as 'who is like God, and Arch-angel', and Gabriel as 'the strength of God' in several lexicons.[11]

It is perhaps not surprising to see that the hierarchy of the angels remained a prominent aspect of belief despite the distaste of Protestant reformers for the formulation; this was, after all, a society that was deeply preoccupied with order and degree.[12] Interestingly though, this particular preoccupation is nowhere near as pronounced in other sources of evidence, which arguably offer an insight into more 'popular' aspects of belief. Personal accounts, ballads and pamphlets suggest that the angels' broader cultural significance lay elsewhere: less importance was attached to angels as abstract celestial role models, and much more attention was focused on their capacities as ministers and protectors of mankind. The notion that angels and men were in a mutually beneficial fellowship is the overriding concern that is conveyed in these texts.

Protection and Defence

The angelic role of defending and protecting humankind is perhaps the most prominent theme to emerge from cheap print, personal and literary sources. In a time of danger or distress, it was a commonplace to react as Hamlet does when first confronted with a spirit in the form of his father, calling on 'Angels and ministers of grace' to defend him, or later to 'save me, and hover o'er me with your wings'.[13] In ballads, adventurous London maidens hope that good angels will guide them; angels 'fight' for virgins and oppressed widows; and murderous assassins 'stampe and curse', convinced that 'some Angel' has kept their victim from them.[14] *The virgin martir*, a play written by Thomas Dekker and Philip Massinger and first published in 1622, is an unusual play in that it provides a rare example of angels appearing as major characters on the seventeenth-century stage. Harpax is 'an euill spirit, following *Theophilus* in the shape of a Secretary', Angelo 'a good spirit, seruing *Darothea* in the habite of a Page'.[15] The play adapts and dramatises the medieval martyr legend of St Dorothy, in the process retaining many hagiographical remnants – a seemingly remarkable, and perhaps unique feat in post-Reformation England. However, as will be demonstrated throughout this chapter, the angel lore associated with the characters in the play is in many ways very conventional. Importantly, in his disguise as Dorothea's page, Angelo is 'euer at her tayle', offering her protection, guidance and encouragement.[16] When Dorothea is threatened with rape by one of her pagan persecutors, and cries out 'Oh guard me Angels', Angelo rushes to her aid, declaring that 'we two/ Are strong enough for such a sickly man' and Dorothea gratefully acknowledges 'that power supernal on whom waites my soule' who is captain over her chastity.[17]

In a touching letter to his new wife, prior to their emigration to New England, the physician John Winthrop consoled his wife with this notion of angelic protection:

> My deare wife be of good courage, it shall goe well with thee and us, the hairs of thy head are numbred, he who gave his onely beloved to dye for thee, will give his Angells charge over thee, therefore rayse you thy thoughts, and be merrye in the Lorde.[18]

As has been discussed, this aspect of belief was central to the reformed conception of the angel, and it also figures prominently in ecclesiastical literature. The belief might also take on more specific characteristics, becoming associated with particular actions or events. A connection with travelling and journeys evidently persisted throughout the period. John Winthorp looked to angels before his dangerous voyage to the Americas, and good angels are similarly evoked on stage at the outset of a journey, such as in Edward Sharpham's thinly veiled satire of James I's court, where Signor Petoune requires a 'whole band of Angels be centinells' on another's journey.[19] In Aphra Behn's Restoration sex comedy, *Sir Patient Fancy*, a character expresses surprise on the entrance of another, asking 'what good Angel conducted you hither?'[20] The archangel Raphael had traditionally been associated with the protection of travellers, and despite Godly objections to the belief, it had persisted in popular culture.[21] The recurrence of the connection in these sources might therefore be expected. Indeed, a late seventeenth-century ballad entitled *A Pleasant new Ballad of Tobias* recounted his journey with Raphael, where the archangel protected him from dangers, equipped him with a medical cure, and offered him advice and encouragement at their destination, securing 'joy and mirth that was not small' for everyone concerned.[22] In another ballad a maiden searches out her lost love, praying to the angels to give her good speed, and verses willing the safe arrival of Queen Mary and King William in Britain in 1688 express the hope that 'Angels too on e'ry sidc' will 'conduct' the monarchs to their rightful places on the throne.[23]

Ballads also reveal a strong patriotic strain where celestial agents were called on to protect and aid the governors of the realm, as with William and Mary during the 1680s. The rhymes ask that the 'King be daily defended/ with Angels guarded where-ever he goes', and that 'Angels preserve him that sits at the Helm/ And teaches how Rulers should Govern a Realm'.[24] The imagery that accompanies these types of ballad also reaffirms the concept that angels provided divine sanction for the monarchs. In the ballad *THE / ROYAL DIALOGUE / OR, / The Courtly Salutation / BETWEEN / King William and Queen Mary*, two angels blowing trumpets and clasping a laurel crown hover above portraits of the king and queen, and in *King WILLIAM'S Courage*, two similar angels hold St Edward's crown over a portrait of the gallant William on horseback.[25] After the recent political 'revolution' these verses could function as propaganda for the hastily installed monarchs, asserting their divinely sanctioned, and properly Protestant right to the throne. Those ballads that imagine the King and Queen's parting when William set sail for war in Flanders, also return to this notion of special angelic protection:

> QUEEN: My Prayers up to Heaven I'll constantly send
> That the blessed sweat [sic] Angels may guard and defend
> Thy dear life from the mallice of insolent foes
> Who, in Flanders, thy glory and honour oppose.[26]

Whilst William and Mary are the focus of most of these ballads, the concept of angelic protection for divinely appointed rulers was evidently an old one, which is alluded to on several occasions by Shakespeare. In *Henry V* the archbishop of Canterbury asks that 'God and his angels guard your sacred throne/ And make you long become it!', and in *Henry VIII* the midwife attending to Anne Boleyn calls on the good angels to 'Fly o'er thy royal head, and shade thy person/ Under their blessed wings'.[27] The outpouring of ballads employing the trope following the accession of William and Mary have much in common with the elegies and tributes that were published after their deaths, suggesting that the themes current in 'high' print culture might also be found in more humble publications, as well as in more popular cultural forms.[28]

Finally, it is worth noting that references to the defence and protection of angels often have a martial tenor. Unlike in material produced by clerics and theologians this was not explicitly linked to the archangel Michael, chief of the heavenly hosts, but was normally more general in tone. At the beginning of 1643 the puritan artisan Nehemiah Wallington was much concerned with the progress of the rebel 'papest', who had recently landed in the West and were seeking to 'roote out and destroy the Prodistant religion'. After some contemplation however, he drew strength from thinking of the revenge that God had taken on his enemies in the past, for 'the Lord can send an Angel as he did one night in the campe of Assure and smote an hundred foure score and five thousand '(2 Kings 19:35).[29] In Shakespeare's *Richard III*, the ghost of George Plantagenet tells the future Henry VII that 'Good angels guard thy battle!', and the duke of Buckingham's ghost warns Richard that 'God and good angels fight on Richmond's side/ And Richard fall in height of all his pride'.[30] The notion that angels would fight on the 'right' side in battle is made more explicit in Richard II, in a grand speech asserting his divine right to be king:

For every man that Bullingbrook hath pressed
To lift shrewd steel against our golden crown
Heaven for his Richard hath in heavenly pay
A glorious angel: then, if angels fight
Weak men must fall, for heaven still guards the right.[31]

Ballads also reflect this association. Queen Mary hopes that when William is in battle, angels will be engaged 'Defending the Life of my Soveraign Lord/ And Victory give to thy Conquering Sword'.[32] More strikingly, in a ballad celebrating the safe return of William from Ireland, this image is conjured up by the balladeer:

Our most Royal Prince in the midst of the fight
When Bullets from Cannons were taking their flight
Good Angels around him his Person did guard
Protecting the life of our Soveraign King.[33]

Amongst these allusions to angelic protection we can therefore see many connections with reformed belief about angels. The emphasis on angels as instruments of God's power, mercy and love underpins the interest in the protective and defensive abilities of celestial beings. Earlier belief associating angels with journeys or battles evidently lingered, but importantly these were often (although not always) rooted in solid scriptural evidence.

The Afterlife

The literature also reveals a healthy concern with angelic responsibilities around the time of death. Alongside a focus on the protective assistance offered by angels in this life, their participation in the afterlife seems to have been of equal concern to contemporaries. Angels were undoubtedly a central element in the heavenly realm envisaged by early modern people, as numerous references in ballads, pamphlets and plays attest. The dominant assumption was that after death the souls of the saved would reside with the angels in heaven, and ballads in particular are full of characters who either wistfully anticipate this post-mortem consolation, or who are assumed to be already receiving it. In *The virgin martir* Dorothy asks Angelo where his father is, and the disguised angel replies that his father is in heaven, and that if Dorothea continues in her dedication to God, then 'You and I both shall meete my father there/ And he shall bid you welcome'.[34] Examples of those hoping for angelic companionship are a clerk from West-Felton, who trusted that 'my soule shall strait ascend the skye/ Where Saints and Angells ever doe rejoyce/ Giving him praises due with heart and voice', and a virtuous maid of Paris, condemned to die for her Protestant faith, who cries:

but Oh my aged Father,
where-ever thou dost lye,

Thou know'st not thy poor daughter,
is ready for to die
but yet amongst the Angels,
in Heaven I hope to dwell
Therefore my loving Father,
I bid thee now farewel.[35]

The clerk of Bodnam, in a ballad that Tessa Watt describes as 'the archtypical ballad of personal faith'; craved on his deathbed 'a robe of Angels cloathing/ that I may still remain/ With thee in heaven where angels sing'.[36] Even more abundant are pronunciations on those who have already departed this life, and their assumed fate. A Godly maid of Leicester departed in peace 'To heaven with Angels to remain' after 'The Lord above gave her release/ from her Afflictions, Grief and Pain'.[37] It is said of a dying man whose counsel is a fit pattern for 'Old and Young, Rich and Poor, Bond and Free' that 'no doubt his soul to heaven is gone/ Where Angels sing and never cease'.[38] In one pious ballad a lamenting lady, foreseeing her own death, bids the world farewell 'Whilst Angels ring my Knell'. The accompanying illustration depicts the subsequent funeral procession, with an angel blowing a trumpet atop the Lady's hearse.[39] Indeed, the sanguine tone of these allusions bears a resemblance to the epitaphs and funeral sermons on Queen Mary and others already discussed.[40] Such optimism is perhaps misplaced however, by the distraught Laertes in *Hamlet*, when in his confrontation with the priest who refuses Ophelia the full burial rites (because of her suspected suicide) he exclaims 'I tell thee, churlish priest, A minist'ring angel shall my sister be, When thou liest howling!'.[41]

Peter Marshall has demonstrated that despite the seemingly severe implications of the reformed rejection of purgatory, funeral sermons and epitaphs were often 'remarkably optimistic in tone, and display a desire ... to accommodate the ineluctable doctrine of election to a deep-seated social impulse to think well of the dead'.[42] References to the glorious angels that will be encountered in heaven certainly support this analysis, but it is also clear that the promise of angelic companionship and the expectation that one would be like the angels after death provided a familiar but striking aspiration model, one that had clearly infiltrated more popular cultures. The counsel in a ballad offering 'Dying Christians Friendly Advice' promised that if the reader had faith in Jesus, 'he will prove your Saviour in the end/ From pains and sorrows he will set you free/ With Saints and Angels you shall happy be'. Similarly a ballad of directions for Christians thought that God would guide penitent sinners 'Where our Souls may live and ever rest/ With heavenly Angels that are blest'.[43]

Another characteristic note of the ballads are the recurring references to angelic singing in heaven. These associations can again find parallels in ecclesiastical discourse, where the singing of angels was equated with the worship of

God.[44] In the verses, people hope to 'live with Christ in perfect joy and peace/ Where Heavenly Angels sing and never cease': the clerk of West-Felton beseeches God to 'Let my Soule with heavenly Angells sing/ Most joyfully to thee my Lord and King'.[45] A pamphlet reporting strange noises heard in the air over a town in Suffolk finished by describing the 'melodius' instruments and 'harmonious' ringing of bells that ended the visitation; significantly the image used to depict these sounds was of an angelic orchestra perched on the clouds above the ear and eye witnesses.[46] In a ballad purportedly giving a 'true relation' of a green angel that appeared to punish a husband who had come home drunk and killed his wife, the angel was accompanied by 'a pleasant Melody' which 'ravisht the hearts of those stood by'.[47] On stage, angels were often accompanied by 'celestial' music, just as earlier appearances of scriptural angels in the mystery cycles had been.[48] Music was an integral part of the staging of *The virgin martir* – Samuel Pepys was so impressed with 'the wind-musique when the angel comes down' at a King's House production in 1667, that he saw the production a further two times, noting in his diary that the music was :

> so sweet that it ravished me, and indeed, in a word, did wrap up my soul so that it made me really sick, just as I have formerly been when in love with my wife; that neither then, nor all the evening going home, and at home, I was able to think of any thing, but remained all night transported, so as I could not believe that ever any musick hath that real command over the soul of a man as this did upon me: and makes me resolve to practice wind-musique, and to make my wife do the like.[49]

The entry is a startling reminder of the power of music and dramatic performance to provoke emotion and to stir the soul. Incidentally, the entry also offers an rare insight into the staging of Restoration drama, Pepys indicating that the actor playing the angel was involved in a rope and pulley descent, and that music was integral to the performance.

The assumption that angels were the stewards of the soul after death is also a strong theme, summed up neatly by Horatio's familiar parting words to Hamlet: 'Goodnight sweet prince, And flights of angels sing thee to thy rest!'.[50] Other characters on stage harboured similar expectations: following the Lady Jantil's death in Margaret Cavendish's *Bell in Campo II*, the chorus sing 'O you Gods pure Angels send her/ Here about her to attend her/ Let them wait and here condoul/ Til receive her spotless Soul', and Walter Montagu's pastoral comedy *The Shepherd's Paradise* finds Moramente speculating that Bellesa's soul 'is gon to visit heaven, and did salute the Angels with a song'.[51] In *The virgin martir* at the moment of Dorothea's beheading, Angelo reveals his true angelic nature to the heroine, and declares that 'I am sent to carry/ Your pure and innocent soule to ioyes eternall'. A stage direction '*Loud Musicke, exit Angelo leauing first laid his hand vp. on their mouthes*' indicates exactly how this could have been represented on stage.[52] In a less serious context, Pepys related a 'good story' told by a dinner companion, of Mr. Newman, a New England minister who preached a funeral sermon foretelling his own death. At the sermon's conclusion, Newman 'did at last bid the angels do their office, and died'.[53]

The consoling message underpinning these references comes across very strongly in those ballads relating to the deaths of pious children. After reassuring her mother that her coming death will be a release from 'sorrow, trouble, care and strife', a 'pious daughter' sees angels all around her deathbed, 'sweet Messengers that waits [*sic*] for me, Who on their Wings will me convey, Where peace and joys will ner decay'. A rare post-Reformation illustration of angels surrounding the girl's deathbed accompanies the verse.[54] The young girl speaks of the comfort that she draws from this vision, 'knowing they my soul will bring, Into the presence of the Lord, where blessed Saints and Angels Si[ng;]'.[55]

The ballad is designed to both give spiritual encouragement to parents, as well as devotional instruction for children, and indicates the widespread belief that God appointed angels to take special care of the young.[56] In a similar vein, a ballad that encourages parents to buy it for the sake of their children, begins by telling of the immaculate piety of a young girl, who spent all of her spare time in 'fervent prayer' and spoke like an angel.[57] She also admonished her fellow children for blaspheming, not respecting their elders, and failing to heed the teachings of the church. Later the girl is greeted by a 'shining Angel' that 'took her by the Hand' and comforted her, telling her that 'in Heaven for you there is a Throne'. This ballad again unusually includes an image of the angel itself, looking severe and gesturing heavenwards. Upon the occasion of her death, a month later, the heavenly angel appeared to her again to take her soul to heaven, to the accompaniment of 'a charming Sound', similar to the 'sweet music' heard in the air at the girl's funeral.

Ballads also include the concept of angelic stewardship after death: the clerk of Bodham was sure that while he lay in his grave 'sleeping', 'Angels have my soule in keeping', and the wronged Lady of another ballad finds that her joys increase and her griefs decay 'For I see the bright Angels which soon will convey, My poor injur'd Soul to the Mansions of Joy'.[58] The association gains its most poignant expression when Balthasar informs Romeo of Juliet's (supposed) death: 'Her body sleeps in Capel's monument, And her immortal part with angels lives'.[59]

The expectation that angels would carry souls to heaven after death permeates both ecclesiastical and more popular writing, and has a firm scriptural precedent in the story of Dives and Lazarus.[60] Notions of angels protecting souls after they have left their 'useless' earthly body behind fit in well with a theological outlook which envisaged the reconciliation of body and soul at the Resurrection – in the meantime, the angels could tend to these 'sleeping' souls.[61] The role that angels would play at the Last Judgement was not forgotten though – one ballad recalls the angelic role of sounding the trumpet so that 'the dead shall heare their voyces/ as they lye in the ground'.[62] The responsibilities that angels were expected to assume are explored in detail in a ballad *The Great TRIBUNAL*, 'a contemplative Description of Resurrection'.[63] The ballad foretells that the angels will be sent out 'To reap and gather in his [God's] Winter-store' of saints, before they sound the trumpet and the dead rise from their graves. Then, the righteous 'By Angels shall be carefully conveyd, From Grace to Glory, for their Peace is made', and they will be ushered through celestial gates by their new companions. Whereas the pen of a cleric can perhaps be detected in the production of this particular ballad, a more personal recollection is provided by the antiquarian Ralph Thoresby. In his visit to the parish church of St John the Baptist, in Knaresborough, Thoresby took the inscriptions of the monuments of the Slingsbys, and was 'much pleased with the serious humour of one, where, above all, stood an angel, with a trumpet, calling *Venite ad judicium*'.[64]

The sources also reveal a continuing association of angels with those suffering a violent death at the hands of others. This was a strain of angelic belief that was strong in both late medieval lives of the saints, and in the martyrologies and pamphlets reporting on executions in the post-Reformation period.[65] Angels are called on to assert the legitimacy of a person's cause or to indicate their innocence, albeit with carrying degrees of success. Some ballads pronounce on the assumed destination of the souls of the departed, using the association as a short hand for the spotlessness of their character. A ballad on the death of the Duke of Grafton in the siege of Cork in 1690 stated that 'In a Religious Cause it was he fell/ Thereof we hope his Loyal Soul will dwell/ Amongst blest Saints and Angels'.[66] For the author of an anti-Catholic verse on the 'barbarous, Execrable, and Bloody Murder of the Earl of Essex', Arthur Capel, there is no question about the ultimate destiny of the duke's soul:

> in Heaven 'tis mounted most high
> Out of the Danger of Rome's Treachery:
> Attended by Angels and Spiritual Charms,
> In Glory and Splendour, free from al Harms.[67]

Angels can also be found at the gallows, protecting those wrongly accused of crimes and bringing the guilty to justice. In a 1605 pamphlet a young man, John Johnson, was falsely accused of theft and sentenced to hang. At the place of execution Johnson behaved immaculately, repenting his sinful life, trusting to be saved through Christ, and hoping for a miracle – not to preserve his life, but to prove his innocence after he was gone. Astoundingly, when his uncle came to the gallows five days later, Johnson was still alive, and he related that an angel of the Lord had placed a stool under his feet, and kept him alive by feeding him in the intervening time.[68] An accompanying image depicts both the stool and the angel attending to Johnson. In a 1651 pamphlet, the servant Anne Green was just as lucky, when she was wrongly hung for murdering her newly born baby. Like Johnson, at the gallows Green hoped for a miracle that would reveal her innocence. After hanging for half an hour, she was removed to the physician's rooms for dissection, but she stirred and began to breath again. She subsequently related that whilst in her trance she had seen a garden of paradise, with 'four little boys with wings, being four angels, saying, Woe unto them that decree unrighteous Decrees ... that the innocent may be their prey'.[69] In *The virgin martir*, Angelo's intervention to protect Dorothea from the effects of the brutal tortures of her captors is unseen by any, and his final appearance in angelic guise at her martyrdom the angel is invisible to all except Dorothea, recalling to mind the intervention of the stool-bearing angel in the John Johnson pamphlet.[70]

Here, the presence of angels serves as a declaration of the innocence of the people involved, and represents God's mercy in action. There is also an underlying political message in the ballads in their encouragement to the keepers of the law to ensure that justice is done. Other protagonists were not so successful in appropriating the cultural power of a belief in angels to their cause. In 1693, the ordinary of Newgate was very troubled by the behaviour of midwife Mary Compton prior to her execution for starving four infants to death. Although he spent a considerable time with her, endeavouring to make her sensible of the 'horrid and barbarous' crimes she had committed, Compton would admit only to being a great sinner, but not to the murders themselves. On the morning of her execution, she claimed that she had made her peace to God and that she was assured of her salvation, because the night before 'an Angel appeared to her and told her she should be saved'. Although Compton was drawing on a long tradition of angelic appearances to prisoners, rooted in a scriptural passage,[71] her behaviour failed to impress the Ordinary or the crowds at her execution. She was said to have 'demeaned herself very stubbornly', because she 'did not hearken to Exhortation as it was hoped', and generally seemed but little affected. With her last breath she denied her accusers, 'to the amazement of those who heard her presume of Gods mercy upon so slight grounds'.[72]

Other examples are more ambiguous. Another victim who failed to successfully overturn the judgement of the authorities was the Franciscan Friar John Forest. In May 1538, the herald Charles Wriothesley wrote in his diary that he had attended the Friar's execution at Smithfield after he was sentenced to death for claiming that Henry VIII was not the Supreme Head of the Church. Despite the best efforts of Bishop Latimer, Forest remained unrepentant to the end, 'obstinatlie standing still and stiffe in his opinions'. When asked by Latimer in what state he would die, Forest declared in a loud voice:

that if an angell should come downe from heaven and shew him any other thing then
that he had beeleved all his life tyme past he would not believe him, and that if his
bodie should be cutt joynt or membre after membre, brent, hanged, or what paine
soever might de donne to his bodie, he wold neaver turne from his old Sect of this
Bishopp of Rome.

Wriothsesley is not impressed by the Friar's steadfastness, describing him vari-
ously as obstinate, forward, and malicious. As far as the diarist is concerned,
Forest death was fitting for such a 'false traitor to his Praynce, an hereticke, and
a seditious person to the Kinges leighe people'.[73]

However, Wriothsesley's hostility to Forest should not blind us to the power
of the Friar's gallows performance and the authority to be drawn by invoking this
scriptural passage.[74] The friar's defiant speech is not mentioned in the account
of Forest's burning included in Foxe's *Actes and Monuments*, and Peter Marshall
has suggested that the crown's repressive policy backfired on this occasion, failing to produce the propaganda triumph the authorities had been anticipating.[75]
A similar phrase appears in Shakespeare's *King John*, in a scene where Hubert
is sent by King John to execute Arthur, the rightful heir to the throne. Hubert
and Arthur have become friends, and Arthur is horrified at the turn of events,
exclaiming that 'if an angel should have come to me/ And told me Hubert
should put out mine eyes/ I would not have believed him'.[76] This suggests not
only that the audience was expected to recognize the scriptural reference, but
also, that, in this instance, they are clearly meant to sympathize with the young,
and quite innocent Arthur. Alexandra Walsham has demonstrated that despite
a general, ingrained reluctance on the part of reformers to endorse the validity
of appearances of angels, there were moments when 'a more upbeat assessment'
triumphed, and visible instances of angelic intervention could be recognized. A
complicated mix of social, cultural, and political factors could come together
to make an apparition credible – although these instances were relatively rare –
but the character and comportment of the witness was always crucial.[77] As these
examples illustrate, where the message coincided with theological and moral priorities angelic apparitions were most likely to be credible.

Godly Angels

The one category of angelic appearances that reformers were more likely to
wholeheartedly endorse was those based on scriptural passages. There are many
ballads that simply translated scriptural events into verse – we have already seen
one based on the apocalyptic vision found in Revelation.[78] References to angels
are also plentiful in ballads that dealt with the Annunciation to Mary and the
later angelic appearance to Joseph,[79] the nativity and the angels' appearance to
the shepherds,[80] and in ballads retelling the story of Christ's resurrection.[81] In

some cases these stories also enforced some of the themes already discussed: a ballad summing up the details of the birth, life, suffering and resurrection of Christ described the 'Songs of Praise' harmonized by the angels and saints in heaven at the nativity, as well as how Christ was 'taken up by Angels bright/ To Heavenly joys at the Ascension.[82] Interestingly, these ballads are also the most likely context in which to find images of angels. In ballads on the Annunciation, angels hover around an image of the Virgin Mary, and in carols and verses dealing with the nativity of Christ, angels are often depicted in the stable or relating the good news to the shepherds, emphasizing positive aspects of the angelic ministry.[83]

The fact that some of these ballads seem to have been penned by clerics would suggest that moralizing ballads set to popular tunes were once again bringing scriptural material into everyday life. Patrick Collinson has noted the popularity of these types of 'Godly ballads' in the context of the 1560s, as well as their decline, when reformed attitudes towards popular media such as the theatre and music hardened in the 1580s and 1590s. By the latter part of the seventeenth century it seems that these types of tunes were once again in vogue, or at least, that ecclesiastics were again comfortable using the medium to disseminate a religious message.[84]

The diffusion of scriptural material was more widespread than Godly ballads however. We have already encountered many allusions to belief that has its roots in passages in the Bible, examples of how scriptural material could become embedded in more popular religious cultures. Certain characteristic beliefs about angels seemed to have gained a wider currency by these means. An example would be the notion of vengeful angels. Recalling the smiting angel that Nehemiah Wallington meditated on in a time of military uncertainty, the purported posthumous spiritual autobiography of Charles I magnanimously beseeched God to sprinkle the polluted souls of his persecutors with the blood of his son, 'that thy destroying Angel may passe over them'.[85] A pamphlet of 1648 described how a man had seen a 'terrible apparition' of an angel 'brandishing a bloodied sword over his head', which was interpreted as a warning that the man, and the nearby town should mend their sinful ways, similarly an angel with a sword of fire was seen in the air above Flanders in 1598.[86]

The fall of the angels also seems to have been a common concept during the period. Ballads attest that the angels fell for the sin of pride, and that legions of angels were expelled from heaven after Satan's rebellion.[87] On stage, a character in Thomas D'Ufrey's tragedy *The Rise and Fall of Massaniello* opined that it was ambition that made angels once rebel 'And from Celestial Throne, sink down to Hell', and Shakespeare's *Henry VIII*, Wolsey commands Thomas Cromwell to 'fling away ambition/ By that sin fell the angels'.[88] In Marlowe's *Doctor Faustus*, Mephistophilis admits that it was for his 'aspiring pride and insolence' that God threw him from the face of Heaven. In Sir George Etherage's comedy *The Man of Mode*, one of the characters 'has a Tongue they say would tempt the/ Angels to a second fall'.[89] Other allusions imply a more detailed knowledge of scriptural angelology: a Godly ballad on the shepherds in scripture notes that 'Jacob gaind the Cherubim/ When the Angel was orecome by him', and 'Charles I' speaks out against the scandalous pamphlets against the king, that 'contrary to the precept of God, and precedent of Angels *speake evill of dignities, and bring railing accusations*'.[90]

Many of the sources also reveal an underlying anxiety about the true nature of angels that exposes a thoroughly Protestant preoccupation with the discernment of spirits. References to angels in association with disguising, mistaking, or 'seeming' are commonplace, and it was clear that this was an element of reformed thought that had widespread currency at the time. An entry in Nehemiah Wallington's diary gets to the heart of the issue:

> The Sabbath day before Ester, 1619 ... Being melancholy I then said that the Divell can com in any likenesse he can com in the liknesse of my showes [shoes], and then I flong away my showes[.] Then I said the Divell can come in the liknes of an Angel of light or in the liknes of Master Robroh: whith that Master Robro oppened the parlor doore. He held my arms because I began to be unruly and told him he was a devil.[91]

Despite the unintentional humour in the entry, Wallington was grappling with the very serious problem that the devil could take a pleasing or familiar shape in order to work his evil. In *Julius Caesar* Brutus confronts the quandary when he sees a vision of a ghost:

> I think it is the weakness of mine eyes
> That shapes this monstrous apparition.
> It comes upon me. Art thou any thing?
> Art thou some god, some angel, or some devil,
> That mak'st my blood cold and my hair to stare?[92]

And this is also the dilemma that lies at the heart of Hamlet's tragedy – the plot pivots on the prince's discernment of the apparition in his father's shape:

> Be thou a spirit of health or goblin damn'd,
> Bring with thee airs from heaven or blasts from hell,
> Be thy intents wicked or charitable,
> Thou comest in such a questionable shape.[93]

Anxieties over angels are not always referred to in such a direct fashion, but they can be detected on many occasions. Good and evil angel are often mentioned in the same breath, suggesting the apprehension and uncertainty that angels provoked, and their proximity in people's minds. On finding out that Romeo has slain Tybalt, Juliet cries 'Beautiful tyrant, Fiend angelical!', and in *Cymbeline*, after Iago first meets Imogen he muses 'though this is a heavenly angel, hell is here'.[94] In *Henry VIII* Queen Katharine is probably justified in telling Wolsey and his attendants that 'Ye have angels' faces, but heaven knows your hearts', and in Margaret Cavendish's *Matrimonial Trouble*, Sir Henry Sage fervently wishes that a character of 'angelical' disposition will not fall from virtue into vice.[95] In *Eikon basilike*, Charles I gloomily mused that 'the Devill of Rebellion, doth commonly turn himself into an Angell of Reformation, and the old Serpent can pretend new Lights', and a 1676 pamphlet is predicated on a similar basis.[96] The pamphlet related the tale of two monks who try to trick a Lutheran shepherd into converting to Catholicism by disguising themselves as two angels. One was 'very gay and beautiful, with a brave pair of wings', the other like a devil. First, the good angel tried to convince the shepherd to embrace Rome with 'fair words and insinuations', but the shepherd resisted, 'possibly remembering that Text, If an Angel from heaven should teach you any other doctrine than what you have received, let him be accursed'. Next, the Devil-monk came up, with 'dreadful noise' to scare him into a conversion. Unfortunately for him, the shepherd's dog attacked him, and he took a fatal blow to the head from his crook. The shepherd swiftly buried the body.[97] The pamphlet ends by expressing the hope that the tale will be a caution to the credulous.

In *The virgin martir* it is impossible not to notice the preoccupation with deceit and disguising that pervades the action. The characters of the good and evil angels remain in disguise for the majority of the drama, and more than one character is tricked into sin by the disguised demon Harpax. Characters repeatedly make references that raise the possibility of deception. Dorothea remarks that Angelo bewitches her with his presence, whereas to Dorothea's persecutors, she is the one engaged in deception – the miraculous preservation of her body during her torture is confirmation that she is a witch, whilst the heavenly instruments that accompany her martyrdom are 'Illusions of the Diuell'. When Theophilus' two daughters try to convert Dorothea to paganism they say that they come as 'good Angels', but the heroine rebuts their claim, exclaiming 'Haue you not clouen feete, are you not diuels?'[98] As with other common expectations about angels, nervousness over discernment, and an ever present uneasiness over the true nature of spirits, made them a natural cultural resource to turn to when penning dramatic texts.

Given that *The virgin martir* contains many startling similarities to the legend of Saint Dorothy, the reformed resonances in the play may help to explain why it was passed by the censor. A hatred of idolatry, and a preference for alms are the most prominent characteristics of Dorothea's piety throughout the play. On several occasions Dorothea denounces the idol worship of her contemporaries, and there is an on stage incident of iconoclasm after the conversion of Theophilus' two daughters, when they 'spit and spurn' at a statue of Jupiter. Alms giving to the poor is an important element of the plot, as well as an indicator of Dorothea's impeccable character.[99] We have also already seen that although Angelo is a guardian angel, he is keen to emphasize that it is by 'God's command' that he has been sent, and the correct angel-lore elsewhere in the play enforces the 'orthodox' character of the angelology. More generally, Angelo's care of Dorothea while she is in prison, and the prototypes of scriptural figures that appear in the text also lend the play a scriptural flavour. The persecuting Theophilus' conversion to Christianity and subsequent martyrdom strongly recall St Paul, and two of Dorothea's servants, who betray her to the governor, are proto-type Judas characters, berated by Angelo for 'Like slaues you sold your soules for golden drosse'.[100]

There is also a broader sense in which *The virgin martir* is attuned to the zeitgeist of early modern England. As Jane Degenhardt has argued, Foxe's *Actes and Monuments* had already provided an extremely popular contextual framework for reading Christian martyrdom in Reformation terms.[101] Indeed, Foxe includes St Dorothy in his immense work, in a list of those that suffered in the tenth and last persecution of the early church.[102] The play should also be considered in a context where there was a long standing, and ongoing anxiety about the question of religious conversion, one which only became increasingly pressing as the decades wore one. The numerous conversions to and from Christianity in *The virgin martir* undoubtedly connected to the contemporary fixation on the ever present seductions of Catholicism and the threat of a national reversion to Catholicism.

Concerns about disguising were thoroughly rooted in a reformed theology that was solely reliant on scripture as a source of authority, and a culture that insisted miracles were extremely rare in the latter days of the church. In combination with the rejection of purgatory, intense anxiety over idolatry, and reformed Protestantism's profound distrust of the eye as a means of divine communication, clergymen argued that visual manifestations of good angels were not what they seemed, and in most cases they were discerned to be the result of demonic delusion.[103] The anxieties and uncertainty that this fostered manifested in broader popular cultures, bringing a reformed preoccupation into a more public arena.

Guardian Angels

In the discussion up to this point, it has been possible to detect many similarities between the belief about angels found in these sources and Protestant angelology. There is little that the reformers would have been likely to object to, and in fact many central Protestant concerns are also to be found in more personal, and non-ecclesiastical sources. However, it also seems that at a more popular level, as might be expected, angelology did not mirror the contours of ecclesiastical theology exactly – belief about angels was absorbed into popular culture in a way that emphasized *some* of the important reforming messages, making use of those aspects that resonated and that made sense within this new context. That is not to say that the reception of reformed angelology was unorthodox, but to acknowledge that religious change was a two way process, in which people remoulded and shifted the conceptual emphasis of the ideas that were presented to them by the Church. In a similar way, lay people were not merely blank slates to be written on by the reformers – older beliefs, expectations and assumptions all contributed to the construction of religious identities at the time. The remainder of this chapter will examine two areas of belief where more popular perceptions appear to have parted company from the 'official' or 'orthodox' conception of angels, seeking to uncover what the significance of these differences might be.

The first area of divergence relates to belief about guardian angels, an aspect of angelology that Calvin and reformed Protestants tended to frown upon.[104] Nevertheless, there is much to suggest that the idea that each person had a special, designated angel watching over them retained its appeal. The characters of Angelo and Harpax in *The virgin martir* testify to the belief, and it is apparent from numerous references in the play that Angelo is Dorothea's particular guardian. Dorothea herself notes that the angel's 'curious eye … euer waites upon my business', and later remarks that 'He must not leaue me, without him I fall'. After he has unmasked himself, Angelo tells Dorothea that 'Your zealous prayers and pious deeds first wonne me/ (But 'twas by his command to whom you sent 'em)/ To guide your steps'.[105] In *Othello*, it is said of Desdemona's father that he would 'curse his better angel from his side/ And fall to reprobance', had he been alive to see his daughter's fate, and many later plays contain similar references to 'my' or 'his' better angel.[106] Characters are comforted by their angel, such as in John Dryden's *Amboyna*, when a character smiles 'as if his Guardian Angel in a dream, told him, he was secure'.[107] On other occasions personal angels are called upon to offer assistance in times of need: in D'Urfey's *Rise and Fall of Massaniello* a character calls on the 'dear Figure of my blessed Angel, that still defends my Life against all Danger' to drag his enemies to their deaths, and in the comedy *The Beaux' Stratagem*, a guardian angel is thanked for guiding its ward successfully.[108] There is also a tendency to use the concept as a metaphor, as when people are referred to as another's guardian: in *Julius Caesar* Anthony is dumbfounded on discovering Brutus' role in Caesar's assassination, remarking in disbelief that 'Brutus, as you know, was Caesar's angel', while a character called Benedick in another D'Urfey comedy remarked that 'Beautiful women were ever my Tutelar and Guardian Angels, that give me an assurance of being ever happy in this world, and immortal in t'other'.[109]

The medieval notion that a person had an *evil* designated angel, seeking to tempt a person into sin, was also a common concept. In *Henry IV, Part II*, Falstaff is confronted by the Lord Chief Justice, who tells him that 'You follow the young prince up and down, like an his evil angel', and a character in an Aphra Behn play remarks dryly to another that 'I had rather have incounter'd my evil Angel than thee'.[110] Perhaps the most famous example of the notion of a person being accompanied throughout life by a pair of angels – one good, one evil – is to be found in Marlowe's *Doctor Faustus*. In the play, a good and evil angel materialise at various junctures to assist or tempt him. The good angel tries to persuade Faustus to lay his magic books aside, 'lest it tempt thy soul' and he encourages Faustus to read the scriptures and exercise contrition, prayer and repentance instead. In contrast, the evil angel encourages Faustus to pursue 'that famous art' whereby he might be made 'Lord and commander' of all the elements, and he inveighs him with thoughts of honour and wealth.[111] There are parallels here with a lengthy and involved account of a possession case in a 1647 publication, where young Margaret Muschamp experiences visits from both good and evil spirits over an extended period.[112] Although Margaret first encounters 'two blessed spirits', she was also sorely tormented by evil spirits: 'behold her two Angels (as she was bold to call them) on her right hand, and her Tormentors on her left'. Margaret is said to be the victim of witchcraft, but throughout her ordeal her good angels would always banish the evil demons that appeared to her.[113]

It is notable that in the sample of ballads examined for this chapter, there is not a single comparable reference to 'my' angel, either good or ill. This is a notable contrast to drama, as well as early dictionaries, where references to guardians, and good and evil angels proliferate. Thomas Thomas' Latin dictionary included a translation of 'Dæmŏnĭum ... an Angell or good spirit'; 'Mānes ... The spirites, soules, and ghostes of the dead: the good and bad angell'; and 'Gĕnĭus ... The good or euil Aungel that painims thought to be appointed to each man, to guide and defend, or to punish them'.[114] These are references to the classical pagan belief in a tutelary god or spirit, allotted to every person at his birth, to govern his fortunes and determine his character. Many other dictionaries also included definitions or translations of 'genius', most affirming that this was 'the angel that waits on a man, be it a good or euill angell'.[115]

Most usually these references are included in language dictionaries, exactly the type of teaching aid that you might expect to be used during a young man's school days. This is a reminder that sermons and theological writings were not the only source of information about spirits. If England was not undergoing an educational 'revolution' during this period, it is still generally agreed that there was a marked expansion in educational facilities as the universities grew and grammar schools proliferated.[116] A strong emphasis on languages, and in particular Latin, might therefore account for the prominence of a concept that was openly disapproved of by many of the ecclesiastical hierarchy – although it should also be noted that the condemnation of guardian angels was by no means universal, even within the Church of England.[117] Grammar-educated Elizabethan playwrights, and classically trained Restoration dramatists evidently came across the classical concept of the 'Genius' during their schooling, and many found the artistic merits of the notion too valuable to resist. Direct references to 'Thy demon ... thy spirit which keeps thee' and 'my good angel, or my Genius' in Shakespeare and Behn's plays would certainly support such an interpretation.[118]

However, it would be specious to suggest that authors of ballads did not also share this educational heritage, so although a classical education might explain the presence of the notion of a guardian or tutelary angel in these theatrical sources, it does not clarify why the concept should be absent from balladry. It would be tempting to think that balladeers thought it best not to wade into the murky theology surrounding the vexed question of guardian angels in printed material such as shorter pamphlets and ballads, because this was aimed at the least literate, and perhaps most impressionable members of the laity, but this would at best be an educated guess.

Human Angels

A second, very prominent characteristic of non-ecclesiastical angelology are the countless occasions on which people are compared to angels in these sources. This type of analogy was persistently applied to both living men and women. Collectively women are referred to as 'Angelical', 'Angell Creatures ... come from Heaven', or 'starres to looke on/ Angells to heare'.[119] However, it is comparisons to individuals that are most striking by virtue of their ubiquity. Romeo's speech beneath Juliet's balcony is a fitting example:

> O speak again, bright angel! For thou art
> As glorious to this night, being o'er my head
> As is a winged messenger of heaven
> Unto the white-upturned wondering eyes
> Of mortals that fall back to gaze on him
> When he bestrides the lazy-pacing clouds
> And sails upon the bosom of the air.[120]

Generally analogies between women and angels are less poetic than Shakespeare's splendid imagery. They are used as shorthand for the flawless reputation of characters and protagonists. In *The Spanish Bawd*, a female character is described as 'but a dissembled Angell, that lives heere amongst us', on other occasions women are said to be 'of an Angelical nature, and not corruptible', 'like an Angel, and almost Divine', or 'as chaste as angels are'.[121] Comparisons to angels are also commonly used to indicate a character's attractiveness. Distraught lovers in ballads lament that 'When first I did thy Beauty see/ O then thou didst appear to be/ an Angel in my Eye', or that their love 'like an Angel doth appear'.[122] An English women is punished for her sinful pride when 'My beauty made me think/ my self an Angel bright/ Framed of heavenly mold/ and not an earthly wight', whilst another recollects that when she first met her love, 'He call'd me Angel, Saint and he/ Did sware for ever true to be'.[123] Women not only look like angels though, they speak like them,[124] sing like them,[125] and woo like them.[126] The analogy even finds its way into the mildly pornographic ballad '*The Swimming Lady ... Being a true Relation of a gay Lady as she was stripping her / self stark naked, and Swimming in a River near Oxford*, when 'The Fishes from all quarters crept/ to see what Angel 'twas'/ She did so like a Vision look/ or fancy in a Dream'.[127]

Although it is less common, there are also instances of comparisons being made between men and angels. In *Henry IV, Part I*, an admirer of young prince Harry's horsemanship remarks that he 'vaulted with such ease into his seat/ As if an angel dropped down from the clouds', and after Belarius and his sons make a heroic stand on the battlefield in *Cymbeline*, a fellow soldier admits that 'Tis thought the old man and his sons were angels'.[128] In a ballad relating the story of an adventurous young apprentice, the people he meets on his travels are so impressed by his character that they think him 'some Angel, sent down from Heaven above', although the apprentice is quick to disabuse them of their error, saying that he is no angel, although he is 'born in famous England/ where Gods word is obeyd'.[129] In other instances, the underlying anxiety about the true nature of those that 'seem' like angels can again be detected: in cautionary ballads about deceitful young men, jilted lovers recall that 'he did appear to me/ An Angel, that does shine so bright', or that 'When he about me clung/ You would think that an Angel sung/ So musical was his Tongue'.[130]

The abundance of these types of comparison in literary sources is a reminder of how ubiquitous the concept of angels was in English cultural life. They also reveal a characteristic belief about angels that has a more secular flavour than those which have been the main focus of this study. Angels were closely associated with both the joys and vagaries of love: the evidence examined here suggests that comparisons to angels borders on cliché, a shorthand for strong emotions, for beauty, or passionate feeling. Given that these sources are mainly literary, it is likely that they have exaggerated the prominence of angels in matters of love, because this is so often the central concern of ballads and plays, as it is to this day. In doing so it may also have drawn undue attention to comparisons between humans and angels - I would not go so far as to say that anthropology was the framing characteristic of Protestant angelology,[131] though clearly the relationship between men and angels was an important concern for these authors. It speaks to a wider interest in the relationship between humankind and angels that was natural in a medium that seeks to explore and understand personal psychology and the human condition. On occasion direct reference is made to this interest. In *Henry VIII* the Chancellor reminds another character that 'we are all men/ In our own natures frail, and capable/ Of our flesh; few are angels', and Hamlet's tortured exclamation: 'What a piece of work is a man! ... in action how like an angel!' indicates the power of the concept.[132] At the outset of this chapter it was noted that generally the dominant concern of personal accounts and more 'popular' literature were with the practical aspects of the angelic ministry, rather than more abstract musings on angels as models of social order or godly comportment. This final theme has however indicated that beyond their theological significance, angels could be a means of exploring aspects of life that were closer to everyday experience, and more abstract than some of the other dominant concerns.

Summary

Beyond official religious teachings, an angel was an important conceptual and cultural 'space', and people harboured a range of expectations concerning angelic characteristics and responsibilities. These expectations chimed with reformed teaching on angels, although it might also be argued that there was nothing particularly 'reformed' about the attitudes expressed in these sources, beyond the ever present anxiety over the true nature of angelic apparitions. Nevertheless, it would be a mistake to ignore the ubiquity of angels in these sources, which is indicative of the significant place they occupied in the early modern mindset. Angels were not only a significant feature of reformed theology, they were also a pervasive presence in broader early modern cultures.

In many ways, this survey can help to flesh out the findings of Alexandra Walsham, who has examined the meanings attached to appearances of early modern angels in England.[133] Walsham finds evidence that many stories of angelic apparition were altered by the educated pastors who recorded them, but she argues that this should not blind us to the extent to which 'Reformed priorities are often interwoven into the very fibre' of the narratives she has examined. The evidence discussed here supplements these findings in several ways. Reformed sensibilities can be detected in those ballads that mention the scriptural appearances of angels, but also in the anxieties over evil angels disguised as angels of light, and in the very correct scriptural material that underpins the angel lore on stage and in print. General assumptions about the divine protection offered by angels, and their responsibilities at the time of death may represent continuities with traditional belief, but these are nonetheless areas that clerical reformers were equally invested in, and eager to promote. On numerous occasions protagonists in ballads and plays call for the *assistance* of angels, but never is there the slightest suggestion that these prayers are directed at the angels themselves. The evidence found here also tempers the providential emphasis that dominates Walsham's narratives, and proffers what might be seen as a more 'positive' perception of angels – the emphasis is on the heavenly companionship and the guardianship of angels, rather than on their roles as divine messengers and punishers (although this is also encountered on occasion).

Finally, this survey has emphasized the importance of angels as a cultural resource, flexible enough to be drawn upon in a large variety of contexts. This could lead to emphasis that was out of sync with the official angelology of the Church of England, though it is a central premise of this study that this official angelology itself was constantly evolving, so this should not merely be interpreted as an example of failed Reformation. The cultural pervasiveness of angels did not diminish throughout the period, and it resonated with both religious and broader cultural developments. The comparison of angels to women is a trend that can also be traced in Renaissance art, where, without any apparent theological adjustments, angels are no longer depicted as masculine or gender neutral as they were in the medieval period, but instead as beautiful, feminine figures.[134] This is the visual inheritance that has dominated to this day. To return to the issue of why guardian angels were mentioned so often on stage, this could plausibly be linked to wider processes whereby angels were becoming more important as a means to explore human experience in greater depth. A central feature of both pre- and post-Reformation angelology had been a preoccupation with the fellowship offered by angels to women and men, reflecting a hope of achieving greater insight into the human condition. The evidence suggests that this aspect of belief was increasingly coming to the fore, as belief about angels was employed to explore and express love, beauty, and the nature of man, often to startling effect.

7 THE EMPIRICAL ANGEL, *c.* 1650–1700

At the end of the seventeenth century, changes in 'natural philosophy' ostensibly represented the biggest menace to angelology since the Reformation. The development of experimental science and the application of reason to theology threatened to undermine the fundamentals of belief in angels and raised questions about their very existence. However, contemporary evidence does not support a paradigm whereby the educated gradually lost their faith in these supernatural creatures because their belief was eroded and destabilized by broader intellectual developments. Similarly, the continuing importance of angels in eighteenth-century England gives the lie to any idea of the earlier collapse of belief, and casts doubt on Max Weber's notion that the 'disenchantment of the world' occurred at this juncture.[1] Historians no longer accept that the Reformation provided the impetus for a process of secularization and the elimination of magic and superstition from human action and behaviour.

This chapter will investigate the broad intellectual trends in natural and mechanical philosophy, placing them in the context of other writings and works relating to angels that took a more 'traditional' approach to the topic. Section one will outline the implications of the new thinking, seeking to uncover what kind of challenge was presented to belief about angels by the growing emphasis (in certain circles) on reason and experiment as a means to ascertain truth. It will try to unpick the reaction to this challenge amongst contemporaries, documenting how mechanical philosophy initially, and perhaps unsurprisingly, did not immediately demolish people's faith in the existence and usefulness of angels. On the contrary, controversial new theories reignited age-old debates on the nature and substance of angels as authors attempted to counter more radical claims and assert the existence of celestial beings.

The second section will place these intellectual concerns in a broader context, recognizing that the attitudes of the elite members of society may not have been reflected in the country at large. It will investigate how mechanical philosophy provoked great anxiety, particularly amongst the clergy, some of whom believed that the new thinking would encourage people to scepticism or even atheism. Debating and questioning the existence of spirits was seen in some quarters to lead naturally to the denial of the existence of God himself. More specifically, questioning the existence of angels left one open to the charge of Sadduceeism, an abusive term originating in the New Testament, whose proponents were believed to deny the resurrection and the immortality of the soul. In reaction to these concerns, clergymen put pen to paper in defence of the existence of angels, some citing their fears about the increasing irreligion of the nation as the motivation behind their work. Several authors went as far as to collect and record apparitions and evidence of angelic activity in the world, building up compilations that were supposed to demonstrate the existence of spirits and counter the claims of the philosophers. There is no doubt that in the longer term, the questions raised by the intellectual developments in this period were to prove detrimental to belief about angels, but at the end of the seventeenth century these future processes were by no means predetermined.

Angels and the 'New Thinking'

The intellectual developments of the sixteenth and seventeenth centuries are popularly summed up in the phrase the 'Scientific Revolution', and are conceived as a fundamental transformation in the natural sciences that both established the foundations of modern science and issued a fundamental challenge to Church dogma and authority.[2] Historians now question the accuracy of describing these developments as a 'revolution' and recognize the danger of projecting a modern understanding of science onto the early modern period, although the significance of intellectual activity during the period is not necessarily diminished by these advances in the historiography. However, a more nuanced picture has emerged that rejects a simplistic and teleological understanding of developments in the period.[3] Scholars recognize that the series of developments and shifts in European thought, the new emphasis on experimental science, and the evolution of mechanical philosophy were not always antagonistic to established religion, and furthermore that orthodox Christians themselves were often the exponents of the 'new thinking'. As Margaret Osler has argued, theology remained a 'central concern to seventeenth-century thinkers, and any proposal to provide new metaphysical foundations for science had to be shown to be theologically acceptable'.[4] This section will investigate the implications and impact of the evolution of natural philosophy in light of this recent scholarship, illustrating that these developments had the capacity both to hinder and stimulate debate and conviction relating to belief about angels.

A strong association of angels with 'scientific' modes of thought was commonplace in early modern England, due to their assumed roles in the government of the spheres. In astrological and occult circles it was widely believed that angels assisted in ordering the universe, and that it might be possible for practitioners to channel these angelic powers. The translation and publication of the German occult writer Henry Cornelius Agrippa's Three books of occult philosophy in 1650 undoubtedly sustained interest in the secrets of ancient wisdom about the natural, celestial and divine spheres. Agrippa argued that angels 'may be procured, and conveyed to us', and he speculated on the ways in which this might be done, 'according to the rules of Naturall Philosophy, and Astronomy'. The German scholar also affirmed that angels ruled over the armies of men, Kingdoms, provinces and beasts, beliefs which should be considered within 'an intellectual climate in which astrology was widely accepted'.[5]

The evidence does not suggest that these ideas suddenly disappeared in the last quarter of the seventeenth century, although new intellectual processes undoubtedly left their mark on this aspect of belief. It was still possible for the astrologer and medical practitioner Richard Kirby and his friend John Bishop to publish in 1687 a Ptolemaic account of the signs of the zodiac, commenting on the natures of the planets and their 'several governing angels'. Kirby and Bishop described each of the planets in turn, relating which sphere and order of the celestial hierarchy of angels it belonged to, and which angels principally governed it – so Saturn belonged to 'the seaventh Orb, Mansion, or Sphere, of the celestial Hierarchy of Angels, in the order of the thrones, whose principal governing Angels ... bearing Rule, are *Cassiel*, or *Zaphkiel, Jophiel*, and *Sabathiel*'. The authors went so far as to claim that it was an angel that appeared to 'the Great Ptolemy' and 'opened unto him the parts of the earth'.[6] Kirby was a successful Whig astrologer, and he dedicated his section of the book to Elias Ashmole, a prominent alchemist and astrologer often consulted by Charles II, notably during the exclusion crisis. Similarly, John Bishop dedicated his share to Robert Boyle, a natural philosopher and one of the original Fellows of the Royal Society.[7] The dedications indicate that the relationship between traditional methods of exploring man's surroundings, such as astrology, and the new natural philosophy, were not viewed by contemporaries as entirely antagonistic, as they have previously been styled by historians.

The sources support this understanding. Thomas Vaughan, who issued tracts on hermetic philosophy and alchemy, argued in 1669 that although there was local motion in the heavenly bodies, it was likely that there was also an intelligence that assisted in the 'continuance or perpetutation' of that movement. What is more, Vaughan asserted that from Richard Hooker and the Christian doctors, through to the 'Platonicks, Peripateticks, Stoicks and all noted Sects of Philosophers', this intelligence was thought to be an angel.[8] However, in 1687, the same year that Kirby and Bishop published their work, the writer and physician Robert Midgley, in *A new treatise of natural philosophy,* argued that having recourse to an angel to 'move, push on, direct, and order the Heaven' was no more necessary than 'to assign a helping Angel to the motion of Animals, and the Vegetation of Plants'. Aristotle's notion of the 'Intelligent Mover' of the stars was in fact God himself, and it was 'ridiculous' to think that the regular or irregular motion of comets could only be explained by the guidance of angels.[9] There was evidently no linear progression from confidence to cynicism, and even if by the end of the century it was no longer possible to find leading and active members of the Royal Society extolling the virtues of astrology, scientists were not the most prominent critics of the art. As Bernard Capp has documented, 'scepticism had not yet developed into indifference'.[10] Ambivalence was certainly the attitude most often expressed towards astrological science. Robert Boyle thus retained a vestigial belief in the idea that the sun, moon and stars have an influence on the earth, and in 1686 stated that 'if Men will needs take in a Being subordinate to God, for the management of the World, it seems more constant to the Holy Scripture, to depute *Angels* to that charge, than *Nature*'.[11] Boyle was evidently not prepared to dismiss the notion of angelical astrology just yet.

Boyle is an excellent example of how intellectual developments that were undermining confidence in astrology were also those that elsewhere were prompting new interest and a refocusing of attention on aspects of belief about angels that had lain dormant for many years. It was natural for men of this milieu to pursue their religious goals by means of intellectual activity, and Boyle was not the only one whose studies sought to gain greater insight into the relationship between God's power, the created realm, and man's perception of it, by utilizing the new experimental methods. Historians have recently begun to probe deeper into Boyle's thought in an attempt to create his 'unified worldview', rather than simply selecting the aspects of his thought that fit into a narrative of progress and modernity.[12] The new aspirations and 'the emergence of a new faith in the potentialities of human initiative' that Keith Thomas has identified had a wide-ranging impact, and almost certainly fuelled attempts to maximise the religious value of the study of the natural world.[13] Boyle was also well aware that reformed natural philosophy was threatened by Thomas Hobbes's mechanical philosophy and the materialistic atheism that Hobbes appeared to exemplify. Boyle's lifelong engagement with natural philosophy was therefore driven by his conviction that the threat of irreligion inherent in the new thinking was best offset by recourse to experimental data. His emphatic denial that human reason was competent to judge the content of revelation in fact placed strict limits on man's finite understanding, for 'where both theology and natural philosophy are concerned, the proper role of human reason is to ascertain and acknowledge its limits'.[14] Thus Boyle's natural philosophy left space for the continued existence of angels, as it was entirely possible that scriptural revelation might appear to be contrary to finite human understanding – angels were in Boyle's categories of the 'inexplicable' or 'incomprehensible'. It is evident then that the 'new thinking' once again drew angels into important theological discussions, as they were argued about and reconsidered in light of the new learning.

One of the ways in which angels assumed a new public role at this time was through their appearance in the work of Thomas Hobbes. As indicated above, Hobbes' ideas were potentially highly corrosive of belief about angels, but his discussion in *Leviathan* often refocused attention on them because other authors were goaded into engaging with his ideas. Hobbes's materialism was the key factor in this – he argued that where angels are mentioned in the Old Testament, in most instances 'Angels were nothing but supernaturall apparitions of the Fancy, raised by the speciall and extraordinary operation of God, thereby to make his presence and commandments known to mankind'.[15] In many other instances the word angel was used to refer to God himself – this was what was meant by the phrase 'the Angel of the Lord' for example, and furthermore Michael referred to Christ, Gabriel to 'nothing but a supernaturall phantasme'.[16] Hobbes concluded that there was no evidence in the Old Testament that angels are either permanent or corporeal, although he then immediately conceded that in the New Testament 'wherein is no suspicion of corruption of the Scripture', references to angels 'have extorted from my feeble Reason, an acknowledgment, and beleef, that there be also Angels substantiall, and permanent', although scripture was not able to prove that they were incorporeal.[17]

Hobbes' equivocation over this question did not spare him criticism from many of his contemporaries.[18] His discussion of angels reignited debates about the nature and substance of angels, traditional queries in angelology which had become less significant in reformed theology. Authors were quick to jump on what they perceived as errors in Hobbes – for example William Lucy, the Arminian Bishop of St David's, argued in 1663, in a work written specifically to confute Hobbes' ideas, that angels 'have a composition in their essence' and that 'their actual understanding is an act'.[19] Other works designed to refute Hobbes' theories also rebutted his claims about angels – John Whitehall in *The Leviathan found out* thought that '"tis more probable and agreeable to the opinion of the generality of the World" that angels assumed bodies on occasion, as opposed to Hobbes' claim that 'Angels have bodies and dimensions'. Whitehall also disputed Hobbes' argument that fallen angels had to have bodies in order that eternal hell-fire could have an effect on them. Whitehall remarked that taken to its logical conclusion this would mean that God was incapable of making 'any other sort of fire that can work upon something not a body'. Whitehall scathingly concluded: 'Mr. Hobbes might as well have said, that if we never had had any fire, God could not have made such a thing as fire'.[20]

Other discussions of the nature of angels were less polemical, but although there was no specific reference to Hobbesian thought within them, it seems likely that interest in the topic was rekindled by the assertions of mechanical

philosophers. Most reiterated that angels were spiritual substances. In 1663
the physician Gideon Harvey noted that 'Angels are constituted by their Forms
without Matter, and for that reason are nominated immaterial'.[21]   Others
discussed the angelic nature at greater length. Edward Polhill, a religious con-
troversialist who specialized in practical reformed theology, wrote of the three
ranks of beings in existence – the spiritual, material and mixed – and stated that
'Angels by Office' belonged to the first, which was the intellectual world. Polhill went on to consider that 'none but the Almighty shoulders can bear them
[angels] up in Being', and also that in contrast to God angels are but 'nullities', 'in
comparison of his Immortality Angels are but smoak'.[22] The Leicestershire clergyman Benjamin Camfield was particularly effusive on the topic, insistent that
they were not 'notions only, Creatures of our brain, Chimera's of our fansie', but
that they were 'true, personal and permanent Subsistences, that have of themselves a real, perfect, and actual Being'. He also returned to the topic in a section
on the nature of spirits, which he defined as 'an incorporeal or bodiless Being,
endued with understanding, will, and active power', in opposition to 'whatever
incompossibility, jargon or non-sense some haughty scorners have talked of, in
the Notion of an immaterial or incorporeal substance'.[23]

It is difficult to find anyone writing in support of Hobbes' thesis, evidence that
the potentially destructive nature of his thinking was yet to make its impact on
belief about angels. In 1675 the bishop of Worcester, Edward Stillingfleet, author
of a monumental work of natural philosophy, did concede that various authorities believed that when the imagination was fixed on divine things, occasionally
'people do really think (as much as men do in dreams) that they are present at
that time with Angels'. He also argued that 'the natural force and power of Imagination will in some tempers produce all the same symptoms and appearances ...
which there are in supernatural elevations'. However, this limited acceptance that
some alleged angels might be the result of illusion or misconception was hardly
a wholesale endorsement of the Hobbesian notion of angels, and was also a common caveat.[24] Even those authors that were attacked by contemporaries for their
materialistic principles held far from straight-forward opinions about the spirit
world. The beliefs of John Webster, a schoolmaster and polemicist who criticized
traditional learning, were strongly condemned by his colleagues, yet on closer
examination they do not necessarily correlate with his opponents' perceptions.
Webster was clear that 'Sacred Scriptures do with infallible certitude teach us,
that both good and bad Spirits have most certainly an Existence', and his opinions
in fact were relatively orthodox when he allowed that although God once made
himself manifest to the Patriarchs 'by the visible appearance of Angels, yet it is no
rational consequence that he doth so now in these days'.[25] The reason that Webster was the focus of such intense criticism was his argument that angels were not
spiritual and incorporeal in substance, but in reality his argument was carefully

nuanced, and the denial was prompted by his concern to differentiate between the First Cause and all other causes. Thus, 'if the Angelical nature were simply and absolutely spiritual and incorporeal, they would be of the same essential Identity with God, which is simply impossible', rather 'Angels must of necessity be of an essence of Alterity, and different from the essence of God'. Webster backed up his assertion by quoting the words of Henry More, who thought 'Angels to be as truly a compound Being consisting soul and body'.[26]

The treatment of Webster is a timely warning not to accept the protestations and exaggerated arguments of contemporary critics of the 'new thinking' without due consideration; the material is often ambivalent and there is not always the evidence to support the claims of those contemporaries who believed they were living in an age of unprecedented irreligion. Webster's protestations of innocence are also worth noting – he pointed out that 'denying the existence of Angels or Spirits; or the Resurrection, doth not infer the denying of the Being of God; nor the denying of the existence of Witches ... infer the denying of Angels or Spirits'. This was because 'the Being of a God is independent of either Angel or Spirit, and doth exist solely by itself', and the two were therefore separable.[27]

The identities of Hobbes' critics are also particularly interesting. The number of physicians writing against his philosophy is marked, and is an indication that the opposition to the new ideas cannot simply be explained away as the reactionary and instinctual response of an embattled church elite. Laymen also disagreed with Hobbes, and other practitioners of the new methods sought to dissociate themselves from his thought, which many of them believed was heretical. Most were in agreement with John Bramhall, a Church of Ireland Bishop who savagely attacked Hobbes in 1658, when he stated 'by taking away all incorporeal substances, he [Hobbes] taketh away God himself'. Bramhall followed Hobbes' opinions to their logical conclusions; if the phrase 'an incorporeal substance' was a contradiction, then:

> to say that an Angel or Spirit, is an incorporeal substance, is to say in effect, that there is no Angel or Spirit at all. By the same reason to say, That God is an incorporeal substance, is to say there is no God at all. Either God is incorporeal, or he is finite, and consists of parts, and consequently is no God. This, That there is no incorporeal spirit, is that main root of Atheism, from which so many lesser branches are daily sprouting up.[28]

Thomas Hobbes differed from many of his contemporaries in that he sought to explain even the human soul and social processes in terms of matter and motion alone. Others rarely went to this extreme – the mechanical philosophy of Pierre Gassendi purported that whilst animals had corporal souls, the human soul was incorporeal; while Renè Descartes' distinction between *res extensa* (the physical world) and *res cogitans* (the thinking being) created a boundary that fell along similar lines. This distinction might explain the exceptionally virulent response that Hobbes provoked, but it might also be true that most churchmen saw the progression from Gassendi's and Descartes's ideas to the materialism of Hobbes as a short and easy step, the threat equally potent. This perception was in fact rooted in reality. Balthasar Bekker, a Dutch Calvinist minister, published a treatise that employed theological and philosophical arguments in order to combat the notion that spirits such as ghosts and angels could influence life on earth. Bekker's arguments were greatly influenced by the Cartesian understanding of the relationship between mind and matter, as the separation of the physical and mental realms left no place for any causal agencies apart from God and man.[29] Thus the initial threat of mechanical philosophy was further realized in later writings, as 'the deanimation of the material world unmistakably kindled the fire of irreligion' and 'the Cartesian ban on active principles put all forms of spiritual intervention at risk'.[30]

Hobbes and his fellow philosophers therefore provided a stimulus to the literature and commentaries relating to angels. Numerous authors went into print in defence of the traditional understanding of angels, based upon the evidence of scripture, and debate on their nature and substance again became prominent.[31] As John Bramhall's words indicate, the 'new thinking' also prompted anxieties and fears about the growing incidence of atheism amongst the population, as there was great concern that mechanical philosophy would encourage more people to question their Christian beliefs. In this context it is easy to understand why such luminaries as Max Weber and Keith Thomas have seen the beginnings of the 'disenchantment of the world' in this period, when numerous tracts poured from the presses denouncing the irreligion and atheism of the time. As has been shown, one of the reactions to these anxieties was an engagement with and refutation of the new ideas on a intellectual level, but there were other solutions and techniques that other Protestant divines adopted in order to counter the perceived threat. Furthermore, angels were to prove an indispensable ally in the defence of belief in the supernatural, and the assault on the mechanical philosophers.

Combating the 'New Thinking'

Thus far the treatment of angels in this chapter has focused upon the significant intellectual developments that shaped angelology in the later seventeenth century. It hardly needs pointing out that the majority of the English laity were unlikely to ever read or to encounter the main ideas in the works of Thomas Hobbes or Rene Descartes, although this should not detract from the impact of intellectual developments at a more popular level. The threat to Christian belief posed by questioning the existence of the supernatural provoked many English Protestant divines into a defence of their systems of belief in writing, an intention they made explicit in the introductions and prefaces that they provided to their works. This tendency was in accord with broader, more deep-rooted concerns about heterodoxy and false belief. Anxieties had traditionally accompanied belief about angels, but following the collapse of the established church unorthodoxy flourished as never before. A measure of the concern can be seen in earlier warnings against offering prayers to angels and reminders of the immortal dangers of worshipping such creatures which were repeated with regular frequency.

For example, Edward Leigh did concede that 'lawfull and moderate reverence' was to be given to angels and that we should 'praise God for them', love them, and 'make them exempla of our lives'. However, he concluded that there was 'generall prohibition of religious worshipping of Angels' in scripture, and he refuted the Papists' claim that religious worship was due to them and that angels would intercede for men. 'Idolotrie is here comitted' was his stern rebuke.[32] Peter Heylyn similarly noted that the worship of angels had been condemned at the Council of Laodicea, and also that in scripture 'Angels themselves ... constantly refused this honour'. John Spencer included in his deliberations a section entitled 'Invocation of Saints and Angells condemned', describing such worship as 'a manifest derogation' and 'robbing of God', and noting that 'more safely and sweetly do I speak in Prayer to my Iesus then to any of the Angels'.[33] Evidently there was no room for compromise or novelty on this aspect of belief. The devilish ability to transform into an angel of light proved particularly useful for those authors seeking to refute some of the radical ideas that were emerging and circulating in the 1650s. Quakers were especially vulnerable in this respect because of their notion of 'inner light' – John Wigan claimed that such beliefs 'not onely open a way for Satan being transformed as an angel of light to suggest unto them as many lyes and erroneous doctrines as he pleaseth', but also, because the light within was to be found in all living creatures, set up more idols, for 'while they do worship that light as God, they do deifie and worship angels'.[34]

Other authors also complemented this message in different genres of writing. The collapse of censorship, combined with the outpouring of radical belief in the 1640s, was accompanied by increasing anxiety about religious unorthodoxy, and books were published that listed and condemned errors in belief and practice. The heresiographers of the time often included in their catalogues of heresies those that were associated particularly with belief about angels. In 1648 Samuel Rutherford listed many religious radicals who included angel worship in their 'antichristian doctrines'. The Libertines and Sadducees were reported to believe 'that Angels, good or ill, are nothing but imaginations, thoughts, and motions of the minde of man', and Familists and antinominians were accused of 'pretended visions, and conferences with the Angels'.[35] Justice of the Peace Richard Braithwaite listed the errors of those 'antient heretics' who believed that the world was made by angels, including in his list Simon Mous, Menander, Saturninu, Basilides and Carpocrates.[36]

Alexander Ross included numerous references to erroneous belief about angels in his *Pansebia*, including that the Jews believed that a good and evil angel stood before each of their synagogues, 'observing who pray and hear most diligently, which was also the reason that 'they hold it a great sin in praying to belch, yawn, spit, or break wind'.[37] The 'Mahumetans' believed that 'every one hath two Angels attending on him, the one at his right hand, the other at his left' (its inclusion indicating Ross' disapproval of such belief), that the moon was on occasion 'impaired by a touch of the Angel Gabriels wing, as he was flying along', and that two Angels with 'angry looks, and flaming firebrands' examined the dying shortly before their end. Simon Magus was pilloried for teaching that 'the world was made by Angels', and this heresy was also said to have 'begot Marconites, Manichees, and the Angelick heretics, who worshipped Angels', and was also attributed to 'Nicholaitans and Gnosticks'. In addition, Ross included the most recent heresies from Rome, 'that we ought to invocate both saints and Angels', and that their churches have 'images also of Angels, which they paint with wings'.[38]

The myriad beliefs that were discussed and indeed refuted in these sources give a hint of the religious and social flux that these authors were experiencing. We have seen how the familiar figure of the angel might serve as a bulwark to support elements of the Protestant faith, and also how they bolstered and legitimized the maintenance of social order despite the absence of the king and the normal representatives of authority. It is also clear that angels were always liable to be hijacked by heretics and 'Gnostics', and the repeated warnings not to invocate angels or commit the sin of idolatry are symptoms of this possibility. The blossoming of novel ideas also exacerbated these fears, and anxieties over the emergence of new sects and confessional strains remained a cause for concern throughout these decades.

However, strongly worded refutations of wrong belief were not the only response to the intellectual flux of the later seventeenth century. Angels assumed an important role in other developments, as Protestant clergyman collected and published stories of the appearances and activities of angels as evidence to counter claims that there could be no such thing as an incorporeal substance. It should be noted that these divines adopted the new methodological techniques and employed them in order to bolster their traditional theological understandings – they gathered experimental data to prove the existence of angels, and reasoned from here to the existence of God and his role in ordering the universe.[39]

Those natural philosophers and clergymen who adopted the experimental methods and turned the weapons of mechanical philosophy against their advocates were part of a broader trend. John Spurr has argued that through the development of 'rational religion', clergymen were convinced that they would be able to use reason to prove the existence of God, and they sought to refute those that argued otherwise. Similarly, Barbara Shapiro has maintained that natural philosophy could provide support for religion, countering the threats posed by atheism and Hobbism by providing proofs for the existence of God and the immortality of the soul. In contrast to the small minority of radical intellectual thinkers that were challenging received wisdom, other men sought to find empirical evidence of the existence of the spirit world.[40] Angels were an exceptionally useful tool in this respect as they were also representative of the workings of God's providence in the world, their benevolent presence signifying an interventionist God at odds with the distant deity of mechanical philosophy. A number of leading clergymen therefore collected information and stories relating to the angelic ministry towards mankind, and published these as empirical proof of the angels' existence and responsibilities. Their concerns and motivation for undertaking such work was often stated explicitly.

The Church of England clergyman Joseph Glanvill prefaced his 1676 essay on 'The *USEFULNESS* of *Real Philosophy* TO *RELIGION*' with the opinion that '*acquaintance* with *Nature* assists *RELIGION* against its greatest enemies, which are *Atheism, Sadducism, Superstition, Enthusiasm*, and the *Humour of Disputing*', before going on to add that one of the main uses of philosophy was to determine 'What a *Spirit* is; and whether there be *Spirits*.' He argued there were angels and souls which 'are *purer* than these *gross* Bodies', that philosophy could prove this, and that by this method of proving the existence of angels and spirits 'a very considerable service is done to Religion: For hereby our Notion of the adorable *Deity* is freed from all *material* grosness'.[41] George Sinclair, who was a natural philosopher, university professor and engineer at different stages of his varied career, in 1685 produced a collection entitled *A choice collection of modern relations proving evidently against the saducees and atheists*. He pondered in his introduction 'what can be the reason of so much *Atheism* in the World?', and his considered opinion was that there were two reasons for it. The first was 'a monstrous rable of men, who following the *Hobbesian* and *Spinosian* Principles, slight Religion, and undervalue the Scripture, because there is such an express mention of Spirits and Angels in it, which their thick and plumbeous capacities cannot conceive'. The second was 'the absurd Principles of the *Cartesian Philosophy*', which did not directly deny the existence of God, but seemed to prove much 'which is Connatural to all men'. His work was intended to counter these claims, and amongst other things, to affirm 'what marvellous works have been performed by Angels'.[42]

Anxieties about irreligion and atheism were not a new phenomenon in post-Reformation England. Michael Hunter has demonstrated that the inclusive concept of 'atheism' encapsulated a range of threatening phenomena that were sensationalized into 'a single, pervasive stereotype' that could serve 'descriptive and prescriptive functions' and colour contemporary perceptions.[43] Although Spurr has since demonstrated that in the Restoration church this stereotype was being sub-divided into more distinct categories of atheists, deists, and Socinians, amongst the individuals in these categories there remained a common assumption that a sinful and debased nature was the ultimate source of scepticism. Thus Hunter's characterizations of the stereotype included those 'free-thinkers' who questioned scripture, espoused a preference for natural over supernatural explanations and that denied the immortality of the soul, characteristics that Hobbes and his colleagues were presumed to embody. The vulnerability of the Restoration church, which Spurr argues was greatly undermined by 'the deficiencies of the clergy, the weakness of her discipline, and the religious diversity of English society', no doubt made anxieties about irreligion particularly acute. Furthermore, the susceptibility of the church was exacerbated by the spirit of 'an age given over to the pleasure of wit, the exercise of reason, the jeering of anticlericalism, and the self-indulgence of libertinism'.[44] In this context, it is not hard to see why anxieties about atheism were especially prominent, and why there was such pressing concern amongst churchmen to combat these developments.

Fortunately for these clergymen and their allies, they felt that the weapons needed to address the threat were within their grasp, and throughout the period churchmen were 'learning how to manipulate the image of the "wit" and how to exploit the figure of the "atheist", in order to rule the conforming, God-fearing laity'.[45] The treatment of angels bears this suggestion out, and several contemporary authors commented upon the peculiar appropriateness of angels to the task. In *A theological discourse of angels* in 1678, Benjamin Camfield stated that 'the Subject insisted on is neither trite in our Language, nor unprofitable; and but too suitable to that Atheistical and degenerate Age we live in, wherein the general disbelief of Spirits ... may well be thought the ground and introduction of all that irreligion and profaneness, which naturally enough follows upon it'. Camfield thought that it was the devil that promoted this kind of infidelity, and that caused men to 'laugh at the Tales of immaterial substances', but it was his intention to 'represent everything according to its proper evidence', so that people might recognize the 'good turns' and 'admirable virtues' of these creatures. In future, men would then be less 'profane, sceptical, and indifferent in our belief, esteem, thoughts and speeches about them'.[46]

Clergymen therefore compiled and published collections that were intended to prove the existence of angels through the evidence provided by those who had experienced them. Among the first to do so was Joseph Hall, bishop of Norwich, who in 1659 published *The invisible world discovered to spirituall eyes,* which is a revealing example of how divines might undertake this task. Hall began by lamenting that he had 'been slack in returning praises to my God, for the continual assistance of those blessed and beneficient spirits', before going on to acknowledge the infinite number of angels that were provided though the 'bountiful provision of the Almighty'.[47] He then considered at length some of the traditional areas of interest – the extent of their power, the capacity of their knowledge, their operations and employment, and the possibility that there was order and degree amongst them. Hall's arguments up to this point are conventional, and follow the pattern set out in earlier Protestant works – scriptural passages provide the basis for his assumptions and conclusions, and there is the usual caution over pronouncing on the 'severall ranks, offices, employments' of angels which is described as a 'soaring conceit': 'they are not to be beleeved that dare to determine' such things.[48]

Hall's treatise then becomes more unorthodox in a section entitled 'The apparitions of Angels'. Here Hall considered a range of reports of angels appearing in latter days. He began by ridiculing those pagan and Catholic authorities that claimed to have seen or been influenced by angels during their lifetimes. Socrates's belief that he was accompanied by a good 'Genii' was ridiculed by Hall, who also wondered 'who can be so fondly credulous, as to believe that Jo. Carrera a young father of the Society [of Jesus], had a daily companion of his Angell in so familiar a fashion', 'Or that the aged Cappuchin Franciscus de Bergamo ... had for eight years together before his death, the assistance of an Angel in a humane shape'. Numerous other Catholic authorities become the target of Hall's scorn and derision, before he conceded that scriptural evidence did demonstrate that angels were once very active in the world, as they were 'in the suceeding times of the Church Primitive'.[49]

> I can easily yield that those retired Saints of the prime ages of the Church had sometimes such heavenly companions, for the consolation of their forced solitude, But withal, I must have leave to hold that the elder the church grew, the more rare was the use of these apparitions, as of other miraculous actions, and events.[50]

In fact, apparitions of angels were now very rare, though 'some few instances our times have been known to yield'.[51] It was his opinion that the 'trade' people had with spirits was now only spiritual, and that there were many times 'insensible helps' from them, though they remained unseen. The miraculous cure of a cripple at St Madron's well in Cornwall was such a case – Hall himself had taken 'a strict and personall examination' of the man, who had been unable to walk for sixteen years, and he was apparently convinced that his restoration was bought about by an 'Author invisible'. There was the tale of a Pastor of Northeuse, John Spangenberge, who no sooner had stepped out of his house 'then the house fell right down in the place', and Hall suggested to his readers that they might also be able to recall occasions when people they were acquainted with 'have faln from very high towers, and into deep pits, past the naturall possibility of hope, who yet have been preserved not from death only, but from hurt: whence could these things be, but by the secret aid of those invisible helpers?'[52]

Although Hall did go on to say that the main care of angels was their ministry to the soul where they were responsible for 'enlightening the understanding'
and 'incouraging our weaknesse', he was evidently convinced of the reality of
their intervention in the world.[53]   Furthermore, he was able to corroborate
this through the testimony of no less a witness than Philip Melanchthon. Hall
related the tale of Simon Grynaeus, a prominent reformer who had offended
a preacher in the city of Speier by accusing him of teaching Popish doctrines.
Whilst eating dinner with Melanchthon in his lodgings, the latter was called
out of the room to speak with a stranger, 'a grave old man of goodly countenance, seemly, and richly attired'. The old man warned Melanchthon that the
preacher had reported Grynaeus, and that officers would soon arrive at the lodgings to carry him to prison. Grynaeus quickly made his escape on the Rhine, just
before the authorities arrived. Hall had taken the tale from Melanchthon's own
Commentary on Daniel, where 'he acknowledges Gods fatherly providence in
sending this Angell of his, for the rescue of his faithful servant'.[54]

It is immediately apparent that Bishop Hall's work represents a new development in the Protestant treatment of angels. Prior to this, although many authors
were insistent that angels played an active part in the world, it was highly unusual for them to single out the specific occasions when this was thought to have
happened. Most were content with documenting the scriptural examples of
angelic inspiration and discussing their ministration and responsibilities in this
context. Hall's distinct approach can be linked directly to the concerns about
atheism and irreligion – in attempting to refute the unbelief of the age he went
further than his predecessors in insisting upon their involvement in the world.
He was providing the evidence on which to base a belief in angels, combining the
incontrovertible proof of Scripture with the experimental evidence of respected
Protestant authorities. Common sense might dictate that this development was
merely the continuation of a trend which had seen the stripped down, minimal
angelology of the immediate post-Reformation period gradually lose its place
as the prominent discourse, to be substituted for the more liberal and expansive angelology of the mid-seventeenth century, where divines were willing to
endorse the notion of guardian angels and other formerly controversial aspects
of doctrine. It is tempting to suppose that once the intense confessional disputes
of the sixteenth century were long gone, clergymen need not feel anxious that
publicly affirming stories of the apparitions of angels might lead the laity into
erroneous ways or provide support for Popish misconceptions.

There may be some truth in this scenario – it is likely that the clergy of the
1660s were more confident than their sixteenth-century predecessors in their
parishioners' Protestant faith. However, this narrative seems unconvincing for
a number of reasons. Most obvious is that when Hall published his work in
1659, confessional wrangles were not a thing of the past: the volatile atmosphere

of the 1640s and 50s had seen the unprecedented fragmentation of systems of belief. It would be a mistake to see Hall's work as a complacent affirmation or continuation of earlier developments – in 1659 the Church of England was yet to be re-established and the Popish Plot and exclusion crisis of the later 1670s were evidence of the persistent, almost hysterical, fear of popery within society. It is also apparent that Hall's work actually did have a distinct confessional bias inherent within it. In rejecting the validity of numerous Catholic accounts of the appearances of angels, whilst affirming the legitimacy of those of Protestant authorities, Hall makes an implicit statement about the relative merits of each. The provenance of these stories is significant – the rejected accounts are from a father of the Society of Jesus, or from '*Isidore* the late *Spanish* Peasant (newly Sainted amongst good company by *Greg.* the 15)', both representative of the spirit of the Counter Reformation, which explains why they were targeted by Hall.[55] Thus although superficially there is not much objective difference between the accounts that Hall rejected and those that he endorsed, there is a definite method in his choices. The use of Melanchthon, a leading early reformer, is particularly significant in this context, and adds extra weight and authority to Hall's arguments whilst emphasizing the different provenances of the accounts.

This argument is supported by the fact that Melanchthon's angel appeared frequently in many other compilations that were designed to demonstrate the existence of the supernatural. Benjamin Camfield retold the account, describing the countenance of the 'Grave old Man' and noting that not only did Melanchthon affirm the appearance of the angel, but also that there was 'the Testimony of many good Men then alive to avouch it'.[56] It was also the first example of angelic intervention that Increase Mather recounted in *An essay for the recording of illustrious providences* in 1684. Mather similarly described 'a Man of very grave and godly countenance', who after speaking 'vanished out of sight'.[57] These authors took a similar approach to Bishop Hall when they sought to affirm the reality of the supernatural by providing evidence for the existence of angels. Camfield also began by discussing scriptural appearances of angels and their responsibilities to mankind whilst acknowledging that 'their doctrinal ministry is not, ordinarily, now to be expected by us'. He then gave some examples of occasions when good men 'have owed their safety and preservation from impendent evils and ruine to the particular warning of Angels'. He discussed at length 'an Holy and Pious Man ... and Acquaintance of Bodinus', who had 'a certain Spirit that did perpetually accompany him', describing how the angel 'by striking his right Ear' would admonish him when he did anything amiss.[58] By the same means of communication the angel would also indicate the character of the people with whom the man met with, or indicate 'if he was about to eat or drink anything that would hurt him' so that he 'was presently raised and strengthened with a spiritual and supernatural Power'.[59]

It is significant that Camfield prefaced his more recent examples of angelic activity by admitting that although God 'may still imploy the holy Angels upon certain Messages, Admonitions, and Instructions', 'the way of Salvation is already prescribed to us'. Camfield's concern was that people might deliberately seek out the assistance of angels, leaving them open to 'Diabolical delusions pretending to be Angelical and Divine Revelations', and he warned his readers 'that a good Angel, an Angel of Light, can never come unto us upon any errand contrary to the revealed Word and Will of God by Jesus Christ, whom they all adore and worship'.[60] This indicates that there remained concerns about how the laity perceived angels, and that divines were not simply content to document stories of apparitions without providing some instruction and guidance as to the meaning and importance of these events. The threat from atheism and mechanical philosophy had certainly caused alarm, but it had not eclipsed more traditional areas of controversy and anxiety relating to belief about angels. Once again the provenance of these accounts is significant. Camfield established the credibility of Amyraldus' account by relating that the author had heard about his angel from Cameron: 'a Divine of Name and Eminence in the Reformed Churches'.[61] The case of Bodin is also worth further consideration: Jean Bodin wrote such a vivid account in *De la Démonomanie des Sorciers* of the friend who was watched over by an angel, that few commentators have doubted that it was Bodin himself.[62] Although Robin Briggs describes the text itself as 'wildly heretical', expressing 'a personal religion that was much closer to Judaism' than Christianity, Bodin articulated very similar concerns to Camfield when it came to the identity of the angel. He was sceptical about the likelihood that people were generally in contact with the angels, and was particularly concerned that when they did appear, they might just be demonical delusions.[63]

The narrative of Bodin's angel was evidently considered to be particularly persuasive as it was recounted in several other works. Increase Mather included Bodinus' 'Relation of a Man that prayed much for the assistance of an Angel', documenting that his prayer was heard, for he was then 'often admonished of his Errors by a Caelestial Monitor' that once 'appeared visibly in the form of a Child; otherwhile in an orb of Light'. Mather is less enthusiastic about the incident, and admitted that 'some fear that this Spirit which he took to be his good *Genius* was a subtle *Cacodaemon*', but Henry More, the most prolific of the Cambridge Platonists, stated that 'I give as much credit' to the tale of a man 'who had the society and assistance of such an Angell or Genius', as to 'any story in Livy or Plutarch'.[64]

These endeavours to collect together experimental evidence of the existence of angels and the supernatural world were quite clearly a reaction to the perceived threat of irreligion and atheism, fuelled in part by the foremost intellectual thinkers of the time. However, the fact remains that the importance of these intellectuals should not be exaggerated in light of what we now know about future developments. The names of the great philosophers and the most important protagonists of the 'Scientific Revolution' are well known to students of history in the twenty-first century, and the eventual significance of their activities is a familiar narrative. However, at the end of the seventeenth century these men were still a minority, and were often considered radical or heretical by the majority of their contemporaries. Hobbes, to his chagrin, was never invited to join the Royal Society because he was seen as too much of a liability by the existing members, and the reaction against his ideas in print is further evidence that the opinions of these thinkers were not shared by the majority of the country.[65] As Euan Cameron has argued, the breakdown of consensus over Aristotelian cosmology and demonology contained the seeds of later developments, but other cultural assumptions needed to fall into place before the logic of the 'New Thinking' was to have what might be termed a 'secularizing' effect.[66]

As has been shown, a much more common position was that held by many of the intellectuals that were the authors of these collections of apparition narratives – the 'scientists' of the day – might employ the experimental method to prove the existence of the spirit world and their studies investigated a number of fields, ranging from metaphysics to astrology. The evidence does not suggest that the rise of rationality utterly destroyed belief in angels; rather, critics took up the weapon of reason 'to fortify and strengthen the Faith of others'.[67] It is also important to remember that although Protestant divines were reacting against the developments in natural philosophy, in a broader sense it was the traditional uses of angels that were most prominent in the literature. Even in those collections that marshalled evidence of the existence of angels in defence of Christianity, tales of angelic appearances in the latter days were far rarer than those that were based on scripture. It was scriptural evidence that formed the basis of these treatises and which provided the bulk of the evidence within them. Confessional anxieties were still an inherent part of these works, and evidence gathered from more diverse sources gives the impression that angels were continuing to fulfil many of the traditional roles that they had assumed through the sixteenth and seventeenth centuries.

Summary

There is no doubt that angels remained an important element of the religious landscape in the late seventeenth century, fulfilling many of the roles and responsibilities that reformed angelology had previously assigned to them. However, the period should not simply be interpreted as a mere continuation of previous trends and emphases. The growth of scepticism and materialism presented a challenge to this angelic belief that was to become increasingly important in the eighteenth century. The changes wrought by the mechanical philosophy were long-term processes, which although they had their roots in the seventeenth century, were to prove gradual and incremental in their effects – there was no sudden collapse in confidence in the supernatural at this juncture. However, these intellectual trends were to have an impact in the short term as they reignited interest in the substance and nature of angels and inspired several clergymen into a defence of the spirit world. Angels, and the scriptural evidence that was the proof of their existence, thus came to be utilized as a bulwark and weapon against what was perceived as a rising tide of irreligion and atheism within the country. This meant that clergymen were more willing to provide concrete evidence of the deeds of angels on earth, a development in reformed angelology that harked back to late medieval religious cultures.

This did not mean, however, that anxieties about idolatry and the abuse of doctrine had disappeared. New stories of the apparitions and activities of angels were inevitably accompanied by caveats and warnings relating to the dangers of angel worship or sinfulness of undue reverence. Nor was the confessionalization of angels a thing of the past. As previous chapters have demonstrated, their pastoral applicability was repeatedly utilized to provide edification and instruction to the laity. It is also evident that angels remained vibrant and caught the attention of many religious controversialists of the time: their appeal had not waned through the political turmoil of the second half of the seventeenth century. Ministers still had confidence in the usefulness of angels as a cultural resource, and they continued to prove adept at exploiting the different facets of their nature in order to inspire greater devotion and commitment to the Christian faith.

CONCLUSION

We must not deny a great truth in Christianity, for fear of giving occasion to Popish consequents and misuse of it.[1]

Richard Baxter's comment encapsulates the reformed attitude to angels throughout the sixteenth and seventeenth centuries, attesting to the positive assimilation of the concept into Reformed theology and mentalities. Although angels were by no means an unproblematic inheritance from late medieval religious cultures, this study has shown that for most reformers, the utility of belief in them far outweighed the more negative associations. Accordingly, angels were utilized for a wide range of purposes and intents in the post-Reformation era. The discussion has traced the course charted by the reformers in order to balance the usefulness of the angelic motif with the 'Popish consequents' that might result from its misuse. This has brought to the fore the continued ubiquity of angels in religious cultures, as they were consistently and persistently utilized as a device by clergymen seeking to convey doctrine and instruction to the laity. It has also located angels in a series of political, cultural and religious sites, focusing not on the development and mutation of a single idea, but rather on the transmission and adaptation of that idea by a diverse range of individuals in both the religious and secular realms, all with their own agendas and aspirations.

In the course of my discussion, I have therefore frequently emphasized the employment of angels for pastoral and didactic functions, as the complex mixture of belief that was attached to angels facilitated their use to tutor the laity in both theology and practice. The foundations for these roles were laid in the late medieval period, when the Catholic Church proved itself particularly adept at exploiting the angelic potential to inspire devotion to the Christian faith. Angels were perceived as fellow worshippers alongside mankind, their ultimate purpose to testify to the majesty and mercy of the godhead and to provide humans with an example of the dedication and obedience that each Christian should strive to achieve. As familiar figures, they were the means by which complex ideas about the nature of sin and salvation, and the quality of God's mercy, were made more approachable, and they offered protection and comfort as ministering spirits that were provided by God to assist weak-minded and sinful humans in the struggle for salvation. As protectors, angels were thought to defend mankind from evil in various ways: they offered spiritual comfort to beleaguered men and women, protected travellers, healed the sick, released men from prison and curbed the assaults of evil demons. This latter function was particularly crucial when it came to the angelic participation in the 'Last Things': because angels were also a prominent presence in the official liturgy relating to death, and they were understood to participate in the cosmic struggle enacted around the death-bed, where good and evil angels competed for custody of the dying person's soul.

Although the dramatic restructuring of the religious landscape in the sixteenth century saw the rejection of the angelic roles of mediation and inter-cession, many of these traditional functions of angels continued to be promoted by reforming clergymen. It was still legitimate to ask God to send his angels to assist men, and the promise of angelic succour and protection and the shared responsibility for the worship of the godhead extended naturally into the post-Reformation era. The retention of the role of angels in soteriology and mortuary culture has been recognized as a particularly significant survival throughout this study. Angels therefore continued to be regarded as a useful devotional aid in the years following the Elizabethan settlement, and the employment of angels in this way persisted throughout the seventeenth century, retaining its importance and showing no sign of decline right up to the 1700s.

Thus angels might be seen as one of the traditional constituents of faith that, once fused with new, reformed ideas, formed the patchwork of belief that post-revisionist scholars recognize as characteristic of the post-Reformation religious landscape. As a traditional element of religious culture with sound scriptural cre-dentials, they were able to help ease the difficult passages of religious transition. Tessa Watt has described this medley of belief as 'distinctively post-Reformation but not thoroughly Protestant', and whilst I agree with the spirit of this approach, a persistent concern of this study has been to emphasize that it is important not to privilege continuity at the expense of change.[2] Although ostensibly angels are an excellent example of a traditional aspect of late medieval religious culture that 'survived' the vicissitudes of reform, this study has demonstrated that this was not because of 'accommodation' by the reformers, and nor did the concept of the angel remain static. This investigation has not simply plotted the for-tunes or popularity of angels over the course of time; rather it has grappled with the broader cultural significance and meanings that angels represented, plac-ing these within the specific social, political and religious realities of the time. Angels were continually re-imagined throughout the period, with particular and differentiated attitudes being imposed upon the motif at various junctures.

Although angels were a familiar and popular concept, the processes of reform managed to redefine them in such a way that they could be utilized explicitly as a conduit for reformed ideas. Reformers re-emphasized certain angelic characteristics that underpinned the reformed mentality and sanctioned their perception of the spiritual universe. Alongside the promotion of the positive benefits of the angelic ministry, reforming clergy linked their discussions of angels to sombre warnings against idolatry and reminders that Christ was the only mediator. They also sought to strip angelology of those aspects that encouraged 'Popish consequents': relegating the importance of the named archangels, casting doubt on the angelic hierarchy and depersonalizing them in such a way that invocation and suspicious rituals were made less likely. As the agents and instruments of the deity, angels were figured in more abstract ways, and represented as the means by which God's providence was enacted upon the world.

The reconfiguring of the notion of an angel in this way indicates an area of consensus amongst Church of England clergymen who could harbour a diverse range of opinions with regard to other aspects of religious cultures. The harmonious representations of angels by these reformers can therefore be described as the 'official line' of the Church of England, and it has been shown how these men were able to consolidate this orthodoxy by using angels to attack aspects of 'papistry', as well as to support a positive projection of the benefits on offer from reformed angels. The notion of the 'reformed angel' assists our understanding of how Protestantism was able to enter the hearts and minds of the populace, and is an example of how changes in theology and doctrine might be experienced by the laity. However, the reformed ideal is only part of the picture. The great versatility of belief associated with angels in fact allowed for alternative representations of angels, and these areas of divergence from the 'official line' of the Established Church reveal much about English religious cultures.

Angels were taken up by churchmen of various stripes in order to bolster their position and support a particular confessional stance. Precisely because angels were not a focal point for intense controversy (in the way that the mass or sacraments were), it was possible for them to become an important ideological resource and weapon in the struggle for the soul of the Church of England and indeed the nation itself. For example, through their association with Arminian and Laudian innovation, they were called upon to play a part in the hardening of religious identities, and were employed by those who were pushing at the official boundaries of the Church at some of its most sensitive points, and breaking the 'rules' of what had once been the Elizabethan consensus. On their own, angels would not inspire a radical version of what the Church of England should be, but their great versatility meant that it was possible for interested parties to use belief about angels to reflect on fundamental questions about doctrine and ceremonial. Those reacting to the emergence and proliferation of Laudianism in the English church therefore sought to attack the protagonists by repeating their warnings about the potential spiritual dangers of angels more vociferously, whilst others tried to overcome the threat that they posed to reformed religion by destroying their surviving physical presence in churches and cathedrals across the country. In the meantime, angels were also being drawn into arguments about the organization and hierarchy of the church, as they were co-opted by Episcopalians and Presbyterians alike to support their distinct visions of what the church should be. Angels were therefore not only the means through which reformed principles might be conveyed to the laity, they were so deeply rooted in all aspects of religious culture that they were excellent tools with which to bolster or subvert confessional identities.

This study has shown that angels were used as an instrument whereby both orthodoxy and ambiguity were expressed, and through which statements were made about the nature of the church itself. They therefore reveal much about the nature of continuity and change in religion over time. The physical and textual continuity of the angelic motif meant that it remained within a restricted framework of belief whose boundaries were formulated along the lines of what was imaginable to contemporaries. However, the flexibility and versatility of the concept meant that within this framework the belief could be exploited for a myriad of uses. This made it possible for an element of 'traditional' belief to become a vehicle for radical change, the means by which unorthodox, and in some cases revolutionary ideas, might find their way back into the religious discourse. This is demonstrated best by the emergence of new and more creative thinking about angels in the 1640s and 50s. These decades saw a renewed and enhanced interest in angels in the context of shifting attitudes and a wider fragmentation of belief. The developments facilitated the emergence of a distinctly Puritan pastoral angelology, one that rehabilitated the notion of specific guardian angels, allowing for the employment of this aspect of belief explicitly in support of the doctrine of predestination. The notion that God had provided guardian angels exclusively for the protection of the elect is thus a demonstration of how angels were transformed into a channel for a paramount Puritan doctrine, one which lay at the heart of their identity.

In similar ways, this study has also demonstrated how angels were employed as a cultural resource to comment on and attempt to influence the social and political issues that were raised by the religious controversies of the later seventeenth century. Ideas of hierarchy and order were particularly prominent in the 1640s and 50s, and the comparing and equating of angels with the great and the good during the Restoration were used to both praise and censure individual political actors. The use of angelic imagery in last dying speeches is indicative of the ways in which angels were commandeered in order to endorse and add authenticity to a cause, and demonstrates how the characteristics of angels lent themselves to political commentary and acted as a useful shorthand in that environment. The employment of angels in concerns about and polemic against Catholicism has emerged as a recurring theme throughout the sixteenth and seventeenth centuries. Fears about the proliferation of dissenting groups and radical sects that came into existence through the fragmentation of Protestantism also persisted, particularly as the angelic motif could be adopted and utilized by those that suffered death at the hands of the government as well as recruited in the name of a variety of different causes.

Finally, this study has shown that despite the vibrancy of belief about angels, shifting intellectual priorities could also have a significant and potentially corrosive effect on them. We have seen how angels were employed following the collapse of the established church in the mid-seventeenth century as a bulwark against radical and 'heretical' belief, a trend that continued towards the end of the century when the development of mechanical philosophy and experimentalism, and the (perceived) surge in atheism appeared to threaten the intellectual viability of angels as never before. The initial impact of these developments was not to immediately discredit belief in supernatural beings; rather, it led to a greater tendency amongst authors to emphasize and elaborate upon the angelic roles and responsibilities. Materialist sceptics were soon faced with a barrage of clergy and laymen who sought to use angels to defend their systems of belief and to provide evidence of the spiritual world. Angels were an exceptionally useful tool in this respect because of their assumed role of enacting God's providence in the world, and clergymen enthusiastically collected stories relating to the angelic ministry to mankind, in the process going further than their predecessors in insisting upon their involvement in the earthly realm.

This discussion has important implications for ongoing debates about the emergence of a 'rational' mind-set and of a modern 'secular' mentality. Alexandra Walsham has recently suggested that thinking in terms of 'cycles of desacrilization and resacrilization' may help to counteract the past tendency in the scholarship for a narrative that emphasizes a linear progression of development from superstition to secularization.[3] The idea of a 'partial re-enchantment of the world' in the later-seventeenth century is held out by the examination of angels during the period. The trend to revisit past debates that had supposedly been extinguished by the Reformation, and the tendency of later Protestants to go further than any of their predecessors in asserting the reality of interaction between the natural and supernatural worlds, both suggest that desacrilization is not as closely tied to the development of Protestantism as has often been assumed. It also demonstrates that the 'religion' that science is often held to evolve in conflict with, is not static or passive, but a dynamic process that could also contribute to, affirm, and inspire 'scientific' theory and methodology. Closer attention to the tangential, the contradictory, and the dissenting voices of the age reveal a fresh receptiveness to the supernatural and sacred that does not contradict but complements our understanding of progress and change in the later seventeenth-century.

With hindsight it is possible to trace the processes of secularization back to the intellectual shifts and developments that were gathering pace in the later seventeenth century, but the preliminary impact of these changes by no means suggests that this was the inevitable outcome. The fate of angels within the progressive 'disenchantment of the world' lies outside the scope of this study, but there is no doubt that a further examination of their roles and significance in the eighteenth century and beyond would be a fruitful avenue of enquiry. Robert Scribner has argued that desacralization may not be as closely tied to the development of Protestantism as has often been assumed, and makes a plea for historians to take account of 'those dissonant elements' which falsify the paradigm of a rationalizing Reformation.[4] Angels have a strong claim to be such an element for a number of reasons. Firstly, they remained a vibrant and versatile cultural resource through which seventeenth-century Englishmen and women were able to conceive and articulate their thoughts and hopes about the world, and their capacity to be continually re-imagined formed one of the chief characteristics of their enduring appeal. That people continually chose to write about angels, often in times of extraordinary upheaval and uncertainty, is symptomatic of the exceptionally ubiquitous nature of this aspect of belief, and there is no indication that the processes of reform had curtailed their importance. The evidence in fact suggests that the turmoil and ferment of the sixteenth and seventeenth centuries provided new and significant roles to angels, alongside their existing pastoral and instructive uses. The angelic trope which had proven so useful to medieval and early modern churchmen was adapted and utilized for a myriad of similar and contrasting uses.

If belief about angels disrupts a teleological historical understanding of the English Reformation and processes of secularization, it also contradicts other deep seated assumptions about the nature of English Protestantism. Whereas revisionist scholarship focused our attention on the destructive consequences of Protestantism, post-revisionist scholarship has begun to shift our attention to the more popular cultural potentialities of the faith. This has allowed recognition of elements of theology and practice that might be considered genuinely 'popular' forms of Protestantism: national fast and prayer days, sermon gadding, catechizing, a new approach to charitable giving and psalm singing, a shared providential understanding of the universe and a virulent anti-Catholicism. Angels should also be incorporated into this understanding, as a versatile element of belief that remained embedded in ecclesiastical and more secular contexts. In particular, in more popular contexts, belief about angels seems to have been characterized by an emphasis on positive associations, constructive resonances that might sit alongside other palatable aspects of reformed belief.

Secondly, it should be noted that to this day, angels have continued to reinvent themselves as a familiar and recognizable element of culture: an Oxford 'Very

Short Introduction' to angels was published as this monograph went to press. The leading cognitive scientist Steven Pinker attested to the powerful nature of the angelic trope by employing it as an organizing principle of his 2011 publication *The Better Angels of Our Nature: The Decline of Violence in History and its Causes.*[5] Angels are evoked with regularity in popular music and films, they are written about in novels and poetry, and those who subscribe to New Age philosophy, as well as some Christians, still look to them for guidance and instruction. In the course of this study the question of whether angels were a 'load-bearing' element of religious cultures was posed, and it has been shown that, in supporting central tenets and proponents of key doctrines, angels assumed a role that provided the basic groundwork for Protestant cultures. It is certainly true that clergymen such as Joseph Glanvill, Benjamin Camfield, Joseph Hall and Henry More were convinced that spirits were essential to the survival of the religious system, and that if belief in angels was undermined then the entire edifice was in danger of collapsing. However, against all their expectations, it was eventually angels that outlasted the dominance of the Church of England, as ideas about them persisted when the effective grip of the established Church on society was all but relinquished. 'Thinking with Angels' remains a useful activity to this day. The concept of winged messengers is one with an ancient heritage in a variety of human cultures, so perhaps angels are a load-bearing *cultural* element, pre-dating and eventually outlasting the early modern period, and they are yet to outlive their usefulness as a cultural resource.

NOTES

Introduction

1. B. Camfield, *A theological discourse of angels and their ministries wherein their existence, nature, number, order and offices are modestly treated of* (London, 1678), sig. A5r.

2. See for example D. Wilson, *Signs and Portents: Monstrous Births from the Middle Ages to the Enlightenment* (London: Routledge, 1993); L. Daston and K. Park, *Wonders and the Order of Nature 1150–1750* (New York: Zone Books, 1997); A. Walsham, *Providence in Early Modern England* (Oxford: Oxford University Press, 1999); K. Cooper and J. Gregory (eds), *Signs, Wonders, Miracles: Representations of Divine Power in the Life of the Church*, Studies in Church History, 41 (Woodbridge: Boydell Press, 2005); J. Shaw, *Miracles in Enlightenment England* (London: Yale University Press, 2006).

3. S. Clark, *Thinking with Demons: The Idea of Witchcraft in Early Modern Europe* (Oxford: Clarendon, 1997), especially chs 3 and 4, pp. 31–68.

4. Earlier important works include C. Haigh, *English Reformations: Religion, Politics and Society under the Tudors* (Oxford: Clarendon, 1993); J. J. Scarisbrick, *The Reformation and the English People* (Oxford: Blackwell, 1984); A. G. Dickens, *The English Reformation*, 2nd edn (London: Batsford, 1989).

5. T. Watt, *Cheap Print and Popular Piety 1550–1640* (Cambridge: Cambridge University Press, 1991), pp. 128 and passim.

6. P. Lake and M. Questier, *The Antichrist's lewd hat: Protestants, Papists and players in post-Reformation England* (New Haven, CT and London: Yale University Press, 2002); J. Maltby, *Prayer book and people in Elizabethan and early Stuart England* (Cambridge: Cambridge University Press, 1998); Watt, *Cheap Print*; Walsham, *Providence*.

7. Walsham, *Providence*, p. 329.

8. P. Bourdieu, *The Field of Cultural Production: Essays on Art and Literature*, ed. R. Johnson (Cambridge: Polity Press, 1993).

9. D. MacCulloch, *Reformation: Europe's House Divided* (London: Penguin, 2003), p. 581.

10. D. MacCulloch, 'Recent Studies on Angels in the Reformation', *Reformation*, 14 (2009), pp. 179–86.

11. E. Duffy, *The Stripping of the Altars: Traditional Religion in England c. 1400–c. 1580* (London: Yale University Press, 1992), pp. 73, 269–71, 244, 345; K. Thomas, *Religion and the Decline of Magic: Studies in Popular Beliefs in Sixteenth and Seventeenth-Century England* (London: Weidenfield & Nicholson, 1971), pp. 101, 166, 273, 281–2, 317, 319–20, 323, 562, 704, 758.

12. See for example D. Harkness, *John Dee's Conversations with Angels: Cabala, Alchemy, and the End of Nature* (Cambridge: Cambridge University Press, 1999); G. Szonyi, *John Dee's Occultism: Magical Exaltation through Powerful Signs* (Albany, NY: SUNY Press, 2004), ch. 7; R. H. West, *Milton and the Angels* (Athens, GA: University of Georgia Press, 1955).

13. D. Keck, *Angels and Angelology in the Middle Ages* (New York: Oxford University Press 1998).

14. R. Johnson, *Saint Michael the Archangel in Medieval Religious Legend* (Woodbridge: Boydell Press, 2005).

15. P. Marshall and A. Walsham (eds), *Angels in the Early Modern World* (Cambridge: Cambridge University Press, 2006)

16. F. Mohamed, *In the Anteroom of Divinity: The Reformation of Angels from Colet to Milton* (Toronto: University of Toronto Press, 2008); J. Raymond, *Milton's Angels: The Early-Modern Imagination* (Oxford: Oxford University Press, 2010).

17. S. A. Meier, 'Angels', in B. Metzger and M. Coogan (eds), *The Oxford Companion to the Bible* (Oxford: Oxford University Press, 1993), p. 27.

18. S. G. F. Brandon, 'Angels: The History of an Idea', *History Today*, 13 (October 1963), pp. 655–65.

19. C. A. Patrides, 'Renaissance Thought on the Celestial Hierarchy: The Decline of a Tradition', *Journal of the History of Ideas*, 20:2 (April, 1959), pp. 155–66.

20. Keck, *Angels*, p. 59.

21. Examples of Michael's role of combating evil appear in Daniel 10:3, Jude 1:9, Revelation 12:7.

22. Keck, *Angels*, p. 63; R. Finucane, *Miracles and Pilgrims, Popular Beliefs in Medieval England* (London: Dent, 1977), p. 41.

23. P. Marshall and A. Walsham, 'Migrations of Angels in the Early Modern World', in Marshall and Walsham (eds), *Angels in the Early Modern World*, pp. 4–5.

1 The Medieval Angel, *c.* 1480–1530

1. For the scriptural basis of belief about angels see above pp. 6–9.

2. Studies which demonstrate the laity's continuing spiritual and financial commitment to the Catholic Church right up to the eve of the Reformation include E. Duffy, *The Stripping of the Altars*; C. Burgess, "A fond thing vainly invented': an essay on Purgatory and pious motive in later medieval England", pp. 56–84. in S. Wright (ed.), *Parish, Church and People: Local Studies in Lay Religion 1350–1750* (London: Hutchinson, 1988); R. Finucane, *Miracles and Pilgrims, Popular Beliefs in Medieval England* (London: Dent, 1977).

3. *The Sarum Missal in English, Part I,* trans. F. Warren (London: De La More Press, 1911), p. 38.

4. Keck, *Angels*, p. 59.

5. Holy, holy, holy, Lord God of Hosts, Heaven and earth are full of your glory, Hosanna in the highest.

6. Keck, *Angels*, pp. 174–9.

7. *Sarum,* trans. Warren, p. 40.

8. The *Use of Sarum* evolved from various descriptive treatises that had been compiled to facilitate the performance of Divine Worship, and it revised and fixed Anglo-Saxon readings of the Roman Rite. Changes were made to the text throughout the period to clarify instructions and to incorporate change of custom or new observances, but the essentials remained.

9. See for example: the Feast of the Crown of Our Lord; the Office for the Conception of the Blessed Virgin; and the Visitation of Mary in *The Sarum Missal in English, Part II*, trans. F. Warren (London: De La More Press, 1911), pp. 70–3, 256, 389.

10. See also: the Common of Many Martyrs; the Common of Saint Peter's Chains, *Sarum, Part I*, trans. Warren, pp. 18–27; *Sarum, Part II*, trans. Warren, pp. 437.

11. See especially Duffy, *The Stripping of the Altars*, Part I.

12. There is also evidence that the *Legenda Aurea* was used as a source book by artists and craftsmen.

13. J. de Voragine, *The Golden Legend: Readings on the Saints, Vol.1*, trans. W. Ryan (Princeton, NJ: Princeton University Press, 1993), p. xiv.

14. S. Powell, 'Mirk, John (*fl. c.*1382–*c.*1414)', *ODNB*, Oxford University Press, 2004 [http://www.oxforddnb.com/view/article/18818, accessed 27 March 2006].

15. Voragine, *Legenda*, pp. 38, 293, 295. See also pp. 380–6.

16. J. Mirk, *Mirk's Festial: A Collection of Homilies by Johannes Mirkus*, ed. T. Erbe (London: Trübner for the Early English Text Society, 1965), pp. 21, 11, 131, 150.

17. Voragine, *Legenda*, pp. 201–211; Mirk, *Festial*, pp. 257–260.

18. Voragine, *Legenda*, pp. 203, 209.

19. See J. Bossy, 'The Mass as a Social Institution 1200–1700', *P&P*, 100 (1983), pp. 29–61.

20. Duffy, *The Stripping of the Altars*, p. 92.

21. Keck, *Angels*, p. 174.

22. Voragine, *Legenda*, Vol. 2, p. 390.

23. See Duffy, *The Stripping of the Altars*, pp. 95–102

24. Voragine, *Legenda*, pp. 207, 209.

25. Ibid., Vol. 2, pp. 208–10.

26. Ibid., Vol. 1, pp. 349, 329, 355; Vol. 2, p. 134.

27. For further discussion of the angels as models of celibacy for the clergy, see P. Marshall, *The Catholic Priesthood and the English Reformation* (Oxford: Clarendon Press, 1994), Chapter 5, pp. 142–173.

28. Voragine, *Legenda*, p. 32, 309, 103, 30, see also Saint Cecillia p. 318.

29. For further discussion of the importance of Mary to individual devotion see above, pp. 23–5.

30. This is a scene that survives on the church wall at Broughton, Cambridgeshire, on misericords at Ely Cathedral, St Mary's Church in Blackburn and Worcester Cathedral, and in one of the woodcuts that illustrated *Mirk's Festial* itself, in a scene that depicts the creation of Eve and the story of the Fall. G. Remnant, *A Catalogue of Misericords in Great Britain* (Oxford: Clarendon Press, 1969), pp. 18, 76, 170; E. Hodnett, *English Woodcuts 1480–1535* (Oxford: Oxford University Press, 1973), fig. 193.

31. Wall painting depicting the appearance to the shepherds at Ashamptstead, Berkshire; warning Joseph at Black Bourton, Oxfordshire; the angel at Jesus's empty tomb at West Chiltington, Sussex; Kempley, Gloucester; Resurrection scenes appear at Pickering, North Yorkshire and Seething, Norfolk. From A. Marshall, 'Medieval Wall Painting in the English Parish Church: A Developing Catalogue', http://www.paintedchurch.org/. For further examples of angelic appearances in depictions of scriptural scenes see E. Tasker, *Encyclopaedia of Medieval Church Art* (London: Batsford, 1993), Chapters 1–3.

32. Duffy, *The Stripping of the Altars*, pp. 68–77.

33. The second scene is the doom painting where Michael appears weighing the souls of the departed, discussed above, pp. 34–5.

34. C. Cave, *Roof Bosses in Medieval Churches: An aspect of Gothic Sculpture* (Cambridge: Cambridge University Press, 1948), pp. 40–42; S. Crewe, *Stained Glass in England 1180–1540* (London: HMSO, 1987), pp. 57–62; Remnant, *A Catalogue of Misericords*, pp. 64, 135, 194. Wall paintings of the Annunciation are very widespread, good surviving examples can be found at Wissington, Gisleham, Barnby and Newton Green in Suffolk; Fring, Norfolk; Tarrant Crawford, Dorset; Salisbury, Wiltshire; Slapton, Northamptonshire; Faversham, Kent.

35. See Duffy, *The Stripping of the Altars*, pp. 256–65.

36. Voragine, *Legenda*, pp. 196–206 Vol. 2, pp. 78–108; 152–169; *Festial*, pp .15–21; 106–114; 221–230.

37. For example, the Angel of the Lord instructed the apostle Andrew to travel to Ethiopia to seek out Matthew; an angel appeared to Seth to tell him that he will have to wait many years before he receives the oil of God's mercy; and Gabriel can be found announcing another birth, this time of John the Baptist.

38. Voragine, *Legenda*, pp. 13, 277, 328, Vol. 2, pp. 154, 275; Mirk, *Festial* pp. 143, 183.

39. Mirk, *Festial*, pp. 230, 222, 224; Voragine, *Legenda* Vol. 2, p. 90.

40. *Sarum, Part II*, trans. Warren, pp. 224–5.

41. Keck, *Angels*, pp. 170–2.

42. Voragine, *Legenda*, p. 197, Mirk, *Festial*, p.221.

43. Voragine, *Legenda* Vol. 2, p. 84.

44. *Sarum, Part II*, trans. Warren, pp. 222–6, 516–7, 537.

45. Mirk, *Festial*, p. 257.

46. For the traditional association of angels with healing powers see Johnson, *Saint Michael the Archangel in Medieval English Legend*, ch. 2.

47. Voragine, *Legenda*, p. 204, 207; Mirk, *Festial*, p. 143.

48. *Sarum, Part II*, trans. Warren, pp. 222–4.

49. Voragine, *Legenda*, p. 208.

50. Ibid., p. 222.

51. *Sarum, Part II*, trans. Warren, pp. 166–8, 171–4.

52. Voragine, *Legenda*, pp. 201–211, quotation p. 205.

53. Mirk, *Festial*, pp. 237, 276.

54. Ibid., pp. 72, 257.

55. Matthew 18:10, Jesus refers to a group of children with the words 'their angels do always behold the face of my Father'; Acts 12:15, Peter is mistaken for 'his angel'.

56. Voragine, *Legenda*, pp. 207–8.

57. Ibid., pp. 362, 171, 32, Vol. 2, p. 196; Mirk, *Festial*, p. 189. See also pp. 209, 276.

58. Voragine, *Legenda*, pp. 86, 106, 225, 316, 317, 322, Vol. 2, pp. 5, 160, 291.

59. Acts 5:19, the angel of the Lord released the apostles from prison, enabling them to continue to spread the good news; Acts 12:15 an angel also released Peter from prison.

60. Voragine, *Legenda*, p. 86; *Sarum, Part II*, trans. Warren, pp. 225, 120–22.

61. Voragine, *Legenda*, pp. 161, 386. See also 'Saint Euphemia', Vol. 2, pp. 182–3.

62. Mirk, *Festial*, pp. 276–7; Voragine, *Legenda*, pp. 336–8.

63. Works addressing medieval mortuary culture include P. Binski, *Medieval Death: Ritual and Representation* (London: British Museum Press, 1996); C. Daniell, *Death and Burial in Medieval England 1066–1550* (London: Routledge, 1997); B. Gordon and P. Marshall, (eds), *The Place of the Dead: Death and Remembrance in Late Medieval and Early Modern Europe* (Cambridge: Cambridge University Press, 2000); P. Marshall, *Beliefs and the Dead in Reformation England* (Oxford: Oxford University Press, 2002).

64. See also Saint Vincent and Saint Quentin, Voragine, *Legenda*, Vol. 1, p. 225, Vol. 2, p. 160.

65. Ibid., Vol. 2, p. 240.

66. Ibid., p. 323.

67. 'A volume of metrical homilies and the lives of the saints in the Northumbrian dialect, Harleian MS.4196', in *Legends of the Holy Rood: Symbols of the Passions and Cross – Poems*, trans. R. Morris (London: Trüber for the Early English Text Society, 1871), pp. 64–5.

68. *Sarum, Part II*, trans. Warren, pp. 127, 182, 174–182.

69. Voragine, *Legenda*, p. 81.

70. Mirk, *Festial*, pp. 222, 260; J. de Voragine, *Legenda aurea sanctorum, sive, Lombardica historia* trans. W. Caxton (London, 1487), sig. CC12r; Voragine, *Legenda*, pp. 209–210.

71. *Sarum, Part II*, trans. Warren, p. 182.

72. J. Alexander and P. Binski (eds), *Age of Chivalry: Art in Plantagenet England 1200–1400* (London: Weidenfeld and Nicolson, 1987), pp. 212–3; Remnant, *Misericords*, pp. 87, 147; Cave, *Roof Bosses*, pp. 102, 42–5.

73. See also the birds that sang on the roof of the house where Saint Elizabeth lay dying, which were taken to be 'angels sent by God to carry her soul to heaven and to honour her body with celestial carolling'. Voragine, *Legenda*, pp. 84, 293, 312.

74. Mirk, *Festial*, pp. 43, 202.

75. *Sarum, Part II*, trans. Warren, p. 174.

76. On the *ars moriendi* see also Binski, *Medieval Death*, pp. 33–46; Duffy, *The Stripping of the Altars*, pp. 314–17. For the role of the angels at the deathbed see P. Marshall, 'Angels around the deathbed: variations on a theme in the English art of dying', in Marshall and Walsham (eds), *Angels in the Early Modern World*.

77. W. Caxton, *Here begynneth a lityll treatise shorte and abredged spekynge of the arte & crafte to knowe well to dye* (London, 1490); see also *The crafte to lyue well and to dye well*, trans. A. Chertsey (London, 1505); Anon, *The Dyenge creature* (London, 1507).

78. Voragine, *Legenda*, pp. 90, 312, 198–200.

79. Mirk, *Festial*, pp. 257–9; Voragine, *Legenda*, pp. 205–6.

80. Images of Michael fighting the dragon are too numerous to list here. Good surviving examples can be found on painted rood screens at Ashton and Ranworth; in the Norman tympanum above the North door at Moreton Valence; on roof bosses at Sherbourne and Tewkesbury Abbeys and at Yeovil, Somerset; and on misericords at Carlisle, Gloucester, and Norfolk Cathedrals. The scene commonly appeared in manuscripts: *Legenda Aurea* and *Mirk's Festial* usually included illuminations on the subject and works such as the Westminster and York Psalters often include beautiful images of the battle.

81. Voragine, *Legenda*, p. 205; Mirk, *Festial*, p. 259.

82. See Keck, *Angels*, pp. 179–84; for a fuller account of the development of the foundation myths see Johnson, *Saint Michael*, chs 2–3.

83. Ibid., passim; Keck, *Angels*, pp. 79–184.

84. Voragine, *Legenda*, pp. 81–2: 'Christ nodded his consent and immediately Michael the archangel came forward and presented Mary's soul before the Lord'; Mirk, *Festial*, p. 224, 'Seynt Myghel beryng our lady sowle yn hys armes, bryghtyr þen þe sonne'.

85. Voragine, *Legenda*, p. 208.

86. Mirk, *Festial*, p. 4; Voragine, *Legenda*, pp. 12, 121, 210.

87. See above p. 19.

88. Other excellent examples of the scene can be found in doom paintings at Catherington, Hampshire; Bishopbounre, Kent; Bartlow, Cambridgeshire; South Leigh, Oxfordshire.

89. A. Gardner, *English Medieval Sculpture* (Cambridge: Cambridge University Press, 1951), p. 260. Examples of angels carrying family arms can be found on roof bosses at Winchester, Tewkesbury, Chichester, Westminster and Blythburgh; and carrying instruments at Westminster, Gloucester, Winchester, York and Norwich. They also frequently appear on misericords, and are featured in the architecture at Southwark, Windsor and Sall. Of particular note is the wonderful series of heavenly musicians still to be seen in the spandrels of the Angel Choir, Lincoln Minster. Cave, *Roof Bosses*, pp. 48–51; Crewe, *Stained Glass*, pp. 57–62; Gardner, *Medieval Sculpture*, pp. 107–145, 259–267; Remnant, *Misericords*; F. Burgess, *English Churchyard Memorials* (London: S.P.C.K., 1979), pp. 173–5.

90. Voragine, *Legenda*, p. 201.

91. Gardner, *Medieval Sculpture*, p. 260.

92. For further discussion on the didactic function of medieval architecture see B. Levy (ed.), *The Bible in the Middle Ages: Its Influence on Literature and Art* (Binghamton, N.Y.: Medieval & Renaissance Texts and Studies, 1992), esp. M. Caviness, 'Biblical Stories in Windows: Were They Bibles for the Poor?', pp. 103–148; Alexander and Binski (eds), *Age of Chivalry*; R. Reynolds, 'Liturgy and the Monument', pp. 57–67 in V. Raguin, K. Brush, P. Draper (eds), *Artistic Integration in Gothic Buildings* (London: University of Toronto Press, 1995).

93. F. Holweck, transcribed by M. Barrett, 'The Five Sacred Wounds', in *Catholic Encyclopedia* [http://www.newadvent.org/cathen/15714a.htm, accessed March 2006]; Voragine, *Legenda*, pp. 61–5.

94. Descriptions and images of these depictions of the Nine Orders can be found in Tasker, *Encyclopaedia of Medieval Church Art*, pp. 178–180.

95. Mirk, *Festial*, pp. 56, 253.

96. Brandon, 'Angels'. V. Flint, *The Rise of Magic in Early Medieval Europe* (Oxford: Clarendon Press, 1993), pp. 126–7, 157–72.

97. These passages appear in Charlemagne's *Admonitio Generalis* of 789 and the collection of capitularies Ansegisus made in early in the ninth century, cited in Flint, *The Rise of Magic*, p. 163. See also Johnson, *Saint Michael,* pp. 42–4.

98. M. Twycross, 'Books for the Unlearned', *Themes in Drama V* (1983), pp. 65–110.

99. See for example Duffy, *The Stripping of the Altars*, pp. 579–82; M. Rubin, 'Corpus Christi Fraternities and Late Medieval Piety', *Studies in Church History*, 23 (1986), pp. 97–109; M. James, 'Ritual, Drama and Social Body in the Late Medieval English Town', *P&P* 98, (February, 1983), pp. 3–29; A. Johnston, 'The Guild of Corpus Christi and the Procession of Corpus Christi in York', *Medieval Studies*, 38 (1976), pp. 372–384.

100. I discuss the significance of angels in drama in more detail in a forthcoming article entitled 'Angels and Belief in the English Mystery Cycles'.

2 The Protestant Angel, *c.* 1530–80

1. Marshall and Walsham (eds), *Angels in the Early Modern World*, p. 13.

2. See above pp. 4–6.

3. MacCulloch, *Reformation*, p. 581.

4. Walsham, *Providence in Early Modern England*, p. 329.

5. 'The Belgic Confession A.D.1561', in P. Schaff, *The Creeds of Christendom with a History and Critical Notes, Vol. 1* (Grand Rapids: Harper and Row, 1877), p. 395, 'Article

12: Of the Creation'; 'The French Confession of Faith A.D. 1559', in Schaff, *Creeds of Christendom*, p. 362, 'Article 5'.

6.   M. Luther, *The last wil and last confession of martyn luthers faith co[n]cerming [sic] the principal articles of religion which are in controversy* (Wesel, 1543), sig. B5v.

7.   Duffy, *The Stripping of the Altars*, pp. 12–52, quotation p. 13.

8.   Church of England, 'The Book of Common Prayer and Administration of the Sacraments and other Rites and Ceremonies in the Church of England', in *Liturgical Services: Liturgies and occasional forms of prayer set forth in the Reign of Queen Elizabeth*, ed. W. K. Clay (Cambridge: Cambridge University Press, 1847), p. 33.

9.   'The Book of Common Prayer 1549', in *The Two Liturgies A.D.1549 and A.D.1552 with other Documents set forth by Authority in the Reign of King Edward VI*, ed. J. Ketley (Cambridge: Cambridge University Press, 1844), p. 89.

10.   J. Calvin, *Institutes of the Christian Religion: a New Translation by H. Beveridge, Vol. 1* (Grand Rapids, Michigan: Wm. B. Eerdmans, 1957), p. 150.

11.   H. Bullinger, 'The Ninth Sermon: Of good and evil spirits', in *The Decades of Henry Bullinger, Minister of the Church of Zurich: The Fourth Decade*, trans. H.I., ed. T. Harding (Cambridge: Cambridge University Press, 1851), pp. 344, 347.

12.   T. Beza, *A booke of Christian questions and answers. Wherein are set foorth the cheef points of the Christian religion in maner of an abridgment*, trans. A. Golding (London, 1572), p. 19r.

13.   E. Allen, *A catechisme* (London, 1548), sig. C5v.

14.   E. Dering, *A briefe and necessary instruction veryre needefull to bee knowen of all housholders* (London, 1572), sig. B3v.

15.   I. Green, *The Christian's ABC: Catechisms and Catechizing in England c.1530–1740* (Oxford: Clarendon Press, 1996), pp. 1–44, quotation p. 43.

16.   Ibid., p. 43.

17.   Historians remain divided on this issue. Christopher Haigh sees catechizing as one of the 'successes' of the Reformation, detecting a gradual improvement in provision. However, in contrast to Green, Haigh does not believe that the expansion of catechizing translated readily into greater religious understanding and conviction. C. Haigh, 'Success and Failure in the English Reformation', *P&P*, 173 (2001), pp. 28–49.

18.   Green, *Christian's ABC*, pp. 3, 383.

19.   The following sample of catechetical works was chosen with reference to Ian Green's list of early modern 'bestsellers', in his *Print and Protestantism in Early Modern England* (Oxford: Oxford University Press, 2000), Appendix 1, pp. 519–672. These catechisms were therefore those that were in wide circulation during the period.

20.   H. Latimer, 'A Sermon made on Christmas Day, by Master Hugh Latimer, At Bexterly, 25 December 1552', in *Sermons and Remains of Hugh Latimer, sometime Bishop of Worcester, Martyr*, ed. George Corrie, PS 20 (Cambridge: Cambridge University Press, 1845), pp. 86–7.

21.   W. Tyndale, 'Exposition of the first epistle of Saint John: Chapter II', in his *Expositions and Notes on Sundry Portions of Holy Scriptures together with the Practice of Prelates,* ed., H. Walter, PS 37 (Cambridge: Cambridge University Press, 1848), p. 169.

22.   J. Bridges, *The supremacie of Christian princes ouer all persons throughout theor dominions* (London, 1573), p. 405.

23.   See also W. Fulke, *D.Heskins, S.Sanders and M.Rastel, accounted (among their faction) three pillers and archpatriarches of the popish synagogue* (London, 1579), pp. 436–7; J. Bradford, 'Confutation of Four Romish Doctrines', in *The Writings of John Bradford,*

containing Sermons, Meditations, Examination, Parker Society Vol. 31 (Cambridge: Cambridge University Press, 1853), p. 281. For other influential Protestants expressing similar sentiments see M. Coverdale, *The Remains of Myles Coverdale,* ed. G. Pearson, PS 22 (Cambridge: Cambridge University Press, 1846), pp. 260–1; J. Jewel, 'Controversy with Harding: the Eighteenth Article', in *The Works of John Jewel: Bishop of Salisbury, Vol 2,* ed. J. Ayre, PS 26 (Cambridge: Cambridge University Press, 1847), pp. 741–2.

24. *The Two Liturgies,* ed. Ketley, p. 474–5; T. Becon, 'The Pomander of Prayer', in *Prayers and Other Pieces of Thomas Becon,* ed. John Eyre, PS 17 (Cambridge: Cambridge University Press, 1844), p. 84; Anon, *A Primer of boke of priuate praier* (London, 1560), sig. X2r-v; Anon, *A primer or booke of private prayer* (London, 1568), sigs. X2r-v, U7r.

25. Calvin, *Institutes,* p. 149.

26. Bullinger, 'The Ninth Sermon', p. 344.

27. J. Calvin, *The forme of common praiers vsed in the churches of Geneua,* trans. W. Huycke (London, 1550), sig. S8r; Dering, *A briefe and necessary instruction,*sig. A5v. Beza, *A booke of Christian questions,* p. 20r.

28. Revelation, 19:10.

29. T. Becon, *The Catechism of Thomas Becon, with other pieces written by him in the reign of King Edward the sixth,* ed. J. Eyre, PS 13 (Cambridge: Cambridge University Press, 1844), p. 59.

30. (J. Jewel), *The second tome of homilies of such matters as were promised, and intitules in the former part of homilies* (London, 1571), p. 244.

31. The distinction between the types of worship was established at the Council of Nicea, 787A.D. For further explanation see M. Aston, *England's Iconoclasts, Volume 1: Laws Against Images* (Oxford: Clarendon Press, 1988), pp. 47–9.

32. (Jewel), *The second tome,* p. 105, my italics.

33. Fulke, *D. Heskins,* p. 604.

34. T. Cranmer, *Miscellaneous Writings and Letters of Thomas Cranmer, Archbishop of Canterbury, martyr, 1556,* ed. J. Cox, PS 24 (Cambridge: Cambridge University Press, 1846), p. 63.

35. Ibid., pp. 63–67.

36. *The Two Liturgies,* ed. Ketley, pp. 131, 136.

37. For further discussion of Raphael and the book of Tobit see above pp. 8, 26, 37, 51, 53, 54, 67–9, 137, 149.

38. For discussion of the significance of the retention of the feast, see above p. 75, 103.

39. A. L. Rowse, *Tudor Cornwall: A Portrait of a Society* (London: Cape, 1957), pp. 164, 186.

40. D. Knowles and R. Hadcock, *Medieval Religious Houses: England and Wales* (Harlow: Longman, 1971), pp. 91, 459.

41. Rowse, *Tudor Cornwall,* p. 186.

42. See above p. 42.

43. Duffy, *The Stripping of the Altars,* pp. 160–1.

44. J. de Voragine, *The golden legend, or, Lives of the saints / as Englished by William Caxton,* Vol. 2 (London: J. M. Dent and Co., 1900), p. 278.

45. Duffy, *The Stripping of the Altars,* pp. 187–8.

46. P. Brown, *The Cult of the Saints: Its Rise and Function in Latin Christianity* (Chicago, IL: University of Chicago Press, 1981), pp. 50–1

47. Brown, *Saints,* pp. 61–3.

48. For further discussion of the association of angels and divine punishment see above pp. 71, 91, 146, 158.

49. For further discussion of the contrast between the nature of Christ and angels, see above pp. 62–3, 133–4.

50. *The Sarum Missal in English, Part II*, trans. F. Warren, (London: De La More Press, 1911), pp. 64–65.

51. J. Foxe, *Acts and Monvments of Martyrs, with a Generall discourse of these latter Persecution* (London, 1563), pp. 958–9.

52. N. Hemmingsen, *A Postill, or, Exposition of the Gospels that are usually red in the churches of God, vpon the Sundayes and feast dayes of Saincts*, trans. A. Golding (1569), p. 326v.

53. J. Bale, *The apology of Johan Bale agaynste a ranke papist anuswering both hym and hys doctours, that neyther their vowes nor yet their priesthode are of the Gospell* [sic], *but of Antichrist* (London, 1550), pp. 134v. Bale returned to the theme in *The first two partes of the actes or unchast examples of the Englysh votaryes gathered out of their owne legenades and chronicles by Johan Bale* (Wesel [London], 1551).

54. Foxe, *Actes*, p. 22.

55. Duffy, *The Stripping of the Altars*, p. 73.

56. W. Bullein, *Bulleins bulwarke of a defence against all sicknesse, soarnesse, and vvoundes that doe dayly assaulte mankinde* (London, 1562), fol. lx, 1r.

57. P. Wallis, 'Bullein, William (*c*.1515–1576)', *ODNB*, Oxford University Press, 2004 [http://www.oxforddnb.com/view/article/3910, accessed 27 Oct 2008].

58. See also Dering, *A briefe and necessary instruction*, sig. B3r.

59. Calvin, *Institutes*, p. 143, Bullinger, 'The Ninth Sermon', p. 329.

60. Calvin, *Institutes*, p. 147.

61. Bullinger, 'The Ninth Sermon', p. 337.

62. Calvin's disdain is explicit in the *Institutes*, where he described discussion of the nature, ranks and number of angels as the 'vain babblings of idle men', which would only result in 'superfluous speculations' and 'nugatory wisdom', p. 144.

63. Ibid., p. 144.

64. For a fuller account of the discrediting of Dionysius see Patrides, 'Renaissance Thought on the Celestial Hierarchy'.

65. Tobit, 12:15.

66. W. Fulke, *A Defence of the Sincere and True Translations of the Holy Scriptures into the English Tongue against the cavils of Gregory Martin*, ed. C. Hartshorne, PS 10 (Cambridge: Cambridge University Press, 1843), pp. 21–3.

67. The collect is the same in each edition of the Prayer Book, *The Two Liturgies*, ed. Ketley, pp. 74, 263; *Liturgical Services*, ed. Clay, p. 176.

68. H. Bull, *Christian Prayers and Meditations* (London, 1568), pp. 234–5.

69. Matthew 18, 1:10; Acts, 12:15.

70. Calvin, *Institutes*, pp. 146–7. Calvin also repeated his warning that notions of good and evil angels 'as a kind of genii' are amongst those aspects of faith that God had not deemed it necessary to elaborate upon, therefore 'it is not worthwhile anxiously to investigate a point which does not greatly concern us'.

71. Bullinger, 'The Ninth Sermon', p. 331. Bullinger in fact does not mention the prospect of *guardian* angels at any point in his sermon on celestial beings.

72. For the association of angels with the Cult of the Virgin Mary and the Cult of the Five Wounds see above pp. 23–5, 36, 57, 65.

73. 'A Proclamation against breakinge or defacing of monuments of antiquitie, being set vp in Churches or other publique places for memory, and not for superstition', 19 Sept. 1560', in *Tudor Royal Proclamations, Vol. 2. The Later Tudors*, eds P. Hughes and J. Larkin (New Haven, CT; London: Yale University Press, 1969), pp. 146–8.

74. Crossley finds evidence that a London shop was the probable source of 'a more carefully modelled type, a little sedate in attitude, but with a winsome expression on the features' found on the chantry chapel of prince Arthur at Worcester and along the cornice of tombs at Ewelme, Windsor, Westminster, Strelly and Hitchin. In contrast in the south-west angels were 'generally half-length and holding shields ... the body clothed with an albe; the wings were brought straight above the head' such as those on canopies at Long Ashton, Wells and Redcliffe: F. Crossley, *English Church Monuments A.D.1150–1550: an introduction to the study of tombs & effigies of the Mediaeval period* (London: B. T. Batsford, 1921), p. 130. See also the illustrations on pp. 140–1, 145. For further evidence that angels remained on both tomb monuments and brasses see also H. Tummers, *Early Secular Effigies in England: the thirteenth century* (Leiden: Brill, 1980), esp. pp. 49–52 where angels are described as 'a most common device'; R. Le Strange, *A Complete Descriptive Guide to British Monumental Brasses* (London: Thames and Hudson, 1972), passim; A. Gardner, *English Medieval Sculpture* (Cambridge: Cambridge University Press, 1951), esp. pp. 107–26. The continuing association of angels with mortuary culture will be further explored later in this chapter.

75. P. Collinson, 'From Iconoclasm to Iconophobia: the Cultural Impact of the Second English Reformation', *The Stenton Lecture 1985* (University of Reading: 1986).

76. Watt, *Cheap Print*, passim.

77. Dowsing's journal is replete with references to the destruction of 'superstitious cherubim' and 'divers angells', too many to list here, but typical entries include: Dennington, 26 September 1644, '10 angels in Sir John Rouse his ile, 9 pictures of angels and crosses, and a cherubim in Sir John Rouse his stool'; or Laxfield, the church where Dowsing was baptized, 17 July 1644, '2 angells in stone, at the steeple's end, and another on the porch, in stone'. Of course, some of the angels that Dowsing encountered may have been Laudian 'innovations', but the editor of the most recent edition of the journal, Trevor Cooper, has undertaken a thorough survey of the churches in question and in many cases has been able to establish the original date of much of what was destroyed. T. Cooper (ed.), *The Journal of William Dowsing: Iconoclasm in East Anglia during the English Civil War* (Woodbridge: Boydell, 2001), pp. 317, 302.

78. Again, there are numerous examples highlighted by Cooper in his edition of Dowsing's journal, see esp. entries: 30: Pullchers or Round Parish, Cambs, 2 January 1644, where 'a host of wooden angels survive'; 46: Withersfield, Cambs, 6 January 1644, where there is a bench end depicting St Michael slaying the dragon; 60: in Saxmundham, Cambs, angels survive on the font, south arcade and west tower window; 247: and in Ufford, Suffolk, 27 January 1644, Dowsing broke down an angel and 12 cherubs in the chancel, yet another 12 remain, untouched.

79. A. Walsham, 'Angels and Idols in England's Long Reformation', in Marshall and Walsham (eds), *Angels in the Early Modern World*, p. 145.

80. Angels on the tabernacle: Exodus, 25:18, 26:1, 36:8, 37:7; angels in Solomon's temple: Kings 1, 6:23. 7:29, 8:6; Chronicles 1, 28:18, Chronicles 2, 3:7, 5:7.

81. J. Calfhill, *An Answer to John Martiall's 'Treatise of the Cross'*, ed. R. Gibbings, PS Vol. 25 (Cambridge: Cambridge University Press, 1846), p. 199.

82. Jewel, 'Controversy with M. Harding', pp. 645–7.

83. Cranmer, *Miscellaneous Writings*, p. 178.
84. Margaret Aston argues that the 1537 *Bishop's Book* was more advanced in its reformed opinion, warning more generally of the spiritual dangers of images, whereas the 1543 *King's Book* appeared to rebut those who would argue against the use of *any* images. The 1547 Royal Injunctions also confined criticism to abused images, but as Aston points out, in practice the criteria for defining 'abused' images was not always clear and was open to interpretation. Aston, *Iconoclasts*, pp. 239–75.
85. T. Rogers, *The Catholic Doctrine of the Church of England: An Exposition of the Thirty-Nine Articles*, ed. J. Perowne, PS 52 (Cambridge: Cambridge University Press, 1854), pp. 221–3.
86. T. Cranmer, *Catechismus, that is to say, a shorte instruction into Christian religion for the synguler commoditie and profyte of childre and yong people* (London, 1548), sig. O5v.
87. Aston, *Iconoclasts*, pp. 392–445.
88. Le Strange, *Complete Descriptive Guide*, pp. 73, 88.
89. Watt, *Cheap Print*, p. 126 and passim.
90. Walsham, 'Angels and Idols', pp. 144, 167 and passim. The point that symbolic religious images did appear to be permissible to some reformers is also made by Aston, *Iconoclasts*, p. 400.
91. Walsham, 'Angels and Idols', p. 232.
92. *The Two Liturgies*, ed. Ketley, pp. 87, 278, 31. See also pp. 221–2. *The Book of Common Prayer*, ed. Clay, p.193. See also p. 58.
93. Latimer, 'A sermon made on Christmas day', p. 86; T. Becon, 'The second sermon upon the saying of the Angel', in *A new postil conteinyng most godly and learned sermons vpon all the Sonday Gospelles*. (London, 1566), sigs. E7v-r. For similar sentiments see Bullinger, *Decades*, p. 342; and J. Habermann, *A dailie exercise of godly meditations drawne out of the pure fountains of the holie Scriptures*, trans. T. Rogers (London, 1579), sig. B7r.
94. Habermann, *A dailie exercise*, sigs. B7r-B8v; Hemmingsen, *A Postill*, p.22r.
95. Cranmer, *Catechimus*, sigs. V5v-r. See also 'A Short Catechism or Plain Instruction' (London, 1553) in *The Two Liturgies*, ed. Ketley, p. 521; or J. Calvin, *The Catechisme or manner to teache children the Christian religion* [Geneva, 1556], sigs. G8v-r.
96. See above p. 52.
97. Allen, *A Catechism*, sigs. G1v-r; Beza, *A booke of Christian questions*, sig. 16v.
98. Becon, 'The second sermon', sig. E4v.
99. Bridges, *The supremacie of Christian princes*, p. 478.
100. Calvin, *Institutes*, pp. 145,147.
101. R. Taverner, *On Saynt Andrewes day the Gospels with brief sermons upon them for al the holy dayes in ye yere* (London, 1542), pp. xivr. Hemmingsen, *A postill*, pp. 19r-20r.
102. Calvin, *Institutes*, pp. 145, 149.
103. Hemmingsen, *A Postill*, pp. 338v-339v.
104. Bullinger, 'The Ninth Sermon', pp. 339–40.
105. *The Two Liturgies*, ed. Ketley, p. 453. Beza also mentioned the notion in *A booke of Christian questions*, sig. D3v, 'concerning the angels ... the lorde useth their seruis in defending his children: and no doubt but they execute their charge as it is inioyned in them, and are careful ... for the welfare of the Godly'. In simpler forms of catechism the idea may have been expressed through one question: 'Are the Angels appointed to serve us? Yes', J. Craig, *A shorte summe of the whole catechisme* (London, 1583), p. 28v.
106. Foxe, *Actes*, p. 442. See also Becon, 'The Second Sermon', sig. E2v: in relating the story of the shepherd in his nativity sermon, he interrupted the flow of the narrative to note

that 'Gods messengers conforte the fearefull'; Calfhill, *An Answer to John Martiall's*, p. 199. 'Angels, from the beginning wrought many virtues for man's behoof'; and Latimer, *Sermons and Remains*, p. 86., 'except God did preserve us from him [the devil] by the ministration of his obedient angels, we should perish ... thanks be unto God, which never ceaseth to provide for us'.

107. Taverner, *On Saynt Andrewes Day*, fol. xxxiiii v.

108. Ibid., fol. xxxiv-xxv

109. Taverner's concerns were supported by Calvin's description of the angelic purpose in *Institutes*, p. 145.

110. M. C. Skeeters, 'Northbrooke, John (fl. 1567–1589)', *ODNB*, Oxford University Press, 2004 [http://www.oxforddnb.com/view/article/20323, accessed 27 Oct 2008]; J. Northbrooke, *Spiritus est vicarious Christi in terra. A breefe and pithie summe of the Christian faith made in the fourme of a confession* (London, 1571), pp. 47v-r.

111. T. Becon, *The gouernaunce of vertue teaching all fayhful Christians, how they oughte daily to leade their lyfe* (London, 1566), sig. L1v.

112. Angelic ministry to condemned prisoners in the hours preceding and during saints' martyrdoms is discussed in Chapter 1 above, p. 28.

113. For the importance of angels to late medieval mortuary culture see above pp. 29–37.

114. P. Marshall, 'Angels around the deathbed: variations on a theme in the English art of dying', in Marshall and Walsham (eds), *Angels in the Early Modern World*, p. 95.

115. Ibid., pp. 91–7.

116. T. Cranmer, *Certayne sermons, or homelies appoynted by the kynges Maiestie* (London, 1547), sig. P4r; Becon, *Sick man's salve*, pp. 6–7.

117. Marshall, 'Angels around the deathbed', p. 103. and passim.

118. Becon, 'The sonday next before Easter', in *A New postil*, p. 195v; Becon, *The flour of Godly praiers*, sig. X1v.

119. J. Bradford, *Godlie meditations upon the Lordes prayer* (London, 1562), sigs. L2v-r; See also Bull, *Christian Prayers*, pp. 181–2, 197.

120. R. Day, *A booke of Christian prayers* (London, 1578), p. 136; Bradford, *Godlie meditations*, sigs. L2v-r.

121. The controversy over guardian angels proved a continual source of debate, see above pp. 74, 100, 107–15, 161–4.

122. See above pp. 57–8.

123. Marshall, 'Angels around the deathbed', p. 103.

124. For the rejection of the book of Tobit from the Protestant canon see above pp. 54–5.

125. J. F. Jackson, 'Hutchinson, Roger (d. 1555)', *ODNB*, Oxford University Press, Sept 2004; online edn, Jan 2008 [http://www.oxforddnb.com/view/article/14287, accessed 27 Oct 2008].

126. R. Hutchinson, *The Works of Roger Hutchinson*, ed. J. Bruce, PS 4 (Cambridge: Cambridge University Press, 1842), pp. 90–1.

127. T. Becon, *The flour of godly praiers* (London, 1550), sig. H7v.

128. Anonymous, *A godly garden out of which most comfortable herbs may be gathered* (London, 1574), p. 71. See also Bull, *Christian Prayers*, p. 134. Bull expanded the idea to give a general sense of God's protection. See also T. Becon, *The Sycke mans salve* (London, 1561), p. 26.

129. Watt, *Cheap Print*, quotation p. 182. See especially Chapter 5.

130. Ibid., pp. 209–10. Watt documents that Toby was part of the stock of godly ballad publishers and lists the painted narrative of his journey on the walls of the White Swan in

Stratford-Upon-Avon (1570–8); an inventory of Wassell Wessells in the Prerogative court of Canterbury which included a 'Storie of Tobias'; and an Essex mercer who died in 1584 who owned a 'little story of Tobias' along with 'other stained cloths' as further evidence to support her claims.

131. Ibid., pp. 185–6.

132. Marshall and Walsham (eds), *Angels in the Early Modern World*, p. 4.

133. Walsham, *Providence*, passim.

134. Hemmingsen, *A Postill*, p. 382r; Calfhill, *An Answer to John Martiall's*, p. 199; Latimer, *Sermons and Remains*, p. 386.

135. *The Two Liturgies*, ed. Ketley, p. 474–5; Becon, *The Pomander of Prayer*, p. 84; Anon, *A Primer of boke of priuate praier*, sig. X2r-v; *A primer or booke of private prayer*, sigs. X2r-v, U7r; R. C., *A briefe and necessary catechisme, concerning the principall points of our Christian religion* (London, 1572), sig. B8r.

136. Foxe, *Actes and Monvments*, pp. 1640, 1643.

137. For a discussion of Foxe's attack on the Mass of the Five Wounds see above pp. 51–2. For the assault on the *Ave Maria*, see above p. 52. For condemnation of the monastic vow to live a chaste life see above p. 52.

138. Foxe, *Actes and Monuments*, pp. 556, 1070.

139. Ibid., pp. 1021, 1449.

140. Ibid., p. 1515.

141. For recent debates on the importance of Foxe's *Actes and Monuments* see especially C. Highley and J. King (eds), *John Foxe and his World* (Aldershot: Ashgate, 2002); D. Loades (ed.), *John Foxe: An Historical Perspective* (Aldershot: Ashgate, 1999); T. Freeman, 'New Perspectives on an Old Book: The Creation and Influence of Foxe's Book of Martyrs', *Journal of Ecclesiastical History*, 49 (1998); D. Loades (ed.), *John Foxe and the English Reformation* (Aldershot: Ashgate, 1997).

142. T. Bright, *An abridgement of the booke of acts and monumentes of the Church: written by that Reuerend Father, Maister Iohn Fox: and now abridged by Timothe Bright* (London, 1589); P. Life, 'Bright, Timothy (1549/50–1615)', *ODNB*, Oxford University Press, Sept 2004; online edn, Jan 2008 [http://www.oxforddnb.com/view/article/3424, accessed 27 Oct 2008]; D. Nussbaum, 'Whitgift's 'Book of Martyrs': Archbishop Whitgift, Timothy Bright and the Elizabethan Struggle over John Foxe's Legacy', in Loades (ed.), *John Foxe: An Historical Perspective*; P. Collinson, 'John Foxe and National Consciousness', in Highly and King (eds.), *John Foxe and his World*, pp. 31–2; P. Collinson, 'John Foxe as Historian', http://www.hrionline.ac.uk/foxe/apparatus/collinsonessay. html (accessed July 2007), and D. Loades, 'The Early Reception', http://www.hrionline. ac.uk/foxe/apparatus/loadesearlyreceptionessay.html#top (accessed July 2007).

143. Loades, 'The Early Reception'.

144. F. Yates, 'Foxe as Propagandist', in her *Ideas and Ideals in the North European Renaissance: Collected Essays*, Vol. III (London: Routledge & Kegan Paul, 1984), p. 34.

145. Collinson, 'John Foxe and National Consciousness', pp. 13, 28.

146. Foxe, *Actes*, p. 1021.

147. See for example 'A prayer and thanksgiving fit for this present time', (1587), p. 604; 'Prayer for the Earl of Leicester' (1587), p. 606. See also prayers requesting the help of a host of angels in *Liturgical Services of the Reign of Queen Elizabeth*, ed. Clay, pp. 629, 637, 648.

148. 'A prayer used in the Queen Majesty's house and Chapel, for the prosperity of the French King and his nobility, assailed by a multitude of notorious rebels that are supported and waged by great forces of foreigners' (1590), in *Liturgical Services*, ed. Clay, p. 653.
149. Ibid., pp. 638, 672–3.
150. Ibid., pp. 667. See also 1598 'A prayer for the safety of the realm', which described 'the very finger of God mightily working herein by his providence and mercy', p. 682.
151. Ibid., pp. 663–4.
152. Ibid., p. 689.
153. See above pp. 55–6.
154. Calvin, *Institutes*, p. 146.
155. Ibid., pp. 144, 149.
156. Walsham, *Providence*, pp. 332–3.
157. D. Cressy, *Bonfires and Bells: National Memory and the Protestant Calendar in Elizabethan and Stuart England* (London: Weidenfeld and Nicholson, 1989), p. xi and passim.
158. Ibid., p. 29.
159. Hemmingsen, 'Postill', pp. 337r-342v; Taverner, *On Saynt Andrewes*, pp. 34r-39v. For the retention of the feast in the *Book of Common Prayer* see *The Two Liturgies*, ed. Ketley, pp. 74,263; and *The Book of Common Prayer*, ed. Clay, p. 176.
160. *Liturgical Services*, ed. Clay, p. 619.
161. Calvin, *Institutes*, pp. 148–9.
162. Foxe, *Actes*, p. 1243. For other examples of similar uses of this biblical passage see also page 1596; Bridges, *The supremacie of Christian Princes*, p. 458; J. Spangenberg, *The sum of diuinitie drawn out of the holy scripture very necessary* (London, 1548), sig. N8v.
163. This conclusion indicates an area of divergence from Kate Harvey's argument that anthropology was 'the framing characteristic' of Protestant intellectual angelology. K. Harvey, 'The role of angels in English Protestant thought 1580 to 1660', Ph.D. diss., (Cambridge, 2005), p. 185 and passim.

3 The Church of England Angel, *c.* 1580–1700

1. P. Collinson, *The Birthpangs of Protestant England: Religious and Cultural Change in the Sixteenth and Seventeenth Centuries* (Basingstoke: Macmillan, 1988), p. ix.
2. Perkins' theology, for example, is described as 'a conventional recital of Calvinist scholasticism in virtually every respect' by M. Jinkins, 'Perkins, William (1558–1602)', *ODNB*, Oxford University Press, Sept 2004; online edn, May 2007 [http://www.oxforddnb.com/view/article/21973, accessed 27 Nov 2008].
3. W. Perkins, *A golden chaine: or The description of theologie containing the order of the causes of saluation and damnation* (London, 1591), pp. 11–2, 232.
4. Ibid., pp. 11, 231–5.
5. The reinterpretation of Perkins' career is discussed at length in W. B. Patterson, 'William Perkins as Apologist for the Church of England', *JEH*, 57 (2006), pp. 252–69. See also I. Breward, *The work of William Perkins* (Abingdon: Sutton Courtenay Press, 1970), Introduction.
6. Patterson, 'William Perkins', p. 268.
7. See L. A. Ferrell, 'William Perkins and Calvinist aesthetics', in C. Highley and J. N. King (eds), *John Foxe and his world* (Aldershot: Ashgate, 2002), pp. 160–82.
8. Patterson, 'William Perkins', pp. 268–9. See also W. Perkins, *An exposition of the Symbole or Creed of the Apostles according to the tenour of the Scriptures* (London, 1595), pp.

73–80; *An exposition of the Lords praier in the way of catechisme* (London, 1593), pp. 42–4; *A declaration of the true manner of knowing Christ Crucified* (London, 1596), p. 7; *A reformed Catholike* (London, 1598), pp. 252–4; *Of the calling of the ministerie two treatises* (London, 1605), sigs. A5v-A6v, pp. 7–10, 66–81; *The combat betvveene Christ and the Diuell displayed* (London, 1606), pp. 4, 31–4, 48, 51–4; *A godly and learned exposition of Christs Sermon in the Mount* (London, 1608), pp. 280–3; *A salve for a sicke man* (London, 1611), pp. 34, 122; *Satans sophistrie ansuuered by our Sauiour Christ and in diuers sermons further manifested* (London, 1694), p. 73–5, 135–139.

9. Perkins, *A godly and learned exposition of Christs Sermon*, pp. 280–3.

10. Perkins, *Exposition of Christs sermon*, p. 282, my italics.

11. L. Andrewes, *The wonderfull combate betweene Christ and Satan* (London, 1592), sigs. 42r, 57r-59r, 98r. See also L. Andrewes, *Scala coeli: Nineteen sermons concerning prayer* (London, 1611), sigs. 71v-r, 152v-156v; L. Andrewes, *A sermon preached at White-hall, on Easter day* (London, 1620), pp. 2–4, 11–16.

12. A. Willet, *Tetrastylon papisticum, that is, the foure principal pillers of papistry* (London, 1593), pp. 54–5, 65, 86, 96, 110, 127–9, 142. See also his *Synopsis Papismi, that is, a generall viewe of papistry* (London, 1592), pp. 299–355 which also uses angels as a prism through which to explore the Catholic and Protestant opinions on worship and invocation of saints and angels; and A. Willet, *A catholicon* (London, 1602), pp. 25–6, 29–32, which discusses the qualities of angels and their fall, with reference to predestination.

13. G. Abbot, *The reasons which Doctour Hill hath brought, for the vpholding of papistry* (London, 1604), pp. 367–9. See also G. Abbot, *An exposition vpon the prophet Ionah, Contained in certaine sermons* (London, 1600), pp. 205, 207, 213–14.

14. A. S. McGrade, 'Hooker, Richard (1554–1600)', *ODNB*, Oxford University Press, 2004 [http://0-www.oxforddnb.com.lib.exeter.ac.uk/view/article/13696, accessed 30 Oct 2011].

15. R. Hooker, *Of the Lavves of ecclesiasticall politie: The First Booke: Concerning Lawes, and their seuerall kindes in generall* (London, 1593), pp. 53–4.

16. N. Ling (ed.), *Politeuphuia: wits common wealth* (London, 1598), sigs. B4r-B5r. See also Francis Meres' 1598 commonplace book, written as a sequel to *Wits common wealth*, which provides further evidence of the stability of the 'official' line on angels. The section reappears, unaltered, in a reprint of the book in 1634. F. Meres, *Palladis tamia: Wits treasury* (London, 1598), sigs. 22v-23v. and F. Meres, *Wits common wealth The second part* (London, 1634), pp. 45–7.

17. T. Tuke, *The practise of the faithfull containing many godly prayers* (London, 1613), pp. 70, 91–2, 172–3, 177, 201–2.

18. J. Norden, *A poore mans rest founded vpon motiues, meditations, and prayers* (London, 1620), pp. 14, 30–1, 43, 82–5, 329.

19. Willet, *Synopsis Papismi*, pp. 291–2.

20. Ling, *Politeuphia*, sig. B5r.

21. R. Rollock, *Lectures vpon the Epistle of Paul to the Colossians* (London, 1603), pp. 208–217.

22. Ibid., pp. 211–2.

23. T. Bastard, *Twelve sermons* (London, 1615), pp. 64–6. See also pp. 49–50.

24. See above pp. 75–6.

25. W. Perkins, *An exposition of the Symbole or Creed of the Apostles* (London, 1595), p. 80.

26. H. Holland, *Spirituall preseruatiues against the pestilence* (London, 1603), pp. 1–2, 5, 53–4, 65–8, 116–29.

27. H. Clapham, *Henoch Clapham his demaundes and answeres touching the pestilience* (London, 1604), pp. 8–12.

28. F. Herring, *A modest defence of the caueat giuen to the wearers of impoisoned amulets* (London, 1604), sigs. A4v-B1v.

29. J. Hall, *Contemplations vpon the principal passages of the holy story* (London, 1614), pp. 315–323, 330–1, 367–8.

30. J. Sears McGee, 'Taylor, Thomas (1576–1632)', *ODNB*, Oxford University Press, Sept 2004; online edn, Jan 2008 [http://www.oxforddnb.com/view/article/27083, accessed 27 Nov 2008].

31. T. Taylor, *Christs combate and conquest* (London, 1618), pp. 8, 12–3, 165–6, 191, 206, 214, 228, 230, 235–41, 347–8, 401–5, 411–13. John Smith expanded the theme in *Essex doue, presenting the vvorld vvith a fevv of her oliue branches* (London, 1629), pp. 21, 70–1, 77, 84, 92, 108, 115–6, 15–7, 35–6, 54, 58, 65–72, 153–55.

32. See above pp. 29–37, 65–7, and P. Marshall, *Beliefs and the Dead in Reformation England* (Oxford: Oxford University Press, 2002), pp. 217, 219, 250–2, 277.

33. Smith, *Essex doue*, pp. 153–4.

34. J. N. *A path-way to penitence with sundry deuout prayers* (London, 1591); H. Smith, *Three prayers* (London, 1591), pp. 18–20. See also Tuke, *The practise of the faithfull*, p. 172. He included in his collection a prayer in the time of sickness, requesting that God 'command thy holy Angels ... to carrie my soule into the bosome of blessed Abraham'.

35. N. Byfield, *The cure of the feare of death* (London, 1618), pp. 69–70, 85–88; N. Byfield, *The marrovv of the oracles of God* (London, 1630), pp. 306, 694–5, 704–6.

36. S. Jerome, *Seauen helpes to Heauen* (London, 1614), pp. 43–44, 54–5, 150, 243, 254–5, 343–4, 354–5, 346, 406, 469.

37. H. Lawrence, *An history of angells being a theological treatise of our communion and warre with them* (London, 1646).

38. Ibid., pp. 23–26.

39. Ibid., pp. 41–2.

40. Ibid., pp. 49–50.

41. S. Clarke, *Medulla Theologia, or the marrow of divinity contained in sundry questions and cases of conscience* (London, 1659), p. 64.

42. J. Gumbleden, *Two sermons: first An ANGEL, in a vision* (London, 1657), pp. 4, 5–7. See also P. Heylyn, *Theologia veterum, or, The summe of Christian theologie* (London, 1654), pp. 70, 176, 317; J. Spencer, *Kaina kai palaia* (London, 1658), pp. 157, 322; T. Watson, *The Christian's Charter* (London, 1654), pp. 85–9; J. Taylor, *Holy living in which are described the means and instruments of obtaining every virtue* (London, 1656), pp. 392, 418, 428; T. Jackson, *Maran atha, or Dominus veniet Commentaries upon the articles of the Creed* (London, 1657), pp. 3312–3, E. Leigh, *Annotations on five poetical books of the Old Testament* (London, 1657), pp. 49, 82; N. Hardy, *The pious votary and prudent traveller characterized in a farewell sermon* (London, 1659), pp. 30–3.

43. Clarke, *Medulla*, pp. 63, 63.

44. J. A. Rivers, *Devout Rhapsodies, in which is Treated, of the Excellencie of Divine Scriptures* (London, 1647), p. 53; Gumbleden, *Two Sermons*, p. 10.

45. E. Leigh, *A treatise of divinity consisting of three books* (London, 1646), pp. 103, 104. For similar examples see also J. Hales, *Golden remains of the ever memorable Mr Iohn Hales of Eton College* (London, 1659), p. 134; W. Ames, *The substance of Christian religion, or, A plaine and easie draught of the Christian catechisme* (London, 1659), p. 134, 288; Heylyn, *Theologia*, p. 73; Taylor, *A collection of offices*, pp. 159r, 185v.

46. I. Ambrose, *Three Great Ordinances of Jesus Christ· viz. 1. War with devils. 2. Ministration of, and communion with angels. 3. Looking unto Jesus* (London, 1662), sigs. A4r, pp. 195–6, 198–9.

47. Ibid., pp. 204–16.

48. Ibid., pp. 219–25.

49. Ibid., pp. 230, 234. The story of the starving mother is reminiscent of the biblical story of Hagar in the wilderness (Gen. 21.14:19), as Ambrose noted. For more on this case see R. Gillespie, 'Imagining Angels in Early Modern Ireland', in Marshall and Walsham, *Angels in the Early Modern World*, pp. 214–32.

50. Ambrose, *Three Great Ordinances*, pp. 242–250.

51. Camfield, *A theological discourse of angels*, pp. 4–49.

52. Ibid., p. 49.

53. Ibid., p. 59.

54. Ibid., p. 78.

55. J. Maynard, *The beauty and order of the creation together with natural and allegorical meditations on the six dayes works of the creation* (London, 1668), pp. 199–205.

56. Ibid., pp. 207–10.

57. Ibid., pp. 211–13.

58. R. Baxter, *The certainty of the worlds of spirits and, consequently, of the immortality of souls of the malice and misery of the devils and the damned* (London, 1691), pp. 8, 11.

59. For more on this see above, chapter 7.

60. W. Johnson, *Deus nobiscum a sermon preached upon a great deliverance at sea* (London, 1664), pp. 5–6, 20–1. The Church of England clergyman David Stokes also evidently thought that angels were useful for instructing the laity: he exhorted his readers to '*follow* the *ardour* and *obedience* of the blessed *Angels*', for 'devotions and Prayers are the surest meanes to procure a Guard of blessed Angels against the greatest dangers', in D. Stokes, *Versus Christianus, or , Directions for private devotions and retirements* (Oxford, 1668), pp. 76, 53.

61. C. Ellis, *A catechism wherein the learner is at once taught to rehearse and prove all the main points of Christian religion* (London, 1674), pp. 8–9.

62. T. Ken, *A manual of prayers for the use of the scholars of Winchester College* (London, 1675), pp. 5, 29.

63. R. Allestree, *Scala sancta: or The exaltation of the soul* (London, 1678), pp. 85–6, 265–6 and pp. 15, 148–50, 159, 240. See also J. Norris, *Reason and religion, or, The grounds and measures of devotion* (London, 1689), pp. 144–5, 155–6; J. Flavel, *An exposition of the assemblies catechism with practical inferences from each question* (London, 1692), pp. 10, 15, 18, 25, 30 1, 48, 56, 94–5, 97, 208–9.

64. A. Horneck, *The happy ascetick, or, The best exercise* (London, 1681), sig. A4r.

65. Ibid., pp. 34–5, 54, 237–8. J. Scott, an Anglican minister whose works examined godly living and prayer, also discussed angels in the third part of *The Christian life part III. Wherein the great duties of justice, mercy, and mortification are fully explained and inforced* (London, 1696). In a section 'Of Helps to Mortification, given us by the Spirit of God', Scott considered at length the 'Aids and Assistances, which the holy Angels give us', noting 'they are ready to succour our Souls, as well as Bodies; and to contribute to our eternal, as well as temporal Interests', pp. 338, 343, 428–9.

66. J. Spencer, *A discourse concerning prodigies wherein the vanity of presages by them is reprehended* ([Cambridge], 1663), pp. 58, 64.

67. W. Kemp, *A brief treatise of the nature, causes, signes, preservation from, and cure of the pestilence* (London, 1665), p. 2.

68. J. Edwards, *The plague of the heart its [brace] nature and quality* (Cambridge, 1665), p. 23. Anon, *London's Lord have mercy upon us* (London, 1665).

69. E. Waterhouse, *A short narrative of the late dreadful fire in London, together with certain considerations remarkable therein* (London, 1667), p. 177.

70. T. Gouge, *A word to sinners, and a word to saints* (London, 1668), pp. 47–8.

71. J. Flavel, *A saint indeed: or The great work of a Christian* (London, 1668), pp. 175–6.

72. T. Vincent, *The death of ministers improved. Or, an exhortation to the inhabitants of Horsley on Glocester-shire, and others, on the much lamented death of that reverend and faithful minister of the Gospel, Mr.Henry Stubbs* (London, 1678), p. 45; T. Watson, *The fight of faith crowned, or, A sermon preached at the funeral of that eminently holy man Mr.Henry Stubs* (London, 1678), p. 15.

73. S. Slater, *A sermon preached (May 16.1680) at the funeral of Mr.Tho.Gilson, late minister of the Gospel* (London, 1680), p. 3; W. Bates, *A funeral-sermon for the reverend, holy and excellent divine, Mr.Richard Baxter* (London, 1692), p. 51. For similar examples see J. Durham, *The blessednesse of the death of these that die in the Lord* (Glasgow, 1681), p. 118; J. Scott, *A sermon preached at the funeral of Dr.William Croun* (London, 1685), pp. 14–5; J. Dunton, *The mourning-ring, in memory of your departed friend* (London, 1692), pp. 49–52.

74. G. Rust, *A funeral sermon preached at the obsequies of the right reverend father in God, Jeremy, Lord Bishop of Down* (London, 1668), pp. 11–12; J. Bunyan, *A confession of my faith and a reason of my practice* (London, 1672), pp. 3–4.

75. S. Slater, *A funeral sermon. Delivered upon occasion of the death of that worthy gentleman John Marsh* (London, 1682), pp.36, 6. See also J. Kettlewell, *Death made comfortable, or, The way to dye well consisting of directions for an holy and an happy death* (London, 1695), pp. 250; Scott, *A sermon preached*, pp. 10–13.

76. These intellectual shifts are described in chapter 7.

4 The Confessionalized Angel, *c.* 1580–1700

1. T. Bilson, *The perpetual gouernment of Christes Church* (London, 1593), p. 235.

2. See for example the opinions of the conformist bishop of Derry, George Downame's *Two sermons, the one commeding the ministerie in generall, the other defending the office of the bishops in particular* (London, 1608), pp. 1–2, 52.

3. J. Barwick, *Certain disquisitions and considerations representing to the conscience* (London, 1644), pp. 15–6. See also P. Hay, *A vision of Balaams asse* (London, 1616), p. 180–6 and Sir T. Brown, *Religio Medici* (London, 1641), pp. 124–6.

4. J. Robinson, *A iustification of separation from the Church of England* (Amsterdam, 1610), pp. 167–8.

5. The congregation of The 'Ancient' Separatist Church of Amsterdam mostly consisted of Elizabethan exiles who united in the late 1590s.

6. H. Ainsworth, *A defence of the Holy Scriptures, worship and ministerie* (Amsterdam, 1609), pp. 111–4.

7. Smectymnuus, *An answer to a booke entitled An hvmble remonstrance* (London, 1641), p. 53. and passim.

8. Ibid., p. 58.
9. W. Prynne, *The substance of a speech made in the House of Commons* (London, 1649), p. 64.
10. See esp. M. Lee Jnr, *Great Britain's Solomon: James VI and I in his Three Kingdoms* (Urbana, IL: University of Illinois Press, 1990) and W. B. Patterson, *King James VI and I and the Reunion of Christendom* (Cambridge: Cambridge University Press, 1997); on ecclesiastical policy see esp. M. Curtis, 'The Hampton Court Conference and its Aftermath', *History*, 46, (1961), pp. 1–16; M. L. Schwarz, 'James I and the Historians: Towards a Reconciliation', *Journal of British Studies*, 13:2 (May, 1973), pp. 114–134; K. Fincham and P. Lake, 'The Ecclesiastical Policy of King James I', *Journal of British Studies*, 24:2 (April, 1985), pp. 169–207; P. Collinson, 'The Jacobean Religious Settlement: The Hampton Court Conference', in H. Tomlinson (ed.), *Before the English Civil War* (London: Macmillan, 1983).
11. See N. Tyacke, *Anti-Calvinists: The Rise of English Arminianism c.1590–1640* (Oxford: Clarendon, 1987), and 'Archbishop Laud', in K. Fincham (ed.), *The Early Stuart Church, 1603–1642* (Basingstoke: Macmillan, 1993).
12. W. Covell, *A iust and temperate defence of the fiue books of ecclesiastical policie* (London, 1603), p. 124.
13. Ibid., pp. 123–8.
14. See K. Fincham and N. Tyacke, *Altars Restored: The Changing Face of English Religious Worship 1547–c.1700* (Oxford: Oxford University Press, 2007).
15. R. Shelford, *Fiue pious and learned discourses* (London, 1635), pp. 17, 8, 16.
16. J. Fisher, *The Priest's duty and dignity* (London, 1636), pp. 40–1; Sir T. Baker, *Meditations and disquisitions upon the Lords Prayer* (London, 1636), p. 6.
17. R. Montagu, *A gagg for the new gospel?* (London, 1624), pp. 195, 197, and *Immediate addresse vnto God alone* (London, 1624), p. 91.
18. Bilson, *The perpetual government*, pp. 235, 290.
19. Fisher, *The Priest's duty*, p. 48.
20. Bilson, *The Perpetual Government*, pp. 290–1, Covell, *A iust and temperate defence*, pp. 125–8., Shelford, *Fiue pious and learned discourses*, pp. 157–167, 185–6, 218–9, 325–6.
21. A. Walsham, 'Angels and Idols in England's Long Reformation', p. 155.
22. Ibid., pp. 154–62.
23. Ibid., pp. 154–8.
24. See A. Milton, *Catholic and Reformed: The Roman and Protestant Churches in English Protestant Thought 1600–1640* (Cambridge: Cambridge University Press, 1995), chapter 2, pp. 93–127; P. Lake, 'Anti-Popery: the Structure of a Prejudice', in R. Cust and A. Hughes, (eds), *The English Civil War* (London: Arnold, 1997). For examples of anti-Popery see esp. T. Cogswell, *The Blessed Revolution: English Politics and the coming of war, 1621–1624* (Cambridge: Cambridge University Press, 1989), pp. 6–12, 50–53 and passim; and A. Walsham, '"The Fatall Vesper": Providentialism and Anti-Popery in Late Jacobean London', *P&P*, 44 (1994), pp. 37–87.
25. Walsham, 'Angels and Idols', p. 157, A. Milton, 'Cosin, John (1595–1672)', *ODNB*, Oxford University Press, 2004 [http://www.oxforddnb.com/view/article/6372, accessed 8 Jan 2008]; J. Spraggon in *Puritan Iconoclasm during the English Civil War* (Woodbridge, Suffolk: Boydell, 2003), pp. 155, 166, 168, 221, 223.
26. W. Prynne, *A briefe survey and censure of Mr Cozens his couzening deuotions* (London, 1628), pp. 4, 8.
27. Ibid., pp. 11, 17, 24–5, 53.

28. J. Ussher, *A sermon preached before the Commos-House of Parliament* [sic] (London, 1624), p. 27. Ussher elaborated on this in *An ansvver to a challenge made by a Iesuite in Ireland* (London, 1624), pp. 413, 426.

29. F. White, *A replie to Iesuit Fishers answere to certaine Questions* (London, 1624), p. 288. See also pp. 295, 314–29.

30. M. Sutcliffe, *A true relation of Englands happinesse* (London, 1629), pp. 10, 150, see also pp. 23–9, 61–8, 146–50. See also J. Stoughton, *XI, choice sermons preached upon selected occasions* (London, 1640), pp. 22–34, 117.

31. Ussher, *An ansvver to a challenge*, pp. 422–6.

32. L. Hughes, *Certaine greevances, vvell vvorthy ... for the satisfying of those that doe clamour, and maliciously revile them that labour to have the errors of the Booke of common prayer reformed* (London, 1640), pp. 19–21.

33. Catholic belief about angels is discussed above, chapter 5.

34. See Spraggon, *Puritan Iconoclasm*, pp. 155, 163, 164.

35. G. Abbot, *Cheapside Crosse censured and condemned by A Letter Sent from the Vice-Chancellor and other Learned Men of the famous University of Oxford* (London, 1641), pp. 9–10.

36. Spraggon, *Puritan Iconoclasm*, pp. 172, 229, 218.

37. *Acts and Ordinances of the Interregnum, 1642–60, from 5th March, 1642 to 30th January, 1649*, Vol. 1, ed. C. H. Firth and R. S. Rait (London: HMSO, 1911), pp. 425–6.

38. Walsham, 'Angels and Idols', p. 158.

39. See above p. 58.

40. Cooper (ed.), *The Journal of William Dowsing*. Of the 272 entries in Dowsing's journal, 77 (just under 30 per cent), mention the destruction or removal of angels.

41. Ibid., defaced fonts at Fen Ditton p. 206, All Saints p. 213, Claydon p. 219, Eyke p. 220, Aldeburgh p. 220, Kelsale, p. 223, St Mary's at the Quay p. 228, Otley p. 250, Litlington p. 269, Nether Parva p. 288, Linstead Magna p. 289, Ringsfield p. 291, Rushmere St Michael p. 227, South Cove p. 295, Baylham p. 247, Offton p. 253, Horham p. 259, Hoxne p. 265, see also p. 188, 165, 258.

42. Ibid., p. 215.

43. Ibid., p. 161.

44. See above pp. 58–9.

45. Spraggon, *Puritan Iconoclasm*, p. 89, 91, 149, 155, 163–4, 172, 218, 223, 224, 229, 240.

46. Walsham, 'Angels and Idols', p. 161.

47. C. Hill, *The World Turned Upside Down: Radical Ideas During the English Revolution* (London: Mourice Temple Smith Ltd., 1972), p. 14.

48. H. Lawrence, *An history of angells being a theological treatise of our communion and warre with them* (London, 1646); R. Dingley, *The Deputation of Angels, or the Angell-Guardian* (London, 1653).

49. J. Raymond, *Pamphlets and Pamphleteering in Early Modern Britain* (Cambridge: Cambridge University Press, 2003), p. 196 and passim.

50. See above pp. 55–6, 74.

51. J. Salkeld, *A Treatise of Angels* (London, 1613), pp. 251–280.

52. T. Venning, 'Lawrence, Henry, appointed Lord Lawrence under the protectorate (1600–1664)', *ODNB*, Oxford University Press, Sept 2004; online edn, Jan 2008 [http://www.oxforddnb.com/view/article/16178, accessed 6 June 2008].

53. Lawrence, *An history*, pp. *3v-r.

54. Ibid., p. *4v.

55. Ibid., my italics, pp. 19–20.
56. Ibid., p. 20.
57. J. Calvin, *Institutes of the Christian Religion: a New Translation by H. Beveridge, Vol. 1* (Grand Rapids, Michigan: Wm. B. Eerdmans, 1957), pp. 146–7.
58. Lawrence, *An history*, p. 22; Calvin, *Institutes*, pp. 146–7.
59. c.f. Lawrence, *An history*, pp. 14, 19–33, 48; Dingley, *The Deputation of Angels*, pp. 17, 42–44, 129. Dingley also refers to Lawrence's work directly, pp. 76, 165.
60. S. Wright, 'Dingley, Robert (1618/19–1660)', *ODNB*, Oxford University Press, 2004 [http://www.oxforddnb.com/view/article/7677, accessed 22 July 2008].
61. Dingley, *Deputation*, p. 19, sigs. A4r, A5v.
62. Ibid., sig. A5r.
63. Ibid., sig. A5r.
64. Ibid., pp. 26, 33.
65. Ibid., pp. 45, 48–52.
66. Ibid., pp. 33, 34–38, 38–40.
67. Ibid., pp. 147–150.
68. Ibid., pp. 161, 76.
69. Ibid., p. 215.
70. Ibid., p. 215, my italics.
71. Z. Bogan, *A view of the threats and punishments recorded in the Scriptures* (London, 1653), pp. 160–1.
72. J. Gumbleden, *Two sermons: first An ANGEL, in a vision* (London, 1657), p. 8, my italics.
73. J. Taylor, *A discovrse of baptisme its institutions and efficacy upon all believers* (London, 1653), p. 20.
74. J. Taylor, *A collection of offices or forms of prayer in cases ordinary and extraordinary* (London, 1657), sig. 119r. See also J. Taylor, *A funeral sermon preached at the obsequies of the Right Hon[oura]ble and most virtuous Lady, the Lady Frances, Countesse of Carbery* (London, 1650), pp. 5–6.
75. Kate Harvey discusses the distinct puritan theology relating to angels in 'The role of angels in English Protestant thought 1580 to 1660', Ph.D. diss., (Cambridge, 2005). She argues that they were seeking to encourage the 'emergence of the angelic potential in the godly of the English nation', and that they assimilated angels into their conception of the linear progress of history towards the true faith: p. 62, and passim.
76. J. Taylor, *Chrisis teleiotike, A discourse of confirmation for the use of the clergy and instruction of the people of Ireland* (Dublin, 1663), sig. B4v.
77. J. Spurr, '"Latitudinarianism" and the Restoration Church', *HJ*, 31:1 (March, 1988), pp. 61–82. See esp. pp. 80–2.
78. J. Spurr, *The Restoration Church of England* (New Haven; London: Yale University Press, 1991), pp. 323–5.
79. B. Worden, 'The Question of Secularization', in A. Houston and S. Pincus (eds.), *A nation transformed: England after the restoration* (Cambridge: Cambridge University Press, 2001), pp. 20–41. Quotation p. 35. See also N. H. Keeble, *The Restoration: England in the 1660s* (Oxford: Blackwell, 2002), pp. 127–8.
80. J. Bryan, *Dwelling with God, the interest and duty of believers in opposition to the complemental, heartless, and reserved religion of the hypocrite* (London, 1670), p. 38; R. Baxter, *The life of faith in three parts* (London, 1670), p. 580. The words are a direct quotation

from the Epistle of Paul to the Hebrews, 1:14, 'Are they not all ministering spirits, sent forth to minister for them who shall be heirs of salvation?'

81. Sir R. Atkyns, *The Lord Chief Baron Atkyn's speech to Sir William Ashurst, Lord-Mayor elect of the city of London* (London, 1693), p. 6, J. Edwards, *A demonstration of the existence and providence of God* (London, 1696), p. 12.

82. Spurr, *The Restoration Church*, pp. 329–32.

83. Lawrence, *An history*, p. 22; Dingley, *Deputation*, pp. 159–160.

84. Ibid., sig. A3v.

85. Ibid., sig. A3r.

86. Ibid., pp. 166–7.

87. Ibid., pp. 167–8, 171, 174.

88. Ibid., pp. 192–8.

89. Ibid., p. 198.

90. Ibid., pp. 200–204.

91. Ibid., pp. 204–7. For further discussion of the concept of toleration in mid-seventeenth century England see B. Worden, 'Toleration and the Cromwellian Protectorate', in W. J. Sheils (ed.), *Persecution and Toleration: papers read at the Twenty-Second Summer Meeting and the Twenty-Third Winter Meeting of the Ecclesiastical History Society* (Oxford: Blackwells, 1984), pp. 199–233.

92. Dingley, *Deputation*, p. 208.

93. Ibid., pp. 208–14.

94. J. Spencer, *Kaina kai palaia* (London, 1658), p. 465.

95. P. Heylyn, *Theologia veterum, or, The summe of Christian theologie* (London, 1654), p. 68. See also R. Gell, *A sermon touching God's government of the world by angels* (London, 1649), p. 19.

96. M. Carter, *Honor rediviuus [sic] or An analysis of honor and armory* (London, 1660), pp. 63–4.

97. T. Barlow, *The origin of kingly and ecclesiastical government* (London, 1681), p. 164.

98. G. Lawson, *Politica sacra, or, A model of civil and ecclesiastical government* (London, 1689), p. 3.

99. Ibid., p. 138.

100. A. Wilson, *The history of Great Britain being the life and reign of King James the First* (London, 1653), p. 44.

101. G. Rust, *A funeral sermon preached at the obsequies of the right reverend father in God, Jeremy, Lord Bishop of Down* (London, 1668), p. 27.

102. T. Vincent, *The death of ministers improved. Or, an exhortation to the inhabitants of Horsley on Glocester-shire, and others, on the much lamented death of that reverend and faithful minister of the Gospel, Mr.Henry Stubbs* (London, 1678), p. 9, T. Watson, *The fight of faith crowned, or, A sermon preached at the funeral of that eminently holy man Mr.Henry Stubs* (London, 1678), p. 28. See also J. Kettlewell, *A funeral sermon for the Right Honourable, the Lady Frances Digby* (London, 1684), sig. A5v; pp. 31–2.

103. E. Fowler, *A discourse of the great disingenuity & unreasonableness of repining at afflicting providence and of the influence which they ought to have upon us* (London, 1695), pp. 36–7.

104. S. Wesley, *Elegies on the Queen and Archbishop* (London, 1695), p. 11.

105. D. Defoe, *The Life of that incomparable princess, Mary* (London, 1695), p. 60.

106. T. D'Urfey, *Gloriana, funeral pindarique poem sacred to the blessed memory of that ever-admir'd and most excellent princess, out late gracious sovereign lady Queen Mary* (London, 1695), pp. 12, 21.

107. J. Gauden, *A pillar of gratitude humbly dedicated to the glory of God the honour of his majesty* (London, 1661), pp. 11, 16.

108. Anon, *England's black tribunal set forth in the triall of K.Charles at a High Court if Justice at Westminster-Hall* (London, 1660), pp. 129, 174, 151–2, 79.

109. See for example A. Horneck, *Gods providence in the midst of confusion set out in a sermon preach'd at the Savoy, January the 30 1681, being the anniversary of the martyrdom of King Charles I* (London, 1682); S. Crossman, *Two sermons preached in the cathedral-church of Bristol, January the 30th 1679/80 and January the 31th 1680/81 being the days of publick humiliation for the execrable murder of King Charles the first* (London, 1681).

110. P. Lake and M. Questier, 'Agency, Appropriation and Rhetoric under the Gallows: Puritans, Romanists and the State in Early Modern England', *P&P*, 153 (1996), pp. 64–107.

111. Lord A. J. Warriston, *The last discourse of the Right Honble the Lord Warestoune, as he delivered it upon the scafford at the Mercat-Cross of Edinburgh* (London, 1664), pp. 3–10.

112. For further discussion of the notion of a 'good death', see R. Houlbrooke, *Death, religion, and the family in England, 1480–1750* (Oxford: Oxford University Press, 1998), Chapter 7.

113. Warriston, *The last discourse*, pp. 13–14.

114. The association with angels can be traced through John Foxe's *Actes and Monuments* and in the narratives of the lives of the saints in the medieval period, see above pp. 28–9, 70.

115. J. Barkstead, *The speeches, discourses, and prayers, of Col. John Barkstead, Col. John Okey, and Mr. Miles Corbet* (London, 1662), pp. 4–12.

116. Ibid., pp. 19, 25, 35, 46, 63, 66–7.

117. T. Alleine, *The life and death of Mr. Joseph Alleine, late teacher of the church at Taunton* (London, 1672), pp. 65–6, 77.

118. Ibid., pp. 94, 77.

119. Anon, *The Dying speeches, letters and prayers &c. of those eminent Protestants who suffered in the west of England (and elsewhere)* (London, 1689), pp. 18, 4, 10.

120. E. Woodward, *The life and death of William Laud* (London, 1645), p. 10.

121. Charles I, *A True copy of the journal of the High Court of Justice for the tryal of K. Charles I / taken by J. Nalson Jan. 4, 1683* (London, 1684), p. IV.

122. J. Gauden, *Cromwell's bloody slaughter-house, or, his damnable designes laid and practised by him and his negro's* (London, 1660), pp. 9–10.

123. H. Denne, *An epistle recommended to all the prisons in this city & nation. To such as chuse restraint rather than the violation of their consciences* (London, 1660), pp. 4, 8.

124. J. Gauden, *A discourse concerning publick oaths, and the lawfulness of swearing in judicial proceedings* (London, 1662), pp. 39–40.

125. S. Fisher, *One antidote more, against that provoking sin of swearing, by reason of which this land now mourneth given forth from under the burden of the oppressed seed of God* (London, 1600), pp. 12–3.

126. F. Howgill, *A copy of a paper sent to John Otway, Justice of the Peace, concerning swearing* (London, 1666), sig. B4r.

127. [E. Fowler], *A friendly conference between a minister and a parishioner of his, inclining to Quakerism wherein the absurd opinions of that sect are detected, and exposed to a just censure* (London, 1676), p. 72.

128. D. Loewenstein, 'Ellwood, Thomas (1639–1713)', *ODNB*, Oxford University Press, Sept 2004; online edn, Jan 2008 [http://www.oxforddnb.com/view/article/8726, accessed 21 Oct 2008]; T. Ellwood, *Truth prevailing and detecting error, or, An answer to*

a book mis-called, *A friendly conference between a minister and a parishioner of his, inclining to Quakerism* (London, 1676), pp. 166–7.

129. Ellwood, *Truth prevailing*, p. 168.

5 The Catholic Angel, *c.* 1550–1700

1. See especially P. Lake, 'Anti-Popery: the Structure of a Prejudice', in R. Cust and A. Hughes (eds), *The English Civil War* (London: Arnold, 1997), pp. 181–210; Walsham, '"The Fatall Vesper"'.

2. See D. Loades, *The Reign of Mary Tudor: Politics, Government and Religion in England 1553–1558* (London: Benn, 1991); Dickens, *The English Reformation*.

3. See W. Wizeman, *The Theology and Spirituality of Mary Tudor's Church* (Aldershot: Ashgate, 2006); L. Wooding, *Rethinking Catholicism in Marian England* (Oxford: Clarendon, 2000); T. M. McCoog, 'Ignatius Loyola and Reginald Pole: a Reconsideration', *JEH* 47 (1996), pp. 45–64; J. Loach, 'The Marian Establishment and the Printing Press', *English Historical Review*, 101 (1986), pp. 135–148; Duffy, *The Stripping of the Altars*.

4. L. Wooding, 'The Marian Restoration and the Mass', E. Duffy and D. Loades (eds), *The Church of Mary Tudor* (Aldershot: Ashgate, 2006), pp. 227–57.

5. Loach, 'The Marian Establishment', esp. pp. 139–142.

6. Duffy, *The Stripping of the Altars*, p. 542.

7. E. Bonner, *A profitable and necessarye doctrine with certayne homelyes* (London, 1555), sigs. D1v-r, H2r.

8. Ibid., sigs. I3r, L2r, Kk4r-Ll1v.

9. Ibid., fol. LVIIIIv.

10. Duffy, *The Stripping of the Altars*, pp. 537–43.

11. R. Valentin, *This prymer of Salisbury vse is se tout a long with houtonyser chyng [sic]/ with many prayers & goodly pyctures in the kalender* (Rouen, 1554), STC 16058, sigs. D3r,E8v, F6r, G2r, P1r; R. Valentin, *Here after foloweth the prymer in Englysshe and in Latin sette out alonge: after the vse of Sarum* (n.p., 1555), STC 16070, sigs. D4r, G2r, H5v; Catholic Church/R. Caly, *The primer in English and Latin, after Salisburie vse: set out at length with manie praiers and goodly pictures: newly imprinted this present yeare* (London, 1555), STC 16073, sigs. C6v; Catholic Church/R. Valentin, *This prymer of Salisbury vse is se tout along with houtonyser chyng [sic]/ with many prayers/ & goodly pyctures in the kalender* (Rouen, 1556), STC 16076, sigs. D2r, E8v, F6r; Catholic Church/J. Wayland, *The prymer in Englishe and Latine after Salisbury vse: set out at length wyth many prayers and goodlye pyctures* (London, 1557), STC16080, sigs. D8r, L3r; Catholic Church/J. Wayland, *The prymer in English and Latin after Salisburys vse set out at length with manye Godly prayers* (London, 1558), STC 16083, sigs. B3r, L2v.

12. Valentin, 16070, sig. E4r; Wayland, 16083, sig. B3r.

13. Valentin, 16070, sig. M1v; Caly, 16073, sig. N6r; Valentin, 16076, sig. K2r; Wayland, 16083, sig. O1r; Wayland, 16080, sig. P1v.

14. Wayland, 16080, sig. F5v. See also Valentin, 16070, sig. E8r and Wayland, 16083, sig. B4r.

15. For Mary's Assumption see Valentin, 16070, sig. I5v and Wayland, 16083, sig. L3r-L4v.

16. Valentin, *Here after foloweth the prymer,* STC 16070, sig. F3v and Wayland, *The prymer in Englishe and Latine,* STC 16080, sig. G1v.

17. Valentin, *This prymer of Salisbury vse,* STC 16058, sig. L8r, and Valentin, *This prymer of Salisbury vse,* STC 16076, sig. L8r.

18. Duffy, *The Stripping of the Altars*, p. 540.

19. L. Pollard, *Fyve homiles of late* (London, 1556) [mis-signed, my pagination p. 32].
20. T. Watson, *Holsome and catholyke doctrine concerninge the seuen Sacramentes of Chrystes Church* (London, 1558), fol. LXXIIIv.
21. J. Martin, *Religious Radicals in Tudor England* (London: Hambledon, 1989), p. 120.
22. M. Huggarde, *A treatise entitled the path waye to the towre of perfection* (London, 1554), sigs. E4v-r.
23. Martin, *Religious Radicals*, ch. 6. Although Martin is very positive about the talents of Miles Huggarde, the artisan is discussed as the 'exceptional case' which highlights the shortcomings of the regime when it came to the printing press.
24. M. Huggarde, *A mirrour of loue* (London, 1555), sigs. B3v-C3r.
25. Pollard, *Fyve homiles*, sig. G1r; R. Edgeworth, *Sermons very fruifull, godly, and learned, preached and sette foorth by Maister Roger Edgeworth* (London, 1557), pp. 76, 213, 279.
26. Edgeworth, *Sermons very fruitfull*, p. 171.
27. W. Peryn, *Spirituall exercyses and goostly meditacions and a neare waye to come to perfection* (London, 1557), sig. L2v.
28. Ibid., sig. K3r.
29. Wizeman, *Theology and Spirituality*, pp. 47–8 and passim.
30. Ibid., p. 245.
31. Duffy, *The Stripping of the Altars*, pp. 529–30.
32. Watson, *Holsome and catholyke doctrine*, fol. CXVr.
33. Edgeworth, *Sermons very fruitfull*, sigs. 313v-r
34. For a more in depth discussion of the importance of celibacy to the special status of the clergy see P. Marshall, *The Catholic Priesthood and the English Reformation* (Oxford: Clarendon Press, 1994), ch. 5, pp. 142–73.
35. Edgeworth, *Sermons very fruitfull*, sigs. 49r-v.
36. J. Bossy, 'The Character of Elizabethan Catholicism', *P&P*, 21 (1962), pp. 39–59.
37. J. Bossy, *The English Catholic Community 1570–1850* (London: Darton, Longman and Todd, 1975), pp. 11, 12, 141 and passim.
38. J. C. H. Aveling, *The Handle and the Axe: The Catholic Recusants in England from Reformation to Emancipation* (London: Blond and Briggs, 1976), pp. 19, 141 and passim.
39. C. Haigh, 'Revisionism, the Reformation and the History of English Catholicism', *JEH*, 36:3 (1985), pp. 394–406; 'From Monopoly to Minority: Catholicism in Early Modern England', *Transactions of the Royal Historical Society*, 5th ser., 31 (1981), pp. 129–47; 'The Fall of a Church of the Rise of a Sect? Post-Reformation Catholicism in England', *HJ*, 21:1 (1978), pp. 181–6.
40. Scarisbrick, *The Reformation and the English People*, pp. 156–9. A. Walsham, *Church Papists: Catholicism, Conformity and Confessional Polemic in Early Modern England* (Woodbridge: Boydell, 1993); M. Questier, *Conversion, Politics and Religion in England 1580–1625* (Cambridge: Cambridge University Press, 1996).
41. P. Lake and M. Questier, 'Agency, Appropriation and Rhetoric under the Gallows: Puritans, Romanists and the State in Early Modern England', *P&P*, 153 (1996), pp. 64–107.
42. P. Lake and M. Questier, *The Antichrist's lewd hat: Protestants, Papists and players in post-Reformation England* (New Haven; London: Yale University Press, 2002).
43. A. Walsham, '"Domme Preachers"? Post-Reformation English Catholicism and the Culture of Print', *P&P*, 168 (2000), pp. 30–71.
44. Wooding, *Rethinking Catholicism*, passim.
45. J. Blom and F. Blom, 'Rainolds , William (1544?–1594)', *ODNB*, Oxford University Press, 2004 [http://www.oxforddnb.com/view/article/23030, accessed 26 Nov 2007].

46. W. Rainolds, *A Refutation of sundery reprehensions, cauils, and false sleights, by which M. Whitaker laboureth to deface the late English translation* (Paris, 1583), pp. 400–1.

47. Ibid., pp. 402–3.

48. Ibid., pp. 500–1.

49. Similar to Loyola's *Spiritual Exercises*, this influential work was a standard item on lists of books secretly distributed in England. V. Houliston, 'Persons [Parsons], Robert (1546–1610)', *ODNB,* Oxford University Press, 2004 [http://www.oxforddnb.com/view/article/21474, accessed 26 Nov 2007].

50. R. Parsons, *The first booke of the Christian Exercise appertayning to resolution* (Rouen, 1582), pp. 36, 84–5, 111, 155.

51. P. Numan, *Miracles lately wrought by the intercession of the glorious Virgin Marie* (Antwerp, 1606), sig. D4v.

52. T. Fitzherbert, *An adioynder to the supplement of Father Robert Persons* (St Omer, 1613), pp. 308, 311.

53. A. de Torquemada, *The Spanish Mandeuile of miracles. Or The garden of curious flowers* (London, 1600), sig. 63v., G. D. Crow, 'Antonio de Torquemada: Spanish Dialogue Writer of the Sixteenth Century', in *Hispania*, 38:3 (September 1955), pp. 265–71.

54. Fitzherbert, *An adioynder*, p. 311.

55. R. Southwell, *An epistle of comfort to the reuerend priestes and to the honourable, worshipfull and other of the layesorte, restrained in Durance for the Catholike Fayth* (Paris, 1587), p. 56v.

56. T. Alfield, *A true reporte of the death and martydome of M. Campion* (London, 1582), pp. 8–9, 22–3.

57. Lake with Questier, *Antichrist's Lewd Hat*, p. 227.

58. 'On the Invocation, veneration, and relics, of saints, and on sacred images', *The canons and decrees of the sacred and Ecumenical Council of Trent,* ed. and trans. J. Waterworth (London: Dolman, 1848), pp. 233–247.

59. Parsons, *The first booke*, pp. 361–4, 432–5.

60. L. de Granada, *The sinners guyde* (London, 1598), pp. 134–5. See also J. Gerard, *Gerards meditations written originally in the Latine tongue*, trans. R. Winterton (Cambridge, 1638), p. 149.

61. G. Piatti, *The happiness of a religious state* (Rouen, 1632), p. 161

62. For angels and the Protestant deathbed see above pp. 65–7, 152, 154.

63. Piatti, *The happiness,* p. 161.

64. Ibid.

65. L. de Granada, *Granadas deuotion, Exactly teaching how a man may truly dedicate and deuote himself vnto God* (London, 1589), pp. 337–41.

66. See above pp. 15–20, 61–2, 99.

67. A. de Molina, *A treatise of the holy sacrifice of the masse* (St Omer, 1623), pp. 154–66.

68. See R. Birely, *The Refashioning of Catholicism, 1450–1700* (Basingstoke: Macmillan, 1999); R. P. Hsia, *The World of Catholic Renewal, 1540–1770* (Cambridge: Cambridge University Press, 1998).

69. Gerard, *Gerards mediations*, p. 146; de Granada, *The sinners guyde*, p.134; J. Sharpe, *The triall of the protestant priuate spirit* (St Omer, 1630), p. 70. See also L. de Granada, *A paradise of prayers* (London, 1614), pp. 4–5.

70. J. Drexel, *The angel-guardian's clock* (Rouen, 1630), pp. 57, 131, 146–57.

71. Ibid., p. 159.

72. Ibid., pp. 54–7. For Raphael see also pp. 190, 195.

73. Ibid., pp. 141–2.

74. Ibid., pp. 189–90, 76.

75. Ibid., 'An ardent Aspiration to all the Angels', p.116; 'O Angel of God', p. 58; 'Prayers to thy Angel-Guardian', p. 80; 'An Aspiration to all the Angels, which may be made by a man readie to yeelde up his last breath', pp. 121–2.

76. Walsham, 'Domme Preachers', p. 80.

77. Ibid., p. 121–2.

78. F. Cervantes, 'Angels conquering and conquered: changing perceptions in Spanish America', in Marshall and Walsham (eds), *Angels in the Early Modern World*, pp. 104–34. More generally Trevor Johnson has documented the energetic promotion of the angelic motif by the Jesuits, 'Guardian Angels and the Society of Jesus', in Marshall and Walsham (eds), *Angels in the Early Modern World*, pp. 191–214.

6 The People's Angel, *c.* 1550–1700

1. A. Eyre, 'A dyurnall, or, Catalogue of all my accions and expences from the 1st of January 1646–[7–]', *Yorkshire diaries and autobiographies, Vol. 1*, ed. H. J. Morehouse (Durham: Surtees Society Publications 65, 1877), p. 53.

2. A. J. Hopper, 'Eyre, Adam (1614–1661)', *ODNB*, Oxford University Press, 2004; online edn, May 2011 [http://0-www.oxforddnb.com.lib.exeter.ac.uk/view/article/76218, accessed 26 Aug 2011].

3. See entries for 15 and 16 August, Eyre, 'A dyurnall', p. 55. For K. Wrightson's discussion of the Eyre marriage see *English Society 1580–1680* (London: Routledge, 2003), pp. 104–6.

4. *The Diary of Samuel Pepys: with an introduction and notes*, ed. G. G. Smith (London: Macmillan, 1906), Thursday 25 December 1662, p. 168, Sunday 9 August 1663, p. 213.

5. J. Hodgson, 'Memoirs of Captain John Hodgson, touching his Conduct in the Civil Wars, &c.', in *Original memoirs, written during the great Civil War; being the life of Sir Henry Slingsby, and memoirs of Capt. Hodgson. With notes, &c* (Edinburgh: J. Ballantyne & Co., 1806), pp. 194–7.

6. E. Coles, *An English Dictionary: Explaining The difficult Terms that are used in Divinity, Husbandry, Physick, Phylosophy, Law, Navigation, Mathematicks, and other Arts and Sciences* (London, 1677), sig. C2r.

7. J. Baret, *An Alveary or Triple Dictionary, in English, Latin, and French: Very profitable for all such as be desirous of any of those three Languages* (London, 1574), sig. D4v; J. Kersey the Younger, *English Dictionary: Or, a Compleat: Collection Of the Most Proper and Significant Words, Commonly used in the Language* (London, 1702), sig. B3r.

8. Coles, *English Dictionary*, sigs. C4r, P1v, Kk3r. Kersey the Younger also included other references to angels in his *English Dictionary*, see 'Jesus', sig. N4v; and 'Seraphical', sig. CC1r.

9. T. Blount, *Glossographia: Or A Dictionary, Interpreting all such Hard Words, whether Hebrew, Greek, Latin, Italian, Spanish, French, Teutonick, Belgick, British or Saxon; as are now used in our refined English Tongue* (London, 1656), sig. U3v. See also: 'Powers', sig. Hh4r; 'Principalities', sig. Ii4v; 'Seraphical' and 'Seraphim', sig. Nn5r; 'Thrones', sig. Rr3v. Some of Blount's definitions appear to have been taken from an earlier collection: J. B., *An English expositour, or Compleat dictionary teaching the interpretation of the hardest words, and most usefull terms of art, used in our language* (Cambridge, 1641), see 'Hierarchie', sig. H6v.

10. E. Phillips, *The nevv vvorld of vvords. Or a general English dictionary Containing the proper significations, and etymologies of all words derived from other languages* (London, 1678), sig. Tt1v. See also: 'Cherubim', sig. K2r, and 'Angelical', sig. C3r.

11. Phillips, *The nevv vvorld*, 'Michael', sig. Hh3v, and 'Gabriel', sig. V3v; Coles, *English Dictionary*, sig. P1v. See also T. Cooper, *Thesaurus linguae Romanae & Britannicae* (London, 1584), 'Gabriel', sig. Iiiiiii3r.

12. For discussions of this preoccupation see Wrightson, *English Society*, chapter 1; D. Underdown, *Revel, Riot and Rebellion: Popular Politics and Culture in England 1603–1660* (Oxford: Oxford University Press, 1985), chapter 2.

13. All references to Shakespeare's plays are to W. Shakespeare, *The RSC Complete Works*, eds, J. Bate and E. Rasmussen (Basingstoke, Macmillan, 2007), *Hamlet*, Iiv, 20, and IIIiv, 106–7. See also W. Shakespeare, *Henry VIII*, IIi, 161, when a gentlemen calls on 'good angels' to keep evil from befalling him; T. D'Urfey, *A common-wealth of women a play* (London, 1686), Captain Marine beseeches 'Heaven and its Angels' to guard Aminta, p. 3; and in F. de Rojas, *The Spanish bavvd, represented in Celestina: or, The tragicke-comedy of Calisto and Melibea*, trans. J. Mabbe (London, 1631), Celestina calls on angels to defend and direct another character, p. 130.

14. L. Price, *The Maydens of Londons brave adventures, / OR, / A Boon Voyage intended for the Sea* (London, [1623–1661?]) R216159; Anon, *A new Ballad, intituled, A Warning to Youth, shewing the lewd life of a Marchants Sonne of London* (London, [1619–29?]) R215905; Anon, *The complaint and lamentation of Mistresse Arden of / Feversham in Kent, who for the loue of one Mosbie, hired certaine Ruffians / and Villaines most cruelly to murder her Husband* (London, [1610–1638?]) S115866.

15. P. Massinger and T. Dekker, *The virgin martir a tragedie. As it hath bin diuers times publickely acted with great applause, by the seruants of his Maiesties Reuels* (London, 1622), B1v.

16. Massinger and Dekker, *The virgin martir*, Iii, D2v.

17. Massinger and Dekker, *The virgin martir*, IVi, H4r.

18. J. Winthorp, 'TO my verye loving Wife Mrs Winthorp the elder at Groton, Suffolk, London, March 10 1629', in *Life and Letters of John Winthrop: Governor of the Massachusetts-Bay Company at their Emigration to New England, 1630*, ed. R. C. Winthrop (Boston, MA: Little Brown, 1864), p. 384.

19. E. Sharpham, *The fleire· As it hath beene often played in the Blacke-Fryers by the Children of the Reuells* (London, 1607), Act 5, sig. H1v. See also W. Shakespeare, *Richard III*, IVi, 94, the Duchess of York to Lady Anne, 'Go thou to Richmond, and good angels tend thee'.

20. A. Behn, *Sir Patient Fancy: a comedy: as it is acted at the Duke's Theatre* (London, 1678), Vi, p. 70.

21. See above, pp. 67–9.

22. Anon, *A pleasant new Ballad of Tobias* [London, 1655–1658].

23. Anon, *Loves fierce desire, and hopes of Recovery. / Or, A true and brief Description of two Resolved Lovers* (London, [1684–86]) R227265; Anon, *Great Britains Earnest Desires / FOR THE / Princess MARYS / Happy Arrival. / Being the Protestants firm Hope and Resolution of the preservation of our / Laws and Liberties* (London, 1689), R188153; Anon, *THE / King's Return from Holland, / AND / His Joyful Reception by His Royal Consort the QUEEN* (London, 1691) R188392.

24. Anon, *The True / Protestants Contemplation: / CONTAINING / Serious Thoughts of the miraculous Deliverance from the intended Invasion: As / likewise the preservation of his Majesties person from the Malice of bloudy Conspirators* (London, 1693) R234290; *Anon,*

The True LOYALIST; / OR, / The Obedient SUBJECT, / A Loyal SONG (London, 1685) R187548.

25. Anon, *THE / ROYAL DIALOGUE / OR, / The Courtly Salutation / BETWEEN / King William and Queen Mary* (London, 1691), R187263; Anon, King *WILLIAM'S Courage, / OR, / Our Royal Monarch's taking Leave of his Queen and Princely / Pallace* (London, 1690), R188381.

26. Anon, *THE / ROYAL DIALOGUE*; see also Anon, *A New Copy of Verses: / UPON / King WILLIAMS / Going / To Flanders, and His / Taking Leave of His Royal Consort / Queen MARY* (London, 1693) R188636.

27. W. Shakespeare, *Henry V*, Iii, 8–9; Shakespeare, *Henry VIII*, Vi, 185–9.

28. The elegies are discussed above, pp. 119–21.

29. *The notebooks of Nehemiah Wallington, 1618–1654: A Selection*, ed. D. Booy (Aldershot: Ashgate, 2007), p. 185.

30. Shakespeare, *Richard III*, Viii, 142, 179–80.

31. W. Shakespeare, *Richard II*, IIIii, 54–7. The passage is also punning on the golden coin (worth ten shillings each) known as an 'angel' from the image of St Michael the archangel pressed into it. Angel coin puns are common in early modern drama, cf. T. Dekker, *Blurt Master Constable,* II.i; T. Dekker, *The Honest Whore*, IV.ii; T. Dekker, *The Wonder of a Kingdom*, I.iv; T. D., *The Bloody Banquet*, II.i; P. Massinger, *The excellent comedy called, The Old Law*, IV.ii; T. Middleton, *A Trick to Catch the Old One*, II.i; T. Middleton, *No Wit, No Help like a Woman's*, I.ii; T. Middleton, *The Roaring Girl*, II.i; T. Middleton and C. Tourneur, *The Revenger's Tragedy*, II.i; W. Shakespeare, Merchant of Venice, II.vii; W. Shakespeare, Merry Wives of Windsor, I.iii & II.ii; (W. Shakespeare), *A Yorkshire Tragedy* ii; E. Sharpham, *The Fleire*, V; G. Villiers, *The rehearsal*, III.i.

32. Anon, *King WILLIAM'S Courage,* R188381.

33. Anon, *The Joy of Protestants / For King William's safe Arrival from the Wars of Ireland … to the unspeakable Joy of all his loving Subjects* (London, 1690), R188358.

34. Massinger and Dekker, *The virgin martir*, I.ii, D3r.

35. Anon, *A Godly Song, entituled, A farewell to the VVorld, made by a / Godly Christian, named Thomas Byll, being the Parish Clerke of West- / Pelton* (London, [1601–40?]), S118574. See also Anon, *Good Admonition Or To al sorts of people this counsell I sing, That in each ones affaire, to take heed's a faire thing/ To the tune of, Magina-Cree* (London, 1630), S4115.

36. Anon, *A very Godly SONG, intituled, the Earnest / Petition of the faithful Christian, being Clerk of Bodnam, made upon his Deathbed, / at the Instant of his Transumation* (London, [1641–1703?]); Watt, *Cheap Print and Popular Piety*, pp. 106–6.

37. Anon, *The Godly Maid of Leicester. / Being a true Relation of Elizabeth Stretton, who lying upon her Deathbed, was wonderfully deli- / vered from the Temptations of Satan* (London, [1684–6]), R234256.

38. Anon, *The Dying Mans good / Counsel to his Children and Friends. / Being a fit pattern for Old and Young, Rich and Poor, Bond and Free to take example by* (London, [1680–95]), R234259.

39. Anon, *The Lamenting Ladies last Farewel to the / WORLD* (London, [1644–82?]), R216013.

40. See above, p. 150.

41. Shakespeare, *Hamlet*, V.i, 190–3.

42. P. Marshall, *Beliefs and the Dead in Reformation England* (Oxford: Oxford University Press, 2002), p. 197.

43. Anon, *THE / Dying Christians friendly Advice. / To Sinners all, and every Christian Friend* (London, 1690–95]) R228197; Anon, *A Godly Guide of Directions / for true penitent Sinners in these troubled times* (London, [1672–96]), R220118.

44. See above pp. 15–16. Peter Marshall also notes that congregational psalm-singing was the metaphor often chosen to express the face-to-face exaltation of the deity in heaven, *Beliefs and the Dead*, p. 215.

45. Anon, *A Looking-Glass for all true Christians. / Very useful and necessary for all people of what degree soever, to look upon in these trouble- / some times of sorrow* (London, [1681–84]), R234261; Anon, *A very Godly SONG*.

46. J. Vicars, *Prodigies and apparitions, or, England waning piece* ([London?], 1643), p. 51. The noises are first reported in Anon, *A Signe from Heaven: or, A fearefull and terrible noise heard in the ayre at Alborow in the county of Suffolk* ([London], 1642).

47. Anon, *Strange and true news from Westmoreland. Being a true relation of one Gabriel Harding* ([London], 1690).

48. For more on the notion of heavenly or celestial music see J. Willis, *Church Music and Protestantism in post-Reformation England* (Farnham: Ashgate, 2010), pp. 16–22.

49. *Diary of Samuel Pepys*, Sunday 16 February 1661, p. 70; Thursday 27 February 1668, pp. 622–3.

50. Shakepeare, *Hamlet*, V.ii, 308–9.

51. M. Cavendish, 'Bell in Campo Part II', IVxix, in *Playes written by the thrice noble, illustrious and excellent princess, the Lady Marchioness of Newcastle* (London, 1662), IV.xix, p. 629; W. Montagu, *The Shepherd's Paradise* (London, 1629 [1659]), V, sig. I1r.

52. Massinger and Dekker, *The virgin martir*, IVi, K2r.

53. *Diary of Samuel Pepys*, Monday 20 January 1668, p. 606.

54. For a discussion of the impact of reform on angels around the deathbed see P. Marshall, 'Angels around the deathbed: a variation on a theme in the English art of dying, in Marshall and Walsham (eds), *Angels in the Early Modern World*, pp. 83–103.

55. Anon, *The Sorrowful Mother, / OR, / The Pious Daughters Last Farewel. / She patiently did run her Race, / believ'd the Word of Truth; / And Death did willingly embrace, / tho' in her blooming Youth* (London, [1685–1688]), R227382.

56. The belief is derived from Matthew, 18:10, 'Take heed that ye despise not one of these little ones; for I say unto you, That in heaven their angels do always behold the face of my Father which is in heaven'.

57. Anon, *The CHILDREN's EXAMPLE. / Shewing, how one Mrs Johnson's Child of Barnet, was tempted by the Devil to forsake GOD* (London, n.d.), R228820.

58. Anon, *A very Godly SONG*; Anon, *The Wronged LADY: / OR, / The Lord's Daughter of Leicestershire, / Who dy'd for the Love of a young Noble-man, who left her after / many solemn Protestations* (London, [1671–1702]), R186893.

59. W. Shakespeare, *Romeo and Juliet*, V.i, 18–19.

60. See above, pp. 29–31, 66–7, 85, 91–2.

61. According to Peter Marshall, the imagery of sleep 'pervades Protestant literature on death and commemoration of the dead to an extraordinary extent', *Beliefs and the Dead*, pp. 220–3. Juliet's 'sleep' is of course mistaken for death.

62. Anon, *A new Ballad intituled, A Bell-man for England, which night and day doth sta ring in all mens hearing, Gods vengeance is at hand. To the tune of, O man in desperation* (London, 1620), S4504.

63. Anon, *The Great TRIBUNAL; or, CHRIST's / glorious appearing in Judgment. Being, a contemplative Description of / Resurrection* (London, n.d.), T35859.

64. 'Come to Judgement'. *The diary of Ralph Thoresby 1677–1724*, ed. J. Hunter (London: S. Bentley, 1830), p. 51.

65. For discussion of these see above pp. 121–5, 138–9.

66. Anon, *Englands Tribute of Tears, / On the Death of his Grace the DUKE of GRAFTON, / Who received his Mortal Wound at the Siege of the City of Cork in Ireland* (London, 1690), R227129.

67. Anon, *On the Barbarous, Execrable, and Bloody / Murder of the Earl of Essex* (London, 1689), R234357.

68. Anon, *A true relation of Go[ds] vvonderfull mercies in preseruing one aliue, which hanged fiue dayes, who was falsely accused* (London, 1605).

69. Anon, *A declaration from Oxford, of Anne Green a young women that was lately, and unjustly hanged in the Castle-yard; but since recovered* (London, 1651).

70. Massinger and Dekker, *The virgin martir*, IVi.

71. See above pp. 28, 65, 70–1.

72. 'Ordinary of Newgate's Account', October 1693 (OA16931023), 'Old Bailey Proceedings Online', www.oldbaileyonline.org (accessed 30 August 2011, version 6.0).

73. C. Wriothesley, *A chronicle of England during the reigns of the Tudors, from A.D. 1485 to 1559, Vol. 1* (Westminster: Camden Society New Series 11, 1875), pp. 78–80.

74. Galatians 1:8. 'But though we, or an angel from heaven, preach any other gospel unto you than that which we have preached unto you, let him be accursed.'

75. J. Foxe, *The Unabridged Acts and Monuments Online* or *TAMO* (1563 edition) (HRI Online Publications, Sheffield, 2011), http//www.johnfoxe.org (accessed August 2011), p. 627. P. Marshall, 'Papist as heretic: The Burning of John Forest, 1538', *HJ*, 41:2 (1998), pp. 351–74 esp. p. 372.

76. W. Shakespeare, *King John*, IV.i, 74–5.

77. A. Walsham, 'Invisible Helpers: Angelic Intervention in Post-Reformation England', *P&P*, 208 (August 2010), pp. 77–130.

78. See above, pp. 155–6.

79. Anon, *A most Excellent Ballad of Ioseph the Carpenter, and the sacred Virgin Mary* (London, [1678–80]), R228250; Anon, *The Angel Gabriel, his Salutation to the Virgin Mary* (London, 1685), R170309.

80. Anon, *The Sinners Redemption. / Wherein is described the blessed Nativity of our Lord Jesus Christ* (London, n.d.), S112947; Anon, *Two pleasant Ditties, one of the Birth, the other of the / Passion of Christ* (London, [1619–1629]), S119328; Anon, *The Shepherds Glory: / OR, A pleasant Song o' th Shepherd Swain* (London, [1672–1696]), R228554.

81. Anon, *A most Godly and Comfortable Ballad of the Glorious Resurrection of our Lord Jesus Christ* (London, [1684–86]), R234243.

82. E. Synge, *The GLORY of MAN's Redemption: / BEING / A new and lively Emblem of the BIRTH, LIVES, SUFFERINGS, RESURRECTION, and glorious / ASCENTION of our blessed Lord and Saviour JESUS CHRIST, Written by the most Reverend / Father in God Edward, Lord Archbishop of Tewham* (London, n.d.), T40844.

83. Images of the Annunciation: Anon, *A godly new ballad, intituled, A douzen of points. A douzen of points, you here may read, whereon each Christian soul may feed* (London, 1686–1688); Anon, *A most Excellent Ballad of Ioseph the Carpenter*; Anon, *FOUR / Choice CAROLS for CHRISTMAS HOLIDAYS* (London, n.d.), T40075; E. Synge, *The GLORY of MAN's Redemption*. Images of the birth of Christ: Anon, *Christus natus est, Christ is born: Angels clap hands, let men forbear to mourn, their saving health is come, for Christ is born* (London, 1631), Wing (2nd edn) / C3970A; Anon, *The Shepherds Glory*.

84. P. Collinson, 'From Iconoclasm to Iconophobia: the Cultural Impact of the Second English Reformation', *The Stenton Lecture 1985* (University of Reading: 1986).

85. [Charles I], *Eikon basilike, The pourtraicture of His Sacred Majestie in his solitudes and sufferings* ([London], 1648), p. 268.

86. L. P., *Strange-predictions related at Catericke in the north of England: by one who saw a vision, and told it himselfe to the company with whom he was drinking healths; how he was struck, and an angel appeared to him with a sword* (London, 1648), pp. 2–3; J. Drucateen, *True newes from [Mecare:] and also out of Worcestershire* (London, 1598), sig. A2v-A3v.

87. J. Vicars, *A Letter for a Christian Family / Directed to all true Christians to Read* (London, [1684–1686]), R227342; Anon, *PARADISE Lost, and PARADISE Regain'd; / BY / The Wonderful WORKS of GOD* (London, [1730–1769]), T43623.

88. T. D'Urfey, *The famous history of the rise and fall of Massaniello* (London, 1700), IIIii, p. 30; Shakespeare, *Henry VIII*, III ii, pp. 513–4.

89. C. Marlowe, *The tragical history of D. Faustus* (London, 1604), sig. B2r; G. Etherage, *The Man of Mode,* (London, 1676), II ii, p. 48. See also Shakespeare, *Macbeth*, IViii, 25.

90. The relevant scriptural passages are: Genesis 32:24–9, where Jacob wrestles the angel; 2 Peter, 2:11, 'Whereas angels, which are greater in power and might, bring not railing accusation against them before the Lord'; Jude 1:9, 'Yet Michael the archangel, when contending with the devil he disputed about the body of Moses, durst not bring against him a railing accusation, but said, The Lord rebuke thee'.

91. Booy, *Notebooks of Nehemiah Wallington,* p. 37.

92. W. Shakespeare, *Julius Caesar,* IV iii, pp. 366–70.

93. Shakespeare, *Hamlet,* I iv, pp. 21–4.

94. Shakespeare, *Romeo and Juliet,* IIIii, 77; W. Shakespeare, *Cymbeline,* IIii, 52.

95. Shakespeare, *Henry VIII,* III i, p. 158; M. Cavendish, 'Matrimonial Trouble, Part II', I i, p. 459 in *Playes.*

96. [Charles I], *Eikon basilike,* p. 235.

97. Anon, *A true relation from Germany, of a Protestant Shepherd's killing a counterfeit devil, that would have perverted him to popery* (London, 1676), pp. 2–3.

98. Massinger and Dekker, *The virgin martir,* II.i, F1v; IV.i, K2v, K3r; III.i, F3r.

99. Ibid., II.i and III.i, G2r.

100. Ibid., V.i and II.i, F1v.

101. J. Degenhardt, "Catholic Martyrdom in Dekker and Massinger's the Virgin Martir and the Early Modern Threat of 'Turning Turk'", *English Literary History,* 73:1 (2006), pp. 83–117. See pp. 93–6.

102. J. Foxe, *The Unabridged Acts and Monuments Online* or *TAMO* (1570 edition) (HRI Online Publications, Sheffield, 2011). [http//www.johnfoxe.org [Accessed: 07.09.11], p. 130.

103. S. Clark, *Vanities of the Eye: Vision in Early Modern European Culture* (Oxford: Oxford University Press, 2007).

104. See above pp. 55, 72–5, 100, 107–17.

105. Massinger and Dekker, *The virgin martir,* I.ii, E1r; III.i, F3v; IV.i, K2r.

106. W. Shakespeare, *Othello,* V.ii, pp. 237–8.

107. J. Dryden, *Amboyna, a tragedy as it is acted at the Theatre-Royal* (London, 1673), III.i, p. 25. See also R. Brome, 'Madd Couple Well Matcht', I.i, sig. B5v in R. Brome, *Five new playes* (London, 1653).

108. D'Urfey, *Rise and Fall,* IV.i, p. 38; G. Farquhar, *The Beaux' Stratagem* (London, 1707), IV, p. 50.

109. Shakespeare, *Julius Caesar*, III.ii, 178; T. D'Urfey, *Sir Barnaby Whigg* (London, 1681), I.i, p. 9.

110. W. Shakespeare, *Henry IV, Part II*, I.ii, 118; A. Behn, *The Dutch Lover a comedy* (London, 1673), II.ii, p. 18.

111. Marlowe, *The tragical history of D. Faustus*. This is also the conceit employed by Shakespeare in Sonnet 144.

112. M. Moore, *Wonderfull newes from the north. Or, A true relation of the sad and grievous torments, inflicted upon the bodies of three children of Mr. George Muschamp* (London, 1650).

113. Ibid., pp. 9–12.

114. T. Thomas, *Dictionarium linguae Latinae et Anglicanae. In hoc opere quid sit præstitum, & ad superiores λεξιχογραφονς adiectum, docebit epistola ad Lectorem* (Cantebrigiae, 1587), sigs. Q3r, BB4r, Mm4r.

115. See Baret, *An Alveary or Triple Dictionary*, 'Angel', sig. D4v; W. B[agnell], *The Mystery of Astronomy Made plain To the meanest Capacity, By An Arithmetical Description of the Terrestrial and Celestial globes* (London, 1655), 'Genius', sig. K6r; T. Blount, *Glossographia: Or A Dictionary, Interpreting all such Hard Words, whether Hebrew, Greek, Latin, Italian, Spanish, French, Teutonick, Belgick, British or Saxon* (London, 1661), 'Genius', sig. S6r; J. Bullokar, *An English Expositor: teaching the interpretation of the hardest words in our language* (London, 1641), 'Genius', sig. H2v; R. Cawdrey, *A Table Alphabeticall, conteyning and teaching the true writing, and vnderstanding of hard vsuall English wordes, borrowed from the Hebrew, Greeke, Latine, or French, &c* (London, 1604), 'Genius', sig. E3r; H. Cockeram, *The English Dictionarie: Or, An Interpreter of hard English Words.* (London, 1623), 'Genius', sig. E7r; T. Cooper, *Thesaurus linguae Romanae & Britannicae tam accurate congestus, vt nihil penè in eo desyderari possit, quod vel Latinè complectatur amplissimus Stephani Thesaurus, vel Anglicè, toties aucta Eliotae Bibliotheca: opera & industria Thomae Cooperi Magdalenensis* (London, 1584), 'Genius', sig. Iii4r, 'Manes', sig. Ffff4r; R. Cotgrave, *A French-English dictionary compil'd by Mr. Randle Cotgrave: with another in English and French. Whereunto are newly added the animadversions and supplements* (London, 1650), 'Ange', sig. E3r; T. Elyot, *The Dictionary of syr Thomas Eliot knyght* (London, 1538), 'Genius', sig. I3v.

116. L. Stone, 'The educational revolution in England 1560–1640', *Past and Present*, 28 (1964), pp. 41–80; Wrightson, *English Society*, pp. 192–207.

117. For a detailed discussion of the full spectrum of views about the existence of guardian angels, see P. Marshall, 'The Guardian Angel in Protestant England, in J. Raymond (ed.), *Conversations with Angels: Essays Towards a History of Spiritual Communication, 1100–1700* (Basingstoke: Palgrave Macmillan, 2011), pp. 295–316.

118. W. Shakespeare, *Anthony and Cleopatra*, II.iii, 20–4; A. Behn, *The Luckey Chance* (London, 1687), IV.i, p. 48.

119. M. Cavendish, 'The Bridals', III.ii, p. 41 in *Plays, never before printed written by the ... Princesse the Duchess of Newcastle* (London, 1668); Anon, *A new Song of a Young mans opinion, of the difference betweene good and bad Women* (London, S125619); Anon, *A Pleasant Comoedie, Wherein is merily shewen: The wit of a Woman* (London, 1604), I.i, G1r.

120. Shakespeare, *Romeo and Juliet*, II.i, 73–9.

121. de Rojas, *The Spanish bavvd*, p.130 ; Anon, *LOVES Unlimitted Power: / Or, Cupids Cruelty* (London, 1685), R188505; Behn, *Dutch Lover*, V.i, p. 88.

122. Anon, *The Frantick LOVER; / Or, The Wandring Young-Man* (London, [1685–88]), R188074; Anon, *The Love-sick / SERVING-MAN* (London, [1675–96?]), R235043.

123. Anon, *Prides Fall; Or, A warning for all English Women* (London, [1684–6]), R234277; Anon, *THE / CONSTANT LADY, / AND / Fals Hearted Squire* (London, [1675–96?]), R174173.

124. Shakespeare, *King John*, Vii, 65; Anon, *The true Lovers Good-morrow* (London, [1684–6]), R233990.

125. T. D'Urfey, *A common-wealth of women a play* (London, 1686), IV, p. 35; J. Dryden, *An Evening's Love* (London, 1671), III, p. 43.

126. W. Shakespeare, *Troilus and Cressida*, Iii, 225.

127. Anon, *The Swimming Lady: / Or, A Wanton Discovery, / Being a true Relation of a gay Lady* (London, [1681–4]), R1687.

128. W. Shakespeare, *Henry IV, Part 1*, IVi, 112–13; Shakespeare, *Cymbeline*, Viii, 91.

129. Anon, *The Honour of a London Prentice. / Wherein is declared his matchless Manhood, and brave Adventures, done by him in / Turkey* (London, [1686–88]), N69951.

130. Anon, *An Excellent New song, / CALLED, The / False hearted young Man / OR, / The Injured Maiden* (London, 1697), R176868; Anon, *The forsaken Maids Frollick / OR, / A Farewell to fond Love, / In which she doth plainly and properly prove* (London, [1666–1700?]), R228230.

131. K. Harvey, 'The Role of Angels in English Protestant Thought 1580–1660', Ph.D thesis (Cambridge, 2005).

132. Shakespeare, *Henry VIII*, Viii, 57–9; Shakespeare, *Hamlet*, III.iii, 284–6.

133. Walsham, 'Invisible Helpers'. Walsham demonstrated that tales of angels appearing to humans can be divided into five categories: aerial apparitions interpreted as warnings; angels that deliver sentences against flagrant sinners; angels that entrust an individual with the task of admonishing a wicked community; angels that are agents of benevolent deliverance; and lastly, angels that assume a medical vocation.

134. E. Gaudie, 'Flights of Angels', *History Today*, 42:12 (Dec., 1992), pp. 13–20.

7 The Empirical Angel, *c.* 1650–1700

1. M. Weber, *The Protestant Ethic and the Spirit of Capitalism*, trans. T. Parsons, (ed.) A. Giddens (London: Routledge, 1992). See esp. R. W. Scribner, "The Reformation, Popular Magic, and the 'Disenchantment of the World'", in *Journal of Interdisciplinary History*, 23:3 (Winter, 1993), pp. 475–94. Scribner suggests that Weber's notion was 'a prime example of the ways in which the nineteenth-century concerns were projected back onto historical understanding of religion in the Reformation', p. 492.

2. For a chief proponent of this view see H. Butterfield, *The Origins of Science, 1300–1800* (London: Bell, 1957).

3. See for example M. Hellyer (ed.), *The Scientific Revolution: the Essential Readings* (Oxford: Blackwell, 2003); P. Dear, *Revolutionizing the sciences : European knowledge and its ambitions, 1500–1700* (Basingstoke: Palgrave, 2001); S. Shapin, *The Scientific Revolution* (Chicago, IL: University of Chicago Press, 1998); J. H. Brooke, *Science and Religion: some historical perspectives* (Cambridge: Cambridge University Press, 1991); D. Goodman & C.A. Russell (eds.), *The Rise of Scientific Europe, 1500–1800* (Sevenoaks; Milton Keynes: Hodder & Stoughton, 1991); R. Millen, 'The manifestation of occult qualities in the scientific revolution', in M. J. Osler, and P. L. Farber, (eds), *Religion, Science and Worldview: Essays in Honour of Richard S. Westfall* (Cambridge: Cambridge University Press, 1985), pp. 185–216; B. Vickers (ed.), *Occult and Scientific Mentalities in the Renaissance* (Cambridge: Cambridge University Press, 1984).

4. M. J. Osler, 'Baptizing Epicurean atomism: Pierre Gassendi on the immortality of the soul', in Osler and Farber, *Religion, Science and Worldview,* pp. 163–83. Quotation p. 164.

5. H. C. Agrippa, *Three books of occult philosophy,* trans. J. F. (London, 1650), pp. 75–6, 77, 78.

6. R. Kirby and J. Bishop, *The marrow of astrology in two books: wherein is contained the natures of the signs and planets, with their several governing angels, according to their respective hierarchies* (London, 1687), pp. 34, 120.

7. Michael Hunter, 'Ashmole, Elias (1617–1692)', *ODNB,* Oxford University Press, Sept 2004; online edn, May 2006 [http://www.oxforddnb.com/view/article/764, accessed 3 Oct 2008]; Michael Hunter, 'Founder members of the Royal Society (*act.* 1660–1663)', *ODNB,* Oxford University Press, May 2006; online edn, May 2008 [http://www.oxforddnb.com/view/theme/59221, accessed 29 Sept 2008].

8. T. Vaughan, *A brief natural history intermixed with variety of philosophical discourses and refutations* (London, 1669), pp. 26–7.

9. R. Midgley, *A new treatise of natural philosophy, free'd from the intricacies of the schools* (London, 1687), pp. 140–1, 146.

10. B. Capp, *Astrology and the Popular Press: English Almanacs 1500–1800* (London: Faber, 1979), pp. 180–90.

11. R. Boyle, *A free enquiry into the vulgarly receiv'd notion of nature made in an essay address'd to a friend* (London, 1686), p. 52.

12. See esp. J. W. Wojcik, *Robert Boyle and the Limits of Reason* (Cambridge: Cambridge University Press, 1997); M. Hunter (ed.), *Robert Boyle Reconsidered* (Cambridge: Cambridge University Press, 1994); L. M. Principe, *The Aspiring Adept: Robert Boyle and his Alchemical Quest* (Princeton, NJ: Princeton University Press, 1998).

13. K. Thomas, *Religion and the Decline of Magic: Studies in Popular Beliefs in Sixteenth and Seventeenth-Century England* (London: Weidenfield & Nicholson, 1971), p. 791–2.

14. Wojcik, *Robert Boyle,* p. 101, see also Chapter 4 and Chapter 7.

15. T. Hobbes, *Leviathan, or, The matter, forme, and power of a common wealth, ecclesiasticall and civil* (London, 1651), pp. 241, see also pp. 211–12.

16. Ibid., p. 213.

17. Ibid., p. 214.

18. For an extensive study of the contemporary reception of Hobbes' work see S. I. Mintz, *The Hunting of Leviathan: Seventeenth-century reactions to the Materialism and Moral Philosophy of Thomas Hobbes* (Cambridge: Cambridge University Press, 1962), esp. Chapters 4 and 5.

19. W. Lucy, *Observations, censures, and confutations of notorious errours in Mr.Hobbes his Leviathan and other his bookes* (London, 1663), p. 407, see also pp. 71, 279, 404.

20. J. Whitehall, *The Leviathan found out* (London, 1679), pp. 104–6.

21. G. Harvey, *Archelogia philosophica nova, or, New principles of philosophy* (London, 1663), p. 6; For similar sentiments, see also physician and apothecary W. Drage, *Daimonomageia a small treatise of sicknesses and diseases from witchcraft, and supernatural causes* (London, 1665), pp. 26–7; and respected physician and author Sir T. Browne, *Religio medici, Observations upon Religio medici* (London, 1682), pp. 77, 208.

22. E. Polhill, *The divine will considered in its eternal decrees, and holy execution of them* (London, 1695), pp. 132, 144–5.

23. Camfield, *A theological discourse of angels,* pp. 4, 13.

24. E. Stillingfleet, *An answer to Mr. Cressy's Epistle apologetical to a person of honour touching his vindication of Dr.Stillingfleet* (London, 1675), pp. 77–8.

25. J. Webster, *The displaying of supposed witchcraft wherein affirmed that there are many sorts of deceivers and impostors* (London, 1677), pp. 42, 105.

26. Ibid., p. 207.

27. Ibid., pp. 38–9.

28. J. Bramhall, *Castigations of Mr. Hobbes his last animadversions, in the case concerning liberty, and universal necessity. With an appendix concerning The catching of leviathan or, The great whale* (London, 1658), pp. 471–2.

29. H. van Ruler, 'Minds, Forms, and Spirits: The Nature of Cartesian Disenchantment', *Journal of the History of Ideas*, 61:3 (July, 2000), pp. 381–395. An abridged translation of the first volume of Bekker's work was published in 1695: B. Bekker, *The world bewitch'd, or, An examination of the common opinions concerning spirits their nature, power, administration and operations, as also the effects men are able to produce by their communication* (London, 1695). Bekker argued that everything in nature's course was dependent upon God's unique power, and that he did not allow semi-deities. Bekker did not however reject the existence of angels altogether, this was left to a the Collegiants – a group of radical merchants and professionals who transformed and disseminated ideas in the Dutch Republic. See A. Fix, 'Angels, Devils, and Evil Spirits in Seventeenth-century Thought: Balthasar Bekker and the Collegiants', *Journal of the History of Ideas*, 50:4 (October–December, 1989), pp. 527–547.

30. van Ruler, 'Minds, Forms, and Spirits', p. 388.

31. For more on the anxieties surrounding the perceived growth of atheism, see M. Hunter (ed.), *Atheism from the Reformation to the Enlightenment* (Oxford: Oxford University Press, 1992).

32. E. Leigh, *A treatise of divinity consisting of three books* (London, 1646), pp. 96, 98.

33. P. Heylyn, *Theologia veterum, or, The summe of Christian theologie* (London, 1654), p. 73; J. Spencer, *Kaina kai palaia* (London, 1658), p. 554. See also H. Hammond, *Of superstition* (London, 1645), pp. 3, 11; H. Hammond, *Of Idolatrie* (London, 1646), pp. 24–5, 27; and D. Dickson, *An exposition of all St. Pauls epistles* (London, 1659), pp. 140, 94.

34. J. Wigan, *Antichrist's strongest hold overturned, or, The foundation of the religion of the people called Quakers* (London, 1651), p. 63.

35. S. Rutherford, *A survey of the spirituall antichrist opening the secrets of familisme and antinomianisme* (London, 1648), pp. 4, 169, 55.

36. R. Braithwaite, *Capitall hereticks, or, The evill angels embattel'd against St.Michael* (London, 1659), pp. 7, 12, 15, 16, 18.

37. A. Ross, *Pansebia, or, A view of all religions in the world with the severall church-government from the creation, to these times* (London, 1655), pp. 30–34.

38. Ibid., pp. 164, 165, 174, 184, 187–8, 436, 472. See also pp. 18–9, 78–9, 192–4, 221–2, 321, 347, 380–1, 426, 472. For other works that voice concern over unorthodox and radical belief about angels see: T. Ady, *A candle in the dark shewing the divine cause of the distractions of the whole nation of England and the Christian world* (London, 1655), pp. 43–6, 55–8, 126–7, 141–2, 145–6; Heylyn, *Theologia*, p. 73; E. Hyde, *A Christian vindication of truth against errour* (London, 1659), pp. 245–358, esp. pp. 333–5; Leigh, *Treatise*, pp. 86–8; J. Mede, *The apostacy of the latter times* (London, 1641), pp. 11–12, 19–20, 24–6, 40, 101, 119; E. Pagitt, *Heresiography, or, A discription of the hereticks and sectaries of these latter times* (London, 1645), pp. 86, 89, 140, 147, 159. Given the frequent reference to angels in these works it is perhaps surprising that angels only merit a passing mention in the most well known heresiography of the time, T. Edwards' *The first*

and second part of Gangraena, or, A catalogue and discovery of many of the errors, heresies, blasphemies and pernicious practices of the sectaries of this time (London, 1646).

39. Alexandra Walsham has noted the 'more strident' tone of publications, as well as the clustering of reported visions of angels in the later Stuart period in 'Invisible Helpers', pp. 54–5.

40. J. Spurr, '"Rational Religion", in Restoration England, *Journal of the History of Ideas*, 49:4 (October–December, 1998), pp. 563–85, quotation p.571; B. Shapiro, 'Natural philosophy and political periodisation: interregnum, restoration and revolution', in A. Houston and S. Pincus (eds), *A nation transformed: England after the restoration* (Cambridge: Cambridge University Press, 2001), pp. 299–327.

41. J. Glanvill, 'The *USEFULNESS* of *Real Philosophy* to *RELIGION*,' in his *Essays on Several important subjects in philosophy and religion* (London, 1676), pp. 6–9.

42. G. Sinclair, *Satan's invisible world discovered, or, A choice collection of modern relations proving evidently against the saducees and atheists of this present age* (Edinburgh, 1685), sigs. A5r, A6v. See also W. Jameson, *Nazianzeni querela et votum justum, The fundamentals of the hierarchy examin'd and disprov'd* (Glasgow, 1697), pp. **2v.

43. M. Hunter, 'The Problem of Atheism in Early Modern England', *Trans. Royal Historical Society*, 5th series, 35 (1985), pp. 135–157.

44. J. Spurr, *The Restoration Church of England* (New Haven; London: Yale University Press, 1991), pp. 219, 249–69. For further discussion see D. Berman, *A History of Atheism in Britain: From Hobbes to Russell* (London: Croom Helm, 1988), Section 2, pp. 48–70; G. E. Aylmer, 'Unbelief in Seventh-Century England', in D. Pennington and K. V. Thomas (eds), *Puritans and Revolutionaries* (Oxford: Clarendon Press, 1978), pp. 22–46. Aylmer notes that Hobbes was treated as 'an actual or virtual atheist', and documents the appearance of 'a new series of more coherent and sophisticated anti-atheistical treatises' from 1652 onwards, pp. 36–7.

45. Spurr, *The Restoration Church*, pp. 228–9.

46. Camfield, *A theological discourse of angels,* sigs. A4v, A5v-r.

47. J. Hall, *The invisible world discovered to spirituall eyes* (London, 1659), pp. 13–14, 20.

48. Ibid., pp. 23, 29, 33, 50, 48.

49. Ibid., pp. 53–4, 54–7, 57.

50. Ibid., pp. 58–9. Note the similarity of Hall's opinion with that of the 'atheist', J. Webster, above pp. 174–6.

51. Ibid., p. 59.

52. Ibid., pp. 64–5.

53. Ibid., pp. 66.

54. Ibid., pp. 59–62.

55. Ibid., pp. 54–5.

56. Camfield, *A theological discourse of angels*, pp. 87–9.

57. I. Mather, *An essay for the recording of illustrious providences wherein their existence, nature, number, order and offices are modestly treated of* (Boston, 1678), pp. 205–5. Isaac Ambrose discusses the case in *Three great ordinances of Jesus Christ viz 1. War with devils. 2. Ministration of, and communion with angels. 3. Looking unto Jesus* (London, 1662), p. 256. For more on Ambrose see above pp. 87–9. Alexandra Walsham also discusses the case of Grynaeus in 'Invisible Helpers'.

58. Bodinus' acquaintance is usually understood as Jean Bodin himself, see above p. 184.

59. Camfield, *A theological discourse of Angels*, pp. 78–80, 87–9, 90–1.

60. Ibid., pp. 83–4.

61. Ibid., p. 90.
62. R. Briggs, 'Dubious Messengers: Bodin's daemon, the spirit world and the Sadducees', in Marshall and Walsham (eds) *Angels in the Early Modern World*, pp. 168–90.
63. Briggs, 'Dubious Messengers', pp. 177–9.
64. Mather, *An essay for the recording*, p. 208; H. More, *An Antidote against atheisme, or, An appeal to the natural faculties of the minde of man* (London, 1653), p. 137. Richard Baxter was also enthusiastic about the tale, describing the 'good Genius' of Bodin's acquaintance, 'that would always given him notice when he did ill, by a stroke', R. Baxter, *The certainty of the worlds of spirits* (London, 1691), p. 62. See also R.B., *The kingdom of darkness: or the history of daemons, specters, witches, apparitions, possessions, disturbances, and other wonderful and supernatural delusions* (London, 1688), p. 187.
65. Hunter, 'Founder members of the Royal Society'.
66. E. Cameron, *Enchanted Europe: Superstition, Reason and Religion*, 1250–170 (Oxford: Oxford University Press, 2010), pp. 22, and part IV.
67. More, *An antidote against atheisme*, p. 164.

Conclusion

1. Richard Baxter on belief about angels, in I. Ambrose, *Three great ordinances, of Jesus Christ· viz. 1. War with devils. 2. Ministration of, and communion with angels. 3. Looking unto Jesus* (London, 1662), p. 332.
2. Watt, *Cheap Print and Popular Piety*, p. 126 and passim.
3. A. Walsham, "Historiographical Reviews: The Reformation and 'The Disenchantment of the World' Reassessed", *HJ*, 51:2 (2008), pp. 497–528.
4. R. W. Scribner, "The Reformation, Popular Magic, and the 'Disenchantment of the World'", in *Journal of Interdisciplinary History*, 23:3 (Winter, 1993), pp. 475–494. Scribner takes issue with Max Weber, Norbert Elias and Michel Foucault, arguing that notions such as the 'Protestant ethic', 'confessionalization' and the 'civilizing process' show no understanding of the 'nature of popular Protestantism', pp. 493–4.
5. D. A. Jones, *Angels: A Very Short Introduction* (Oxford: Oxford University Press, 2011); S. Pinker, *The Better Angels of Our Nature: The Decline of Violence in History and its Causes* (London: Allen Lane, 2011).

WORKS CITED

Primary Printed Sources

Abbot, G., *An exposition vpon the prophet Ionah, Contained in certaine sermons* (London, 1600).

—, *Cheapside Crosse censured and condemned by A Letter Sent from the Vice-Chancellor and other Learned Men of the famous University of Oxford* (London, 1641).

—, *The reasons which Doctour Hill hath brought, for the vpholding of papistry* (London, 1604).

Acts and Ordinances of the Interregnum, 1642–60, from 5th March, 1642 to 30th January, 1649, Vol.1, eds C. H. Firth and R. S. Rait (London: HMSO, 1911).

Ady, T., *A candle in the dark shewing the divine cause of the distractions of the whole nation of England and the Christian world* (London, 1655).

Agrippa, H. C., *Three books of occult philosophy*, trans. J. F. (London, 1650).

Ainsworth, H., *A defence of the Holy Scriptures, worship and ministerie* (Amsterdam, 1609).

Alfield, T., *A true reporte of the death and martydome of M. Campion* (London, 1582).

Alleine, T., *The life and death of Mr. Joseph Alleine, late teacher of the church at Taunton* (London, 1672).

Allen, E., *A catechisme* (London, 1548).

Allestree, R., *Scala sancta: or The exaltation of the soul* (London, 1678).

Ambrose, I., *Three Great Ordinances of Jesus Christ· viz. 1. War with devils. 2. Ministration of, and communion with angels. 3. Looking unto Jesus* (London, 1662).

Ames, W., *The substance of Christian religion, or, A plaine and easie draught of the Christian catechisme* (London, 1659).

Andrewes, L., *The wonderfull combate betweene Christ and Satan* (London, 1592).

—, *Scala coeli: Nineteen sermons concerning prayer* (London, 1611).

—, *A sermon preached at White-hall, on Easter day* (London, 1620).

Anon, *The CHILDREN's EXAMPLE. / Shewing, how one Mrs Johnson's Child of Barnet, was tempted by the Devil to forsake GOD* (London, n.d.), R228820.

—, *Christus natus est, Christ is born: Angels clap hands, let men forbear to mourn, their saving health is come, for Christ is born* (London, 1631), Wing (2nd edn) / C3970A.

—, *The complaint and lamentation of Mistresse Arden of / Feversham in Kent, who for the loue of one Mosbie, hired certaine Ruffians / and Villaines most cruelly to murder her Husband* (London, [1610–1638?]) S115866.

—, *THE / CONSTANT LADY, / AND / Fals Hearted Squire* (London, [1675–96?]), R174173.

—, *A declaration from Oxford, of Anne Green a young women that was lately, and unjustly hanged in the Castle-yard; but since recovered* (London, 1651).

—, *THE / Dying Christians friendly Advice. / To Sinners all, and every Christian Friend, / This my advice I freely recommend. / And wish them all while they have time and breath, / To make Provision for to meet with Death* (London, 1690–1695]) R228197.

—, *The Dyenge creature* (London, 1507).

—, *The Dying Mans good / Counsel to his Children and Friends. / Being a fit pattern for Old and Young, Rich and Poor, Bond and Free to take example by* (London, [1680–1695]) R234259.

—, *The Dying speeches, letters and prayers &c. of those eminent Protestants who suffered in the west of England (and elsewhere)* (London, 1689).

—, *England's black tribunal set forth in the triall of K.Charles at a High Court if Justice at Westminster-Hall* (London, 1660).

—, *Englands Tribute of Tears, / On the Death of his Grace the DUKE of GRAFTON, / Who received his Mortal Wound at the Siege of the City of Cork in Ireland* (London, 1690), R227129.

—, *An Excellent New song, / CALLED, The / False hearted young Man / OR, / The Injured Maiden* (London, 1697), R176868.

—, *The forsaken Maids Frollick / OR, / A Farewell to fond Love, / In which she doth plainly and properly prove* (London, [1666–1700?]), R228230.

—, *FOUR / Choice CAROLS for CHRISTMAS HOLIDAYS* (London, n.d.), T40075.

—, *The Frantick LOVER; / Or, The Wandring Young-Man* (London, [1685–88]), R188074.

—, *A godly garden out of which most comfortable herbs may be gathered* (London, 1574).

—, *A Godly Guide of Directions / for true penitent Sinners in these troubled times* (London, [1672–1696]), R220118.

—, *The Godly Maid of Leicester. / Being a true Relation of Elizabeth Stretton, who lying upon her Deathbed, was wonderfully deli- / vered from the Temptations of Satan* (London, [1684–86]), R234256.

—, *A godly new ballad, intituled, A douzen of points. A douzen of points, you here may read, whereon each Christian soul may feed* (London, 1686–8).

—, *A Godly Song, entituled, A farewell to the VVorld, made by a / Godly Christian, named Thomas Byll, being the Parish Clerke of West- / Pelton* (London, [1601–40?]), S118574.

—, *Good Admonition Or To al sorts of people this counsell I sing, That in each ones affaire, to take heed's a faire thing/ To the tune of, Magina-Cree* (London, 1630).

—, *Great Britains Earnest Desires / FOR THE / Princess MARYS / Happy Arrival. / Being the Protestants firm Hope and Resolution of the preservation of our / Laws and Liberties* (London, 1689), R188153.

—, *The Great TRIBUNAL; or, CHRIST's / glorious appearing in Judgment. Being, a contemplative Description of / Resurrection* (London, n.d.), T35859.

—, *Here begynneth a lytell treatyse of the Dyenge creature enfected with syknes vncurable with many sorowfull complayntes* (London, 1507).

—, *The Honour of a London Prentice. / Wherein is declared his matchless Manhood, and brave Adventures, done by him in / Turkey* (London, [1686–88]), N69951.

—, *The Joy of Protestants / For King William's safe Arrival from the Wars of Ireland ... to the unspeakable Joy of all his loving Subjects* (London, 1690), R188358.

—, *THE / King's Return from Holland, / AND / His Joyful Reception by His Royal Consort the QUEEN* (London, 1691) R188392.

—, *King WILLIAM'S Courage, / OR, / Our Royal Monarch's taking Leave of his Queen and Princely / Pallace* (London, 1690), R188381.

—, *The Lamenting Ladies last Farewel to the / WORLD* (London, [1644–1682?]), R216013.

—, *London's Lord have mercy upon us* (London, 1665).

—, *A Looking-Glass for all true Christians. / Very useful and necessary for all people of what degree soever, to look upon in these trouble- / some times of sorrow* (London, [1681–84]), R234261.

—, *The Love-sick / SERVING-MAN* (London, [1675–96?]), R235043.

—, *Loves fierce desire, and hopes of Recovery. / Or, A true and brief Description of two Resolved Lovers* (London, [1684–86]) R227265.

—, *LOVES Unlimitted Power: / Or, Cupids Cruelty* (London, 1685), R188505.

—, *A most Excellent Ballad of Ioseph the Carpenter, and the sacred Virgin Mary* (London, [1678–80]), R228250.

—, *A most Godly and Comfortable Ballad of the Glorious Resurrection of our Lord Jesus Christ* (London, [1684–86]), R234243.

—, *A new Ballad intituled, A Bell-man for England, which night and day doth sta ring in all mens hearing, Gods vengeance is at hand. To the tune of, O man in desperation* (London, 1620) S4504.

—, *A new Ballad, intituled, A Warning to Youth, shewing the lewd life of a Marchants Sonne of London* (London, [1619–29?]) R215905.

—, *A New Copy of Verses: / UPON / King WILLIAMS / Going / To Flanders, and His / Taking Leave of His Royal Consort / Queen MARY* (London, 1693) R188636.

—, *A new Song of a Young mans opinion, of the difference betweene good and bad Women* (London, n.d.), S125619.

—, *On the Barbarous, Execrable, and Bloody / Murder of the Earl of Essex* (London, 1689), R234357.

—, *PARADISE Lost, and PARADISE Regain'd; / BY / The Wonderful WORKS of GOD* (London, [1730–69]), T43623.

—, *A Pleasant Comoedie, Wherein is merily shewen: The wit of a Woman* (London, 1604).

—, *A pleasant new Ballad of Tobias, wherein is shewed the wonderful things that chanced unto him in his youth, and how he wedded a yong Damsel that had had seven husbands, and, never enjoyed their company, who were all slain by a wicked Spirit. To a new tune* [London, 1655–8].

—, *Prides Fall; Or, A warning for all English Women* (London, [1684–6]), R234277.

—, *A primer or booke of private prayer* (London, 1568).

—, *A Primer of boke of priuate praier* (London, 1560).

—, *THE / ROYAL DIALOGUE / OR, / The Courtly Salutation / BETWEEN / King William and Queen Mary* (London, 1691), R187263.

—, *The Shepherds Glory: / OR, A pleasant Song o' th Shepherd Swain* (London, [1672–1696]), R228554.

—, *A Signe from Heaven: or, A fearefull and terrible noise heard in the ayre at Alborow in the county of Suffolk* ([London], 1642).

—, *The Sinners Redemption. / Wherein is described the blessed Nativity of our Lord Jesus Christ* (London, n.d.), S112947.

—, *The Sorrowful Mother, / OR, / The Pious Daughters Last Farewel. / She patiently did run her Race, / believ'd the Word of Truth; / And Death did willingly embrace, / tho' in her blooming Youth* (London, [1685–1688]), R227382.

—, *The Swimming Lady: / Or, A Wanton Discovery, / Being a true Relation of a gay Lady* (London, [1681–4]), R1687.

—, *The true Lovers Good-morrow* (London, [1684–6]), R233990.

—, *A true relation from Germany, of a Protestant Shepherd's killing a counterfeit devil, that would have perverted him to popery* (London, 1676).

—, *Two pleasant Ditties, one of the Birth, the other of the / Passion of Christ* (London, [1619–1629]), S119328.

—, *Strange and true news from Westmoreland. Being a true relation of one Gabriel Harding* ([London], 1690).

—, *True Love Rewarded with Cruelty* (London, [1672–96?]), R228611.

—, *The True LOYALIST; / OR, / The Obedient SUBJECT, / A Loyal SONG* (London, 1685) R187548.

—, *The True / Protestants Contemplation: / CONTAINING / Serious Thoughts of the miraculous Deliverance from the intended Invasion: As / likewise the preservation of his Majesties person from the Malice of bloudy Conspirators* (London, 1693) R234290.

—, *A true relation of Go[ds] vvonderfull mercies in preseruing one aliue, which hanged fiue dayes, who was falsely accused* (London, 1605).

—, *A very Godly SONG, intituled, the Earnest / Petition of the faithful Christian, being Clerk of Bodnam, made upon his Deathbed, / at the Instant of his Transumation* (London, [1641–1703?]).

—, *The Wronged LADY: / OR, / The Lord's Daughter of Leicestershire, / Who dy'd for the Love of a young Noble-man, who left her after / many solemn Protestations* (London, [1671–1702]), R186893.

Atkyns, Sir R., *The Lord Chief Baron Atkyn's speech to Sir William Ashurst, Lord-Mayor elect of the city of London* (London, 1693).

B., J., *An English expositour, or Compleat dictionary teaching the interpretation of the hardest words, and most usefull terms of art, used in our language* (Cambridge, 1641).

B[agnell], W., *The Mystery of Astronomy Made plain To the meanest Capacity, By An Arithmetical Description of the Terrestrial and Celestial globes* (London, 1655).

Baker, Sir T., *Meditations and disquisitions upon the Lords Prayer* (London, 1636).

Bale, J., *The apology of Johan Bale agaynste a ranke papist anuswering both hym and hys doctours, that neyther their vowes nor yet their priesthode areof the Gospell* [sic], *but of Antichrist* (London, 1550).

—, Bale, J., *The first two partes of the actes or unchast examples of the Englysh votaryes gathered out of their owne legenades and chronicles by Johan Bale* (Wesel [London], 1551).

Baret, J., *An Alveary or Triple Dictionary, in English, Latin, and French: Very profitable for all such as be desirous of any of those three Languages* (London, 1574).

Barkstead, J., *The speeches, discourses, and prayers, of Col. John Barkstead, Col. John Okey, and Mr. Miles Corbet* (London, 1662).

Barlow, T., *The origin of kingly and ecclesiastical government* (London, 1681).

Barwick, J., *Certain disquisitions and considerations representing to the conscience* (London, 1644).

Bastard, T., *Twelve sermons* (London, 1615).

Bates, W., *A funeral-sermon for the reverend, holy and excellent divine, Mr.Richard Baxter* (London, 1692).

Baxter, R., *The life of faith in three parts* (London, 1670).

—, *The certainty of the worlds of spirits and, consequently, of the immortality of souls of the malice and misery of the devils and the damned* (London, 1691).

Becon, T., *The flour of godly praiers* (London, 1550).

—, *A new postil conteinyng most godly and learned sermons vpon all the Sonday Gospelles.* (London, 1566).

—, *Prayers and Other Pieces of Thomas Becon*, ed. John Eyre, PS 17 (Cambridge: Cambridge University Press, 1844).

—, *The Catechism of Thomas Becon, with other pieces written by him in the reign of King Edward the sixth*, ed. J. Eyre, PS 13 (Cambridge: Cambridge University Press, 1844).

—, *The Sycke mans salve* (London, 1561).

B., R., *The kingdom of darkness: or the history of daemons, specters, witches, apparitions, possessions, disturbances, and other wonderful and supernatural delusions* (London, 1688).

Behn, A., *The Dutch Lover a comedy* (London, 1673).

—, *Sir Patient Fancy: a comedy: as it is acted at the Duke's Theatre* (London, 1678).

—, *The Luckey Chance* (London, 1687).

Bekker, B., *The world bewitch'd, or, An examination of the common opinions concerning spirits their nature, power, administration and operations, as also the effects men are able to produce by their communication* (London, 1695).

Beza, T., *A booke of Christian questions and answers*, trans. Arthur Golding (London, 1572).

Bilson, T., *The perpetual gouernment of Christes Church* (London, 1593).

Blount, T., *Glossographia: Or A Dictionary, Interpreting all such Hard Words, whether Hebrew, Greek, Latin, Italian, Spanish, French, Teutonick, Belgick, British or Saxon* (London, 1661).

—, *Glossographia: Or A Dictionary, Interpreting all such Hard Words, whether Hebrew, Greek, Latin, Italian, Spanish, French, Teutonick, Belgick, British or Saxon; as are now used in our refined English Tongue* (London, 1656).

Bogan, Z., *A view of the threats and punishments recorded in the Scriptures* (London, 1653).

Bonner, E., *A profitable and necessarye doctrine with certayne homelyes* (London, 1555).

Boyle, R., *A free enquiry into the vulgarly receiv'd notion of nature made in an essay address'd to a friend* (London, 1686).

Bradford, J., *Godlie meditations upon the Lordes prayer* (London, 1562).

Bradford, J., *The Writings of John Bradford, containing Sermons, Meditations, Examination*, PS 31 (Cambridge: Cambridge University Press, 1853).

Braithwaite, R., *Capitall hereticks, or, The evill angels embattel'd against St.Michael* (London, 1659).

Bramhall, J., *Castigations of Mr. Hobbes his last animadversions, in the case concerning liberty, and universal necessity. With an appendix concerning The catching of leviathan or, The great whale* (London, 1658).

Bridges, J., *The supremacie of Christian princes ouer all persons throughout theor dominions* (London, 1573).

Bright, T., *An abridgement of the booke of acts and monumentes of the Church: written by that Reuerend Father, Maister Iohn Fox: and now abridged by Timothe Bright* (London, 1589).

Brome, R., *Five new playes* (London, 1653).

Brown, Sir T., *Religio medici, Observations upon Religio medici* (London, 1682).

Bryan, J., *Dwelling with God, the interest and duty of believers in opposition to the complemental, heartless, and reserved religion of the hypocrite* (London, 1670).

Bull, H., *Christian Prayers and Meditations* (London, 1568).

Bullein, W., *Bulleins bulwarke of a defence against all sicknesse, soarnesse, and vvoundes that doe dayly assaulte mankinde* (London, 1562).

Bullinger, H., *The Decades of Henry Bullinger, Minister of the Church of Zurich: The Fourth Decade*, trans. H.I., ed. T. Harding (Cambridge: Cambridge University Press, 1851).

Bullokar, J., *An English Expositor: teaching the interpretation of the hardest words in our language* (London, 1641).

Bunyan, J., *A confession of my faith and a reason of my practice* (London, 1672).

Byfield, N., *The cure of the feare of death* (London, 1618).

—, *The marrovv of the oracles of God* (London, 1630).

C., R., A *briefe and necessary catechisme, concerning the principall points of our Christian religion* (London, 1572).

Calfhill, J., *An Answer to John Martiall's 'Treatise of the Cross'*, ed. Richard Gibbings, PS 25 (Cambridge: Cambridge University Press, 1846).

Calvin, J., *The forme of common praiers vsed in the churches of Geneua*, trans. W. Huycke (London, 1550).

—, *The Catechisme or manner to teache children the Christian religion* [Geneva, 1556].

—, *Institutes of the Christian Religion: a New Translation by H. Beveridge, Vol. 1* (Grand Rapids, Michigan: Wm. B. Eerdmans, 1957).

Camfield, B., *A theological discourse of angels and their ministries wherein their existence, nature, number, order and offices are modestly treated of* (London, 1678).

Carter, M., *Honor rediviuus [sic] or An analysis of honor and armory* (London, 1660).

Catholic Church/R. Caly, *The primer in English and Latin, after Salisburie vse: set out at length with manie praiers and goodly pictures: newly imprinted this present yeare* (London, 1555), STC 16073.

Catholic Church/ R.Valentin, *This prymer of Salisbury vse is se tout a long with houtonyser chyng [sic]/ with many prayers & goodly pyctures in the kalender* (Rouen, 1554), STC 16058.

—, *Here after foloweth the prymer in Englysshe and in Latin sette out alonge: after the vse of Sarum* (n.p., 1555), STC 16070.

—, *This prymer of Salisbury vse is se tout along with houtonyser chyng [sic]/ with many prayers/ & goodly pyctures in the kalender* (Rouen, 1556), STC 16076.

Catholic Church/J. Wayland, *The prymer in Englishe and Latine after Salisbury vse: set out at length wyth many prayers and goodlye pyctures* (London, 1557), STC16080.

—, *The prymer in English and Latin after Salisburys vse set out at length with manye Godly prayers* (London, 1558), STC 16083.

Cavendish, M., *Playes written by the thrice noble, illustrious and excellent princess, the Lady Marchioness of Newcastle* (London, 1662).

—, *Plays, never before printed written by the ... Princesse the Duchess of Newcastle* (London, 1668).

Cawdrey, R., *A Table Alphabeticall, conteyning and teaching the true writing, and vnderstanding of hard vsuall English wordes, borrowed from the Hebrew, Greeke, Latine, or French, &c* (London, 1604).

Caxton, W., *Here begynneth a lityll treatise shorte and abredged spekynge of the arte & crafte to knowe well to dye* (London, 1490).

[Charles I], *Eikon basilike, The pourtraicture of His Sacred Majestie in his solitudes and sufferings* ([London], 1648).

—, *A True copy of the journal of the High Court of Justice for the tryal of K. Charles I / taken by J.Nalson Jan. 4, 1683* (London, 1684).

Chertsey, A., *The crafte to lyue well and to dye well* (London, 1505).

Clapham, H., *Henoch Clapham his demaundes and answeres touching the pestilience* (London, 1604).

Clarke, S., *Medulla Theologia, or the marrow of divinity contained in sundry questions and cases of conscience* (London, 1659).

Cockeram, H., *The English Dictionarie: Or, An Interpreter of hard English Words.* (London, 1623).

Coles, E., *An English Dictionary: Explaining The difficult Terms that are used in Divinity, Husbandry, Physick, Phylosophy, Law, Navigation, Mathematicks, and other Arts and Sciences* (London, 1677).

Cooper, H., *Thesaurus linguae Romanae & Britannicae tam accurate congestus, vt nihil penè in eo desyderari possit, quod vel Latinè complectatur amplissimus Stephani Thesaurus, vel Anglicè, toties aucta Eliotae Bibliotheca: opera & industria Thomae Cooperi Magdalenensis* (London, 1584).

Cooper, T., *Thesaurus linguae Romanae & Britannicae* (London, 1584).

Cosin, J., *A collection of private deuotions: in the practise of the ancient church Called the houres of prayer* (London, 1627).

Cotgrave, R., *A French-English dictionary compil'd by Mr. Randle Cotgrave: with another in English and French. Whereunto are newly added the animadversions and supplements* (London, 1650).

Covell, W., *A iust and temperate defence of the fiue books of ecclesiastical policie* (London, 1603).

Coverdale, M., *The Remains of Myles Coverdale*, ed. G. Pearson, PS 22 (Cambridge: Cambridge University Press, 1846).

Craig, J., *A shorte summe of the whole catechisme* (London, 1583).

Cranmer, T., *Certayne sermons, or homelies appoynted by the kynges Maiestie* (London, 1547).

—, *Catechismus, that is to say, a shorte instruction into Christian religion for the synguler commoditie and profyte of childre and yong people* (London, 1548).

—, *Miscellaneous Writings and Letters of Thomas Cranmer, Archbishop of Canterbury, martyr, 1556*, ed. J. Cox, PS 24 (Cambridge: Cambridge University Press, 1846).

Crossman, S., *Two sermons preached in the cathedral-church of Bristol, January the 30th 1679/80 and January the 31th 1680/81 being the days of publick humiliation for the execrable murder of King Charles the first* (London, 1681).

Day, R., *A booke of Christian prayers* (London, 1578).

Defoe, D., *The Life of that incomparable princess, Mary* (London, 1695).

Denne, H., *An epistle recommended to all the prisons in this city & nation. To such as chuse restraint rather than the violation of their consciences* (London, 1660).

Dering, E., *A briefe and necessary instruction veryre needefull to bee knowen of all housholders* (London, 1572).

Dickson, D., *An exposition of all St. Pauls epistles* (London, 1659).

Dingley, R., *The Deputation of Angels, or the Angell-Guardian* (London, 1653).

Downame, G., *Two sermons, the one commeding the ministerie in generall, the other defending the office of the bishops in particular* (London, 1608).

Drage, W., *Daimonomageia a small treatise of sicknesses and diseases from witchcraft, and supernatural causes* (London, 1665).

Drexel, J., *The angel-guardian's clock* (Rouen, 1630).

Drucateen, J., *True newes from [Mecare:] and also out of Worcestershire* (London, 1598).

Dryden, J., *An Evening's Love* (London, 1671).

—, *Amboyna, a tragedy as it is acted at the Theatre-Royal* (London, 1673).

Dunton, J., *The mourning-ring, in memory of your departed friend* (London, 1692).

Durham, J., *The blessednesse of the death of these that die in the Lord* (Glasgow, 1681).

Edgeworth, R., *Sermons very fruifull, godly, and learned, preached and sette foorth by Maister Roger Edgeworth* (London, 1557).

Edwards, J., *The plague of the heart its [brace] nature and quality* (Cambridge, 1665).

—, *A demonstration of the existence and providence of God* (London, 1696).

Edwards, T., *The first and second part of Gangraena, or, A catalogue and discovery of many of the errors, heresies, blasphemies and pernicious practices of the sectaries of this time* (London, 1646).

Ellis, C., *A catechism wherein the learner is at once taught to rehearse and prove all the main points of Christian religion* (London, 1674).

Ellwood, T., *Truth prevailing and detecting error, or, An answer to a book mis-called, A friendly conference between a minister and a parishioner of his, inclining to Quakerism* (London, 1676).

Elyot, T., *The Dictionary of syr Thomas Eliot knyght* (London, 1538).

Etherage, G., *The Man of Mode,* (London, 1676).

Eyre, A., 'A dyurnall, or, Catalogue of all my accions and expences from the 1st of January 1646–[7–]', *Yorkshire diaries and autobiographies, Vol. 1*, ed. H. J. Morehouse (Durham: Surtees Society Publications 65, 1877).

Farquhar, G., *The Beaux' Stratagem* (London, 1707).

Fisher, J., *The Priest's duty and dignity* (London, 1636).

Fisher, S., *One antidote more, against that provoking sin of swearing, by reason of which this land now mourneth given forth from under the burden of the oppressed seed of God* (London, 1600).

Fitzherbert, T., *An adioynder to the supplement of Father Robert Persons* (St Omer, 1613).

Flavel, J., *A saint indeed: or The great work of a Christian* (London, 1668).

—, *An exposition of the assemblies catechism with practical inferences from each question* (London, 1692).

[Fowler, E.,], *A friendly conference between a minister and a parishioner of his, inclining to Quakerism wherein the absurd opinions of that sect are detected, and exposed to a just censure* (London, 1676).

Fowler, E., *A discourse of the great disingenuity & unreasonableness of repining at afflicting providence and of the influence which they ought to have upon us* (London, 1695).

Foxe, J., *Acts and Monvments of Martyrs, with a Generall discourse of these latter Persecution* (London, 1563).

Fulke, W., *D. Heskins, S. Sanders and M. Rastel, accounted (among their faction) three pillers and archpatriarches of the popish synagogue* (London, 1579).

—, *A Defence of the Sincere and True Translations of the Holy Scriptures into the English Tongue against the cavils of Gregory Martin*, ed. Charles Hartshorne, PS 10 (Cambridge: Cambridge University Press, 1843).

Gauden, J., *Cromwell's bloody slaughter-house, or, his damnable designes laid and practised by him and his negro's* (London, 1660).

—, *A pillar of gratitude humbly dedicated to the glory of God the honour of his majesty* (London, 1661).

—, *A discourse concerning publick oaths, and the lawfulness of swearing in judicial proceedings* (London, 1662).

Gell, R., *A sermon touching God's government of the world by angels* (London, 1649).

Gerard, J., *Gerards meditations written originally in the Latine tongue*, trans. R. Winterton (Cambridge, 1638).

Glanvill, J., 'The *USEFULNESS* of *Real Philosophy* to *RELIGION*' in his *Essays on Several important subjects in philosophy and religion* (London, 1676).

Gouge, T., *A word to sinners, and a word to saints* (London, 1668).

de Granada, L., *Granadas deuotion, Exactly teaching how a man may truly dedicate and deuote himself vnto God* (London, 1589).

—, *The sinners guyde* (London, 1598).

—, *A paradise of prayers* (London, 1614).

Gumbleden, J., *Two sermons: first An ANGEL, in a vision* (London, 1657).

Habermann, J., *A dailie exercise of godly meditations drawne out of the pure fountains of the holie Scriptures*, trans. T. Rogers (London, 1579).

Hales, J., *Golden remains of the ever memorable Mr Iohn Hales of Eton College* (London, 1659).

Hall, J., *Contemplations vpon the principal passages of the holy story* (London, 1614).

Hall, J., *The invisible world discovered to spirituall eyes* (London, 1659).

Hammond, H., *Of Idolatrie* (London, 1646).

Hardy, N., *The pious votary and prudent traveller characterized in a farewell sermon* (London, 1659).

Harvey, G., *Archelogia philosophica nova, or, New principles of philosophy* (London, 1663).

Hay, P., *A vision of Balaams asse* (London, 1616).

Hemmingsen, N., *A Postill, or, Exposition of the Gospels that are usually red in the churches of God, vpon the Sundayes and feast dayes of Saincts*, trans. A. Golding (London, 1569).

Heylyn, P., *Theologia veterum, or, The summe of Christian theologie* (London, 1654).

Herring, F., *A modest defence of the caueat giuen to the wearers of impoisoned amulets* (London, 1604).

Hobbes, T., *Leviathan, or, The matter, forme, and power of a common wealth, ecclesiasticall and civil* (London, 1651).

Hodgson, J., 'Memoirs of Captain John Hodgson, touching his Conduct in the Civil Wars, &c.' in *Original memoirs, written during the great Civil War; being the life of Sir Henry Slingsby, and memoirs of Capt. Hodgson. With notes, &c* (Edinburgh: J. Ballantyne & Co., 1806), pp. 194–7.

Holland, H., *Spirituall preseruatiues against the pestilience* (London, 1603).

Hooker, R., *Of the Lavves of ecclesiasticall politie: The First Booke: Concerning Lawes, and their seuerall kindes in generall* (London, 1593).

Horneck, A., *The happy ascetick, or, The best exercise* (London, 1681).

—, *Gods providence in the midst of confusion set out in a sermon preach'd at the Savoy, January the 30 1681, being the anniversary of the martyrdom of King Charles I* (London, 1682).

Howgill, F., *A copy of a paper sent to John Otway, Justice of the Peace, concerning swearing* (London, 1666).

Huggarde, M., *A treatise entitled the path waye to the towre of perfection* (London, 1554).

—, *A mirrour of loue* (London, 1555)

Hughes, L. *Certaine greevances, vvell vvorthy the serious consideration of the right honorable and high Court of Parliament* (London, 1640).

Hutchinson, R., *The Works of Roger Hutchinson*, ed. J. Bruce, PS 4 (Cambridge: Cambridge University Press, 1842).

Hyde, E., *A Christian vindication of truth against errour* (London, 1659).

Jackson, T., *Maran atha, or Dominus veniet Commentaries upon the articles of the Creed* (London, 1657).

Jameson, W., *Nazianzeni querela et votum justum, The fundamentals of the hierarchy examin'd and disprov'd* (Glasgow, 1697).

Jerome, S., *Seauen helpes to Heauen* (London, 1614).

(Jewel, J.), *The second tome of homilies of such matters as were promised, and intitules in the former part of homilies* (London, 1571).

Jewel, J., *The Works of John Jewel: Bishop of Salisbury, Vol 2*, ed. J. Ayre, PS 26 (Cambridge: Cambridge University Press, 1847).

—, *A defence of the Apologie of the Churche of Englande conteininge an answeare to a certaine booke lately set foorthe by M. Hardinge* (London, 1567).

Johnson, W., *Deus nobiscum a sermon preached upon a great deliverance at sea* (London, 1664).

Kemp, W., *A brief treatise of the nature, causes, signes, preservation from, and cure of the pestilence* (London, 1665).

Ken, T., *A manual of prayers for the use of the scholars of Winchester College* (London, 1675).

Kersey the Younger, J., *English Dictionary: Or, a Compleat: Collection Of the Most Proper and Significant Words, Commonly used in the Language* (London, 1702).

Kettlewell, J., *A funeral sermon for the Right Honourable, the Lady Frances Digby* (London, 1684).

—, *Death made comfortable, or, The way to dye well consisting of directions for an holy and an happy death* (London, 1695).

Kirby, R., and Bishop, J., *The marrow of astrology in two books: wherein is contained the natures of the signes and planets, with their several governing angels, according to their respective hierarchies* (London, 1687).

Latimer, H., *Sermons and Remains of Hugh Latimer, sometime Bishop of Worcester, Martyr*, ed. George Corrie, PS 20 (Cambridge: Cambridge University Press, 1845).

Lawrence, H., *An history of angells being a theological treatise of our communion and warre with them* (London, 1646).

Lawson, G., *Politica sacra, or, A model of civil and ecclesiastical government* (London, 1689).

Leigh, E., *A treatise of divinity consisting of three books* (London, 1646).

—, *Annotations on five poetical books of the Old Testament* (London, 1657).

Legends of the Holy Rood: Symbols of the Passions and Cross – Poems, trans. R. Morris (London: Trüber for the Early English Text Society, 1871).

Legenda aurea sanctorum, sive, Lombardica historia, [W. Caxton,] (London, 1483).

Life and Letters of John Winthrop: Governor of the Massachusetts-Bay Company at their Emigration to New England, 1630, ed. R. C. Winthrop (Boston, MA: Little Brown, 1864).

Ling, N. ed., *Politeuphuia: wits common wealth* (London, 1598).

Liturgical Services: Liturgies and occasional forms of prayer set forth in the Reign of Queen Elizabeth, ed. W. K. Clay (Cambridge: Cambridge University Press, 1847).

Lucy, W., *Observations, censures, and confutations of notorious errours in Mr.Hobbes his Leviathan and other his bookes* (London, 1663).

Luther, M., *The last wil and last confession of martyn luthers faith co[n]cerming [sic] the principal articles of religion which are in controversy* (Wesel, 1543).

—, *Legenda aurea sanctorum, sive, Lombardica historia*, trans. W. Caxton (London, 1487).

Marlowe, C., *The tragical history of D. Faustus* (London, 1604).

Massinger, P. and Dekker, T., *The virgin martir a tragedie. As it hath bin diuers times publickely acted with great applause, by the seruants of his Maiesties Reuels* (London, 1622).

Mather, I., *An essay for the recording of illustrious providences wherein their existence, nature, number, order and offices are modestly treated of* (Boston, 1678).

Maynard, J., *The beauty and order of the creation together with natural and allegorical meditations on the six dayes works of the creation* (London, 1668).

Mede, J., *The apostacy of the latter times* (London, 1641).

Meres, F., *Palladis tamia: Wits treasury* (London, 1598).

—, *Wits common wealth The second part* (London, 1634).

Midgley, R., *A new treatise of natural philosophy, free'd from the intricacies of the schools* (London, 1687).

Mirk, J., *Mirk's Festial: A Collection of Homilies by Johannes Mirkus*, ed. T. Erbe (London: Trübner for the Early English Text Society, 1965).

de Molina, A., *A treatise of the holy sacrifice of the masse* (St Omer, 1623).

Montagu, R., *A gagg for the new gospel?* (London, 1624).

—, *Immediate addresse vnto God alone* (London, 1624).

Montagu, W., *The Shepherd's Paradise* (London, 1629 [1659]).

Moore, M., *Wonderfull newes from the north. Or, A true relation of the sad and grievous torments, inflicted upon the bodies of three children of Mr. George Muschamp* (London, 1650).

More, H., *An Antidote against atheisme, or, An appeal to the natural faculties of the minde of man* (London, 1653).

N., J., *A path-way to penitence with sundry deuout prayers* (London, 1591).

Norden, J., *A poore mans rest founded vpon motiues, meditations, and prayers* (London, 1620).

Norris, J., *Reason and religion, or, The grounds and measures of devotion* (London, 1689).

Northbrooke, J., *Spiritus est vicarious Christi in terra. A breefe and pithie summe of the Christian faith made in the fourme of a confession* (London, 1571).

The notebooks of Nehemiah Wallington, 1618–1654: A Selection, ed. D. Booy (Aldershot: Ashgate, 2007).

Numan, P., *Miracles lately wrought by the intercession of the glorious Virgin Marie* (Antwerp, 1606).

P., L., *Strange-predictions related at Catericke in the north of England: by one who saw a vision, and told it himselfe to the company with whom he was drinking healths; how he was struck, and an angel appeared to him with a sword* (London, 1648).

Pagitt, E., *Heresiography, or, A discription of the hereticks and sectaries of these latter times* (London, 1645).

Parsons, R., *The first booke of the Christian Exercise appertayning to resolution* (Rouen, 1582).

Peryn, W., *Spirituall exercyses and goostly meditacions and a neare waye to come to perfection* (London, 1557).

Perkins, W., *An exposition of the Symbole or Creed of the Apostles according to the tenour of the Scriptures* (London, 1595).

—, *A golden chaine: or The description of theologie containing the order of the causes of saluation and damnation* (London, 1591).

—, *An exposition of the Lords praier in the way of catechisme* (London, 1593).

—, *An exposition of the Symbole or Creed of the Apostles* (London, 1595).

—, *A declaration of the true manner of knowing Christ Crucified* (London, 1596).

—, *A reformed Catholike* (London, 1598), pp. 252–4; *Of the calling of the ministerie two treatises* (London, 1605).

—, *The combat betvveene Christ and the Diuell displayed* (London, 1606).

—, *A godly and learned exposition of Christs Sermon in the Mount* (London, 1608).

—, *A salve for a sicke man* (London, 1611).

—, *Satans sophistrie ansuuered by our Sauiour Christ and in diuers sermons further manifested* (London, 1694).

Phillips, E., *The nevv vvorld of vvords. Or a general English dictionary Containing the proper significations, and etymologies of all words derived from other languages* (London, 1678).

Piatti, G., *The happiness of a religious state* (Rouen, 1632).

Polhill, E., *The divine will considered in its eternal decrees, and holy execution of them* (London, 1695).

Pollard, L., *Fyve homiles of late* (London, 1556).

Price, L., *The Maydens of Londons brave adventures, / OR, / A Boon Voyage intended for the Sea* (London, [1623–1661?]) R216159.

Prynne, W., *A briefe survey and censure of Mr Cozens his couzening deuotions* (London, 1628).

—, *The substance of a speech made in the House of Commons* (London, 1649).

Rainolds, W., *A refutation of sundery reprehensions, cauils, and false sleights, by which M. Whitaker laboureth to deface the late English translation* (Paris, 1583).

Rivers, J. A., *Devout Rhapsodies, in which is Treated, of the Excellencie of Divine Scriptures* (London, 1647).

Robinson, J., *A iustification of separation from the Church of England* (Amsterdam, 1610).

Rogers, T., *The Catholic Doctrine of the Church of England: An Exposition of the Thirty-Nine Articles*, ed. J. Perowne, PS 52 (Cambridge: Cambridge University Press, 1854).

de Rojas, F., *The Spanish bavvd, represented in Celestina: or, The tragicke-comedy of Calisto and Melibea*, trans. J. Mabbe (London, 1631).

Rollock, R., *Lectures vpon the Epistle of Paul to the Colossians* (London, 1603).

Ross, A., *Pansebia, or, A view of all religions in the world with the severall church-government from the creation, to these times* (London, 1655).

Rust, G., *A funeral sermon preached at the obsequies of the right reverend father in God, Jeremy, Lord Bishop of Down* (London, 1668).

Rutherford, S., *A survey of the spirituall antichrist opening the secrets of familisme and antinomianisme* (London, 1648).

Salkeld, J., *A Treatise of Angels* (London, 1613).

Schaff, P., *The Creeds of Christendom with a History and Critical Notes, Vol 1* (Grand Rapids: Harper and Row, 1877).

Scott, J., *A sermon preached at the funeral of Dr.William Croun* (London, 1685).

—, *The Christian life part III. Wherein the great duties of justice, mercy, and mortification are fully explained and inforced* (London, 1696).

Shakespeare, W., *The RSC Complete Works*, eds, J. Bate and E. Rasmussen (Basingstoke, Macmillan, 2007).

Sharpe, J., *The triall of the protestant priuate spirit* (St Omer, 1630).

Sharpham, E., *The fleire· As it hath beene often played in the Blacke-Fryers by the Children of the Reuells* (London, 1607).

Shelford, R., *Fiue pious and learned discourses* (London, 1635).

Sinclair, G. *Satan's invisible world discovered, or, A choice collection of modern relations proving evidently against the saducees and atheists of this present age* (Edinburgh, 1685).

Slater, S., *A sermon preached (May 16.1680) at the funeral of Mr.Tho.Gilson, late minister of the Gospel* (London, 1680).

—, *A funeral sermon. Delivered upon occasion of the death of that worthy gentleman John Marsh* (London, 1682).

Smectymnuus, *An answer to a booke entitled An hvmble remonstrance* (London, 1641).

Smith, H., *Three prayers* (London, 1591).

Smith, J., *Essex doue, presenting the vvorld vvith a fevv of her oliue branches* (London, 1629).

Spangenberg, J., *The sum of diuinitie drawn out of the holy scripture very necessary* (London, 1548).

Spencer, J., *Kaina kai palaia* (London, 1658).

—, *A discourse concerning prodigies wherein the vanity of presages by them is reprehended* ([Cambridge], 1663).

Stillingfleet, E., *An answer to Mr. Cressy's Epistle apologetical to a person of honour touching his vindication of Dr.Stillingfleet* (London, 1675).

Stokes, D., *Versus Christianus, or , Directions for private devotions and retirements* (Oxford, 1668).

Stoughton, J., *XI, choice sermons preached upon selected occasions* (London, 1640).

Synge, E., *The GLORY of MAN's Redemption: / BEING / A new and lively Emblem of the BIRTH, LIVES, SUFFERINGS, RESURRECTION, and glorious / ASCENTION of our blessed Lord and Saviour JESUS CHRIST* (London, n.d.), T40844.

Sutcliffe, M., *A true relation of Englands happinesse* (London, 1629).

Taverner, R., *On Saynt Andrewes day the Gospels with brief sermons upon them for al the holy dayes in ye yere* (London, 1542).

Taylor, J., *A funeral sermon preached at the obsequies of the Right Hon[oura]ble and most virtuous Lady, the Lady Frances, Countesse of Carbery* (London, 1650).

—, *A discovrse of baptisme its institutions and efficacy upon all believers* (London, 1653).

—, *Holy living in which are described the means and instruments of obtaining every virtue* (London, 1656).

—, *A collection of offices or forms of prayer in cases ordinary and extraordinary* (London, 1657).

—, *Chrisis teleiotike, A discourse of confirmation for the use of the clergy and instruction of the people of Ireland* (Dublin, 1663).

Taylor, T., *Christs combate and conquest* (London, 1618).

The canons and decrees of the sacred and Ecumenical Council of Trent, ed. and trans. J. Waterworth (London: Dolman, 1848).

The Diary of Ralph Thoresby 1677–1724, ed. J. Hunter (London: S. Bentley, 1830).

The Diary of Samuel Pepys: with an introduction and notes, ed. G. G. Smith (London: Macmillan, 1906).

The Sarum Missal in English, Part I, trans. F. Warren (London: De La More Press, 1911).

The Sarum Missal in English, Part II, trans. F. Warren (London: De La More Press, 1911).

The Two Liturgies A.D.1549 and A.D.1552 with other Documents set forth by Authority in the Reign of King Edward VI, ed. J. Ketley (Cambridge: Cambridge University Press, 1844).

Thomas, T., *Dictionarium linguae Latinae et Anglicanae. In hoc opere quid sit præstitum, & ad superiores λεξιχογραφονς adiectum, docebit epistola ad Lectorem* (Cantebrigiae, 1587).

de Torquemada, A., *The Spanish Mandeuile of miracles. Or The garden of curious flowers* (London, 1600).

Tudor Royal Proclamations, Vol. 2. The Later Tudors, eds P. Hughes and J. Larkin (New Haven; London: Yale University Press, 1969).

Tuke, T., *The practise of the faithfull containing many godly prayers* (London, 1613).

Tyndale, W., *Expositions and Notes on Sundry Portions of Holy Scriptures together with the Practice of Prelates* ed. H. Walter, PS 37 (Cambridge: Cambridge University Press, 1848).

D' Urfey, T., *Sir Barnaby Whigg* (London, 1681).

—, *A common-wealth of women a play* (London, 1686).

—, *Gloriana, funeral pindarique poem sacred to the blessed memory of that ever-admir'd and most excellent princess, out late gracious sovereign lady Queen Mary* (London, 1695).

—, *The famous history of the rise and fall of Massaniello* (London, 1700).

Ussher, J., *A sermon preached before the Commos-House of Parliament* [sic] (London, 1624).

—, *An ansvver to a challenge made by a Iesuite in Ireland* (London, 1624).

Vaughan, T., *A brief natural history intermixed with variety of philosophical discourses and refutations* (London, 1669).

de Voragine, Jacobus, *The Golden Legend: Readings on the Saints, Vol.1*, trans. W. Ryan (Princeton, NJ: Princeton University Press, 1993).

—, *The golden legend, or, Lives of the saints / as Englished by William Caxton,* Vol. 2 (London: J. M. Dent and Co., 1900).

Vezelius, T. B., *A booke of Christian questions and answers. Wherein are set foorth the cheef points of the Christian religion in maner of an abridgment*, trans. A. Golding (London, 1572).

Vicars, J., *Prodigies and apparitions, or, England waning piece* ([London?], 1643).

—, *A Letter for a Christian Family / Directed to all true Christians to Read* (London, [1684–1686]), R227342.

Vincent, T., *The death of ministers improved. Or, an exhortation to the inhabitants of Horsley on Glocester-shire, and others, on the much lamented death of that reverend and faithful minister of the Gospel, Mr.Henry Stubbs* (London, 1678).

Warriston, Lord A. J., *The last discourse of the Right Honble the Lord Warestoune, as he delivered it upon the scafford at the Mercat-Cross of Edinburgh* (London, 1664).

Waterhouse, E., *A short narrative of the late dreadful fire in London, together with certain considerations remarkable therein* (London, 1667).

Watson, T., *Holsome and catholyke doctrine concerninge the seuen Sacramentes of Chrystes Church* (London, 1558).

—, *The Christian's Charter* (London, 1654).

—, *The fight of faith crowned, or, A sermon preached at the funeral of that eminently holy man Mr.Henry Stubs* (London, 1678).

Webster, J., *The displaying of supposed witchcraft wherein affirmed that there are many sorts of deceivers and impostors* (London, 1677).

Wesley, S., *Elegies on the Queen and Archbishop* (London, 1695).

White, F., *A replie to Iesuit Fishers answere to certaine Questions* (London, 1624).

Whitehall, J., *The Leviathan found out* (London, 1679).

Wigan, J., *Antichrist's strongest hold overturned, or, The foundation of the religion of the people called Quakers* (London, 1651).

Willet, A., *Synopsis Papismi, that is, a generall viewe of papistry* (London, 1592).

—, *Tetrastylon papisticum, that is, the foure principal pillers of papistry* (London, 1593).

—, *A catholicon* (London, 1602).

Wilson, A., *The history of Great Britain being the life and reign of King James the First* (London, 1653).

Woodward, E., *The life and death of William Laud* (London, 1645).

Wriothesley, C., *A chronicle of England during the reigns of the Tudors, from A.D. 1485 to 1559, Vol. 1* (Westminster: Camden Society New Series 11, 1875).

Secondary Sources

Alexander, J., and Binski, P. (eds), *Age of Chivalry: Art in Plantagenet England 1200–1400* (London: Royal Academy of Arts in association with Weidenfeld and Nicolson, 1987).

Aston, M., *England's Iconoclasts, Volume 1: Laws Against Images* (Oxford: Clarendon Press, 1988).

Aveling, J. C. H., *The Handle and the Axe: The Catholic Recusants in England from Reformation to Emancipation* (London: Blond and Briggs, 1976).

Aylmer, G. E., 'Unbelief in Seventh-Century England', in D. Pennington and K. V. Thomas (eds), *Puritans and Revolutionaries* (Oxford: Clarendon Press, 1978), pp. 22–46.

Berman, D., *A History of Atheism in Britain: From Hobbes to Russell* (London: Croom Helm, 1988).

Binski, P., *Medieval Death: Ritual and Representation* (London: British Museum Press, 1996).

Birely, R., *The Refashioning of Catholicism, 1450–1700* (Basingstoke: Macmillan, 1999).

Bossy, J., 'The Character of Elizabethan Catholicism', *P&P*, 21 (1962), pp. 39–59.

—, *The English Catholic Community 1570–1850* (London: Darton, Longman and Todd, 1975).

—, 'The Mass as a Social Institution 1200–1700', *P&P*, 100 (1983), pp. 29–61.

Bourdieu, P., *The Field of Cultural Production: Essays on Art and Literature*, ed. R. Johnson (Cambridge: Polity Press, 1993).

Brandon, S. G. F., 'Angels: The History of an Idea', *History Today*, 13 (October 1963), pp. 655–65.

Breward, I., *The work of William Perkins* (Abingdon: Sutton Courtenay Press, 1970).

Briggs, R., 'Dubious Messengers: Bodin's daemon, the spirit world and the Sadducees', in P. Marshall and A. Walsham (eds) *Angels in the Early Modern World* (Cambridge: Cambridge University Press, 2006), pp. 168–90.

Brooke, J. H., *Science and Religion: some historical perspectives* (Cambridge: Cambridge University Press, 1991).

Brown, P., *The Cult of the Saints: Its Rise and Function in Latin Christianity* (Chicago, IL: University of Chicago Press, 1981).

Burgess, C., "A fond thing vainly invented": an essay on Purgatory and pious motive in later medieval England', in S. Wright (ed.), *Parish, Church and People: Local Studies in Lay Religion 1350–1750* (London: Hutchinson, 1988), pp. 56–84.

Burgess, F., *English Churchyard Memorials* (London: S.P.C.K., 1979).

Butterfield, H., *The Origins of Science, 1300–1800* (London: Bell, 1957).

Cameron, E., *Enchanted Europe: Superstition, Reason and Religion*, 1250–170 (Oxford: Oxford University Press, 2010).

Capp, B., *Astrology and the Popular Press: English Almanacs 1500–1800* (London: Faber, 1979).

Cave, C., *Roof Bosses in Medieval Churches: An aspect of Gothic Sculpture* (Cambridge: Cambridge University Press, 1948).

Cervantes, F., 'Angels conquering and conquered: changing perceptions in Spanish America' in P. Marshall and A. Walsham (eds), *Angels in the Early Modern World* (Cambridge: Cambridge University Press, 2006), pp. 104–34.

Clark, S., *Thinking with Demons: The Idea of Witchcraft in Early Modern Europe* (Oxford: Clarendon, 1997).

—, *Vanities of the Eye: Vision in Early Modern European Culture* (Oxford: Oxford University Press, 2007).

Cogswell, T., *The Blessed Revolution: English Politics and the coming of war, 1621–1624* (Cambridge: Cambridge University Press, 1989).

Collinson, P., 'The Jacobean Religious Settlement: The Hampton Court Conference', in H. Tomlinson (ed.), *Before the English Civil War* (London: Macmillan, 1983).

—, 'From Iconoclasm to Iconophobia: the Cultural Impact of the Second English Reformation', *The Stenton Lecture 1985* (University of Reading: 1986).

—, *The Birthpangs of Protestant England: Religious and Cultural Change in the Sixteenth and Seventeenth Centuries* (Basingstoke: Macmillan, 1988).

Cooper, K., and J. Gregory (eds), *Signs, Wonders, Miracles: Representations of Divine Power in the Life of the Church*, Studies in Church History, 41 (Woodbridge: Boydell Press, 2005).

Cooper, T. (ed.), *The Journal of William Dowsing: Iconoclasm in East Anglia during the English Civil War* (Woodbridge: Boydell, 2001).

Crow, G. D., 'Antonio de Torquemada: Spanish Dialogue Writer of the Sixteenth Century' in *Hispania*, 38:3 (September, 1955), pp. 265–71.

Curtis, M., 'The Hampton Court Conference and its Aftermath', *History*, 46, (1961), pp. 1–16.

Cressy, D., *Bonfires and Bells: National Memory and the Protestant Calendar in Elizabethan and Stuart England* (London: Weidenfeld and Nicholson, 1989).

Crewe, S., *Stained Glass in England 1180–1540* (London: HMSO, 1987).

Crossley, F., *English Church Monuments A.D.1150–1550: an introduction to the study of tombs & effigies of the Mediaeval period* (London: B. T. Batsford, 1921).

Daniell, C., *Death and Burial in Medieval England 1066–1550* (London: Routledge, 1997).

Daston, L., and K. Park, *Wonders and the Order of Nature 1150–1750* (New York: Zone Books, 1997).

Dear, P., *Revolutionizing the sciences: European knowledge and its ambitions, 1500–1700* (Basingstoke: Palgrave, 2001).

Degenhardt, J., "Catholic Martyrdom in Dekker and Massinger's the Virgin Martir and the Early Modern Threat of 'Turning Turk'", *English Literary History*, 73:1 (2006), pp. 83–117.

Dickens, A. G., *The English Reformation*, 2nd edn (London: Batsford, 1989).

Duffy, E., *The Stripping of the Altars: Traditional Religion in England c.1400–c.1580* (London: Yale University Press, 1992).

Fincham, K., and Lake, P., 'The Ecclesiastical Policy of King James I', *Journal of British Studies*, 24:2 (April, 1985), pp. 169–207.

Fincham, K., and N. Tyacke, N., *Altars Restored: The Changing Face of English Religious Worship 1547–c.1700* (Oxford: Oxford University Press, 2007).

Finucane, R., *Miracles and Pilgrims, Popular Beliefs in Medieval England* (London: Dent, 1977).

Fix, A., 'Angels, Devils, and Evil Spirits in Seventeenth-century Thought: Balthasar Bekker and the Collegiants', *Journal of the History of Ideas*, 50:4 (October–December, 1989), pp. 527–47.

Flint, V., *The Rise of Magic in Early Medieval Europe* (Oxford: Clarendon Press, 1993).

Freeman, T., 'New Perspectives on an Old Book: The Creation and Influence of Foxe's Book of Martyrs', *JEH*, 49 (1998), pp. 317–28.

Gardner, A., *English Medieval Sculpture* (Cambridge: Cambridge University Press, 1951).

Gaudie, E., 'Flights of Angels', *History Today*, 42:12 (December, 1992), pp. 13–20.

Goodman, D., and Russell, C.A.(eds), *The Rise of Scientific Europe, 1500–1800* (Sevenoaks; Milton Keynes: Hodder & Stoughton, 1991).

Gordon, B., and P. Marshall, P. (eds), *The Place of the Dead: Death and Remembrance in Late Medieval and Early Modern Europe* (Cambridge: Cambridge University Press, 2000).

Green, I., *The Christian's ABC: Catechisms and Catechizing in England c.1530–1740* (Oxford: Clarendon Press, 1996).

—, *Print and Protestantism in Early Modern England* (Oxford: Oxford University Press, 2000).

Haigh, C., 'The Fall of a Church of the Rise of a Sect? Post-Reformation Catholicism in England', *HJ*, 21:1 (1978), pp. 181–6.

—, 'From Monopoly to Minority: Catholicism in Early Modern England', *Transactions of the Royal Historical Society*, 5th ser., 31 (1981), pp. 129–47.

—, 'Revisionism, the Reformation and the History of English Catholicism', *JEH*, 36:3 (1985), pp. 394–406.

—, *English Reformations: Religion, Politics and Society under the Tudors* (Oxford: Clarendon, 1993).

—, 'Success and Failure in the English Reformation', *P&P*, 173 (2001), pp. 28–49.

Harkness, D., *John Dee's Conversations with Angels: Cabala, Alchemy, and the End of Nature* (Cambridge: Cambridge University Press, 1999).

Harvey, K., 'The Role of Angels in English Protestant thought 1580 to 1660', Ph.D. diss., (Cambridge, 2005).

Hellyer, M. (ed.), *The Scientific Revolution: the Essential Readings* (Oxford: Blackwell, 2003).

Highley, C., and King, J. (eds), *John Foxe and his World* (Aldershot: Ashgate, 2002).

Hill, C., *The World Turned Upside Down: Radical Ideas During the English Revolution* (London: Mourice Temple Smith Ltd, 1972).

Hodnett, E., *English Woodcuts 1480–1535* (Oxford: Oxford University Press, 1973).

Houlbrooke, R., *Death, religion, and the family in England, 1480–1750* (Oxford: Oxford University Press, 1998).

Houston, A., and Pincus, S. (eds.), *A Nation Transformed: England after the Restoration* (Cambridge: Cambridge University Press, 2001).

Hunter, M. 'The Problem of Atheism in Early Modern England', trans. *Royal Historical Society*, 5th series, 35 (1985), pp. 135–57.

—, (ed.), *Atheism from the Reformation to the Enlightenment* (Oxford: Oxford University Press, 1992).

—, *Robert Boyle Reconsidered* (Cambridge: Cambridge University Press, 1994).

Hsia, R. P., *The World of Catholic Renewal, 1540–1770* (Cambridge: Cambridge University Press, 1998).

James, M., 'Ritual, Drama and Social Body in the Late Medieval English Town', *P&P*, 98 (February, 1983), pp. 3–29.

Johnson, R., *Saint Michael the Archangel in Medieval English Legend* (Woodbridge: Boydell Press, 2005).

Johnson, T., 'Guardian Angels and the Society of Jesus' in P. Marshall and A. Walsham, *Angels in the Early Modern World* (Cambridge: Cambridge University Press, 2006), pp. 191–214.

Johnston, A., 'The Guild of Corpus Christi and the Procession of Corpus Christi in York', *Medieval Studies, 38* (1976), pp. 372–84.

Keck, D., *Angels and Angelology in the Middle Ages* (New York: Oxford University Press, 1998).

Keeble, N. H., *The Restoration: England in the 1660s* (Oxford: Blackwell, 2002).

Knowles, D., and Hadcock, R., *Medieval Religious Houses: England and Wales* (Harlow: Longman, 1971).

Lake, P., 'Anti-Popery: the Structure of a Prejudice' in R. Cust and A. Hughes, (eds), *The English Civil War* (London: Arnold, 1997), pp. 181–210.

Lake P., and Questier, M., 'Agency, Appropriation and Rhetoric under the Gallows: Puritans, Romanists and the State in Early Modern England', *P&P*, 153 (1996), pp. 64–107.

—, *The Antichrist's lewd hat: Protestants, Papists and players in post-Reformation England* (New Haven; London: Yale University Press, 2002).

Lee Jnr, M., *Great Britain's Solomon: James VI and I in his Three Kingdoms* (Urbana: University of Illinois Press, 1990).

Le Strange, R., *A Complete Descriptive Guide to British Monumental Brasses* (London: Thames and Hudson, 1972).

Levy, B. (ed.), *The Bible in the Middle Ages: Its Influence on Literature and Art* (Binghamton, N.Y.: Medieval & Renaissance Texts and Studies, 1992).

Loach, J., 'The Marian Establishment and the Printing Press', *English Historical Review*, 101 (1986), pp. 135–48.

Loades, D., *The Reign of Mary Tudor: Politics, Government and Religion in England 1553–1558* (London: Benn, 1991).

— (ed.), *John Foxe and the English Reformation* (Aldershot: Ashgate, 1997).

—, *John Foxe: An Historical Perspective* (Aldershot: Ashgate, 1999).

McCoog, T. M., 'Ignatius Loyola and Reginald Pole: a Reconsideration', *JEH*, 47 (1996), pp. 45–64.

MacCulloch, D., *Reformation: Europe's House Divided* (London: Penguin, 2003)

—, 'Recent Studies on Angels in the Reformation', *Reformation*, 14 (2009), pp. 179–86.

Maltby, J., *Prayer book and people in Elizabethan and early Stuart England* (Cambridge: Cambridge University Press, 1998).

Marshall, P., *The Catholic Priesthood and the English Reformation* (Oxford: Clarendon Press, 1994).

—, 'Papist as heretic: The Burning of John Forest, 1538', *HJ*, 41:2 (1998), pp. 351–74.

—, *Beliefs and the Dead in Reformation England* (Oxford: Oxford University Press, 2002).

—, 'Angels Around the Deathbed: a Variation on a Theme in the English Art of Dying', in P. Marshall and A. Walsham (eds), *Angels in the Early Modern World* (Cambridge: Cambridge University Press, 2006), pp. 83–103.

—, 'The Guardian Angel in Protestant England', in J. Raymond (ed.), *Conversations with Angels: Essays Towards a History of Spiritual Communication, 1100–1700* (Basingstoke: Palgrave Macmillan, 2011), pp. 295–316.

Marshall, P., and A. Walsham (eds), *Angels in the Early Modern World* (Cambridge: Cambridge University Press, 2006).

Martin, J., *Religious Radicals in Tudor England* (London: Hambledon, 1989).

Meier, S. A., 'Angels' in Bruce Metzger and Michael Coogan (eds), *The Oxford Companion to the Bible* (Oxford: Oxford University Press, 1993).

Millen, R., 'The manifestation of occult qualities in the scientific revolution', in M. J. Osler, and P. L. Farber, (eds), *Religion, Science and Worldview: Essays in Honour of Richard S. Westfall* (Cambridge: Cambridge University Press, 1985), pp. 185–216.

Milton, A., *Catholic and Reformed: The Roman and Protestant Churches in English Protestant Thought 1600–1640* (Cambridge: Cambridge University Press, 1995).

Mintz, S. I., *The Hunting of Leviathan: Seventeenth-century reactions to the Materialism and Moral Philosophy of Thomas Hobbes* (Cambridge: Cambridge University Press, 1962).

Mohamed, F., *In the Anteroom of Divinity: The Reformation of Angels from Colet to Milton* (Toronto: University of Toronto Press, 2008).

Osler, M., J., 'Baptizing Epicurean atomism: Pierre Gassendi on the immortality of the soul', in M. J. Osler and P. L. Farber, *Religion, Science and Worldview* (Cambridge: Cambridge University Press, 1985), pp. 163–83.

Patrides, C. A., 'Renaissance Thought on the Celestial Hierarchy: The Decline of a Tradition', *Journal of the History of Ideas*, 20:2 (April, 1959), pp. 155–66.

Patterson, W. B., *King James VI and I and the Reunion of Christendom* (Cambridge: Cambridge University Press, 1997).

—, 'William Perkins as Apologist for the Church of England', *JEH*, 57 (2006), pp. 252–69.

Principe, L. M., *The Aspiring Adept: Robert Boyle and his Alchemical Quest* (Princeton, NJ: Princeton University Press, 1998).

Questier, M., *Conversion, Politics and Religion in England 1580–1625* (Cambridge: Cambridge University Press, 1996).

Raymond, J., *Pamphlets and Pamphleteering in Early Modern Britain* (Cambridge: Cambridge University Press, 2003).

—, *Milton's Angels: The Early-Modern Imagination* (Oxford: Oxford University Press, 2010).

Remnant, G., *A Catalogue of Misericords in Great Britain* (Oxford: Clarendon Press, 1969).

Reynolds, R., 'Liturgy and the Monument', in V. Raguin, K. Brush, P. Draper (eds), *Artistic Integration in Gothic Buildings* (London: University of Toronto Press, 1995), pp. 57–67.

Rowse, A. L., *Tudor Cornwall: A Portrait of a Society* (London: Cape, 1957).

Rubin, M., 'Corpus Christi Fraternities and Late Medieval Piety', *Studies in Church History*, 23 (1986).

van Ruler, H., 'Minds, Forms, and Spirits: The Nature of Cartesian Disenchantment', *Journal of the History of Ideas*, 61:3 (July, 2000), pp. 381–395.

Scarisbrick, J.J., *The Reformation and the English People* (Oxford, 1984)

Scribner, R. W., "The Reformation, Popular Magic, and the 'Disenchantment of the World'", in *Journal of Interdisciplinary History*, 23:3 (Winter, 1993), pp. 475–494.

Schwarz, M. L., 'James I and the Historians: Towards a Reconciliation', *Journal of British Studies*, 13:2 (May, 1973), pp. 114–34.

Shapin, S., *The Scientific Revolution* (Chicago, IL: University of Chicago Press, 1998).

Shapiro, B., 'Natural Philosophy and Political Periodisation: Interregnum, Restoration and Revolution', in A. Houston and S. Pincus (eds), *A nation transformed: England after the restoration* (Cambridge: Cambridge University Press, 2001), pp. 299–327.

Shaw, J., *Miracles in Enlightenment England* (London: Yale University Press, 2006).

Southwell, R., *An epistle of comfort to the reuerend priestes and to the honourable, worshipfull and other of the layesorte, restrained in Durance for the Catholike Fayth* (Paris, 1587).

Spraggon, J., *Puritan Iconoclasm during the English Civil War* (Woodbridge, Suffolk: Boydell, 2003).

Spurr, J., "'Latitudinarianism' and the Restoration Church", *IIJ*, 31:1 (March, 1988), pp. 61–82.

—, "'Rational Religion' in Restoration England, *Journal of the History of Ideas*, 49:4 (Oct-Dec, 1998), pp. 563–85.

—, *The Restoration Church of England* (New Haven; London: Yale University Press, 1991).

Stone, L., 'The Educational Revolution in England 1560–1640', *P&P*, 28 (1964) pp. 41–80.

Szonyi, G., *John Dee's Occultism: Magical Exaltation through Powerful Signs* (Albany NY: SUNY Press, 2004).

Tasker, E., *Encyclopaedia of Medieval Church Art* (London: Batsford, 1993).

Thomas, K., *Religion and the Decline of Magic: Studies in Popular Beliefs in Sixteenth and Seventeenth-Century England* (London: Weidenfield & Nicholson, 1971).

Tummers, H., *Early Secular Effigies in England: the thirteenth century* (Leiden: Brill, 1980).

Twycross, M., 'Books for the Unlearned', *Themes in Drama V* (1983), pp. 65–110.

Tyacke, N., *Anti-Calvinists: The Rise of English Arminianism c. 1590–1640* (Oxford: Clarendon, 1987), pp. 51–70.

—, 'Archbishop Laud', in K. Fincham (ed.), *The Early Stuart Church, 1603–1642* (Basingstoke: Macmillan, 1993).

Underdown, D., *Revel, Riot and Rebellion: Popular Politics and Culture in England 1603–1660* (Oxford: Oxford University Press, 1985).

Vickers, B. (ed.), *Occult and Scientific Mentalities in the Renaissance* (Cambridge: Cambridge University Press, 1984).

Walsham, A., *Church Papists: Catholicism, Conformity and Confessional Polemic in Early Modern England* (Woodbridge: Boydell, 1993).

—, '"The Fatall Vesper": Providentialism and Anti-Popery in Late Jacobean London', *P&P*, 44 (1994), pp. 37–87.

—, *Providence in Early Modern England* (Oxford: Oxford University Press, 1999).

—, '"Domme Preachers"? Post-Reformation English Catholicism and the Culture of Print', *P&P*, 168 (2000), pp. 30–71.

—, 'Angels and Idols in England's Long Reformation', in P. Marshall and A. Walsham (eds), *Angels in the Early Modern World* (Cambridge: Cambridge University Press, 2006), pp. 134–67.

—, 'Historiographical Reviews: The Reformation and "The Disenchantment of the World" Reassessed', *HJ*, 51:2 (2008), pp. 497–528.

—, 'Invisible Helpers: Angelic Intervention in Post-Reformation England', *P&P*, 208 (August 2010), pp. 77–130.

Watt, T., *Cheap Print and Popular Piety 1550–1640* (Cambridge: Cambridge University Press, 1991).

Weber, M., *The Protestant Ethic and the Spirit of Capitalism,* trans. T. Parsons, (ed.) A. Giddens (London: Routledge, 1992).

West, R. H., *Milton and the Angels* (Athens, GA: University of Georgia Press,1955).

Willis, J., *Church Music and Protestantism in post-Reformation England* (Farnham: Ashgate, 2010).

Wilson, D., *Signs and Portents: Monstrous Births from the Middle Ages to the Enlightenment* (London: Routledge, 1993).

Wizeman, W., *The Theology and Spirituality of Mary Tudor's Church* (Aldershot: Ashgate, 2006).

Wojcik, J. W., *Robert Boyle and the Limits of Reason* (Cambridge: Cambridge University Press, 1997).

Wooding, L., *Rethinking Catholicism in Marian England* (Oxford: Clarendon, 2000).

—, 'The Marian Restoration and the Mass', E. Duffy and D. Loades (eds), *The Church of Mary Tudor* (Aldershot: Ashgate, 2006), pp. 227–57.

Worden, B., 'Toleration and the Cromwellian Protectorate', in W. J. Sheils (ed.), *Persecution and Toleration: papers read at the Twenty-Second Summer Meeting and the Twenty-Third Winter Meeting of the Ecclesiastical History Society* (Oxford: Blackwells, 1984).

Wrightson, K., *English Society 1580–1680* (London: Routledge, 2003).

Yates, F., *Ideas and Ideals in the North European Renaissance: Collected Essays*, Vol. III (London: Routledge & Kegan Paul, 1984).

Websites

A. Marshall, 'Medieval Wall Painting in the English Parish Church: A Developing Catalogue', http://www.paintedchurch.org/ (accessed 2006).

'Catholic Encyclopedia', http://www.newadvent.org/cathen/15714a.htm (accessed March 2006).

'John Foxe's The Acts and Monuments Online, http://www.hrionline.ac.uk/foxe (accessed July 2007).

'Old Bailey Proceedings Online', www.oldbaileyonline.org (accessed 30 August 2011, version 6.0).

INDEX